C0-AJQ-580

EXECUTIVE AND ORGANIZATIONAL CONTINUITY

SURESH SRIVASTVA
RONALD E. FRY
and Associates

EXECUTIVE AND ORGANIZATIONAL CONTINUITY

Managing the Paradoxes of Stability and Change

Jossey-Bass Publishers · San Francisco

658.406
S 774

Copyright © 1992 by Jossey-Bass Inc., Publishers, 350 Sansome Street, San Francisco, California 94104. Copyright under International, Pan American, and Universal Copyright Conventions. All rights reserved. No part of this book may be reproduced in any form — except for brief quotation (not to exceed 1,000 words) in a review or professional work — without permission in writing from the publishers.

For sales outside the United States, contact Maxwell Macmillan International Publishing Group, 866 Third Avenue, New York, New York 10022

Manufactured in the United States of America

 The paper used in this book is acid-free and meets the State of California requirements for recycled paper (50 percent recycled waste, including 10 percent postconsumer waste), which are the strictest guidelines for recycled paper currently in use in the United States.

Library of Congress Cataloging-in-Publication Data

Srivastva, Suresh, date.
    Executive and organizational continuity : managing the paradoxes of stability and change / Suresh Srivastva, Ronald E. Fry, and associates. — 1st ed.
       p.   cm. — (The Jossey-Bass management series)
    Includes bibliographical references and index.
    ISBN 1-55542-444-9
    1. Organizational effectiveness. 2. Organizational change.
3. Continuity. 4. Quality of work life. I. Fry, Ronald E. (Ronald Eugene) II. Title. III. Series.
HD58.9.S733 1992
658.4'06 — dc20

92-5932
CIP

FIRST EDITION
HB Printing   10 9 8 7 6 5 4 3 2 1   *Code 9245*

The Jossey-Bass
Management Series

Consulting Editors
Organizations and Management

WARREN BENNIS
University of Southern California

RICHARD O. MASON
Southern Methodist University

IAN I. MITROFF
University of Southern California

Contents

Preface

Executive and Organizational Continuity is about how and why executives value and try to preserve the ongoing quality of life in their organizations — issues that will be increasingly crucial to organizational success in the future. The book explores ways of thinking about and achieving *continuity* — the force that bonds the organization's members together through cooperative acts — in everyday work life. This source of connectedness is at best taken for granted and at worst undervalued in today's overall preoccupation with change and quest for competitive advantage, new market niches, faster product innovation cycles, and shorter management tenures in key positions. Rather than being beneficial, these tendencies destroy meaningful experiences in the workplace, undo work relationships that nurture adult development, and truncate the learning process. In short, managers and employees alike must beware of changing for the sake of change alone.

This book stresses a different approach. It urges that as we and our organizations change we preserve the best of what has preceded us, so that the future we create is life giving: proactive, not reactive; developmental, not merely instrumental; holistic, not segmented; appreciative, not evaluative; and hopeful, not despairing. Organizations exist, at least in theory, to allow us to engage with others in ways that provide meaning, learning opportunities, and a collective purpose through which we experience joy, trust, and dependability. For this to happen, organizational leaders must recognize and establish a sense of ongoingness or connectedness between the past and the future, a goal that is best accomplished when change is managed with continuity in mind.

Background

This volume is the culmination of a symposium held at the Weatherhead School of Management at Case Western Reserve University in December 1990. We felt that the time was ripe for those concerned with the quality of organizational life to venture beyond the tendency of conventional theory to focus only on the entropic side of organizations, on those natural processes of compromise and deterioration that are part of any system. Many studies have emphasized these problematic features of collective existence but have forgone any in-depth analysis of the life-enhancing factors. Faced with such a one-sided view, we felt compelled to conduct a more holistic inquiry that would encompass the seemingly paradoxical experiences of organizational life. In the midst of chaotic events and unprecedented developments, our search is for knowledge that enables change to be nourishing; our call is for scholarship of "that which holds us together."

In previous efforts to shed light on the world of executive functioning (Srivastva and Associates, 1983, 1986, 1988; Srivastva, Cooperrider, and Associates, 1990), we have tried to provide forums that would counter this current trend. We have emphasized the life-giving aspects of executive work and the generative, health-enhancing agenda of organizations. This kind of holistic view requires simultaneous attention to what William James (1907) referred to as the affective, conative, and cognitive realms of human experience. By means of this threefold approach we have been drawn to examine aspects of leading and managing that address the "feeling" or "tone" of an enterprise, which is what enables employees to see themselves as central, significant, and exceptional, and to see their work as challenging and collectively changing for an exciting purpose.

In the course of our recent research into the nature of the CEO experience (Jonas, Fry, and Srivastva, 1989, 1990), research involving extensive interviews with and case histories of twenty-three chief executive officers, we observed several patterns that have helped shape this volume. As caretakers of their organization's culture, the CEOs we studied were unanimous in their perception that one of their key roles was to set and maintain the "tone" of the company. At the same time, they underscored their intention of changing the organization toward some specific end. Within this apparent duality of consistency and change, several other tendencies piqued our curiosity. The executives' accounts of changes were not always orderly; there was an untidiness to their views on how to make changes happen. They were often attracted to crises, partly because the (unexpectedly) difficult agenda of providing a stable reference point for employees was either suspended or made easier by the unambiguous demands of the immediate situation. These and other patterns began to signal a topic that has been neglected in organizational research: How is continuity achieved in one's work life? When and why is change effective and accepted as good? How do people embrace new ideas while retaining their expertise and sense of self-reliance?

During this period of inquiry, our involvement with a nearby insurance organization was pivotal in helping us clarify the topic for this volume. The organization was experiencing record profits and enormous growth — adding dozens of new management positions every month and expanding its businesses by opening new branch offices. Yet it was experiencing increasing turnover, relying on a workforce in which the tenure of the average worker was less than four years. Many felt that the company was on the verge of collapse. It was here that we first articulated for ourselves the interrelationship between transition, novelty, and continuity. The adaptive change and innovation taking place at the insurance company were positive developments. But the sense of continuity was being destroyed. The disruptive changes were proliferating and leadership credibility was waning in the face of random innovations introduced at an ever-accelerating pace. How can an organization like this keep its sense of progress and achievement at the same time that it maintains its sense of stability and directedness? It seemed to us that "continuity" signaled a possible answer and provided new terrain worth exploring.

Finally, we decided to focus on the topic of continuity because of what we believe to be a noble imperative facing this generation's managers. Organizational continuity will cause managers, and for that matter all of us, to be concerned with organizational leadership that brings about sustainable development for the global good. The World Commission on Environment and Development (1987, pp. 8–9) has defined *sustainable development* as progress or development "that meets the needs and aspirations of the present without compromising the ability of future generations to meet their own needs." We see continuity management as a key factor in helping today's executives act on a vision for the future in which people will be increasingly able to meet their collective needs and aspirations.

Audience

Executive and Organizational Continuity has appeal for both academics and executives. For the educator, it views age-old issues of stability and change from new and diverse perspectives. It is the most recent addition to a series of books (Srivastva and Associates, 1983, 1986, 1988; Srivastva, Cooperrider, and Associates, 1990) that is dedicated to constructing a state-of-the-art portrait of the executive experience. For the executive, this book is an invitation to rethink the conventional wisdom about managing change. It provides compelling new insights into a core dilemma for today's leaders—how to use change to shape a better future without destroying the past practices and values that contribute to today's success.

This book should also appeal to our research colleagues. It questions whether we have in fact advanced our understanding of change in social systems over the past decade and proposes a new research agenda to truly broaden our understanding of organizational change and preservation. It also embraces the complexity of organizational life. We hope that this look into executive and organizational continuity will significantly alter the lenses through which we study organizational renewal and growth in the twenty-first century.

Overview of the Contents

In the Introduction, we call into question the acontextual nature of current theories of change. We propose that by focusing on continuity we can better understand and manage the simultaneous needs in organizational life to adhere to time-tested and value-driven procedures while changing to adapt to the environment or to improve. The remaining chapters of the book address three important aspects of leading and managing change: the *search* for the meaning of continuity, the *valuing* of those things that should be continuous, and the *development* of continuity into the future.

Part One, "Searching for Continuity," consists of three chapters. They focus on how we should define continuity, where we should look for it, and how we should begin to articulate for ourselves or our organizations what it is that connects the past to the present. Chapter One sets the stage by drawing our attention to our own life stories, which are shown to be stories either of continuous evolution or of sporadic, shocklike change. Mary Catherine Bateson asserts that the executive agenda is to interpret the world of the organization in both continuous and discontinuous terms and warns us that to do either while ignoring the other can lead to pathological results.

Chapter Two also relies on the life story as a vehicle for understanding the nature of continuity, or what it is that links past to present and present to future. Mary McCanney Gergen challenges our popular views of continuity as being heavily male dominated. Her creative analysis of popular autobiographies by men demonstrates the linear, deterministic, rational, and impersonal manner in which the subjects tell their stories. This style differs markedly from the chaotic, fluid, personal, and untidy orientation of women's accounts. The author then discusses the parallels between women's stories and chaos theory and considers the implications of both for modern organizations.

Chapter Three differs from the two preceding chapters in its level of analysis. It deals with the stories of two organizations over decades. The analysis of these case histories challenges some of the postmodern tenets of organizing. A deeper look into the historical relationships between the organization and its region, community, and labor associations reveals the validity of a style of organizing different from those deemed successful in the current literature. The primary emphasis here, as in the other chapters in this book, is on the importance of the historical perspective as a means of understanding current issues and opportunities.

Part Two, "Valuing Continuity," comprises three chapters, which discuss the choices involved in applying the lessons of history to the challenges of the future. Each of the three chapters explores how we come to value continuity and incorporate it into our lives: how we choose which practice or time-tested idea to preserve and which to alter or discard. Chapter Four focuses on the primary goal or core practice of the enterprise as the basis for handling the dilemmas of the executive role. Barry Schwartz questions the promotion of economic imperialism, calling attention to its destructive impact on the intrinsically good or idealistic aspects of the organization.

Chapter Five pursues a similar intrinsic-extrinsic dichotomy: traditionalism versus rationalism, or the tendency to focus exclusively on outcomes. Paul F. Salipante, Jr., presents the concept of *evaluative traditionality* as a compromise embracing time-tested practices in the context of ongoing adaptation. The result is "continuity-in-change."

This part ends, as did Part One, with a cross-cultural focus. In Chapter Six, Leonard H. Lynn brings to life the lessons suggested in Chapters Four and Five in his description of a Japanese steelmaker's approach to major organizational transformation. We see how tradition is preserved as changes are incorporated by the company. We also see how core practices in social relationships are maintained even as core businesses begin to change.

The four chapters in Part Three, "Developing Continuity," all adopt a more prescriptive tone. They help us deal with these questions: How can we change without causing undue disruption or destruction to intrinsically held values? How can we foster both stability and change, both continuation and innovation? Chapter Seven discusses the relationship between means and ends, and suggests that the essence of continuity is a vision consistently espoused by organizational leaders about the ends to be achieved. Jonathan I. Klein and George F. Farris develop a set of guiding principles for establishing ends while providing flexible means toward those ends. They describe the effective executive as both a captain (as regards ends) and a catalyst (as regards means) and highlight the constructive tension that this dual role creates.

In Chapter Eight, Robert E. Quinn, Gretchen M. Spreitzer, and Stuart L. Hart examine the leader's style or behavior, showing that continuity is an experience of integrating the extremes rather than choosing one over the other. The authors challenge much of the binary thinking in popular management models (task versus people; Theory X versus Theory Y) and call for an "interpenetration" of our dominant views of leaders' behavior. The result is a new notion of effective leader behavior characterized by *tough love* and *practical vision*. The authors argue in favor of a leadership style that has previously been seen as polarized and has not been usefully integrated into practice.

Chapter Nine suggests structural and systemic remedies for the change-continuity duality in organizational life. Paul A. L. Evans compares system maturation with adult development and shows how lessons from the latter can be applied to organizations to achieve a mature state of dynamic balance between continuity and change, looseness and tightness, and so on. He presents a variety of examples of how organizations have handled complexity and its resultant tensions and provides recommendations for how other companies can do the same.

Chapter Ten also addresses the tensions that occur when an organization is faced with apparent duality: this time innovation versus continuity. Kathryn M. Bartol discusses the impact of reward systems on our inclination to focus either on stable (past-to-present) or on innovative (present-to-future) practices. She also considers the implications for the pay and reward systems that are most likely to support incremental creativity: those which encourage support of both time-tested practices *and* the generation of new ideas.

Finally, in the Conclusion, Suresh Srivastva and Craig G. Wishart summarize several of the themes that run through the entire volume and challenge us with the proposition that all change serves continuity; that to put into effect our vision of the future we must first seek to preserve that which we most value from the past.

Acknowledgments

In addition to the featured authors who contributed original chapters to this book, our friends and colleagues have offered continuous good will, unstinting support, and thoughtful input that we greatly value. We are fortunate to have faculty colleagues in the Department of Organizational Behavior in the Weatherhead School of Management at Case Western Reserve University who both provide continuity of support and challenge us to explore new perspectives and ways of understanding organizational life. They are Lisa Berlinger, Diana Bilimoria, Richard Boyatzis, Susan Case, David Cooperrider, David Kolb, Eric Neilsen, William Pasmore, and Donald Wolfe. The symposium that provided the initial dialogue and critique for the authors to help them refine their chapters could not have taken place without the contributions of the people mentioned or without the active assistance of the doctoral students from our integrative seminar. Julie Cox, Kathy Gurley, Bruce Hanson, Veronica Hopper, Pamela Johnson, Leonel Maia, Cynthia Staehle, Ram Tenkasi, Tojo Thachankery, Timothy Wilmot, and Craig Wishart all acted as "shadow scholars" to our invited authors and were instrumental in providing a community for scholarly inquiry and exciting learning. Three of our colleagues — Diana Bilimoria, Kathy Gurley, and Craig Wishart — carried out the immense task of organizing the symposium. Their diligence, commitment, and dependability were critical to our success. Dean Scott Cowen of the Weatherhead School of Management provided much of the financial support as well as consistent institutional encouragement for this kind of scholarly inquiry. We are grateful to all — and to many other unmentioned friends who were significant sources of continuity throughout this effort.

Warren Bennis, Richard O. Mason, and Ian I. Mitroff, consulting editors for the Jossey-Bass Management Series, continue to be thoughtful, supportive, and generous with their ideas and time. William Hicks, editor of the Management Series, has remained a true friend, colleague, and guide throughout this entire process. His courage and his commitment to making new developments in management thinking known are two assets in our efforts to realize the best for organizations in the twenty-first century. Finally, our administrative staff—Bonnie Reynolds and, most important, Retta Holdorf—deserve special thanks for their help during the symposium and in the subsequent preparation of this manuscript.

Cleveland, Ohio   Suresh Srivastva
March 1992   Ronald E. Fry

The Authors

Kathryn M. Bartol is professor of organizational behavior and human resource management at the University of Maryland, College Park. She received her Ph.D. degree (1972) from Michigan State University in organizational behavior and human resource management. Bartol is past president of the Academy of Management and is a fellow of the Academy of Management, the American Psychological Association, and the American Psychological Society. She is the author of the book *Male and Female Leaders in Small Work Groups* (1973).

Mary Catherine Bateson is Clarence J. Robinson Professor in anthropology and English at George Mason University. She received her Ph.D. degree (1963) from Harvard University in linguistics and Middle Eastern studies. Bateson has taught at Harvard, Northeastern University, and Amherst College and has taught and done research in Iran and the Philippines. Her books include *With a Daughter's Eye: A Memoir of Margaret Mead and Gregory Bateson* (1984), *Thinking AIDS* (1988, with G. Bateson), and *Composing a Life* (1989).

Paul A. L. Evans is professor and department chair of organizational behavior at the European Institute of Business Administration (INSEAD) in Fontainebleau, France. He received his Ph.D. degree (1974) from the Sloan School of Management at the Massachusetts Institute of Technology in management and organizational psychology. His current research interests include human resource management from a general management perspective and the organization of complex multinational enterprises. Evans's books include *Must Success Cost So Much?* (1981) and *Human Resource Management in International Firms: Change, Globalization, Innovation* (1989, with Y. Doz).

George F. Farris is acting dean and professor of organization management in the Graduate School of Management at Rutgers University, where he also directs the Technology Management Research Center. He received his Ph.D. degree (1966) from the University of Michigan in psychology. Farris's research interests include technical leadership, the informal organization in research and development, and strategic decision making in developing new technology. He is currently on the editorial boards of *IEEE Transactions on Engineering Management* and the *Journal of Engineering and Technology Management.*

Ronald E. Fry is associate professor of organizational behavior in the Weatherhead School of Management at Case Western Reserve University, where he is also director of the Executive MBA Program. He received his Ph.D. degree (1978) from the Massachusetts Institute of Technology in management. Fry's research interests include the study of effective groups and management of fundamental change in organizations. He has coauthored several books, including *Managing Human Resources in Health Care Organizations: An Applied Approach* (1978, with I. Rubin and M. Plovnick), *Improving the Coordination of Care: A Program for Health Team Development* (1975, with I. Rubin and M. Plovnick), and *Exercises, Cases, and Readings in Organization Development* (1982, with M. Plovnick and W. W. Burke).

Mary McCanney Gergen is associate professor at Pennsylvania State University. She received her Ph.D. degree (1980) from Temple University in psychology. Gergen's recent research has focused on narrative constructions of biography and the differences between how men and women tell their life stories in popular autobiographies. She is coeditor of *Historical Social Psychology* (1984, with K. Gergen).

Stuart L. Hart is assistant professor of corporate strategy and organizational behavior in the Graduate School of Business and Management at the University of Michigan. He received his Ph.D. degree (1983) from the University of Michigan in planning. His current research interests include the strategy-making process and executive leadership, with an emphasis on the management of technology and innovation. Hart's books include *Revival in the Rust Belt* (1987, with D. Denison) and *Strategic Technology Management* (forthcoming, with P. Dussauge and B. Ramanantsoa).

Jonathan I. Klein is assistant professor of organizational behavior in the Graduate School of Management at Rutgers University. He received his Ph.D. degree (1987) from the University of Southern California in business administration. Klein's recent research efforts have been devoted to developing a new theory of work motivation and behavior. In addition to teaching, he has consulted for both public and private organizations in the areas of organizational and job design, performance appraisal, and reward systems.

Ray Loveridge is professor and head of strategic management and policy studies at Aston University in Birmingham, England. He received a diploma from Ruskin College at Oxford University (1963) in politics and economics, an M.S.C. degree (1967) from the University of London, and an M.A. degree (1969) from Cambridge University in economics. Loveridge's most recent books include *Information Technology in European Services* (1990), *The Strategic Management of Technological Innovation* (1990), and *Continuity and Change in the National Health Service* (1991).

Leonard H. Lynn is associate professor of management policy in the Weatherhead School of Management at Case Western Reserve University. He received his Ph.D. degree (1980) from the

University of Michigan in sociology. His dominant research interest is the comparisons in technology policy and management between the United States and Japan. He is the author of *How Japan Innovates: A Comparison with the U.S. in the Case of Oxygen Steelmaking* (1982) and coauthor of *Organizing Business: Trade Associations in America and Japan* (1988, with T. McKeown).

Robert E. Quinn is chair of the Department of Organizational Behavior and Human Resource Management in the School of Business Administration at the University of Michigan. He received his Ph.D. degree (1974) from Brigham Young University in organizational behavior and applied behavioral science. His research covers the areas of management, organizational theory, organizational development, organizational behavior, executive skill development, and group dynamics. Quinn is the author of six books, including *Beyond Rational Management: Mastering the Paradoxes and Competing Demands of High Performance* (1988) and *Becoming a Master Manager: A Competency-Based Framework* (1990).

Paul F. Salipante, Jr., is associate professor of industrial relations and head of the division of labor and human resource policy in the Weatherhead School of Management at Case Western Reserve University. He received his Ph.D. degree (1975) from the University of Chicago in business. His current research interests include organizational tradition, cross-cultural differences, employee grievances, and individual conceptualizations and behavior in employment relationships.

Barry Schwartz is professor of psychology and former head of the Department of Psychology at Swarthmore College. He received his Ph.D. degree (1971) from the University of Pennsylvania in experimental psychology. His research interests include learning and motivation, with a focus on biological constraints on learning and on the undermining of intrinsic motivation by extrinsic incentives. Schwartz's books include *The Battle for Human Nature* (1986), *The Psychology of Learning and Behavior* (1989), and *Learning and Memory* (1991, with D. Riesberg).

Gretchen M. Spreitzer is a Ph.D. candidate in organizational behavior and human resource management in the School of Business Administration at the University of Michigan. She received her B.A. degree (1987) from Miami University (Ohio) in systems analysis. Spreitzer's current research involves exploring the role of managerial change and empowerment in organizational revitalization.

Suresh Srivastva is professor of organizational behavior in the Weatherhead School of Management at Case Western Reserve University. He received his Ph.D. degree (1960) from the University of Michigan in social psychology. He is the author of numerous articles in the area of psychology and management problems. Srivastva's major books include *Executive Power* (1986, with others), *Executive Integrity* (1988, with others), and *Appreciative Management and Leadership* (1990, with D. Cooperrider and others).

Craig G. Wishart is a Ph.D. candidate in the Department of Organizational Behavior in the Weatherhead School of Management at Case Western Reserve University. He received his B.S. degree (1989) from the University of Pittsburgh in psychology. His research interests focus on the role of tradition in postmodern organizations.

Continuity and Change in Organizational Life

Ronald E. Fry, Suresh Srivastva

In recent years, the images of executives as "changemasters" and "pathfinders," as "gamesmen" and "entrepreneurs," and as "visionaries" and "transformational leaders" have captured the popular imagination. The modernist spirit, as embodied in each of these notions, had predominantly been one of novelty, of chaos, of innovation, of change. Indeed, the *idea of change* dominates the landscape of modern life, most certainly including life at the workplace. Executives everywhere continue to be called on to envision alternatives that have not yet existed, to break the shackles of conventional notions of what is possible, to ignite the spirit of collective renewal, and to harness turbulent environmental forces to help transform their organizations in new and different ways. But in what ways? As Daniel Bell (1976) reflects on it, the thing that is so singularly apparent about this emphasis on change, "the tradition of the new," is that novelty has apparently taken on value in and of itself. The avant-garde has become the cherished and customary way of life.

This book stems from the premise that while the management of *novelty* and management of *transition* form two major executive agendas in all of today's social systems, it is a third agenda — the management of *continuity* — that provides for meaningful and purposeful change and that brings value to new ideas.

1

But this latter agenda is largely overlooked in the modernist predilection for change. In our look to the future, we, as academics and practitioners alike, have been enamored with concepts of transformation, innovation, and change. Simply put, we want and expect executives everywhere to make the new happen.

But toward which ends? Change in the service of which values? Transition for the sake of which noble purposes? As people in all walks of life have been both dazzled and exhausted by novelty, they (we) are beginning to express a hidden hunger for continuity and community, for responsiveness and dependability, and for the strength of identity that comes from a true sense that today's life experience is integrally connected to both the wisdom of the past and promise for the future (Gergen, 1991). Continuity management, we propose, is a pivotal force in organizational existence and thus in virtually every executive act. But we understand so little about the nature of continuity in what many have called these chaotic, "postmodern" times. And we have yet to spell out exactly what continuity management means in organizational and process-oriented (nonstatic) terms. Our purpose in this volume, therefore, is to develop the notion of continuity further and to explore the premise that *continuity is central to the executive role in bringing about organizational health.*

Why Continuity?

Continuity is the connectedness over time among organizational efforts and a sense or experience of ongoingness that links the past to the present and the present to future hopes and ideals. Our studies have revealed continuity to be a critical objective of executive functioning (Jonas, Fry, and Srivastva, 1990) and a key characteristic of healthy, renewing organizations (Bouwen and Fry, 1988). For nearly all of today's and tomorrow's organizations, it is a foregone conclusion that change is ubiquitous. It is and will be the norm. The "winners" will be managed by those who "love change," "embrace chaos," "bust bureaucracies," "pathfind" where no one else dares, and so on, if we are to accept the tenets of the current management literature. This may well describe some of what has to occur, but why and how? With increasing frequency, we also see and hear of change programs that fail (Beer, Eisenstat, and Spector, 1990) because they are too disruptive, threatening, or confusing to those who actually need to change. Instead of being transformational, a change program is experienced first as a discontinuity to be avoided or coped with. Instead of being a brilliant, exciting innovation that captures the collective imagination and aspirations of a group, a new idea is perceived to devalue tried-and-true practices or years of personal investment and commitment to proven ways of doing things. Something would appear to be lacking in our understanding and/or practice of organizational change and development.

When we assess the current state of theory and practice regarding the management of change, we can see that continuity is necessary to accomplish change that is transformational and to foster innovation that is valued by the organization and its constituents. Friedlander and Brown (1974) concluded in a major review of the organizational change literature that there had been a failure to produce a theory of change arising from the change process itself. A stream of subsequent reviews of the change literature have converged toward the conclusion that our models and understanding of effective change management are ahistorical and acontextual (for example, Pettigrew, 1985; Faucheaux, Amato, and Laurent, 1982; Alderfer, 1977). Let us consider some of these observations in more depth, to show how continuity management can help us advance our knowledge and praxis.

1. Studies of change continue to be, for the most part, episodic — more likely *an* episode about *a* change rather than analysis of the dynamics of several changes or *changing* (Pettigrew, 1985). This snapshot quality of our models and case illustrations gives rise to linear, sequential explanations of the process of change (for example, Lippitt, Watson, and Westley, 1958; Bennis, Benne, and Chin, 1976), the dynamics of organizational growth and development (Beckhard, 1969; Greiner, 1967, 1972), and the action-research methodology to facilitate planned change

(Kolb and Frohman, 1970). While most of these and other authors cite caveats to guard against literal translation of their models, the overall emphasis of the literature is on a sequential order of events to accomplish getting from A to B. Cause and effect is interpreted from left to right, or top to bottom, albeit with feedback arrows to denote the possibility of iterations. The possibility that change in social systems does not begin, grow, and end, that one simultaneously has a felt need to change and a resistance to doing so, that change may be spontaneous versus planned, that intentional agendas to innovate are actually untidy, sporadic, and subject to change, all seem to be beyond the grasp of our theories and models, yet apparent to all of us (to some degree) every day. Thus, the attention to continuity requires ongoing efforts on the part of executives and researchers to embrace the complexity of organizational life; the continual and simultaneous tension between time-tested practices and the need to change them; the ambiguities inherent in moving from ideals and visions to pragmatic change plans; and the delicate balance of time and energy directed to past (learning), present (doing), and future (planning) in every organizational interaction and activity. The complex, problematic nature of group and organizational life and the issue of why choices are made (not which choices) become the agenda for the executive who attends to continuity.

2. The studies from which we draw our theories about organizational change seldom span a chronological time frame broad enough to enable us to consider alternative reasons (causes) for the results being observed, or to foresee all the possible consequences of the interventions taken. While the latter has received increasing attention in debates about short- versus long-term time horizons for future goals, for example, and differentiation of degrees or depth of change (Golembiewski, Billingsley, and Yeager, 1975), the historical impact on studies of change is conspicuously absent. Notable exceptions are Pettigrew's (1985) encompassing analysis of organizational evolution at ICI and Alderfer's (1977) mention of a few studies that noted historical trends as reasons for the success or failure of OD interventions (that is, organizational development worked better in nonunion

settings and in stable suburban school settings without urban unrest). But the current models of change or transition management remain centered on moving from now toward a future state (Beckhard and Harris, 1977; Nadler, 1987). Schein's (1985b) notion of organizational culture is useful to us here. It is the intergenerational transmission of basic assumptions that define the taken-for-granted aspects of daily work life that, in turn, give identity to the organization and its environment, as well as to its members. Without consideration of history, culture is denied and any planned change, therefore, risks the destruction of the bonding agent that holds things together (usually productively in some parts and not in others). Perhaps only in severe "turnaround" or initial creation scenarios can ignorance of the past be so cavalierly tolerated, if not celebrated, as in the case of our society's current fascination with Iacocca, Jobs, Walton, Buffett, and so on. For most organizations today, the inescapable fact is that history (particularly of relationships) shapes one's current choices and, therefore, one's stance toward the future. To understand people's readiness and capability for change, we must investigate what Schein refers to as the learned responses to their reference group's problems of survival in its environment (in or out of the organization) and that group's challenges to become internally cohesive. With the increasing diversity of the workforce and bimodal age distribution, these learned products of past group experiences are going to have greater and greater impact on if and how organizations change. In the case of age diversity, for instance, the new members' stake in the old practices and the old members' stake in the new must be brought to the surface and understood before a "felt need" can be assumed, let alone acted on. Executive, group, and organizational continuity therefore involves concern for the intergenerational transmission of organizational life. It is concerned with recognition, celebration, and creation of moral, inspirational, and normative standards that provide the cultural cohesion required for continued organizational (group) life.

3. Studies of change in organizations typically exclude more interrelationships, interdependencies, environmental contingencies, relationship factors, and so on than they include.

Alternatively, large-scale analyses to discover common characteristics or factors that differentiated eleven successful change efforts from fourteen unsuccessful change efforts led Franklin (1976) to conclude that there was little support for a set of characteristics or antecedents that are either absolutely necessary or sufficient to determine successful and unsuccessful change in organizations. In other words, it depends; context matters. Faucheaux, Amato, and Laurent (1982) similarly chided the U.S.-dominated literature on planned change for its superficial treatment of context, particularly with respect to cultural biases. While the works of Hofstede (1980) and others have gnawed away at this particular barrier, Faucheaux, Amato, and Laurent's (1982, p. 366) challenge lingers: that the field of organizational change can only develop if it ventures into its own context. Those interested in understanding organizational change must ensure that whenever a piece of reality is exposed, the context from which it came is never lost from view. We can see this issue today in the spread of knowledge or technology transfer between countries. The current adoption of Japan's quality control practices by Western industries is both curious and enlightening. First, why were only the Japanese able to benefit from the statistical process control "technology" when it was first made available in both Japan and the West? And second, having decided it was worth adopting, why did (do) so many Western organizations believe that only the technological aspect of the innovation should be copied or transferred, not the social dimension? This limited view of the change in Japanese industry has led many executives to make the bitter discovery of the hidden context behind the Japanese success story. The point here is that we all suffer from attempts to derive universal truths about effective organizational change without tempering them with important differences and without further qualifying those with unique exceptions. All levels of inquiry into and recognition of contextual factors increase our ability to develop relevant theory about change. Organizational continuity is a systems matter involving the organization's (group's) linkages with its environment — past, present, and future. Continuity in open systems requires recognition of the social, technical, and ecological consequences of an organization's (group's) actions and of its attempts to become a vital participant in the conditions of its community, economy, and ecosystem.

4. Part of the failure to appreciate contextual nuances in change efforts stems from the boundedness of our frames for understanding organizational life. Perry's studies of the epistemological development of adults (reported in Salner, 1986) suggest phases that parallel the development of change in organizations. He defines three basic levels of development: dualism, multiplicity, and contextual relativism. In Perry's first phase, *dualism,* a clear distinction exists between the self and the external world. Knowledge resides in the external world, where differences are reduced to true-false, right-wrong categories. Ambiguity is irritating and is viewed as an unnecessary confusion and a failure to find the appropriate authoritative reference. Faucheaux, Amato, and Laurent (1982) likened the field of organization change and development to this stage. They noted that the dominant paradigms in the literature were bipolar: scientific management versus human relations; Theory X versus Theory Y; managers versus managed; organization versus environment; organization man versus complex man; rational versus emotional; and so on. Perry's second developmental phase, *multiplicity,* results from the pluralistic social influences on the dualistic thinker. Many truths now exist, there is more than one way to solve a problem, but to avoid unnecessary conflict, the self satisfices by saying, "You see it your way; I see it mine." Multiplicity in change theories is represented in the recent plethora of situational and contingency approaches that attempt to consider more (than two) variables or factors and prescribe different "fits" as the "right" solution for a given instance. Sociotechnical systems and various situational management and decision models are examples. They often lead to the conclusion that "it depends" on the subjective perceptions of the manager about situational characteristics; the self is left to a subjective choice compared to the dualist's reliance on external absolutes. Perry's third stage, *contextual relativism,* is where the self strives for understanding in ways that allow him or her to choose or value one outcome over another. This stage represents an in-

creased awareness that contexts are important to defining truth and value. Pluralism is accepted as a condition (as in multiplicity), but intellectual standards and reasoned commitment are now paramount. Many of the commentaries in the literature cited in this discussion seem to yearn for this stage. Attention to continuity is necessarily dialectical and interactive. It calls forth the interpersonal transmission of ideas, intentions, and meaning in daily work and allows for exploration and experimentation with shared views. It searches for truth not in the world (as the dualistic thinker), nor in the self (as the multiplistic thinker), but in the interaction between oneself and the world that results from committed acts in that world.

5. Our notions about managing change are heavily deterministic or outcome oriented. While we tend to want to view organizations more as open systems (for example, Katz and Kahn, 1978; Pasmore, 1988; Weick, 1969), our change theories or strategies are more concerned with entropic characteristics of closed systems than with the equifinality of change in open systems (Nonaka, 1988). We read everywhere about *what* to become or change to, not *why* or *how*. The fixation on a specific target, goal, list of attributes, or fit with an environmental condition necessarily draws attention to resistance as a major force to be managed. Choices among strategies for change that do speak to the change process are heavily concerned with managing resistance (Kotter and Schlesinger, 1979). That is, they focus on minimizing loss of energy through resistance rather than creation or mobilization of energy via a different framework for organizational growth. (See, for example, Srivastva, Cooperrider, and Associates, 1990.) The long-standing notion of opposing forces toward change from Lewin's (1951) classic contributions to this field may have conditioned our views unnecessarily toward a preoccupation with the resistant side of human nature in changing times. We lose sight of the fact that, even when we stay the "same," we are changing, growing, maturing, and so on. At another level, our most widely used strategies for change are rooted in intentions that are deterministic, disruptive, or both. Chin and Benne (1976) trace our change strategies to three basic roots. The rational-empirical model that underlies liberal edu-

cation, scientific approaches to management, and expert or authoritarian views of what is right is clearly deterministic (antiequifinal) in nature. The power-coercive model that underlies many of the community development and sociopolitical change strategies is less deterministic, perhaps, but overtly disruptive in its intent. Finally, the normative-reeducative model that underlies most organization development efforts and planned change methodologies in organized systems is heavily rooted in the therapeutic search for pathology and its remedy. While practitioners in this area devote much attention to humanistic growth and potential, their methods and models are nonetheless based on a presumption of pathos. The management of continuity relates to an alternate way of thinking and knowing that apprehends the unity of time and space not in simple deterministic terms (emphasizing causal, mechanistic thinking). Continuity management is important precisely because of its nondetermination or open (versus closed) future.

The point of this discussion is not to set up current theories of planned change as a "strawperson" to summarily attack, but rather to highlight our view that while the cup is partly full (with useful models, guidelines, experiences), it is also partly empty. We propose the notion of continuity management to fill up more of our cup of understanding of organizational change and growth.

Turning Our Frame of Change Upside Down

The contributions to this volume represent a diverse, creative, and provocative investigation of the notions of continuity expressed earlier. Taken together, they add up to nothing less than an upside-down (or is it right side–up?!) view of change. The metamessage from the chapters that follow is that leaders, managers, members, and scholars should consider the proposition that all effective change in organizations is in the service of continuity, not simply for deterministic goals or future ends; that it is possible we have gotten our conceptions of the change process backward. As John Gardner writes in *Self-Renewal: The Individual and the Innovative Society* (1981, p. 5), "Our thinking about growth and decay is dominated by the image of a single life span, animal or vegetable. Seedling, full flower, and death. . . . But for an ever renewing society, the appropriate image is a total garden, a balanced aquarium, or other ecological system. Some things are being born, other things are flourishing, still other things are dying — but the system lives on." Organizations are collections of individual and group lives-in-progress. What changes, what remains the same, and ideas that flourish all make up what continues on. Understanding in depth those things that continue, the source and content of the ongoingness of organizational life, is our focus here. The verb *continue* comes from the Latin root *continere,* which means "to hold together." The contributors to this volume all call on us to examine what it is that holds us together to better understand and guide organizational change.

How can we look with a different eye at the dynamics of organizational or group development? How does an awareness of continuity alter the way we manage, lead, or create change? Each contribution that follows details some aspect of these questions. All the contributions emphasize the need to move away from sequential and linear approaches to change and toward a process of *searching for, valuing,* and *developing* continuity.

Searching for continuity means exploring the genesis and history of the organization (group) to find shared views of "what it is that has held (now holds) us together." It is the articulation of the core logic, core tasks, or primary practice(s) of the enterprise as well as investigation of where they came from and how they are currently maintained or reinforced. This search can have many possible results. In some cases, it may bring to light a technologically based routine or mechanism that has been and still is central to the organization's existence. In other cases, it could highlight certain values or attitudes shared by older members of the workforce. In still other cases, it could call attention to the CEO's persona as it embodies the spirit of the firm. This search recognizes the importance of history and of pluralistic views about what has truly been important in sustaining a sense of ongoingness. One outcome could be to bring out a need to change things: to refocus on training or recruitment of talent to perform core tasks, to review a strategic plan in light of the consensus on core values or assumptions, and so on.

Valuing continuity implies making reasoned choices about which things in our history are most important to carry forward. Valuing is a process of articulating choices that arise from simultaneous consideration of past influences on the present and present desires to shape the future. It is the drive for "contextual relativism" that was described above. We are not passive observers of history as if it is the determining factor in our lives but separate from us. We need to assess the lessons from our exploration of the historical patterns and then decide how we wish to act. In choosing among complex options, we signal a purpose, and when we act toward that purpose, we signal what we value. When we choose to act based in part on our understanding of prior acts and on what was valued in the past, we are carrying forward, transferring from past to future, certain priorities, beliefs, values, and so on that, by definition, are holding us together. As we will see, this is rarely an experience of "business as usual." On the contrary, valuing continuity often involves a difficult confrontation with seemingly contradictory options.

Developing continuity is the proactive engagement with others to construe the world of the workplace in ways that invite and excite cooperative acts. It encompasses leader and follower acts, behaviors of managers and those managed. It consists of agendas and processes that embrace ambiguity, equifinality, and diversity, and, at the same time, it involves a search for courses of action that first, do the least damage to continuity, and second, next create the most meaning or significance in the context of shaping a desired future.

Managing or attending to continuity requires all three of the orientations just described. The various chapters in this book are grouped and sequenced according to their emphasis in helping the reader to understand why and how to search for, value, and develop continuity in executive and organizational life.

Detailed Overview of the Contents

The chapters in the book are original works by a distinguished and diverse group of scholars and professionals who responded to an invitation to explore the ongoing, life-sustaining, generative forces that exist in organizations as a result, in part, of executive action. While the style, focus, time frame, and context differ from chapter to chapter, one thread strongly connects all of these contributions. Each author comes through with a sincere caring for the quality of human experience that occurs in daily work: it was for this that they were selected and invited to contribute to this effort. Their work is arranged in three sections, as mentioned above, to help convey an alternative approach to how we view organizational change and evolution. First, we consider where and how to *search for* continuity in order to discover how the past has brought us to the present. Next we consider the *valuing* of continuity: what to consider and how to choose what is best or most appropriate to carry forward as we face and enact the future. Finally, we consider different ways of actually *developing* and maintaining continuity so that it allows effective change and renewal to take place.

Part One: "Searching for Continuity"

Our contributors to this part, Mary Catherine Bateson, Mary McCanney Gergen, and Ray Loveridge, unite in helping us to answer the question, "Where do I begin to look to discover or uncover whatever has created a sense of continuity or ongoingness in me (or my organization) today?" They each challenge us to look beyond what is easily taken for granted or socially conditioned in order to discover new ways in which our lives (organizations) in progress have, in fact, progressed. They also display an appreciation for the power of history that is central to the subject of continuity: how we select and reconstruct the past in terms of present problems and future desires.

The editors' personal experiences in conveying the power of history to executives has been enlightening. We determined from our studies of CEOs that the job, in part, calls for one to be a custodian of the organization's culture, which presupposes the ability to link past to present and future needs and opportunities. Based on this, for the past seven years we have routinely assigned a major term project to our executive MBAs that requires them to do a historical analysis of the leadership practices and underlying beliefs in their organization. We are routinely greeted with dismay, sighs, expectations of boredom, denial that it is a relevant task, or assertions that they already know what it is important to know. To our delight, the overwhelming majority report afterward in a self-reflective vein (or on course evaluations) that this was one of, if not the most useful and eye-opening assignments of their entire curriculum. They feel empowered, more identified with their organization, and more free to choose those aspects of the current state they wish to personally commit to preserving. There is a sense in this experience and in the three chapters in this section that if we are willing to leave habitual biases or familiar lenses on the table and look into the past with open, nonjudgmental eyes, we need not fear "Pandora's box." We will, instead, discover a "treasure chest."

　　Mary Catherine Bateson, in Chapter One, defines the terrain for our journey in search of continuity. She provides a perfect beginning point when she asserts the agenda for any executive or leader: to interpret situations in terms of continuity and discontinuity. That it is possible to do both in any circumstance may sound trivial, at first glance. We are confronted soon, however, with the probability that the same is true of our own lives. In a gentle but informed manner, Bateson confronts our habitual tendency to associate what we and others are today with continuous or discontinuous explanations: constructions of the past that have resulted in the present. The fact that these interpretations are social constructions and that they can exist concurrently presents us with both opportunity (for innovation) and danger (in terms of pathological patterns, where too much change or too much consistency causes new problems). She leaves us with a finer concern for balancing continuity with discontinuity. Waterman (1987) calls it a delicate *im*balance. As Bateson warns, we must avoid changes that require less flexibility (in the name of continuity) and find constancy that involves deeper change in variables that are essential to survival. Finally, Bateson contributes to the general frame-breaking tenor of this book by calling on us to look at ourselves (and others) from the alternate stance (continuous or discontinuous). In the symposium in which all the contributors gathered to dialogue about their ideas, Bateson brought this message home with a timely anecdote. As she was leaving her hotel on campus that morning to attend the symposium, she found herself standing alongside another visitor while waiting to be picked up. She cordially asked him, "Are you here to talk about continuity?" "No," he replied, "I'm interested in change; I'm a geneticist."

Mary McCanney Gergen follows in Chapter Two with a creative and provocative exploration of how the stories of our lives in progress can have meaning for the way we view organizational continuity. She concurs with Bateson that our life stories, and therefore an organization's story, are socially construed and subject to alternative or even opposing interpretations. Gergen's novel research on autobiographies of prominent social, political, and business figures in our society, however, takes us further to expose underlying differences between men's and women's stories. In men's constructions of their pasts, we are shown how continuity is conceived in linear, sequential, continuous-time, predictable, and stable terms. This may not surprise the reader who was sympathetic to our earlier discussion of the current state of our knowledge and theories about change. Since male authors dominate that literature, we could expect that the linear, deterministic, and sequential nature of change models is the result of male influence as well. From her study of women's autobiographies, Gergen extracts a different set of characteristics: multifaceted, reflexive, tentative, oscillating, fuzzy, and discontinuous. To say more about her insights into either set of stories would rob the reader of the evocative experience of actually reading her work. The challenge she presents us with is to consider the possibility that women's stories, which overlap in many respects with chaos science, may be more instructive than men's stories in our attempts to make sense of group or organizational evolution. As we search for the roots of continuity in various contexts, Gergen offers us a thoughtful caution to avoid entrapping ourselves with old ways of knowing. Why not conceive of continuity itself to reside in erratic, untidy, fluctuating, ambivalent, chaotic conditions? Gergen's

propositions regarding how organizations would look or function from this standpoint become increasingly more attractive,
given the popular calls for managers to "embrace chaos," "love
change," and so on.

Next comes Ray Loveridge's contribution in Chapter
Three. At first glance, this chapter is far afield from the self-
reflective, biographical path that Bateson and Gergen take to
uncovering continuity. Indeed, his focus is on interorganizational and transorganizational linkages and relations that survive over time. He steers us to more macrolevel thinking about
the roots and sources of continuity in organizational evolution.
Yet one of his primary themes echoes the first two chapters: the
power of historical reflection in shaping our values and behavior
in organizations. In a sense, Loveridge stands in thoughtful opposition to the postmodernist view that bureaucratic hierarchies
have jaded our ability to organize effectively. He is not advocat-
ing blind faith in traditional forms of organizing, but rather a
complex review of how current organization structures and practices are nested in other structures and hierarchies such as labor
or trade associations, local community traditions, and regional
economic conditions. He cautions us not to readily adopt the
apparent postmodernist trends to "chunk up" our organizations
into smaller, more autonomous, decentralized, "quasi-organi-
zations" with temporary partnerships and interorganizational
alliances just to respond more quickly and directly to market
opportunities. While this approach *may* be the extension of continuity (holism and interdependency) between U.S. or British
organizations and their societies, the view is different from, say,
a Japanese or German perspective. Loveridge supports his analysis by contrasting the histories of two major European firms
involved in original equipment manufacturing for motor vehicles. The two case histories emphasize the lessons learned (and
missed) from viewing interorganization relationships with care
and from a historical perspective.

The juxtaposition of Loveridge's level and unit of analysis with that of Bateson and Gergen in Part One is intentional.
At the individual, group, system, and societal level, the voice
in these chapters is for the empowering nature of historicity.

Both the executive and the scholar of organizational life must become historians. The thoughtful investigation of how the past has shaped the present can be empowering, as shown by these authors, because it opens up new perspectives, affirms the care given to certain traditions or values, and provides more depth of understanding to support future choices.

Part Two: "Valuing Continuity"

As we uncover the lessons of history and the threads of continuity in our lives in progress, we confront choices that must be made. For things to flow, grow, continue, they must change. We have to act to create meaning and experience efficacy in organizational life. The contributors to this part — Barry Schwartz, Paul F. Salipante, Jr., and Leonard H. Lynn — help us to examine this choice-making or valuing process in managing continuity. They explore why we must determine what is the right or the best or the most desirable practice and give us some useful guides for framing our choices. The strong message shared by these three chapters is that the management of continuity is, in essence, an exercise of *caring* for what is right, be it at the interpersonal, group, or organizational level. Continuity management, as demonstrated by these authors, is a virtuous agenda that transforms past reasons for connectedness in social systems to possibilities for future ongoingness. It is this "transformation" that is central to each of the three chapters in Part Two.

In Chapter Four, Barry Schwartz begins with an eloquent demonstration of how attention to continuity in a social system — here a softball game — creates choicepoints or dilemmas that cannot be managed without consensus about the fundamental goals or purposes of the organized effort. He moves on to a provocative critique of the dominance of "economic imperialism" in organizational life, noting ways that it systematically destroys or perverts the intrinsic goods and goals of a practice. This notion of core "practice" is as central to continuity as is adaptation to changing times and externalities. When practices are (need to be) transformed, however, Schwartz argues that the energy for this evolution should come from internal sources, from the participants in the practice. Thus, organizational adaptation is value driven from intrinsic beliefs about what is best, or ideal, rather than being instrumentally shaped by impersonal adherence to an externally based "value" attached to economic ends.

In Chapter Five, Paul F. Salipante, Jr., suggests that traditionality in organization become a stronger voice in determining what will be valued and pursued in the future. Like Schwartz, he sees an internal-external dichotomy in our current thinking about organization development. He argues that the current focus on flexibility, adapting to change, finding niches in turbulent environments, and so forth unjustly denigrates or obscures the values inherent in traditions. He shows that traditionality — utilizing past beliefs and practices in shaping current action — can coexist with a basic change orientation. Thus, he questions the premise that organizations *must* be predominantly rational and provides examples of when and how traditionality (by definition, nonrational because it is passed on via subjective, personal experience) has been central to the organization's successful continuation. He challenges our typical mindset by proposing a paradigm that merges traditionality with rationality: *evaluative traditionality*. From this perspective, organizations manage continuity by means of thinking and decision processes that balance the positive elements of both models. To create continuity-in-change, Salipante urges the affirmation and use of traditionality to make sure that organization plans and efforts remain connected to the personally felt values that have been shaped and nurtured through traditions. People thus feel a "part of a movement or cause" in the organization.

The third contribution to this section, by Leonard H. Lynn, extends this valuing of tradition in organizations to the Japanese experience. In Chapter Six, Lynn reviews Japanese business practices and uses a detailed case history and analysis of one of Japan's leading steelmakers to examine the commonsense notion that holding on to the old can result in an inability to change or remain competitive. He focuses on hiring, training, personnel, and decision processes to illustrate the complex interrelationship between continuity and change. What stands out in his discussion is the priority given to work relationships in achieving a slow but steady assimilation of new people and ideas. In bringing about a major strategic shift to new businesses and a drastic alteration of their product mix, this organization appears to proceed "more slowly" than its global counterparts without losing competitive advantage. Indeed, Lynn gives us practical evidence that the organization's leadership acts as if its key stakeholders are the employees and managers; hence their concern for undue disruption of the positive, bonding characteristics of their culture (traditionality). Constructive change is occurring. New ideas and skills are being introduced, but not at the expense of the learned capabilities, cohesion, and values of the core of the institution. In this sense, Lynn's discourse, like that of Schwartz in Chapter Four, suggests that change could well be viewed as being *in the service of* continuity. In other words, we can effectively change social systems by choosing to act based on valued agendas that are embodied in the members (old and new) of the system and thereby maintain purpose.

The diverse social-system context represented in these three chapters adds strength to the common call from Schwartz, Salipante, and Lynn for processes that explicitly articulate what has worked best and why, as guides for changing organizations. Purpose, mission, or vision, while capturing the opportunity of the future, must also preserve whatever has been of value in holding the organization together so far.

Part Three: "Developing Continuity"

Attention to continuity exposes the complex and often-paradoxical nature of group and organizational life. The contributors to this part—Jonathan I. Klein, George F. Farris, Robert E. Quinn, Gretchen M. Spreitzer, Stuart L. Hart, Paul A. L. Evans, and Kathryn M. Bartol—break new ground for us by suggesting prescriptions for *how* to create processes that address seemingly bipolar or contradictory realities. The language of these chapters is intentionally full of what Bateson calls the "double binds": continuity-in-innovation, tough love, practical vision, vital stability, stable mobility, changing sameness, and the like. All these authors address the question, "How do we honestly face the paradoxical duality (or multiplicity) of continuity *and* change, of continuity *and* innovation, and maintain a 'tension' that is creative and life giving?"

In Chapter Seven, Jonathan I. Klein and George F. Farris turn upside down our popular, deterministic orientation to create continuity of means toward an end. They suggest that managing continuity really calls for a "means-ends chain" throughout the organization's structures that ensures continuity of ends and flexibility of means. This is an important agenda, because it recognizes the equifinality of organizational change in a pragmatic sense. For Klein and Farris, continuity is the consistency of goals or purpose, across leadership levels over time. They suggest that common notions of continuity of means are often driven by habit (our way is the only way to do it) or inertia, which are often antithetical to change. Likewise, adaptability to the environment has often driven flexibility in goals for the sake of novelty and resulted in destructive disruption. To counter these patterns, Klein and Farris develop a *utility principle of leadership* and a *telescope principle of decision making*. They then explain how executives can utilize these principles in achieving continuity of decisions at the system, organization, people, and task levels. Finally, their views of the executive's role in managing these continuities pose a "paradoxical" challenge to be both a captain (of ends) and a catalyst (for means), to direct (control) and facilitate (empower). This complexity in the managerial role gives rise to potential interpersonal and intraorganizational conflicts. Rather than as problems to be avoided, Klein and Farris see these potential conflicts as necessary and productive if they give rise to deliberation in the organization about means versus ends.

In Chapter Eight, Robert E. Quinn, Getchen M. Spreitzer, and Stuart L. Hart continue to explore the leader's role and dilemmas in managing continuity. They see the experience of continuity as the feeling of "bothness" compared to the feeling of oppositeness (either-or choice). They introduce the concept of *interpenetration* as a means of countering the limitations of bipolar thinking. The idea of interpenetration emphasizes the simultaneous operation of opposites; it treats polar opposites (stability-change; people-tasks) as parts of the whole. Their chapter communicates the insights from a creative and rigorous research program to explore and test the relevance of two kinds of interpenetration that arise from attempts to deal with the paradox of continuity in organizational life: productive teamwork and practical revitalization. They suggest pragmatic measures or indicators of these orientations, which have previously been treated as mostly bipolar (product versus relationship; practical versus visionary). The results of their research to date provide compelling evidence that continuity management requires the executive to be skilled at both *tough love* and *practical visioning.* The promise of these notions is the counterpoint they provide to the current proliferation of competency-based and situation-management training models. While the latter tend to treat competencies as independent and variably useful, depending on level, task complexity, work relationships, and so forth, Quinn, Spreitzer, and Hart lay a realistic foundation for the behavioral aspects of the ideal, that elusive "9–9 manager" that is too often discounted as "merely" an ideal abstraction to strive toward. In this chapter, we see how attention to continuity eventually compels the executive to *be* that ideal.

The last two chapters in Part Three shift our attention from leader/executive actions to systems and structures to promote continuity. In Chapter Nine, Paul A. L. Evans addresses the change-continuity *duality* of organizational life and suggests through a detailed discussion of multidisciplinary studies that this characteristic of organizations is rooted in human nature and all social systems. Thus he offers more support for viewing organized efforts as the continuation of lives in progress. Our bias toward duality is again challenged in Evans's discourse as he argues that the typical means of dealing with duality — namely, pendular shifts of emphasis or sequencing — are linked to developmental adapting strategies in adults. It is as if we cannot expect organizations to manage continuity well (that is, to deal with stability *and* change) until all their members reach advanced stages of their own development. Perhaps then it is possible to view dualities in a different, more integrated (or interpenetrated, to use Quinn, Spreitzer, and Hart's notion in the previous chapter) and "fused" fashion.

For example, how or when could we expect executives to not treat resistance to change as an opposing force but rather embrace that voice as part and parcel of the duality in the situation? Evans suggests we need not wait for the individual adult to mature. Attention to continuity can, in fact, be a catalyst for transition to a different treatment of duality in life, inside and outside the organization. His prescriptions are aimed at systems and procedures that build in to everyday work life the articulation and appearance of "constructive tensions" brought about by the continuity-change choicepoints. Specifically and pragmatically, he introduces the concepts of *layering* and *decision architecture*, which are derived from observations of adult development, to deal with dualities. These approaches can guide the organization in achieving a *dynamic balance* between continuity and change, centralization and decentralization, loose and tight controls, and so on. Layering involves creation of new, complementary capabilities "on top of" existing ones to encompass more diversity and handle more complexity (Lynn's Japanese steelmaker, Chapter Six, demonstrates this well) and implies, among other things, new attention to how executives frame and use questions to construe what is going on and what should happen next. Evans presents three methods of decision architecture — multifocalism and reconciliation processes, complementarity in team decision making, and procedural justice — together with practical examples and suggestions for implementation. It is important to note the premise that underlies these system interventions. Evans is inviting us to intentionally embrace dualities in organizations as necessary and vital sources of tension. He believes that the experience of such tensions between opposites can be the catalyst for learning, new ideas, renewal, and excitement. In this sense, this chapter is a welcome reminder that continuity is *not* sameness or comfort; it is, however, life giving.

Kathryn M. Bartol examines the duality of continuity and innovation in Chapter Ten. She is concerned with the apparent tendency for organizations to overemphasize continuity with the past at the expense of future innovation. She addresses the question, "How can organizations preserve an appropriate degree of continuity and yet promote the necessary amount of innovation for success?" Her focus is on pay or reward systems as a mechanism for promoting continuity *and* innovation at the same time. This discussion helps us to treat continuity holistically. Rather than arguing for the connectedness of past and present (history) as one agenda and of present and future (plans, performance goals, visions) as another, she recommends recognition and reward systems that tie these together as the key to effective, incremental innovation. Referring to numerous studies that examine the intrinsic and extrinsic motivational factors relevant to the stages of the innovating process, Bartol illustrates the effect of reward systems on the delicate nature of creativity. Additionally, she discusses the potential advantages and disadvantages of various payment systems (outcome-based pay, merit plans, price-rate incentives, profit sharing, gain sharing, non-traditional bonus plans, special awards, and person-based pay systems) for promoting innovation. As the organizational strategy varies from requiring moderate (incremental) to substantial (radical) creativity, so does the attractiveness of these various reward systems. This review and comparison is noteworthy both because of its comprehensive nature and because of its context. Bartol compares and analyzes these practices with respect to their impact on the generation of new ideas *and* their influence on time-tested and proven practices.

In the Conclusion, Suresh Srivastva and Craig G. Wishart provide both a summary of the themes that recur throughout the book and a launching point for the reader's future investigation and application of the continuity concept. In this chapter, we come full circle back to our earlier discussion of change. The authors carefully craft their case for the acceptance of a new frame of reference for understanding the change processes of social systems. Their emphasis on continuity as the foundation of all change is compelling if we are to truly embrace the crucial leadership challenge for the twenty-first century: how to preserve the valued systems and practices of the past so that present aspirations for the future can be pursued, while shaping a future that does not limit the ability of future generations to fulfill their aspirations. In other words, the authors argue for a perspective that frees us to explore change processes that are inherently proactive, generative, creative, and purposeful, not just adaptive to external conditions. If we consider change to be, first and foremost, in the service of preserving continuity, then new questions, opportunities, and avenues of action emerge. We cannot stay the same because necessary dialogue about the source or essence of continuity creates new understandings and ambiguities. Creative tensions between old and new, loose and tight, centralized and autonomous, and creative and proven surface, compelling us to make collective choices. These choices signify what is important, exciting, and life giving. Thus, as the organization "acts," it both preserves its values and changes with purpose and passion for the future.

Implications for Executives

For the reader who finds herself or himself in never-ending "white water" (Vaill, 1989) or momentarily in the "eye of the storm," this injunction to pay more attention to continuity in your own and your organization's experience may sound trivial, irrational, or even foolhardy. But managing continuity is *not* staying the same or denying the need to change. Continuity is *not* the opposite of change. We believe that continuity is the key to organizational health. It enlightens our ideas and conceptions about how to "be well" (not how to treat disease). It challenges us to ponder how we are changing when we seem to maintain tried-and-true routines or practices, or how we maintain sameness while we alter goals, procedures, and practices. Waterman shares a wonderful personal anecdote to illustrate this at the beginning of his book *The Renewal Factor* (1987, p. 1):

> My family and I travel extensively. We like variety, new experiences, and rarely go back to a place we've been. The exception is Kona Village in Hawaii. We have been there ten times and will probably keep going back as long as it retains its special charm. I asked [   ], one of Kona's managers, how they maintained such amazing consistency over the 15 years we had been vacationing there.

> He smiled and said, "You've changed a lot in those years, haven't you? . . . There's your answer. Kona Village is not the same as it was. The guests run the place. You only see it as unchanging because we have been lucky enough to do a good job of tracking tastes and needs of people like you." Kona Village is both old and new. [Its management] knows how to retain the best of the past and still change with the times.

Paying attention to continuity in executive and organizational life compels the executive to embrace *learning* as a constant agenda, along with performing and developing. Learning, whether individually or organizationally, requires looking at what is analogous and unique in our current state. This necessitates forums and dialogue that provide time and space to experience the knowledge that is not only expressed orally and in writing but is also tacit — embedded in example, story, metaphor, gesture, and so forth. It is at this level of exchange that continuity can be discovered, nurtured, and passed on. As every chapter in this book exemplifies, this learning orientation results in a never-ending rephrasing and reframing of the basic questions and observations one is experiencing. Through just this reflective and interactive process, managers can be watchdogs to avoid change that is unduly disruptive or disconnected from aspirations and ideals that are carried forward from past experiences. In addition, the same process can prevent past practices from becoming habit and can foster choiceful renewal of practices or values that help shape the future and connect with the present.

So in continuity management we embrace the purposeful intent to renew ourselves and our organizations, we align with the priority of learning through and from our experiences with others, and we signal a clarion call to organizations and executives of the twenty-first century: preserve the past to ensure the future; conceive the future to enact the present; and transform the present to provide linkages that hold together the past, the present, and the future.

PART ONE

Searching for Continuity

The three chapters comprising this part focus on what continuity is, how we can articulate for ourselves and our organizations exactly what it is that connects the past to the present, and where we should begin to look for it. This inquiry is essentially historical in nature. Each of the contributions to this part tells a story or discusses storytelling as a legitimate means of recognizing and even celebrating the things that hold our experience together in some meaningful way.

For Bateson in Chapter One, continuity (and discontinuity) become interpretive frameworks for viewing one's life in progress. She asserts that our understanding of the present and expectations for the future are determined by how we have viewed our pasts in terms of continuous (or discontinuous) explanations. For her, the job of the executive or leader involves interpreting the situation of the organization in terms of continuous and discontinuous explanations, metaphors, or models. The fact that these interpretations are social constructions leads to the realization that continuous and discontinuous explanations can coexist. It is therefore important for the leader to make choices that give meaning and hope to the current situation. Bateson also warns us of the dysfunctional consequences of relying too much on either perspective, where the view of past success (or failure) is attributed to too much consistency or too much change.

In Chapter Two, Gergen suggests that stories of our lives in progress (autobiographies) can enhance our ways of viewing continuity in organizations. Through an analysis of how men and women construe their lives differently, she offers alternative ways of looking into past organizational experiences to determine what is important or unique to carry forward into the future. As a counterpoint to the linear, predictive, sequential, goal-oriented model of continuity derived from men's stories, we are challenged to consider the multifaceted, tentative, fuzzy, oscillating tenor of women's stories as a valid interpretive framework for understanding what it is that links life's (or the organization's) experiences. In this context, continuity is viewed in dynamic (versus stable) terms; it resides in erratic, untidy, fluid, and ambivalent conditions. This way of conceptualizing the continuous nature of things may well be better suited to the modern call for executives to "love change," "embrace chaos," and so on.

The third contribution to this section, by Loveridge, is a story of another kind. In contrast to the self-reflective, biographical approach to continuity taken in the first two chapters, Chapter Three compares the stories of two major European firms involved in original equipment manufacturing for motor vehicles. These case histories illustrate how current organizational structures and practices are embedded in other system structures and hierarchies such as labor or trade associations, local traditions, and regional economic circumstances. Loveridge's analysis suggests that it is the appreciation, maintenance, and nurturance of these alliances and networks that extend continuity from the past into the future. We are reminded in this chapter that continuity is contextually based and thus that historical reflection and inquiry are essential in shaping the perspectives we draw on in functioning within, and changing, our organizations.

Chapter One

The Construction
of Continuity

Mary Catherine Bateson

The term *continuity* refers to a degree of sameness, primarily to sameness sustained through time. There are few situations in which it is not possible to discern both continuity and discontinuity, and indeed, they are two sides of the same coin. Often the distinction is a matter of interpretation. The leadership issue in any organization or community, I believe, is to work with the relationship between continuity and discontinuity so that the benefits of both are available.

Continuity/Discontinuity in Individual Lives

I have recently been experimenting with the following workshop exercise dealing with continuities and discontinuities in individual life histories that I developed for participants in a computer conference on "Emergent Ambitions." I asked them to provide two brief life stories, one of which was to be focused on discontinuity:

1. How would you tell the story of your life as an elaboration of the following statement: Everything I have ever done has been heading me for where I am today . . .

27

2. How would you tell the story of your life as
    an elaboration of this other statement: After
    lots of surprises and choices (and perhaps in-
    terruptions and disappointments), I have ar-
    rived somewhere I could never have antici-
    pated . . .

The questions were presented in the same communication, along with a pair of samples:

1A: "I already thought of myself as a future writer,
even in high school, and there has hardly been a
year since college when I have not published something, so now I have a joint appointment in Anthropology and English and I take off half of every
year to write. Many of my students are aspiring
writers."
2A: "I planned in high school to be a poet, but I
gave up writing poetry in college and the only writing I did for many years was academic. But when
I became unemployed because of the Iranian revolution shortly after my mother died, I chose the
strategy of writing a memoir, and suddenly as a
result, I found I had a reputation as a writer of
nonfiction. Now I am considering switching again
and writing a novel."

The context, the program, the title of the seminar, and
so on would have tilted responses in the direction of change if
I had not asked for two versions. The purpose of the exercise
was not to determine each individual's preferred way of con-
struing his or her life history, but to allow each one to discover
the existence of alternative interpretations, to experience an "old
woman/young woman" set of alternative interpretations in her
own life.
    Even in our change-emphasizing culture, some contexts
favor emphasis on the threads of continuity in life histories.
Obituaries and heroic biographies (this is important, for these

are the stories held up for emulation) often emphasize continuity and report early signs of achievement to come: Henry Ford is said to have lost his heart to the first horseless carriage he saw as a child; St. Teresa of Avila is said to have tried to run away to be martyred by the Moors; mothers of musicians describe their children's response to the radio. You see, these stories suggest he or she was always on the path to this particular kind of greatness. Such models of achievement propose a single rising curve of development, prefigured in childhood, prepared by education, overcoming obstacles, and moving upward, often with significant defined milestones: partnership for a lawyer, tenure for a professor, properly spaced promotions for a military officer, a vice presidency, perhaps, for a rising executive. In this type of story, if the milestones do not occur in the appropriate rhythm, cease, or slow down, a career is stalled. Here we have two kinds of continuity: a continuity of focus whereby a particular skill or dedication is maintained and a continuity of change, steady rise along a given trajectory.

These narratives contrast with another popular subtype, where the plot involves a major shift, the turning of a corner. This plot type is most common in "confession" narratives like those of St. Augustine, Malcolm X, or Crashing Thunder, which depend on accentuating early badness before a turnaround. Yet most modern readers of St. Augustine are struck by the continuities behind the conversion plot. Other such narratives involve a critical meeting, immigration, a technological breakthrough. Such turning-point narratives play a continuing and perhaps increasing role in our culture. An example would be the development of 12-step programs, which require that the individual model his or her experience so that a moment is identified as touching bottom, after which ascent becomes possible. Similarly, we typically deal with other transitions in life by emphasizing the discontinuity involved, for instance, by amplifying the hostility in the disintegration of a marriage. The drama involved in the assertion of total change may be a useful motivating factor; yet one who has the experience of being born again may have to face all the groping learning of an infant. For a whole range of topics, we seem to have difficulty conceptualizing gradual change. The development of an autonomous human individual involves multiple watersheds and gradual transitions. There are half a dozen points at which one might identify gestation, but this society is locked in debate to determine a single point of absolute contrast between stages.

The steady-achievement narrative and the conversion narrative provide clear, unambiguous plot lines, whatever suspense and dangers are built in along the way. Implicit in each — or often enough explicit — is some kind of goal toward which a life is directed. We do not as a culture value those stories that involve zigzag or spiral rhythms, multiple starts and stops, new beginnings and recyclings of earlier elements. A common question in job interviews is "What do you want to be doing in five years?" "Nothing I can now imagine" is not a winning answer. In my recent work on the ways in which women combine commitments to career and family (Bateson, 1989, 1991), I have been struck by how common such stories are and how frequently they are denigrated or disparaged. While much of the organizational behavior literature focuses on innovation, personnel officers may still discriminate against individuals whose résumés do not show a clear progression, and young people worry about getting "on track." My recent work has involved developing ways to affirm underlying continuities in lives of constant readaptation, continuities of learning and creativity.

For the computer seminar I described earlier, most members of the group discovered that either interpretation — continuity or discontinuity — was possible, in spite of habitual preferences. Some constructed two stories by focusing on different aspects of their lives (same spouse, different job). Some noticed that apparent discontinuity was increased or reduced by semantic selection ("I have always been a writer" versus "I used to write poetry, but now I am a journalist"). Some noticed continuities to change itself ("I have always enjoyed tackling the unknown" or "I have always expected my work to provide interest and challenge"), others in styles of action ("It's always been important for me to work with people"); others used metaphors of continuous variation such as surfing ("one wave after another"). Many go through shifts in their major activities but seldom recognize that they have shifted not to something new but to something prefigured in minor activities. As one participant said, "After all, the laws of physics never change." But one might equally have said, "Sure I've been an engineer for thirty years, but meanwhile consider the turnover in my body's cells."

Interpretations Combining
Continuity and Discontinuity

If, as my experience suggests, there is wide interpretive latitude in discerning themes of continuity and discontinuity in particular events, and if the choice of a particular mode of interpretation is influenced by cultural models and preferences, our understanding of the relationship between continuity and discontinuity in management must include the dimension of interpretation. We need a theory that explores the usefulness of alternative interpretations in different situations. Arguably, it is in the interest of management to make sure that both interpretations are viable. The reshaping of the Atlantic and Pacific Tea Company into the modern A&P depended on the affirmation that the company had been and would continue to be a food company. Thus a choice of management strategies may involve a deliberate choice of certain factors or definitions to be held constant and certain factors to be varied. Both deserve explicit attention. Beyond the issue of general cultural preferences in interpretation, individuals must find values in the experience of both continuity and discontinuity. Each may sometimes be freeing. Each may sometimes be pathological.

Some degree of continuity would seem to be essential to an individual's sense of security, security that makes other dimensions of change bearable. When I was an infant, my mother formulated the following rule: It is all right to leave the baby in a strange place with a familiar person, or in a familiar place with a strange person, but too frightening when both are strange. In fact, we never moved, but great numbers of people moved through the household. When my daughter was little, my husband and I moved frequently, but she had a much smaller number of caretakers. At some deep level in the personality, perhaps, all change evokes the danger of abandonment. For individuals in states of high vulnerability, the insecurity associated with discontinuity can sometimes be triggered by minute changes. Clients in psychotherapy, which is, after all, a process designed to produce change, sometimes spend weeks struggling with their reactions to a change in the furniture arrangement in a consulting room or a new hairstyle adopted by the therapist. Often individuals construct symbols of continuity that can be carried with them, as parents may consciously encourage the development of so-called "transitional objects" (security blankets) for children who face the insecurities of multiple caretakers or travel. In the same way, immigrants coming to America or pioneers moving West have always carried with them at least a few objects that provide a link with the past: photographs, ritual objects such as candlesticks, a Bible, a figurine hat, moved from mantel to mantel, converts a new house into a home. Similarly, we associate the carrying of a "lucky piece" with the wanderer or adventurer.

Continuities that provide a sense of security during periods of change may also be a great deal more abstract. An account of the experience of Iowa farmers who lost their farms (and identities) to mortgage foreclosures suggested that the wives were quicker to adapt than their husbands—but while the men had lost their homes, their livelihoods, and their identities, the women had lost only the first two. Their identities as wives provided a basis for new ways of caring for and supporting their husbands.

One benefit that flows from a sense of continuity is a great deal more proactive than the maintenance of security or identity, and this is the capacity to transfer learning. If a situation is construed as totally new and different, earlier learning may be seen as irrelevant. The transfer of learning relies on some recognized element of continuity—a woman describing her patchwork of careers for me recently noted that she had found a continuity between work as a kindergarten teacher, a teacher of the deaf, and dean of "Greek life" (fraternities) on a university campus! The capacity to adjust to a radical change in one's situation by recognizing continuities is a critical survival skill. If I recognize my situation today as different but in some sense comparable to my situation yesterday, I can translate yesterday's skills and yesterday's learnings. I will make neither the mistake of trying to start from scratch nor that of simply replicating previous patterns.

Gender stereotypes often suggest that female roles emphasize continuity (this is called "keeping the home fires burning"), whereas males venture forth. Similarly, we often speak as if women pass on tradition, while paternal care provides new challenges. There is no doubt some truth to this cultural division of labor, yet actually, if one examines activities rather than labels, traditional female roles involve a high degree of adaptation to change, while many men (and many women outside the home) ply the same trade for a lifetime with little new learning.

Along with the odd distortion, which is now often commented on, of women who used to say, "I don't work, I'm just a housewife," there is a second, usually unremarked distortion when women say, "I've been doing the same thing for the last fifteen years, just looking after our kids and keeping house." If a corporate assignment changes and involves new skills and increased responsibility, the title often changes as well, and the discontinuity (and success in bridging that discontinuity) is noted. But you rarely hear someone say, "I was getting pretty good at being the mother of an infant, but my new assignment, caring for a toddler, is still really challenging." Mother of one becomes mother of two? Mother of an adolescent? Mother-in-law? Part of the agony of caring for a severely retarded child may be the lack of change, the lack of milestones, and, conversely, the recognition and celebration of change in a developing infant may be a critical dynamic within the continuity of the human family. My suspicion is that women are still somewhat less likely to initiate than men, but more likely to find ways to adapt when change is imposed on them.

Thus it is simplistic to associate continuity or discontinuity with either gender. Pressures in both directions can come from either parent. Pity the child whose father has been fixated since his birth on having someone follow in his footsteps, as well as the child whose mother has been fixated on having someone free to follow the career she was not allowed.

Parents, like managers, play a key role in determining whether a given process is defined as continuity or discontinuity. My daughter said when she was about fourteen, having decided to be an actress, "Mummy, it must be awfully hard on you and Daddy that I don't want to do any of the same things you and Daddy do and Grandma and Granddad." Well, you don't know with an adolescent whether the sense of continuity is critical at a given moment or the sense of rebellion, but I crossed my fingers and said, "You can't be a good actress unless you are an observer of human behavior and unless you think about the range of human experiences and motivations. Actually what we do has a lot in common." I was lucky, since apparently what I said then was useful. American families have traditionally combined continuity and change when the sons of garage mechanics have become engineers and their sons have become physicists. In contrast with this, I have had a number of conversations with members of Israeli kibbutzim, bewailing the fact that their children do not want to follow in their footsteps and choose instead to leave the kibbutz, even to go abroad. When I ask them, "Did you grow up on a kibbutz?", they respond, "Oh, no, my father was a shopkeeper in the city and was very religious." The children are, in fact, following in the parents' footsteps by leaving. When a corporation gets a new CEO, is this necessarily an example of discontinuity? It is, but there is also discontinuity involved if a CEO gives up smoking. At the same time, continuity is not hard to find when a new CEO steps in; in America today he is likely to be yet another white male. There is a choice of interpretations, but finding the appropriate balance is the key to an effective transition.

This balance may be critical to survival. Recently, I was invited to speak at a national conference of midlife women, members of a Catholic teaching order. They all belonged to the age cohort that entered the order before the reforms in the Catholic Church; when they entered, they were cloistered, wore old-fashioned habits, were taught to avoid all personal conversation. Today they live in apartments, some alone, some with other members, develop friendships, dress as they please. As high school and college teachers they were always well educated, but today they can choose their assignments, and many work in other social service professions. From one five-year cohort, as many as four out of five left the order. Interestingly enough, some of those who left did so because of too much change, others because of too little (I do not know in what proportion). The question arises, under those circumstances, who stays? One hypothesis would suggest that they are the weakest, those for whom any security is better than autonomy, or those who simply drift, and no doubt there are some who could be looked at in this way. But the ones I conversed with (there is an endemic problem in ethnography that one has the richest interactions with the liveliest people) fit a different category. They were women who had been able to recognize continuity in discontinuity, to accept a radical change in the pattern of their lives and assert that the commitment they were expressing was still changing and yet at a deeper level remained the same.

The Eriksonian version of the life cycle can easily be used to argue for openness to change in the adult years, since the life stage of *generativity* involves as much emphasis on giving birth to the new as on maintaining the past. Arguably, effective parenting involves both the transmission of continuities and the openness to individual particularity and development; it involves providing a base of security and continuing identity and freeing the individual for risk and experimentation. The definition of any stage of the life cycle only as a plateau, without a dimension of growth, seems likely to lead to stagnation and discontent. The famous "midlife crisis," as well as much of the senility observed in the elderly, may be an artifact of such a cultural and organizational misdefinition.

I use two metaphors frequently in thinking about the combination of continuity and creativity in the ways that individuals "compose" their lives. One is linguistic: in speaking, we follow culturally transmitted rules of grammar, but these allow totally original utterances (in fact, the generation of sentences never before spoken is the norm). The other is that set of art forms referred to as improvisational, such as jazz or Homeric recitation, which actually depend on endless practice and the recombining of previously learned components so that each performance is both new and practiced. Effective parenting involves the transmission of these skills.

In a sense, all behavior depends on this recognition of continuity within discontinuity. A story used to be told about the cyberneticist Norbert Wiener. He was riding in a car driven slowly by a student through narrow streets when they knocked over a child chasing a ball. The student pulled over, helped the child — who was only slightly bruised — to her feet, took her into a pharmacy, bought her a bandaid and a lollipop, and called her mother. (Today he might call a lawyer.) Wiener had not moved. "You have hit a small child before with your car?" he asked. The student said, "My God, no, heaven forbid." "But then how did you know what to do?" In fact, to know what to do in a novel situation, he had to use a truly vast amount of existing knowledge: law, folk psychology, first aid, how to use a telephone. Even in completely new situations, response depends on recognizing continuity.

Alternative interpretations of most situations in terms of continuity and discontinuity exist, then, and the choice of emphasis in interpretation is related to personality or mental state (the patient in therapy versus the adventurer who says, "I have always enjoyed starting something new"). This choice is also related to cultural definitions of what counts as the same and what counts as different, and to the acts of labeling that occur during transitions. Thus, continuity and discontinuity are socially constructed categories. The trick of successful innovation may be to offer both at the same time.

Logical Levels

Beyond the issues of definition and symbolism and the need to include both kinds of interpretation, however, real issues in combining the appropriate levels for maintenance and for change arise. All change can be interpreted as an effort to maintain some constancy, perhaps a very abstract constancy such as survival or profitability. Much that we do in the name of stability leads to drastic change: the Vietnam War, for instance. The nuns who stayed through the reforms were asserting, *plus ça change plus c'est la même chose.* Those who resist change often suffer the reverse, *plus c'est la même chose, plus ça change.*

All around the world today, we find processes of change underway where the key challenge to leadership is to make rapid change tolerable by providing affirmations of underlying continuity. Thus, for example, Ethiopian Jews arriving in Israel are able to bear the most radical change by saying they have come home. But in situation after situation, some still find discontinuity so unthinkable that they are driven to reactionary behavior. In resisting change in this way, they fail to recognize that when some item is held constant, while the context varies, constancy is an illusion. It is not surprising that a reversion to extreme nationalism and anti-Semitism is occurring in the former Soviet Union, but the meaning of these regressive responses is different as we approach the year 2000. The traditional garments worn by nuns or Hasidim were only slightly different from general patterns of dress when they were adopted, but freezing these styles created new situations of extreme differentiation. Similarly, fundamentalists, threatened by frightening and overwhelming change, assert that they are practicing the "true" religion, but because they assert the truth of the words of scripture in the context of modern notions of truth and falsehood (which they share), they are in effect asserting something new.

Any reader of my summary of alternative narratives will have noticed a variable relationship between the continuity dimension and the discontinuity dimension: sometimes these are at the same level of abstraction, but more often they are at different levels. We can see contrasts between superficial change within profound continuity, and superficial continuity within profound change. In evolution, an abstract constancy (survival) is maintained by the possibility of multiple small changes (adaptation). Lamarckian evolution (the inheritance of acquired characteristics) would be fatal because of the loss of flexibility involved: A dog grows thicker fur when exposed to a cold climate because it has the trait "adjustable fur thickness." If after several generations in a cold climate the offspring have "acquired" that characteristic, then one constancy, the capacity to adjust fur thickness, has been replaced by another, "fixed heavy fur thickness." But the animal can no longer adjust to a warmer climate. A tightrope walker maintains his balance by changing the angle of the balancing pole he carries. Freeze the angle of the pole and he will fall. Symbolically, superficial tokens of continuity may be immensely comforting during transitions, but the maintenance of superficial continuity carries great dangers. In a balanced cybernetic system, of course, the very changes or adjustments produced by negative or corrective feedback maintain a fundamental constancy, while the changes in a regenerative or positive feedback system do not.

Pathologies of Continuity and Change

Some ways of connecting continuity and change may be pathological. This is illustrated by two kinds of addiction, which should perhaps be distinguished. In one kind of addiction, typical of many smokers whose consumption remains level, the behavior that maintains a constant level of nicotine intoxication through the day nevertheless brings about cumulative and often fatal changes in heart and lungs. In this type of addiction, the relationship between levels is distorted: a superficial constancy is maintained at the cost of more profound change.

The same term — *addiction* — is also used for a rather different pathology in the relationship between constancy and change. A family of acquired needs exists where the need is not for a given substance but for a constant change in the supply of that substance, which must steadily increase because of various forms of habituation and changes in threshold. This description applies to some forms of alcohol and heroin use, to arms races, and to the American economy, which is addicted to increases in GNP. In these forms of addiction, more and more of something is required in order to feel good. Anorexics must get thinner and thinner in order to feel slim. More and more missiles are needed in order to feel secure. Pornography must be progressively more horrendous to continue to titillate. Some treatments of addiction involve replacing an escalating need for a destructive substance with a stable need for one that carries a reduced cost, such as methadone or daily attendance at Alcoholics Anonymous meetings.

An addictive potential exists in all pleasures that do not carry a natural satiety. Once money is invented, for example, wealth apparently becomes addictive, for the wealthy are never wealthy enough. However, the use of the term *addiction* always carries the judgment that the change produced is in some sense degenerative. Some readers would no doubt disagree about the ecological and other costs of an addiction to growth. I suspect, however, that at least some kinds of affirmation of constant change must fall outside of this definition: constant learning, for instance. And yet we might argue that the modern vulnerability to boredom is the long-term result of an addiction to change and variation. These are kinds of shifts that are very important to find ways to think about.

Conclusion

Continuity and discontinuity are defined by relationships: between past and present. The efficacy of a particular balance of continuity and discontinuity depends on the relationship between a given system and its context and on relationships between systemic and logical levels. Because these are relational concepts, we should beware of reifying as a prescriptive "good" for either an organization or a life.

From the point of view of composing a life or managing a corporation, the kind of double vision I suggested at the beginning of the chapter seems to be very important: the ability to recognize any situation as representing both continuity and change and to express that double recognition to fit the needs of individuals. But at a more profound level, we need to recognize and avoid those kinds of change that reduce flexibility and those kinds of constancy that involve deeper change in variables essential to survival. The issue of freedom seems to turn up to a striking degree in thinking about continuity and discontinuity. On the one hand, the freedom to survive and flourish and sustain an ongoing sense of identity is essential. But on the other hand, continuities such as those of addiction can become prisons.

Chapter Two

Metaphors for Chaos, Stories of Continuity: Building a New Organizational Theory

Mary McCanney Gergen

We dream in narrative, remember, anticipate, hope, despair, believe, doubt, plan, revise, criticize, construct, gossip, learn, hate, and love by narrative.

— Hardy, 1968, p. 5

I think of history as a story and myself as a storyteller.

— Tuchman, 1979, p. 144

The construction is nothing more than an improvisation.

— Rosenwald, 1988, p. 256

The storyteller, biographer, historian, and organizational leader have much in common. Whether to amuse, edify, clarify, or inspire, all of them need stories through which to communicate with their audience. Like them, each of us makes sense of our lives, our worlds, our experiences via the repertoire of stories available to us. Formed and informed as we are in the languages and cultures of our youths and later lives, we spin our tales of self and others, orchestrated by the forms that have been set before us. Through myths, fairy tales, fables, legends, novels, dramas, musicals, comic strips, and films, to mention some forms, we become acquainted with the possible variations of storied lives. These stories give us models of possibilities for becoming, and, with invisible ease, captivate us. Because of their intimate and long-standing connection to our lives, we overlook them; they have become transparencies. The words we speak often seem to be spontaneous and freely chosen. Yet we are servants to the forms set down before us. Through them we tell the stories of childhood, school days, adolescence, first loves, separations, families, careers, midlife crises, and old age. Stories, in sum, enable us to "know" ourselves and to become (Gergen and Gergen, 1988).

These socially constructed narratives we tell of our lives are rooted not only in our repertoire of experience but also in our interactions with others. Each of us brings to every interaction the sum of our experience. Then the negotiation begins. Because of the interactive interchange that produces these constructions, stories are open to continuous alterations as temporal and interactive processes change. Each narrative, as the joint product of people in relationships, sustains, enhances, and/or impedes the flow of other actions. A happy story cannot easily lead to failure. And so, too, the reverse. Each story told prevents others from a telling. Each one told has many iterations. No story is final.

Social scientists have recently begun to explore the potentials of narratives as forms for inquiry, often as a result of increasing dissatisfaction with more traditional forms of empirical study. Psychologists, in particular, have become involved in the study of how individuals construct their lives via narratives (M. Gergen, forthcoming; McAdams, 1985; Runyon, 1983; Sarbin, 1986; Schaie, 1989). Additionally, social scientists have drawn from philosophers and historians of science the idea that scientific pursuits in general can be understood in terms of narrative lines (Knorr-Cetina, 1981; Latour, 1987). Scientific investigations, for example, are frequently described as forms of mystery stories. The researcher is hot on the trail of an unsolved mystery. In the posture of Sherlock Holmes, the scientist detects false leads, dead ends, and crucial evidence, and through "elementary" logical deduction and brilliant insight, the researcher finally solves the case. In turning away from a natural science vision of knowledge, narratologists have just begun to suggest the range of potentials that linguistic devices have in formulating various phenomena and their relationships. Gareth Morgan (1986), an organizational theorist, for example, discusses the power of metaphors in shaping the ways in which members of organizations know who they are, what they belong to, and how they interact.

Many theorists, particularly those in literary theory and criticism (Frye, 1957; Propp, 1968), historiography (White, 1957), and the social sciences (Mandler, 1984; Gergen, 1989), have tried to define the well-formed narrative (whether for use in individual lives, organizational frames, or scientific investigations). In summarizing these core characteristics, Kenneth Gergen and I have suggested that to produce a paradigmatic narrative in contemporary Western culture, one must generally include at least five basic features. The storyteller must (1) establish a valued endpoint to the story; for example, a company must have a profitable year. Once established, (2) the events selected for inclusion in the story must be somehow relevant to that goal, while diverse or tangential materials are excluded. The love affair of the mail clerk and the vice president of human resources must not be noted in the annual report, but the annual sales figures must be. These events are, at the same time, (3) ordered by some principle of intelligibility, the most frequent one being chronologically. One would not randomly present sales figures. But beyond chronicling events, the storyteller (4) establishes causal linkages between these events. The sales figures are tied to explanatory events — the simpler, the better. Finally, the storyteller (5) gives signs that indicate the beginning and end of the tale. The annual report has an introduction and a conclusion. Thus, the listener knows that other forms of discourse and action may ensue.

In addition, our analyses have indicated that the storyteller has limited options in terms of the overall pattern or trajectories of these stories. Three general forms are the basis of all stories:

the progressive narrative, when the progress toward the goal becomes increasingly more positive; the regressive narrative, when these fortunes are in decline; or the stability narrative, when the tides of fortune are level, as in a "happily ever after" ending. Combinations of these three forms constitute the varieties of stories found in Western cultures today: the tragedy, comedy, or melodrama (Gergen and Gergen, 1983, 1986, 1988).

Beyond these properties, narratives are often divided into types according to their content, their characters, and the ways in which the tides of fortune swing for the heroes in their tales. Joseph Campbell (1956, 1972), the great scholar of ancient myth, suggests that all stories can be compressed into one, a universal myth or monomyth, from which all others derive. This tale should sound familiar — the young hero must leave his land and people to set out on a quest. This sacred challenge leads him into dark and dangerous territories, where he battles fierce and wily enemies, resists great temptations, and overcomes adversity. Finally, after intense suffering, travail, and courage, he achieves his goal and is handsomely rewarded. In important respects, the hero's tale exemplifies what Lyotard (1984) has called the grand narrative of progress. This form exemplifies the well-made narrative, containing the five cardinal attributes delineated above. What is crucial to recall from these analyses of narrative form is that the nature of the form, the composition of the story, what may and may not be included, where the dramatic points, highlights, climaxes, and endings must be, are dependent not on the happenings of people's lives but on the nature of the narrative form itself. Thus, in some very important way, the narrative form determines the nature of the life. As Paul de Man (1979, p. 920) has said, "We assume that life produces the autobiography as an act produces its consequences, but can we not suggest, with equal justice, that the autobiography project may itself produce and determine life?"

While it may seem reasonable that individual lives may be produced through story form, and that history and biography can be seen as narratives, it is often less evident that scientific theories dealing with broader or more abstract entities are subject to the same formulations as individual lives. Yet why should the stories of social groups, organizations, and institutions be any different? From this perspective, it is inevitable that scientific theories are also born from the cultural traditions belonging to the groups that share, apply, and recreate them. No group with a culture, regardless of its centrality, power, or claims to rationality, can escape being identified and characterized within the languages of the culture. As Michael Sprinker (1980, p. 325) has described it, "Every text [and every theory] is an articulation of the relations between texts, a product of intertextuality, a weaving together of what has already been produced elsewhere in discontinuous form." Thus, sociologists link together the forms of prior generations; anthropologists follow closely in the footsteps of their predecessors; organizational theorists forage among the formulations of other players from the recent past. In psychology, one might suggest that Piaget's theories of cognitive development have been described as a story of heroic proportions — the upward struggle to a new and higher level of integration for the child. In contrast, Freud's theories provide us a melodramatic struggle with darkness that is never totally won, while Carl Rogers delineates the story with a happy ending where unconditional love may continually flow (Gergen and Gergen, 1983).

The question in the present context concerns organizational continuity. The need for this focus stems from a perceived imbalance favoring change over continuity in organizational studies especially. In recent years, organizational practitioners and theorists have been fascinated by images of "razzle-dazzle" leaders (the "changemasters," "pathfinders," and "gamesmen," for example), leaders who tend to be enamored of concepts of transformation and innovation and change. In contrast, as Srivastva and Fry have written, "We are beginning to express a hidden hunger for continuity and community, for responsiveness and dependability, and for the strength of identity that comes when life is integrally connected to both the wisdom of the past and concern for the future" (letter of invitation to the Case Western Reserve University Continuity Symposium, June 6, 1990). What are we to make of this charge? How shall we respond? From a narratological perspective, what are needed are new stories of organizations, stories that will recognize the central import of continuity in executive interactions. The dilemma arises when we try to imagine creating these new forms, because we too are dependent on stories previously told. From what stories should we heap together a new form? Must we create a new hero whose quest is continuity? Or are there other ways to tell the tale of organizational continuity and executive life? Might we find intriguing elisions, novel conjunctions, and unsettling forms in some other "tale world" to put together new possibilities around this theme? We can give it a try.

I come to this call for new stories of continuity by way of autobiography (M. Gergen, forthcoming). I am interested in how famous people in our society tell their life stories. I see these storytelling forms as basic narrative models for our own lives. These stories not only shape the form of individual human lives but are molds for telling other stories as well. Of particular interest here is the question of how one might, as an organizational scientist, use life stories to define organizational continuity in new ways. To understand these narrative forms, we will begin by looking at men's stories; their form dominates the scene in science as well as social life. The dominance of a single, linear, progressive form of continuity in men's stories will be underscored. I will suggest that the type of continuity that issues forth from these narratives affects how organizations also view continuity in their story lines. The limits of these stories will be highlighted, too. An exposition of women's stories will reveal that they contain far different notions of continuity — forms that are not singular, linear, or progressive. To make the distinction between the gendered stories clear and to illustrate the potential of women's stories, I will then contrast the two. Through the introduction of the metaphors of chaos science, the limits of traditional men's/science narrative forms are transcended. In conclusion, I suggest that organizational leaders and scientists might benefit from viewing continuity within a new narrative form — one that emerges from the metaphors of chaos science.

Men's Stories: Life as Career

What does the reader discern about form when she looks at popular autobiographies of famous men? From what kind of narrative form is the story constituted? Do well-known men tell their own life stories as heroes, or do they wonder at the tides of fortune that have thrust them into the limelight? Are these lives compact renditions of a single theme or a melange of professional and personal concerns, with each taking the major part of the narrative as time and fortunes shift? To answer these questions, I analyzed a group of popular autobiographies primarily published in the 1980s in the United States. In this section, I will concentrate on the life stories of Lee Iacocca, J. Paul Getty, Donald Trump, Ahmad Rashad, Chuck Yeager, Thomas Watson, Jr., Edward Koch, and Richard Feynman. In addition, we will note the content by which the form is revealed. In this context I used quantitative methods of analysis — for example, counting the instances of achievement-related passages in each book. However, I found the lengthy and tedious process of dissecting pages of prose into categories of content and form more destructive and uninformative concerning the flow of the book's overall form than helpful. Thus, I have chosen to abandon these formalized techniques in favor of a qualitatively tuned method that attempts to encompass the narrative form in a more integrated manner. Each method gains and loses in certain ways. The precision and apparent reliability of the first method is lost, but the interpretive strength of the latter in maintaining the holistic integrity of the book is apparent. Moreover, the finding that men and women tell their stories differently is so striking that no statistical framework seems necessary once one begins to read for the gendered pattern of narrative form.

Leibowitz (1989, p. xiv) says that "the grand theme of American autobiography, almost its fixation, is the quest for distinction." Popular autobiographies of men are very similar to each other in form and theme; they constitute variations on the plot of Joseph Campbell's monomyth. Following the rules for the well-formed narrative, these autobiographies center on one chain of events. They also tend to be linear, aimed in a teleological sense at an explicit goal state or end point established by the author. The events described in any detail are strongly connected to this goal, and tangential events are ignored, truncated, or attached to the major thrust of events. Often the events of this narrative are ordered chronologically. The movement of the stories tends to be progressive in form, building from a lower level of satisfaction or success to a higher plane. In the classic sense, the story has a comic or happy-ending form. From lowly origins, difficult beginnings, or otherwise challenging circumstances, through a realm of struggle, dedication, vision, discipline, and hard work, the author emerges victorious. These stories are usually characterized by one or two major climaxes, around which the entire story is built. These are frequently situated near the end of the book. In most cases the ending suggests a leveling off, possibly a transition to other goals, but not a downturn of events. There is seldom any hint of irony, self-doubt, distraction, displeasure, indulgence, or oscillating in the continuities that link the initiation of the story in the past via the present and into the future. That is, the hero does not relinquish his goal once he becomes committed to it.

Chuck Yeager's autobiography is centered on his rise from a barefoot and ignorant "hillbilly" boy to a distinguished American pilot. The heroic dimensions of his story are the focus of his tale, with particular emphasis on the contrast of his meager origins with his triumphant achievement, which merited attention from presidents and prime ministers. The form that concentrates exclusively on his life as a pilot allows him little opportunity to bring in other aspects of his life. Yeager's book is so "lean and mean" in his tellings that inserts produced by other people were introduced to soften the effect. His wife, for example, is introduced to recall personal life events, such as their courtship, marriage, and family life. She writes about finding out that Chuck intended to marry her when his mother mentioned it in a letter. She adds, "The night before the wedding, he finally proposed, in his own way: 'I don't have much, so I can't promise you much except maybe a little cabin up in some hollar'" (Yeager and James, 1985, p. 99).

Richard Feynman (1986, p. 3), the Nobel Prize–winning physicist, begins his story this way: "When I was about 11 or 12, I set up a lab in my house." One might think that Feynman had sprung from a satellite or some other mechanical object, since his story of his origins is almost completely detached from anything but physics lessons. A sprinkling of other stories concerning his interests in art, music, and sex occur in his book, but they are most often included to show him as a physicist who can outsmart most others, in their areas, while remaining committed to his number one involvement: physics.

Ahmad Rashad's book *Rashad* is also arranged primarily around the monomythic tale of his rise to football stardom and the rewards he reaped as a result. The focus on football is clearly signaled in his opening phrase: "I've spent most of my life working on Sunday mornings, and I'm not even a man of the cloth" (Rashad, 1988, p. 1). What deviates from the norm in this kickoff is a suggestion that the hero has a sense of humor. The hero's tale is rarely a source of amusement!

J. Paul Getty's autobiography (1986), like those of Donald Trump, Thomas Watson, Jr., and Lee Iacocca, is dominated by the goals of business success. For Getty, the quest for oil and the development of his company despite the foils of nature; for Trump, the making of the bigger and bigger deals against the competition of other bidders; for Watson, the growth of IBM to colossal stature; and for Iacocca, the creation of more and more successful automobile ventures in an often-hostile world set up the goal states that orient the trajectory of the autobiographies. As Iacocca (1984, p. xiv) begins, "You're about to read the history of a man who's had more than his share of successes." The need to keep the form of the narrative simple leads to an interesting coda in Iacocca's book. He wants to describe his role in spearheading the drive to save the Statue of Liberty, as chair of the Statue of Liberty–Ellis Island Centennial Commission. But he describes this part of his life, which he apparently perceives as a totally different goal state from the automobile success story, separately in an epilogue, as a miniature narrative at the conclusion of the other tale. In form, it mimics the larger book, and it has the appearance of being tacked on, as is a chapter in which he gives his opinions on how to save American business from the Japanese. What is interesting about these two parts is that they cannot be accommodated into the main portion of the book because the form is too rigid to allow for "extraneous" discussion. In these autobiographies, the level of continuity expressed by the narrow, linear, progressive, and nonrecursive line of the aerodynamic story form is rigorously followed almost without exception.

While it would theoretically be possible for a story line as described above to be created around any significant life goal, the nature of the monomythic form is such that the content, at least at an abstract level, coalesces with the form. The monomyth is not just a description of a narrative form, but it is also a particular story. The overarching theme of this story is the pursuit of a vision despite hardships. Translated into the modern era, this theme becomes the success story, with the career as the vehicle for advancing the dream. A necessary attribute is a sense of continuity from one causal element in the story to another. What evolves as a result of this discipline of continuity within the linear form is a story of the hero in search of his career goal. Whatever is irrelevant to this topic is lost or slighted.

Let me illustrate this conclusion with two topics that one might presume to be important in the formation of a life story but that are endangered species in these books: close relationships and the body. From reading these stories, one might conclude that the hero has no investment in emotional relationships with others and no body (except, as in the case of Rashad, as professional equipment). The tangential nature of close relationships may be illustrated by these firsthand tellings.

Lee Iacocca on the death of his wife: As he explains, Mary, his wife of over twenty-five years, was a diabetic. Her condition worsened over the years; after two heart attacks, one in 1978 and the other in 1980, she died at the age of fifty-seven in 1983. According to Iacocca (1984, p. 301), each of her heart attacks came following a crisis period in his career, first at Ford and later at Chrysler: "Above all, a person with diabetes has to avoid stress. Unfortunately, with the path I had chosen to follow, this was virtually impossible."

Richard Feynman on the death of his wife: Feynman's wife was fatally ill with tuberculosis and was moved to a sanatorium in Albuquerque, New Mexico, so that she could be fairly near him while he worked on the Manhattan Project to build the atomic bomb in Los Alamos. The day she was dying, he borrowed a car to go to her bedside. "When I got back (yet another tire went flat on the way) they asked me what happened. 'She's dead. And how's the program going?' They caught on right away that I didn't want to moon over it" (Feynman, 1986, p. 113).

Ahmad Rashad's second marriage: "One day we just up and went over to Las Vegas. We had a quickie marriage in one of those Wedding Bell Chapels. Ironically, I recognized the guy sweeping the floor of the place — he had been on my high school track team but didn't remember me. What I remember most about the ceremony is that when I said, 'I do,' what flashed through my mind was, 'I don't.'" (Rashad, 1988, p. 181).

Donald Trump, describing his family: "I have a father who has always been a rock. . . . And I'm as much of a rock as my father. . . . My mother is as much of a rock as my father. . . . When I finally did get married, I married a very beautiful woman, but a woman who also happens to be a rock" (Trump, 1987, pp. 96–97).

Thomas Watson, Jr., who married his youthful sweetheart, Olive, goes chapters without mentioning her. Finally, near the end of the book (Watson and Petre, 1990), he tells how she has walked out on him and how he manages to get her back.

One possible explanation for why emotional attachment is missing in these narratives is that these men rarely express any emotion about anything: family, friends, or work. However, this is not entirely convincing. When it comes to discussing the struggle to achieve, one can find signs of caring, involvement, and deep attachment.

J. Paul Getty (1986, p. 28) describes drilling his first great oil well: "The sense of elation and triumph was — and is — always there. It stems from knowing that one has beaten nature's incalculable odds by finding and capturing a most elusive (and often a dangerous and malevolent) prey."

Lee Iacocca (1984, p. 65) describes his experience as general manager of Ford as the happiest period of his life: "For my colleagues and me, this was fire-in-the-belly time. We were high from smoking our own brand — a combination of hard work and big dreams."

Thomas Watson, Jr., describes his self-accounting on the anniversary of his father's death as follows: "I would spend a quiet evening taking stock of what IBM had accomplished in his absence, and then say to Olive, 'That's another year I've made it alone.' By then IBM was two and a half times as big as when Dad left it — over two billion dollars a year in sales . . . and the value of our stock had quintupled. . . . For those five years I hadn't let anybody share the spotlight with me. Inside and outside the company I wanted to establish that Tom Watson, Jr. meant IBM, and I guarded my power carefully" (Watson and Petre, 1990, p. 342).

The tenor of these emotive monologues is often similar to that of athletes during sports contests: exhilaration, pride, joy, anger, and revenge. In general, emotions are inscribed along with the deeds that constitute the heroic story. The missing voices of emotion are those that center on relationships outside of work, particularly love, longing, sadness, shame, and pathos. Watson's autobiography contains hints of grave emotional problems that are revealed in more detail than one normally finds in men's stories: "I did not understand how to change pace when I left the office. . . . When I saw I could not bend my wife and children to my will, I'd feel totally thwarted and boxed in. Those were the blackest moments of my adult life" (Watson and Petre, 1990, p. 315). The loss of control in the family setting that Watson describes may suggest why so many "heroes" prefer life at the office.

Traditionally, the function of the autobiography has been to illustrate an exemplary life that others might emulate (Stone, 1982). The notion of what was appropriate to the story has been rigidly enforced by historians and arbiters of good taste. For most men, the autobiography has been a forum for describing abstract and idealized lives dedicated to principles and professions. One of the outcomes of a focus on goal states is that materials tangential to this goal are pared away. While it is difficult to illustrate the absence of topics in men's autobiographies, it is possible to compare the presence of these topics in women's autobiographies and thus to note a deficit. One area of omission in men's stories relates to their embodied status as human beings. These men only rarely describe their bodies in any form, and when they are mentioned, it is most often only to offer some explanation about their impact on other goals. Even sexual activities, which are usually regarded as the province of active, aggressive men, are scarcely mentioned in these stories. These heroes do not seem to have sex lives. In the male sample, J. Paul Getty (1986, p. 50) revealed his first sexual experience in the most detail: "Another classmate and I played truant . . . for a dalliance with two willing damsels we had met the previous week at a fiercely chaperoned dance. In my classmate's words, this initiatory experience was everything it was cracked up to be — and then some. I agreed wholeheartedly." This reluctance to reveal secrets of the flesh is particularly noticeable among the business leaders. The restriction of the story form to the one thin career line all but prohibits the inclusion of "body talk" in the autobiography. The major conclusion one might draw is that men of heroic stature define themselves by their wills, minds, and imaginations, and not by their physical "containers." Their identities are shaped by their ideas, not their carnal condition. Only when they require the services of their bodies for some task are the bodies of interest.

How do these writers suggest that their identities are distinct from their flesh? Here is how Chuck Yeager discusses the fun the pilots had at Pancho's, an ill-reputed bar near the airfield base: "Being in our early 20's, we were in good physical shape and at the height of our recuperative powers — which we had to be to survive those nights. That was our Golden Age of flying and fun. By the time we reached 30, our bodies *forced moderation* on us" (Yeager and James, 1985, p. 180; italics added).

The body as an instrumental means to achievement is clearly indicated in many passages in footballer Rashad's story (1988, p. 156): "Every back who carries the ball a lot gets beat up pretty badly, in almost every game. . . . A running back's not hurt unless he's got a busted leg. If something is bruised or pulled, the guy can play. If something's broken and it can be taped together, the guy can play. That's what's expected of a runner."

In these examples, we see that the body is not the "I," but the instrument of the "I." It is the vehicle to get the job done. The "I" is elsewhere.

The Monomyth and the Study
of Organizational Continuity

In the preceding section, the cardinal characteristics of men's autobiographies were illustrated. We saw that the single, linear, progressive form is crucial to these autobiographies and that they are organized around the career trajectory. The single, linear, forward formulation reflects the central mode of autobiographies. The point of illustrating these stories has been to suggest that they have some relevance to the concept of continuity, and more precisely, to an understanding of approaches to continuity in organizations. In my view, the narrative of the male autobiography closely corresponds to the conventional definition of *continuity*. This definition stresses the immediate connection of events uninterrupted in time, so that they form a continuous or connected whole. Emphasis is on prolonging or maintaining a position of relative stability over time. Related words include *endurance, persistence, perseverance,* and *stability.* The connection among events is seen as linear, singular, and unidirectional. That which precedes must be causally related to that which follows. Continuity, like the male autobiography, then, is within an arrow of time that is flowing from past via present to future temporal events. There are no bifurcations, doubling backs, or reflexive renewals in the system. The "straight arrow" never bends or bursts.

These conceptions of continuity on the one hand and the narrative line on the other thus seem to be part of the same worldview and to be complementary to one another. The male myth itself is a microcosm of a continuous world order, in that it is the story of the connecting of the new hero to the historical tradition. The hero functions to protect the continuity of the realm against disorderly forces that seek to undermine it. The rewards of conquering the challenging forces of darkness most often include the honor of continuing the line of the prior hero, father figure, or CEO. In this sense, the hero is a conservative force helping to maintain social order. Watson's autobiography is a stunning example of this. His entire existence is predicated on carrying the torch his father had ignited.

Men's stories, not surprisingly, promote the maintenance

of social order and progress. Organizations can also function in this heroic capacity. By carrying out traditions of value, maintaining established practices, resisting external influences, excluding marginal social groups, abhorring disorderly influences, and fighting known adversaries, they can anticipate continued rewards from established sources and can attain status in traditional orders. Continuity studied from this perspective has as its goal the repression of or resistance to systemic upheaval and disordered change. In fact, any sudden or unpredicted change would be unsettling and disturbing and thus a threat to the system.

In this context, those who value continuity may find themselves perceived as opposed to the exciting world of change and discontinuity. Yet I would argue that these traditional assumptions limit our ways of thinking. To expand these horizons, it will be helpful to introduce stories of women's lives. We will be especially sensitive to how the molding of women's stories from an amalgamation of other stories provides a more multifaceted approach to continuity for those interested in executive actions, as organizational psychologists, managers, or invested onlookers.

Women's Stories: The Cauldron of Narrative Forms

One might, at first, assume that successful women in our culture tell their life stories as men do—that is, as monomyths in form and content. While this may seem to be a "logical" assumption, readers should be suspicious of where traditional logic leads, at least within the context of this chapter. In women's autobiographies, we are not likely to find the simple, linear, unidirectional, progressive form that we glimpsed in the previous section. Instead, we frequently encounter complexity and chaos.

In contrast to the men's stories, women's accounts are often characterized by multifaceted story lines rather than single ones. Women do not keep a career line foremost in their stories at all times, relegating the purely "personal" to brief asides and subordinating the meaning of their personal lives to the relevant career dimensions, as men's stories often do. Women's stories combine many subplots, with themes oscillating between the various important points of interest. No one theme is exclusive or primary. The story may shift among an emphasis on a love relationship, the birth of a child, conflicts between self and others, career successes and setbacks, friendships, parental well-being, physical appearance, emotional stability, and moral concerns. It may be cut into seemingly disparate and disconnected parts, as one theme comes to dominate and others fade. Unlike men's stories, where the tide of fortune is almost always treated as a unitary force, women's stories may feature a progressive escalation of the plot in one area, while at other times the plot may be regressive. Often the self the author presents within her story is marked by insecurity and ambivalence about her choices, abilities, and outcomes. This uncertainty contrasts with the stance of the typical male author, who does not tell a self-reflexive story but almost always projects outward, seemingly unaware of himself as a central figure in an ongoing drama. In a woman's story, the narrative line is not only multiple, but the lines themselves are often "fuzzy" rather than smooth. Many examples of the multifaceted, reflexive, tentative, complex, and oscillating autobiography could be given. A few will have to suffice.

In this section, I will draw on the autobiographies of Sydney Biddle Barrows, Joan Baez, Nien Cheng, Linda Ellerbee, Martina Navratilova, and Beverly Sills. I chose these sources to parallel the men's sample, although no autobiographies of women as "captains of industry" or politics were available. Most of the women's autobiographies begin with histories of their families and their place within them. Grandparents, parents, siblings, and children are all considered relevant starting points. In close proximity, however, one finds another story that reveals the achievement dimension of their lives. Each autobiography emphasizes the blending of the two themes of love and work.

Sydney Biddle Barrows (1986, p. 1), infamous, perhaps, for her dual role as a Mayflower descendant and as the owner of an "escort" service, begins her book by relating her family's place in American Colonial history: "The Annual Meeting of the Society of Mayflower Descendants begins with a roll call of New England's first settlers. . . . According to a tradition in my father's family, I could have stood up for John Howland. . . . My mother's family, however, had documented our direct descent from Elder William Brewster, the minister who served as spiritual head of the brave little group that sailed into Plymouth Rock on November 21, 1620." This opening section stands in stark contrast (not entirely unintentional, I am sure), to the preface, which reveals that the police are cracking down on Barrows for running a prostitution ring.

Martina Navratilova (1985), in the prologue to her book, recounts the following exchange with her father: "'I'm always going to look like a boy,' I cried. 'Don't worry,' he told me. 'You're a late bloomer. I can tell you're going to be pretty when you grow up. . . . ' Also he told me I would win Wimbledon some day. I believed that part." Dual aspects of Navratilova's life — as woman and as champion — are highlighted in this early vignette.

Nien Cheng, author of the bestseller *Life and Death in Shanghai* (1986, p. 1), a story about her arrest and imprisonment during the Cultural Revolution in China, combines her family concerns with her work identity: "I now move back in time and space to a hot summer's night in July, 1966, to the study of my old home in Shanghai. My daughter was asleep in her bedroom, the servants had gone to their quarters, and I was alone in my study." In a modest explanation of her work, she mentions that after her husband's death she took his place working for Shell International Petroleum Corporation; her duties included advising the general manager on how to "resolve problems without either sacrificing the dignity of Shell or causing the Chinese officials to lose face. . . . Whenever the general manager went on home leave or to Beijing . . . I acted as general manager" (Cheng, 1986, p. 5). Again, her story begins with a blend of family engagement and work involvement.

Women authors tend to interpret their success differently from male authors. Women's autobiographies place much less emphasis on heroic struggle; they are more likely to tell the story of someone who has been given lucky breaks, opportunities, advantages, and the support of mentors and loved ones, who have made it all possible. As noted above, Cheng describes herself merely as a substitute for her dead husband. He was responsible for the success; she merely serves in his place.

In another example, Joan Baez (1987, p. 11) begins her preface by saying that "I was born gifted. I can speak of my gifts with little or no modesty, but with tremendous gratitude, precisely because they are gifts, and not things which I created or actions about which I might be proud." A woman author rarely accepts achievements that have singled her out for fame at face value, in the way men do. She is much more likely to be concerned with the moral implications of her success, especially with the consequences of her actions for others she cares about. In the typical monomyth, heroes appear to take for granted that what they have done is very important and/or very good, even when the cost to loved ones and others is extremely high. Trump, for example, never questions whether spending one's life making bigger and bigger deals is a socially valuable activity; Feynman loses no sleep over his contributions to the creation of the atomic bomb. Yeager (Yeager and James, 1985, p. 80), on receiving orders to strafe German civilians, frankly states, "We were ordered to commit an atrocity, pure and simple. . . . I remember . . . whispering to [a friend], 'If we're gonna do things like this, we sure as hell better make certain we're on the winning side.' That's still my view."

Women often consider their achievements open to question. Barrows is defensive about the social value of escort services, particularly her own, throughout her book. After describing her operation as "successful, elegant, honest and fun," she states that "I had no 'moral' problems because escort services filled a human and age-old need" (Barrows, 1986, p. 49). Later she adds (p. 267) that "there was a warrant out for my arrest. The charge, as expected, was promoting prostitution—a felony. I wasn't surprised, but I was angry that the authorities were making such a fuss about it all. Yes, I might have done something illegal, but I certainly hadn't done anything *bad*." Perhaps one might argue that her business put her in an especially vulnerable position in terms of social censure, but defending the moral aspect of her work seems critical to her throughout her book.

Baez describes her image in a whimsical, somewhat self-parodying vein, as the "Queen of Folk" and "Ms. World Peace." She criticizes herself (1987, p. 318) as well: "Granted I was known for being a benevolent and good queen, for taking risks, giving away money, caring for the poor, going to jail for my beliefs, and sacrificing my career for more meaningful things. But nonetheless, I had become accustomed to special treatment and had developed some unconscious habits which I still retain and recognize only if someone gently points them out to me."

In terms of story forms, women authors constantly measure and discuss their life's activities in terms of moral justifications. But while men's stories seem based on strong codes of conduct, they do not contain scenes of moral deliberation or questions about the value of their positions and actions. An exception is their occasional "lip service" to being sorry they have neglected their families, but this seems perfunctory, since they never alter the behavioral patterns that produce the neglect.

For women writers, career successes are often tempered by other goals, which can range from maintaining relationships to having fun. Beverly Sills, discussing a very successful television show in which she costarred with Carol Burnett, relates how unhappy she was when it was finished, not because she would lose income or her high ratings as a television star, but because it meant that she and Carol "would have nobody to play with the next day" (Sills and Linderman, 1987, p. 280). Navratilova gave up skiing to avoid injury, but she later took it up again despite the risk. She commented (1985, p. 320) that "in recent years I've wanted to feel the wind on my face again. . . . I wasn't willing to wait God-knows-how-many years to stop playing and start living."

Women usually are more sensitive than men to the impact of their career commitments on others. They do not stick to their goals unwaveringly, as males are more likely to. Even at the pinnacle of success, women will often give up their career goals if they are harmful to personal relationships. Navratilova (1985, p. 218) says that after her breakup with writer Rita Mae Brown, "Trying to live with Rita Mae, I had tossed part of my career over the side, like a sled driver trying to lighten the load to outrace the wolves. I had given away part of myself and now I had to get it back." Sills, on moving to Cleveland to be with her new husband, said that "I began reevaluating whether or not I truly wanted a career as an opera singer. I decided I didn't. . . . I was 28 years old, and I wanted to have a baby" (Sills and Linderman, 1987, p. 120). In addition, the women authors rarely see their achievements as sole undertakings, driven by their own motivation, despite adversaries, as men often do. Women are more inclined not to take full credit for their accomplishments, but to share the basis of their success with others. The acknowledgment pages of women's books are filled with respect and thankfulness to others for their help and support. For example, Navratilova (1985, p. 162) credits her opponents with helping to improve her game: "You're totally out for yourself, to win a match, yet you're dependent on your opponent to some degree for the type of match it is, and how well you play. You need the opponent; without her you do not exist." (Koch and Iacocca never said anything so nice about their professional rivals!) And in sharp contrast to the male writers, women often dedicate their performances to others' dreams for them. Navratilova describes her first victory at Wimbledon as "fulfilling her father's dreams." Sills dedicates her book "To Mom, who had a dream; to Pete who fulfilled the dream; to Muffy, who is a dream" (Sills and Linderman, 1987). Perhaps the relevant contrast for women and men storytellers is between the dimensions of interdependence and autonomy. Women's motives seem more integrated or merged with the lives of significant others, while men's are separated and autonomous.

Earlier, the contrast between men's and women's stories in terms of embodiment was suggested. Male characters are identified by their projects, goals, and dreams, all abstract idealizations, while women tell their stories from an embodied position. Unlike men, who tend to see their identities as defined by their "minds," "spirits," or "wills," women's stories indicate a diffuse identity that is contiguous with their bodies. Embodied events are central to women's identity development (Jaggar and Bordo, 1989). Thus women's autobiographies often discuss the significance of breast development, initiation into sexual relations, illnesses, and issues related to sleeping, eating, hair growth, height, weight, and other aspects of personal appearance in detail with reference to self-concept and identity. A few relevant passages bear this out. Navratilova (1985, p. 62) notes that "my new weight gave me some curves I'd never thought I'd have, and they gave me the idea that I was a full-grown woman at 17. I'd finally gotten my period a few years before, along with some lectures on sex, mostly from my father." Baez (1987, p. 78) describes her first and only lesbian relationship as follows: "One night we kissed, ever so lightly and briefly in the privacy of our little motel cottage. All my puritanical lineage loomed up in my face, wagging a finger of disapproval." Cheng (1986, p. 324) presents this graphic picture of her physical condition over the years of her internment by the Communist regime: "Around my wrists where the handcuffs had cut into my flesh, blood and pus continued to ooze out of the wounds. My nails were purple in color and felt as if they were going to fall off. . . . I tried to curl up my fingers but could not because they were the size of carrots. I prayed to God to help me recover the use of my hands." Barrows (1986, 320–321) describes how she raised money for her defense fund by organizing the Mayflower Defense Fund Ball: "I was looking forward to the party, but I didn't have a thing to wear." Eventually a designer lent her a dress, a "pink taffeta strapless gown that I wore with a pearl-and-diamond choker and the same white elbow-length kid gloves that I had worn as a debutante 14 years earlier."

These examples illustrate typical features of women's autobiographies. From my necessarily brief analyses, it is evident that men and women tell two different kinds of stories. According to many literary critics, not only are these stories different from one another, but the form used by women violates the traditional standards of scholarship set down for the autobiography (Stone, 1982). According to Estelle Jelinek (1980, p. 10), a feminist critic of traditional forms, "The emphasis by women on the personal, especially on other people rather than on their work life, their professional success, or their connectedness to current political or intellectual history, clearly contradicts the established criterion about the content of autobiography." Because the ordered story form used by male heroes is presumed available to any literate member of the society, one might wonder why women's stories seem to be so "corrupted" and "disruptive" — at least from the establishment point of view.

Feminist theorists have developed many interpretations of women's lives that might answer this question. An investigation of the causes for different narrative lines, however, is beyond the scope of this chapter. Perhaps it is as Carol Gilligan (1982) suggests, that women's involvement in relationships, as well as their commitment to caring for and being responsible for others, precludes a simple career story. Or socialist feminists may be correct in ascribing these stories to oppressive conditions for women in a capitalist society (Hartsock, 1983; Smith, 1987). Alternatively, women's ways of knowing and of telling may be geared to different experiential worlds (Belenky, Clinchy, Golderberger, and Tarule, 1986). Other theorists have suggested that early childhood experiences create the male-female personality differences that are reflected in various cultural forms (for example, Chodorow, 1978; Dinnerstein, 1976), that patriarchal domination produces deference in women (Brownmiller, 1975; Griffin, 1979), or that traditional cultural forms are inappropriate or inadequate for telling women's lives (Burke, 1978; DuPlessis, 1985; Jelinek, 1980; Mason, 1980; Rabuzzi, 1988; Russ, 1972). This latter suggestion holds the most promise from my perspective. Women's stories are pastiches of other stories, evolving from a cultural gap where no woman's story can be found. The traditional story of women as homemakers and others proves inadequate to the telling of public achievement outside the home.

Women's Stories and Chaos Metaphors

The stories that women tell challenge the form of the heroic male story. They violate rules that have been rationalized as the guiding form for Western cultural myths. While this may at first appear to be a dangerous and threatening activity, undermining the values of stability and continuity from one period to another, an alternative approach may in fact be desirable.

One of the central aspects of the traditional story form that is undermined in women's autobiographies is the adherence to the notion of the single goal state. Women's stories are often oriented to several, sometimes very diverse, goals. Many strands traverse the temporal and spatial planes; the potential of each goal to draw attention is temporary and relative to others. Various plot lines are juxtaposed and interconnected. Progressive, regressive, and stability narratives are interrelated. Thus, the mood or emotional tone of the stories also shifts in more erratic ways than in the men's tales. I often note the reflexivity of women's voices. Circling back on the events reported, reinterpreting the meaning of earlier events in light of later ones, women's stories are replete with renegotiated meaning of life events. The need to keep to the path is never as strong as in men's tales. With their emphasis on flexibility, multiplicity, reflexivity, women's life stories can be interpreted in more varied ways than the single-focus, progressive, goal-directed men's stories can.

Every metaphor one chooses has the strength of revealing connections and similarities between two apparently diverse objects. The omission of other metaphors can obscure other potentially important characteristics of the object of interest. By inscribing these stories with a new metaphor, one from which an altered concept of organizational continuity can more readily emerge, old associations will be blocked, but new aspects can emerge. As I see it, the linear, goal-directed, game metaphors associated with men's stories are convergent with those of *normal science* practices (borrowing this term from Kuhn, 1970) and traditional views of organizational processes. The metaphors of mazelike, complex, perhaps confusing women's stories have much in common with the new chaos approaches to science (Gleick, 1987; Prigogine and Stengers, 1984; Briggs and Peat, 1989). It is interesting to ponder what might emerge as we explore the potential of metaphors from chaos science for organizational continuity. Can women's stories become models for new theorizing in organizational studies?

To create general laws, the conventional natural sciences, particularly physics, have depended on their capacities to derive pure forms from irregular configurations of data—a tactic that is necessary to produce data that are amenable to mathematical manipulations. For the scientist, the general strategy has been to constrain irregular, messy, and idiosyncratic data to the idealized forms necessary to accomplish scientific procedures and to regard the deviations from perfection as "errors." In addition, the traditional science strategy has been to seek the smallest constituent part of an entity to understand it. This analytical strategy is premised on the belief that the parts, once understood, can be put back together again into a larger entity. In this system, the study of relationships, holistic elements, and "flow" among undefined smaller entities is avoided, if possible. The third element of the traditional natural science enterprise is the search for causal chains. All causes precede effects in classical scientific work. The enterprise of science is dedicated chiefly to discovering the order that is presumed to be regulating the universe at every level. Chaotic events are considered to be merely disguises of perfect order—order at a higher level of sophistication than is now known or events that are not amenable to scientific investigation. Most scientific enterprises disdain discontinuities, nonlinear causation, self-generating systems, and other irregularities that interfere with linear cause-effect chains. To return to the subject of narratives, the way men's stories have been told bears a strong resemblance to how the physical world has been described by natural scientists. In many respects, one can also apply the constraints of the normal scientific enterprises metaphorically to the narratives that men have developed for their lives. Men's told lives and their creation—natural science—are extremely similar from a narrative standpoint.

Within chaos science, many of these natural science assumptions are challenged. For example, the assumption that small errors cancel out or can be set aside is not made automatically within chaos science, as it is in normal science. In fact, sometimes small perturbations at one point have been shown to create gigantic effects at another. This phenomenon is well known within chaos sciences as the "butterfly effect"—a butterfly flapping its wings in Hong Kong produces a tornado in Texas. In another example, within chaos science the details of collected data are often scanned for imperfections and irregularities. Pure form is not privileged over irregular, "impure" form but may even be considered an ill-serving illusion produced by normal science. Among chaos scientists, linearity, simple notions of causation, and atemporality (notions that influence classical formulations to varying degrees) are often rejected in favor of circularity, multiple origins, and temporal specificity. History matters for the chaos scientist and is discarded by the normal scientist. Events in chaos science can be denoted as depending on oscillations, irregularity, and reflexivity. Sometimes things happen; sometimes they don't.

Women's stories are well served by the tropes of chaos science. Their assemblage of small, irregular, interwoven fragments effectively fit the metaphor of oscillating forms of changing dimensions, expanding and contracting over time. Women's narratives might also be described in the language of chaos science as full of "strange attractors in phase space." This chaos metaphor suggests that points of place or theme within the story are often returned to after the storyteller has wandered off on new and different paths. Chaos theory also refers to conditions that produce bifurcations in a state. These unstable conditions with high-intensity elements that suddenly produce a break, after which each segment can branch off and reverberate at its own rate of change, form an interesting metaphor for change. Chaos theory also addresses turbulence; as a flow of liquid speeds or slows, its reactions to perturbations also shift. Whether something produces whirls and eddies or merely slides around a barrier depends on external conditions. Yet the male monomyth seems far from this metaphor world. The progress of heroes rarely is construed as a life cascading with whirlpools, vortices, or frothing rills. The metaphors of chaos science — perturbations, oscillations, bifurcations, and turbulence — suggest the forms of women's stories, not men's.

Women's stories have traditionally been regarded by critics as immature, domestic, and ill-formed. Yet they seem to take on a legitimate form if described with the novel metaphors that chaos theories provide. Once this distinction is recognized, we are ready for the question that is central to this chapter: What

can these chaos metaphors offer to organizational theorists studying continuity? And beyond this, what can chaos metaphors do
for those who influence the flow in organizational life?

Organizational Continuity and the Metaphor of Chaos

As Gareth Morgan (1986) has demonstrated, theories of organizations depend on the metaphors with which we construct
them. In his landmark book, Morgan entertains the possibilities
and limitations that result from the application to organizations
of various metaphors: machine, organism, psychic prison, and
others. He also covers the metaphors of flux, self-producing systems, and dialectical change. His analysis anticipates the possibility of applying metaphors from chaos science to organizational theory. The range of metaphors from chaos science that
might enrich theories of organizations, in particular those related
to continuity, is vast. In our earlier survey of men's and women's
autobiographies, we saw how several of these metaphors foster
an understanding of women's lives. In conclusion, I would like
only to offer an analysis of one visual image taken from the work
on turbulence to illustrate how chaos metaphors might be applied to the issue of organizational continuity. The image shown
in Figure 2.1 is suggestive of chaotic flow in a turbulent environment. If you imagine a winding stream, punctuated with rocks,
beginning to swell with the melted snows of springtime, and
with a person floating on a raft with the currents, the image
may take on fuller dimensions for you.

The Metaphor of Turbulence
in Life and Organizations

What can this metaphorical image tell us about ourselves, our
lives, and the organization? The conditions surrounding and
including us are always subject to change. As we flow through
time, we become a part of different vistas. Sometimes we are
embroiled in turbulent and fast-flowing change, and sometimes
we are in smoother, less turbulent currents. Though we seem
to be headed in one direction, the course of our path is curved

Figure 2.1. Metaphoric Image of Sensitive Chaos.

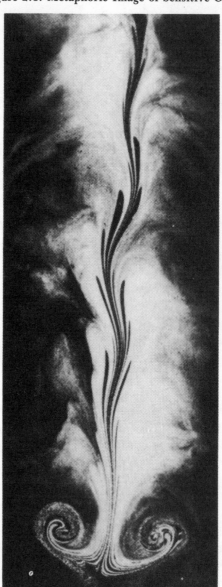

Source: T. Schwenk, *Sensitive Chaos,* Rudolf Steiner Press, Sussex,
Fourth Impression 1990. Reprinted with permission.

and shifting, sometimes recursive, but rarely straight. Sometimes we may be going around in circles (and may not even know it). What is continuous is not a specific set of coordinates, but a changing set of directional goals. We weave (or do we tack?) back and forth according to the way we experience the flow, but we still move from one place to another. Sometimes we seem to be in the center of the flood, while at others we skirt the edge. We have no rules that require us to stand firm against the flow. (We have no Principles.) We travel where the flux seems to go. While for most of the journey we seem to be one, a continuous entity, the unity is not simply of one but is a conjunction of many. The continuity of the whole is composed via melding, as diverse currents fold into the mainstream. The new currents conform to the direction of the prior form but offer the diversity of the origins. The course depends on the new as well as the old.

My image of the process centers on the unified, interwoven, complicated whole. Thus a form of continuity is sustained. Continuity becomes defined as the integration of various chaotic events that pulsate, shift, and merge at the borders with changing, yet more stable, entities. Rather than being a firm boundary between the internal and the external, the border is fuzzy and blurred. What is and is not a part of any one thing is never fully specified or specifiable. All is seen as overlapping and osmotic. This disorderly connectiveness need not break down or split apart: however, it may transpose and recompose. In this metaphorical illustration, a bifurcation does occur. How are we to understand this? Perhaps conditions change sufficiently that the oneness thins or splits into two. A parting develops in which certain parts peel off in one direction and others in another. Perhaps in spinning off, two new elements will be born, each of which will find new paths. Paradoxically, each can exist with uniqueness, but in unity as well.

The metaphor of the flow is compatible with continuity as described by Srivastva: "Organizational continuity is a system matter involving the organization's linkages with its environment — past, present, and future. Continuity management relates to a way of knowing and thinking that apprehends the unity of time and space not in simple, determinist terms (emphasizing causal-mechanistic thinking), nor in terms of a kind of future determinism. . . . Continuity management is important precisely because of the non-determination or open versus closed future. Continuity management involves, therefore, a continuous interplay between the social construction of the open, nonobjective past and the social construction of the future" (letter of invitation to the Case Western Reserve University Continuity Symposium, June 6, 1990).

Conclusions

I shall conclude with several recommendations for organizational leaders concerning new visions of organizational continuity. If organizations are viewed from the metaphorical perspective of chaos science, as turbulent and laminar flows in a stream of time, new worlds open up that suggest many forms of understanding and paths of action not previously considered. Five departures from existing conventions are especially important:

1. A sense of organizational continuity is not dependent on "real-world continuity," but gains its credibility through social construction processes within the group. Participants within the organization define continuity through the telling of its history to its members and others. In all, no single segment of an organization can ultimately bring about the construction of continuity alone. Its reality depends on the agreement of all relevant voices; no further authority can be claimed, nor can its existence be otherwise proven.

2. Unlike traditional forms of continuity that are rigidly formed around specific policies, practices, and personnel, successful stories of continuity are connected to more abstract entities, such as long-term goals, images, and self-conceptions. Continuity so developed is more substantial than continuity constructed around specific aspects of prior activities, because it is more readily open to reinterpretation and change. The most feasible constructions of reality are those that accept the potential of many concrete activities to fulfill the superordinate goals. Thus, customer orientation can refer to pricing practices in one

era and service in another. The main pitfall to avoid is rigidity in patterns for its own sake.

3. While adapting to changing conditions has often been viewed as a "necessary evil" in traditional approaches to continuity, surviving organizations have typically gone with the tides of historical change (as constructed by the group's "historians"). However, within "chaos"-defined views of continuity, not only must an organization be willing to adapt to change, but it must be willing to be erratic in the pursuit of specific goals or in the maintenance of any particular state. Rather than press for an unwavering commitment to a direction or to a steady progression toward a goal, this approach suggests that the opposite is often desirable. Organizations may need to heed several possibilities at a time — sometimes pushing in one direction, then falling back and regrouping for another. Spurts of dynamism may alternate with periods of calm. Making a virtue of perseverance and constant activity may be viewed as a maladaptive strategy. Prioritizing once and for all may become a shortsighted and self-defeating project.

Organizations need to relinquish surety, even in such basic matters as identity and the boundaries between self and others. Organizations need to accept the possibility of a changing definition of self and of a "fuzzy," unstable permeability as the boundary conditions between one current state of being and future states of being. At their frontiers, organizations become integrated with others in symbiotic, open-ended activities. Entities may even oscillate between identity states. In times of great fluidity, organizations may discover that they are better able to maintain their higher-order goals by splitting into new functional areas with differing operational styles and interests. One facet of the company might merge with a competitor and proceed in a very formal manner, while another might spin off into an eclectic hyperspace as a leaderless group. Bifurcation in the service of continuity requires a form of social construction that resists the traditional binary logic of oppositions and polarities. Thus, an organization may paradoxically be continuous and discontinuous, one and many, simultaneously.

4. A characteristic of traditional organizations with an

emphasis on continuity has been strong hierarchical, often inherited, positions of power. One might argue that the emphasis on this form of continuity has served primarily to protect vested interests and privilege. Continuity based on rigid lines of authority and power is antithetical to a chaos formulation. To refresh an organization's strength while maintaining a connection to its self-constituted superordinate goals and past history, new members drawn from diverse backgrounds must join in the construction processes. Newcomers are vital to the organization because they are the carriers of cultural change. They are the bearers of new information and styles of being. This energy and knowledge must be preserved. No artificial barriers supported by traditional practices and habit should filter out new voices. Including diverse group members alters the organization in ways that preserve its existence while maintaining much of its basic composition. Under highly turbulent conditions, phases of ambiguity, confusion, and identity diffusion set in that may temporarily impede group cohesiveness. However, these turbulent periods are useful in creating new integrations of the organization and eventually lead to new stories of continuity.

5. Traditionally, organizations have expected to plan and predict the future, usually by extrapolating from the performances of the past. Time and again long-term planners, enamored of the prospects of packaging human existence into precise mathematical models, have set upon this task with relish. But these efforts have usually failed. In a social system organized with chaos metaphors, organizational leadership will benefit from the notion that changes can be conceptualized as unexpected forms at unanticipated rates, as can stability. Members of the organization cannot necessarily predict all important changes, even if they try to do so. The nature of change should not be viewed as linear, incremental, or predictable, in most cases. The organization that will survive is the one that is best able to construct a reality that includes unanticipated, erratic permutations of existing circumstances.

These five points are suggestive of the ways that metaphors derived from chaos science might enrich theorizing about continuity within organizational studies. Each could be greatly expanded. Other facets of chaos science could yield other emphases as well. We should be wary of our habitual tendency to formulate stories of life, of social science, and of organizations according to the male monomyth, as well as of related tendencies in the natural sciences. I do not believe all such monomyths should be curtailed, although we might find them tiresome after so many centuries. I suggest that the stories of women's lives that are compatible with chaos science be explored for their relevance to organizational life. Who knows what a few butterflies in flight might do!

Chapter Three

Crisis and Continuity: Reviewing the Past to Preview the Future

Ray Loveridge

Constant revolutionizing of production, uninterrupted disturbance of all social conditions, everlasting uncertainty and agitation distinguish the bourgeois epoch from all earlier ones. All fixed, fast-frozen relations . . . all swept away, all new formed ones become antiquated before they can ossify. All that is solid melts into air, all that is holy is profaned.

> —*Marx and Engels, 1888, pp. 53–54*

Nothing is predictable. Currency-exchange transactions now total 80 trillion pounds a year, only 4 trillion pounds of which is required to finance trade in goods and services. The rest is essentially currency speculation, one reason that the overall financial situation has been labeled the 'Casino Society.' . . . So we don't know from day to day the price of energy or money. . . . We don't know whether merging or demerging makes more sense. . . . We don't know who our competitors will be, or where they will come from.

> —*Peters, 1988, p. 9*

> How can you learn a language without accepting
> a tradition and authority?
>
> — *Sachs, 1990*

For the last quarter of a century the organized boundaries that form the structures of industrialized society have been under severe strain. The wave of social dissent that threatened to engulf American society in the late 1960s appears to have rolled across the so-called Socialist bloc and reduced the Berlin Wall to a cloud of asbestos dust. In the analysis of some scholarly observers, both phenomena may be described as part of the transformation of a modernist mode of social organization into modes of postmodernism. The Vietnam War protests, the Black Power insurrection, and the reduction of East European command economies to chaotic anarchies, though all significant in their own right, are also seen as symptomatic of a wider frustration with the centralization and growing atrophy in governments and in corporate administrations.

Postmodernist theorists such as Baudrillard (1983) and Bauman (1987) see this frustration as having worked out its solutions through the marketplace. The hegemony of mass production and of the commodification of the environment is thought to have given place to an individuation of consumption. This has been expressed in the niche marketing now common among modern producers of goods and services. But the individual consumer has learned to impress a free-floating symbolic significance on commodified products. Thirty years ago, pop groups began an anarchism in the use of language that is seen by these French sociologists to have spread to all areas of consumerism.

In this chapter, the postmodernist view of a consumerist revolution is set against other perspectives. These typify current forms of organization as *continuing* modes of producer control over larger global markets as neomodernist. Moreover, the paradoxical success of traditional relationship structures such as those existing in so-called "industrial districts" of Japan and Europe are seen to have provided the adaptability required to survive in rapidly changing market contexts. I suggest that the new models of effective organization have arisen out of the adaptability required to survive in rapidly changing market contexts as well as out of the continuities in community values and beliefs once described by Durkheim ([1893] 1964) as *organic solidarity*.

The Postmodern Organization

Postmodernist theorists such as Aglietta (1979) maintain that the widespread rejection of a standardized life-style created a crisis in Western capitalism, geared as it was to mass production and organized as it was around functionally specialized bureaucracies. In particular, the giant automobile manufacturers that had pioneered so-called scientific management seemed to stagger from crisis to crisis in the 1970s as more and more of their markets were taken over by their more flexibly organized competitors from Japan. Unable to cope with the uncertainties created by the new environmental turbulence, they were forced to make drastic changes in their own modes of governance over the next decade. Authority became devolved to operating units, decision making was decentralized, and operations were globally fragmented. In particular, activities that either were not central to the core design capabilities of the operating unit or were used infrequently, were either spun off or out-sourced (Shutt and Whittington, 1987).

The aim of the new arrangements was not simply cost reduction, but the achievement of flexibility in meeting market needs and obtaining new creativity or a synergistic response to rapidly changing tastes in the product market. In this context, a surprising reversion to the past was thought to be taking place. Within the operational unit, the division of labor was seen to allow a much greater span of tasks to be undertaken at all hierarchical levels. Emphasis was given to collective functions and to teamwork — including interpersonal skills. The integration of product marketing, design, and production that had been the hallmark of the preindustrial form of artisanal organization was believed to be reappearing in a postmodernist form. This was most clearly evident in the so-called "simultaneous engineering" modes employed by many Japanese producers. In the West, this has been presented as an assault on internal departmental boundaries that had been allowed to grow up between core activities of the firm (Kanter, 1983). A variety of remedies have been deployed, including centrally created design projects such as those formed by General Motors for the K-car and more recently for the Saturn project. More often, the integration of functions has involved the devolution of R&D to local business units, where development engineers have been able to share the same geographic and social space as that assigned to marketing and production managers and together to interact with groups of operatives in the delivery of the product or service (Whittington, 1990).

Perhaps equally important as a characteristic of postmodernism has been the development of what Miles and Snow (1986) describe as "dynamic networking." Joint ventures or strategic alliances have become a familiar feature of global trading, especially those involving at least one large multinational corporation (MNC). The logic underlying these alliances often derives from a wish to explore new technologies and/or new markets in a manner that allows a mutual sharing of the very high risks involved. Many observers have commented on the paradoxical mixture of collaboration and contest involved in the creation and management of such ventures (Doz, 1986).

The most generally accepted view among economic analysts is that intercorporate partnerships are undertaken in an opportunistic and instrumental manner. Miles and Snow themselves describe the postmodern corporation as a "switchboard" through which appropriate effective connections can be made. Like medieval middlemen, MNCs scan the global marketplace for means of connecting networks of inventory suppliers to networks of customer-users. But like all such intermediaries, they are forced by their own uncertainties to form nonbinding alliances, both vertically with suppliers and distributors and horizontally with potential competitors based on a commonly shared incomprehension of the next source of change.

The Neomodernist Backlash

This postmodernist interpretation of the last quarter century of business history has received wide support from scholars ranging from mainstream organizational theorists to radical economists and sociologists such as Piore and Sabel (1984). Others remain skeptical (Giddens, 1990). True, the global economy has been through a major upheaval over the last twenty-five years. True also that in many fields of creative activity the uncertainties experienced over this period have found expression in a range of diverse strategies often labeled either as modernist or as postmodernist. Exactly what is meant by either term is the subject of ongoing debate. Some of this uncertainty shows through in the interdisciplinary use of archetypes of postmodernism. Clegg (1990), for example, uses Norman Foster's famous Lloyds Building as an example of postmodernist architecture because of its "inside-out" structure. Foster himself regards the building as a good example of modernism, displaying as it does its functional plumbing in a way that allows the structure to be easily adaptable. In other words, Clegg, the sociologist, emphasizes the transitoriness of the surface appearance; Foster, the architect, sees his creation as representing the adaptability of functionalism. Baudrillard (1983) and other social philosophers such as Bauman (1987) see the individual consumer as having achieved an awareness and ability to provide his or her own meaning to goods, whether produced in the form of music, architecture, or automobiles. This, rather than the speed of technological change alone, is at the root of the anomie or lack of norms experienced by corporate executives.

Skeptics, on the other hand, find little in the recent global marketing of "world cars" such as the revamped Ford Escort or GM Astra or in the universal orchestration of fads such as Teenage Mutant Ninja Turtles to suggest a newly emancipated consumer. For neomodernists such as Giddens (1990), the power of the consumer to maintain a market fluidity is not yet proven. The present turbulence is characteristic of historical epochs of rapid technological change of a generic nature. In the 1890s and 1930s, power shifted to the consumer, as both producers and distributors tried to come to terms with rapid innovations. These occurred in the area of energy generation, for example with the development of electricity utilities, and in transportation, where, for instance, the internal combustion engine created a multiplicity of automobile and airplane manufacturers (Abernathy, Clark, and Kantrow, 1983; Chandler, 1990). To be sure, the effects of information technology are likely, ultimately, to be more revolutionary than any previous advance in technology. Also, the extension of information technology applications is likely to continue to challenge organizational forms for as long as it is possible to forecast. But the underlying motive for organization within industrial societies tends to be that of control, or the predictive use of power. Current applications of information technology, even in the service sector, often appear to be dominated by the need for standardized outcomes and for monitoring performance in relation to such standards (Child and Loveridge, 1990).

Perhaps the most influential of the neomodernists, though not normally described in these terms, are the so-called new institutional economists. They begin with the assumption of an opportunistic marketplace in which there are few contestants and imperfect information (Williamson, 1975). In the original exposition of the theory, Williamson sees the corporate entrepreneur as trying to retain control over scarce and idiosyncratic assets (knowledge) within the most cost-effective form of available governance (control) structures. Like Chandler (1990), he points to the longevity and remarkable adaptability shown by the largest corporate bureaucracies.

In later extensions of the theory, entrepreneurs are regarded as predatory. Each partner to collaborative arrangements is actually attempting to appropriate the idiosyncratic or tacit knowledge possessed by the other (Teece, 1986; Mowry, 1987). Thus, strategic alliances are interpreted as a possible means of exploiting the other party's unique assets. Evidence from joint ventures undertaken over the last decade does, in fact, suggest a certain asymmetry in outcomes — to the point where one or the other party eventually takes over the venture and, sometimes, the other partner as well (Mowry, 1987)! In this way, we can see ultimate financial *control* within global organizations as becoming increasingly concentrated in spite of devolution of operational *responsibility*. The use of information technology in metering performance can be viewed as complementing both tendencies as well as enabling portfolio management to be more successfully coordinated at the center.

Recent work by Ouchi (1984) has acknowledged the ex-

istence of "clan" or of the continued existence of nonopportunis-
tic, effectively based relationships in industrial societies. These
closed groups nevertheless work to monopolize their advantages
or to defend their members' interests within the industrial markets. Ouchi makes little attempt to provide a theoretical under-
pinning for the existence of "clans," but the allusions to the
normatively bound networks of Japanese companies and to the
artisanal networks of industrial districts are clear enough.

Existence of Voice

Central to the achievement of so-called "tight-loose" relationships within new forms of organization (Peters and Waterman,
1982) is the achievement of a commitment to the coordination
of activities based on mutual trust. Over a wide range of its
independent operations, each party is free to exploit its individual assets, including those obtained or held mutually, but
with regard to rules of conduct that are implicitly held to exist
by both parties, whatever the explicit contract between them.
These types of relationships are, as the appellation *clan* attached
to them by Ouchi suggests, most often to be found within traditional communities. They have discovered a high level of internal complementarity in activity and interdependency in relationships over several generations of experience. Usually this
awareness has been kept alive by the existence of an external
threat or opportunity shared by the whole collectivity, such as
lack of resources in the case of the peasant regions of Japan or
the German state of Baden-Württemberg or the Italian region
of Emilia Romagna.

A number of observers, most notably Ouchi (1984) and
Piore and Sabel (1984), claim to have discovered competitive
collaboration to be present, not only in the vertical integration
of the supply of component services to manufacturers within
particular regions, but also horizontally through local association of suppliers. Trade associations have, of course, existed for
defensive purposes or as pressure groups for many years. What
is unique about the suppliers located within the industrial dis-

tricts described by Piore and Sabel is the complementarity between their skills and products and the manner in which they collaborate in a proactive way in their marketing. Moreover, the strength of each individual enterprise lies in the fact that it achieves an artisanal integration of functions within its own internal organization.

For the most part, these industrial districts are composed of small artisanal family-owned businesses. The basis for their collaboration is thought to have been worked out at a number of levels, from a sharing of value-oriented institutions such as the Catholic Church and Communist Party (a curious alliance in the history of the Emilia Romagna region), interventionary city and regional administrations (particularly important in providing technology transfer in Baden-Württemberg), and long-lasting artisanal associations with national recognition and state-provided privileges (Segenberger, Loveman, and Piore, 1990).

But more paradoxical still has been the apparent embeddedness of many of the most successful parties to global alliances between multinational corporations in their *local* supply networks. These operate within the traditions of a particular geographic region, most especially those of Japan (Best, 1990). For example, the use of *kyoryokukai* associations of local components suppliers by larger Japanese assemblers is the normal means of coordinating their activities. These are believed to have developed within a set of shared network norms established over a long period of time, sometimes traced to the deferential ordering of the *samurai* and, later, of the *zaibatsu*.

However, the assumption of familial allegiance does not exclude exploitation, as any feminist writer would be quick to remind us. Indeed, the interpretation of the relations existing between large and small firms in Japan by most Western observers up until the last decade was one in which the former were perceived to be exploiting the latter within what was normally described as a "dual market" (McMillan, 1984). Sabel's (1982) original interpretation of the workings of the markets within European industrial districts also adopted this interpretation.

Writing in 1979, Edwards described the emergence of a

new consciousness among large manufacturers like General Motors of the need for strategies of labor market segmentation. Specifically, he refers to the movement of manufacturing facilities to the Sun Belt states of the United States, to the employment of nonunionized women in line jobs formerly occupied by men, and of the selection of new recruits or candidates for career advancement on the basis of personality or attitudinal orientation rather than simply on skill or technical aptitude. Other writers have described such attempts to obtain a socially normative basis for compliance in the workforce over the last decade as a search for a neo–human relations form of *self*-control among operatives. For the neomodernist, such self-legislation or *Eigengesetzlichkeit* represents a new high point in cultural hegemony (Lash, 1990).

Others describe cellular or autonomous group working deployed in new modes of manufacture or service delivery as being constrained in choice of task, timing, or method by an immediate threat of competition from external subcontractors. At the same time, they are offered a possible path to survival through complying with the requirement to move around a series of highly programmed tasks (Elger and Fairbrother, 1990). Furthermore, the nature of the cellular organization often leaves such tasks easily translatable into automated "systemofacture" once the technical problems involved in information technology interfaces have been overcome and the relative prices of labor and machines make it worthwhile to do so (Kaplinsky, 1984).

It might appear that, as Helper (1990) points out, interparty commitment may be obtained in a variety of ways. In the case of the large Japanese *keiretzu* groups, this usually includes a mutual equity stake in the ownership of other firms in the group. Helper also stresses the nature and mutuality of information exchange involved in the creation of consultative coordination between firms. Using Hirschman's (1970) terms, she suggests that the Japanese mode of subcontracting includes the right to "voice" within the relationship, as against a simple "exiting" into the free market if the relationship is unsatisfactory. The crucial distinction between what are sometimes described as the Fordist modes that formerly prevailed in automobile manufacture and the present post-Fordist relations between assemblers and suppliers is the shift that has taken place in dependencies. This follows when customer and supplier share design information and, more important, design *capability* (Chaillou, 1977). Helper suggests that the Big Three auto assemblers in the United States have consciously attempted to move toward the sharing of design capability with their principal or "preferred" suppliers: the latter now have a "voice" in the core design activities of auto assemblers.

Central to all these explanations of the new significance accorded to collaboration between corporate giants and between small enterprises is a realization of their mutual dependency, either on each other or in the creation of new ventures. This spirit of mutuality is to be seen in the manner in which large-scale European assemblers such as Benetton and Bosch actively encourage suppliers to use knowledge gained in the design of their products to extend the products and services offered to *other* clients. Helper observes that in practice, component suppliers in the United States have found it difficult to trust their new partners, if only because of the asymmetry of costs, or risks, involved. The large assemblers rarely enter into long-term contracts with their suppliers, while expecting the latter to undertake investment in high-tech capital equipment often dedicated to their narrow requirements. In a smaller study of auto component suppliers in the British West Midlands, Turnbull (1989) encountered similar attitudes of mistrust among parties to "new" forms of intercorporate and intracorporate working relationships.

Clearly the transfer of the social technology by which Japanese firms have gained preeminence in many areas of manufacturing requires more than the codification of product and production engineering techniques in a way that enables their learning by rote. Any form of effective long-term control of social activity must involve some understanding of the values, beliefs, archetypes, and analogies that frame behavioral recipes. Many management writers point to the fact that the techniques deployed by successful Japanese and European firms were first formulated by American writers on group working and quality control (for example, see Deming, 1982). Why, therefore, should they not be reimported and utilized in their original form within their country of origin? One answer might be that most organization prescriptions propagated in the managerial literature are offered as implied critiques of existing practices within a country or locality. The fact that such practices have changed but slowly in the face of academic criticism is, perhaps, testament both to the social embeddedness of the former practices and the ineffective modes of education adopted by academics. But equally, the rapid assimilation of such prescriptions in countries *outside* of their country of origin might indicate both the motivation to gain advantage among potential competitors together with a greater matching of their preexisting social structures with those being prescribed or a greater ability to adapt because of their lack of formal structure.

In the next section, I offer a brief comparison of the histories of two corporations to illustrate their learning responses to successive epochs of sociotechnological change. One, Robert Bosch GmbH, was founded in 1886 in Baden-Württemberg — one of the industrial districts of Germany. The other, Joseph Lucas (now Lucas Industries), was founded in 1875 in the British West Midlands. In this case, investigators have viewed relations between collaborators as lacking the trust required of postmodernist alliances. The mode of inquiry adopted has been triangulated across several data sources (Pettigrew, 1985), but it is offered here as an illustration of historical cosmogony in the manner suggested by Barrett and Srivastva (1991).

Two Case Histories in Strategic Transformation

The choice of companies stems from the strategic position that both occupy in the European auto components chain. Both manufacture electronic and electrical equipment that is essential for engine, body, and braking control within motor vehicles. While the largest auto assemblers have some specialist capability in this area (for example, GM Delco), their reliance on specialist out-sources — such as Bendix in the United States — for innovation is easily proven in the historical records of the industry (Abernathy, Clark, and Kantrow, 1983). The number of patents

currently held by Bosch in the United States trails only the largest
Japanese auto and electronics manufacturers and Ford Motor
Company itself, while Lucas has long held a place in the top
ten innovators in the United Kingdom. Both companies figure
among the top remaining manufacturers in their respective countries. Lucas had sales of $6 billion in 1988 and Bosch had sales
of $18.5 billion, with their respective numbers of employees in
rough proportion.

The first Lucas company was formed by a Birmingham
silversmith turned oil salesman. He purchased the design of a
new lamp, which he redesigned to make it capable of line assembly by formerly unskilled labor. Bosch set up his first workshop in Stuttgart in 1886, after completing an apprenticeship
as a mechanical engineer and then embarking on a voyage of
self-education through employment with Edison in the United
States and Siemens in Britain. He undertook the installation
and servicing of gas engines, telephones, and telegraphic machines. He designed his first magneto ignition for a client in
1887. By 1900, it was installed in the first airship as well as in
Daimler and Dion-Bouton automobiles. Over the next fourteen
years, the growth of the firm was phenomenal; from around fifty
employees it grew to nearly 5,000, and plants were set up in
Springfield, Ohio and Yokohama, Japan. Over the same period,
Lucas also evolved from a firm of some 100 workers, largely
employed in the production of lamps and bicycles, to five times
that number. From the 1890s, an increasing proportion of the
workforce was employed in producing car lighting, starters, and
spark plugs. The outbreak of World War I found British airplanes and motor vehicles largely dependent on Bosch magnetos.
The son of Lucas's founder brought in the largest existing supplier of a replica of the Bosch magneto design; by 1918 Lucas
had grown to 4,000 employees largely based in Birmingham,
England.

Both founders built "model factories" toward the end of
the last century and later became proselytizers of Fordist philos-
ophies of mass production. In the case of Lucas, the founding
ideals were passed through family succession until the untimely
demise of the founder's grandson in 1948. Robert Bosch himself

lived until 1942 and passed control to an independent trust to take over in 1964. It is evident that Bosch saw Fordism in its widest sense as creating the basis for consumer emancipation. Not only was he a pioneer of the eight-hour day and high-wage employment, but he actually wrote to Henry Ford suggesting a joint endeavor to avert World War II. He gave much of his early profits to the Stuttgart Technical University and later established and endowed the leading medical hospital in the region. While Lucas combined a similar style of patriarchalism with pioneering modes of scientific management, the scale and professionalism in which both were carried out were incomparably different.

In part, this was explained by the nature of their financial circumstances. Lucas had become a publicly quoted company in the 1900s, while Bosch, though a joint stock company from 1917, remained indebted to local banks, whose long-term commitment to the entrepreneur enabled his continued capital growth. However, Bosch's momentum largely derived from the scale of the inventions produced within his design team (the most important of which was fuel injection, first for diesel engines, then for the Daimler-Benz internal combustion engines that powered, among other airplanes, the Messerschmidt 109). The ability of his management team to create new markets for new products powered by electric motors matched their design skills. These went far beyond their original industrial users. In the midst of the German economic crisis, Bosch diversified into power tools and entered into joint ventures in television (1929), photography and cinematography (1932), and telephones and radios (1933). The company began to manufacture refrigerators in the latter year and in the 1950s rebuilt its factories to supply the expanding demand for domestic kitchen machines. The enforced demise of the German aircraft industry caused the company to abandon production of aircraft engines.

From Hierarchy to Markets

Meanwhile, Lucas expanded across a variety of nonstandardized components supplied to the more than thirty auto assemblers in Britain (and the Commonwealth). It did so largely by a process of adapting the product inventions and methods of leading manufacturers in the United States, Germany, and France, often improving them to the extent of exchanging licenses with these competitors in what amounted to an informal global cartel. Its major strategic growth was determined by the acquisition of other firms that were specialist designers such as CAV (carburetors and later fuel injection), which in 1930 led the company into a joint venture with Bosch that lasted until 1938. Also, through acquisition Lucas enlarged its commitment to aircraft components manufacture. This was a direction that might be seen to sit uneasily with the mass production philosophy of the company's leadership. However, in 1941 the Rover automobile company was asked to build the first British turbojet, and Lucas became a principal contractor in this venture. By the late 1960s, the company had become one of the companies chosen by the Labour administration of the day to rationalize the British aerospace industry. With the continued help of government subsidies, it acquired most of the existing British plant and design capability in aerospace body and engine control systems.

Unlike Bosch, the British company developed no significant link to consumer markets (other than through after-sales). Its dependency on final assemblers became increasingly marked over the 1970s, when both the British motor vehicle and aerospace sectors went into rapid decline. The period was one in which industrial conflict brought interruptions at every stage of the supply chain within both sectors. The company's attempts at centralized control became increasingly ineffective. By the mid 1970s, the chief executives of the main operating companies (product divisions) were reported as being "too busy" to attend the group's strategic planning body (Nockolds, 1976). Earlier in the 1960s the electrical company (now automotive division) had lost its niche in the development of semiconductors in engine control applications — one of the few occasions when it was ahead of its international rivals — through its failure to sell their applications either to the British motor manufacturers or in other uses such as medical equipment. (Its main financial returns were from licenses to GM Delco and Motorola; Golding, 1972.)

In 1981, the company suffered its first loss on annual operations. The effect on the board was traumatic. The CEOs retired and two other members were appointed as joint managing directors. There followed a debate that was foreclosed in 1982, when the French government prevented the group from acquiring total control over the major producer of electromechanical components in that country. The advocate of European expansion resigned, leaving the present CEO, Tony Gill, to implement his strategy of devolution of operational control to business units. Following a practice already adopted in the aerospace division in the 1970s, each unit had to set benchmarks representing the achieved performance of its best competitor, against which it would itself be judged from the center. The means of doing so was provided by a formula for the reorganization of production around the JIT/Total Quality principles of Taiichi Ohno (Toyota). The agent of change was a former professor of production engineering, John Parnaby, who set up a systems engineering consultancy group within the company for this purpose.

By 1990, the cellular system of manufacturing had been adopted by two-thirds of the 150 or so remaining businesses, with varying degrees of success. Lucas had become known as one of the most "Japanized" of British companies, both in its attempts to reorganize its internal operations and its relations with suppliers and customers. Profit levels had been restored (and more important in the United Kingdom, so had dividends). Gill announced record levels of investment in R&D over the year 1989–90 (one reason, perhaps, why Lucas quoted share prices remained low). Critics point to the relative lack of enthusiasm for cellular manufacture among shop floor workers (Turnbull, 1986), particularly among craftspeople, many of whose trade skills have been merged in the new grade of "manufacturing technician" and who also have to undertake unskilled work as members of the *kan-ban* team. Senior management see problems stemming from the insistence of "area coordinators" on behaving like supervisors (which for the most part they formerly were) in "chasing" production. Among suppliers also there is an evident feeling of coercion, the more so because the sole remaining British-owned assembler, Rover Cars, has since 1982 been making public threats of cutting off suppliers who did not adopt their selected mode of CAD/CAM in the implementation of *their* JIT system. (Much the same phenomenon is reported by Helper [1990] in the U.S. car industry.)

Underlying much of the early unease among Lucas dependents could be the apparent arbitrariness with which business units were disposed of in the mid 1980s or reestablished as joint ventures by central fiat—even after achieving their benchmark targets. The Group Board, advised at first by INSEAD academics, evidently determined to expand through acquisition into the U.S. aerospace industry in order to become main contractors to Boeing and McDonnell as well as to Air Bus in Europe. After a period during which it provided access to the markets created by Japanese automobile operations in Britain by selling stakes in its "commodity" business, the group has evidently determined to focus on two high-value-added areas of vehicular subsystems—braking and fuel injection—and to maintain significant business in Germany and France.

From Hierarchy to Hierarchy

By contrast to the trauma in Lucas, the Bosch organization seems to have been barely ruffled by the global crises of the last quarter of a century. Production growth slowed but profits continued to mount over the whole period. Like Lucas, the Bosch Group had always sought to internalize key manufacturing processes, but the very diversity of its products created a much greater network of subcontractors. Over the decade of the 1970s, Bosch adopted a greater formalization in its monitoring and selectivity of subcontractors. Like Lucas, the Bosch Group had developed a strategic capability in the design of machine tools, which it utilized in a steady adoption of Flexible Manufacturing Systems across a wide variety of production lines during the 1980s. (Lucas announced its abandonment of hardware production in 1990 after a series of unhappy attempts at automation. Parnaby has always eschewed machine-based systems, preferring to use information technology in the coordination of project management and design.)

The automation process in Bosch production lines has

been accompanied by changes in the academic and work-based education through which all apprenticed and graduate staff have passed. As a consequence, there has been little or no change in the hierarchy of occupations and accompanying certification required to pass from one level to another. (All posts advertised in the group newspaper are preceded by the academic and trade qualification required.) Within each grade, an enormous change in the tasks undertaken has occurred, however. These have been agreed on with the Works Council and Supervisory Board internally, and externally with the appropriate local Chamber of Trade, the technical high schools and technical universities, and, through them, with the Federal Institute for Vocational Education and Training. The regional officers of the Metal Workers Union also have been informed. During the 1960s, most plants recruited a significant proportion of Turkish and Greek *Gastarbeiter* to line jobs. In the 1980s, they or their successors went through a companywide education program designed to provide a base for the acquisition of information technology skills, but also to extend their wider frame of reference (Lucas has recently launched a more modest version).

Strategically since 1959, Bosch has been organized into fourteen product divisions, and on the accession of a new CEO, Hans Merkle, in 1963 the company set up a planning and control system that was further divided in 1968 to form product subdivisions, each with a CEO. This latter administrative structure has remained virtually unchanged since that time (Dyas and Thanheiser, 1976; Hillebrand, 1989). Each division is managed from group headquarters by four functional managers (administration, engineering, marketing, and purchasing) who work as a team under the administrator.

Authority remains extremely concentrated. Each month, the managers of German strategic business units meet in planning sessions at headquarters with two representatives of the seventy overseas units in order to make ten-minute illustrated presentations on trends in the unit operations (prepared and circulated at least two days before). In addition, a similar plenary meeting debates the three-year rolling plan of each unit at budgetary meetings each fall. An enormous amount of executive time is spent in planning and monitoring strategy. Other advisory divisional groups shape strategic directions, but the weekly board meeting of administrators (whose attendance is mandatory) works on an agenda set by the group CEO. Over its lifetime, the company has had only four chief executives. The last one, who retired in 1984, remains on the supervisory board and lives next door to the present one, both in modest suburban villas near the head office.

Research is largely a group-financed activity (90 percent) located near the headquarters building. It has generally employed something over ten times as many "scientific" and "developmental" staff as has Lucas Group research. These people appear to work in relative isolation from production units, even though up to 80 percent of the work done has been generated upward from the plants. A major bridge was created through the conscious development of corporate sales teams in the 1960s whose job was, and is, to be the liaison with Bosch's largest ongoing customer-users in the development of existing and proposed new products. These four-person teams have to negotiate with their subdivisions and then directly with divisional management for an R&D budgetary allocation for this purpose. Needless to say, the sales team are all graduate engineers with management education.

The recent trading performance of Bosch displays the dilemma facing all Western manufacturers of electronic consumer goods. Its products are constantly being undercut in price by Far Eastern manufacturers. In spite of movement of some production to Pacific Basin countries, high home costs, especially labor costs, make continued competition difficult in domestic utensils, radio, television, and videocamera markets. Lack of an appropriate public infrastructure makes the sale of its most inventive products in autonavigation and telecommunications problematic over the next decade, by which time Japanese competitors may offer better value. In Europe it faces three major competitors in motor component supply, but globally, Nippon Denso and Sumitomo, both members of *keiretsu* groupings, provide more formidable future contestants. Bosch helped to create the former company for the Toyota group and has retained close links across several joint ventures. Lucas is similarly linked to Sumitomo.

Industrial Order and Industrial Dynamism

It would be easy to explain the greater relative success of Bosch when compared with Lucas as being due to the conservatism and lack of creativity among the latter's management, especially between the demise of the founding family and the accession of the present CEO, Tony Gill. But this would be too psychological and perhaps would give too much importance to the admittedly remarkable characteristics of Bosch and the people Gill attracted around him in executive and technical posts.

To look for a wider structural explanation, one needs to compare the institutions of the West Midlands and of Baden-Württemberg that shaped the foundation and growth of the two organizations. The population of these regions is approximately the same, although the latter region is much greater in area. Both have a very high proportion of small businesses engaged in engineering, tool making, and garment manufacturing (a recent importation to the West Midlands). Both regions were involved with the production of light machines, especially bicycles, at an early date, and it should not be surprising that the earliest automobile designs emanated from Württemberg or that Daimler chose to establish his first overseas plant in the West Midlands in the 1890s. The history of the industry's development in both regions was marked by conflict in the early years between competing suppliers, between suppliers and manufacturers, and between labor and management.

The factory system adopted by Bosch and by what became Daimler-Benz clearly challenged the established craft regulation of the work process in Württemberg. These emergent orchestrators of local industry responded, not with sustained confrontation (a widespread strike occurred in 1913), but by putting into effect a legislative structure designed to implement a system of vocational education enacted by regional governments throughout the new German Federation in the late nineteenth century. The integration of artisan control over technical tasks within a bureaucratized system and the complementary movement of professional education into the technical universities was not accomplished without some amount of coercion (Gispen, 1990). The central regulatory role of the communally based Chambers of Trade and of Commerce has been given a corporate seal of approval by subsequent governments.

Herrigel (1990) attributes much of the recent industrial success of Württemberg to the existence of an associational framework that allows small businesses to "socialize" the risks of innovation. He particularly emphasizes the proactive role played by the VDMA or Machine Tool Manufacturers Association in providing an elaborate R&D service, especially in marketing, and in creating bridges into local universities and technical high schools. The VDMA and similar associations provide forums for coordination and standard setting between vertically divided specialist contractors and, most important, between large-scale assemblers and smaller suppliers. These forums have also provided a frame within which the regional Christian Democratic administration under Lothar Späth was able to shape incentives toward explicit objectives in technology transfer. Unlike similar efforts in Britain and the United States, these have not simply offered separately justified subsidies to individual firms. Nor have they been directed at attracting so-called high-tech investment with little commonality with the existing infrastructure of social knowledge and skills. Rather, the policy of Späth's administration, which has been in power since 1978, has been directed at raising the levels of education and communally provided services to match the needs of technological advance within a prevailing industrial structure.

By contrast, the environment provided by the West Midlands was one marked by disputes and acrimony (Turner, 1973). Like that of Michigan and Ohio described by Helper (1990), the supply chain was horizontally divided into specialist processes that became increasingly dependent on the motor vehicle industry in spite of their "jobbing" origins. The car industry became a barometer of short-term changes in the national economy, and the effects of downturns were passed rapidly down the supply chain within contracts that could easily be suspended.

The earnings of line operatives were geared to these short-term and somewhat arbitrary cycles, by payment-by-results systems. The very arbitrariness of the changes became translated into the aggressive pursuit of financial rewards during the short boom periods. In turn, this led to the greatly inflated power of local shop stewards within a formally unregulated system of workplace bargaining (Loveridge, 1981).

Assemblers were more numerous and smaller than in the United States and Germany (though not Japan) and adopted (unlike Japan) a policy of dual sourcing as a cover against risk. They nevertheless retained a wish to control the design of their own components and generally resented Lucas's attempts both to standardize design and to introduce its own innovations. Their dependency on Lucas led to severe public confrontations. Most of their smaller suppliers were actually bought out by larger groups in the 1930s and 1960s. These groups continued to specialize in a few stages of production, but even world manufacturers such as GKN (Guest, Keen, and Nettlefold, of the Midlands Metalworking Group) preferred to leave the individual businesses to operate in a largely autonomous way. At the end of the 1970s, GKN consisted of no fewer than 274 separately registered companies, most of which traded under the name of the founder. In this way the federal grouping could "dual-source" customers from several establishments whose employees and even senior management owed their first loyalty to the local "family" firm and its customers.

This "tight-loose" control system provided a number of advantages for the individual firm. A major one was the fractionation of labor, particularly craftworkers' unions. Overall, the effect on the environment shared with other firms was to ensure its continued turbulence. There was little that a centrally controlled firm such as Lucas could do either to ensure predictability in its own operational inputs and outputs or to form coalitions of suppliers in its continuous negotiations with the largest assemblers: Morris, Austin, Ford, and GM Vauxhall.

One of the ongoing struggles inherited by Midlands engineering employers in the late nineteenth century was the struggle to control the apprenticeship system. This was formally closed by a general lockout in 1922, which the Engineering Employers

Federation (EEF) won. It continued to preoccupy the activities of the latter organization right up to the 1980s, by which time the apprenticeship system had lost much of its former significance. Again, Lucas was an exception in the support it gave both to maintaining a high level of apprentice training and (even more significant in British industry) of rewarding the academic education that was supposed to complement the workshop training. Lucas also remained outside of the EEF, preferring to deal with unions at a divisional and plant level (though somewhat ambiguously, within a kind of Works Council).

The Thatcher decade brought a decimation of Midlands engineering and metal processing plants. Overall employment in the industry has been reduced by half and at Lucas by 40 percent. As a consequence, the workplace power of trade unions has been significantly reduced. The pioneering attempt to introduce cellular manufacturing in a Birmingham plant of Lucas in 1983 was done by directly balloting employees over the heads of union officials. The EEF has ceased to regard collective bargaining (or rather grievance handling) as its major function. Instead, it provides a modest management consultancy function as well as acting as an agent in government-administered operative training schemes and in management education. The Birmingham City Council, as well as those of other cities, has provided an important focus for the development of economic activity, most important in service and leisure, in garment making, and, not least, in the Aston Science Park. It would be difficult to accord any of these recent developments an institutional significance comparable to that of the Späth initiatives in Württemberg.

Discussion

It would be easy to suggest that the devolution of operational authority within Lucas has been no more than an intelligent matching of organizational configuration to contingencies presented in the immediate and indeed the national context of the firm. To do so would, of course, ignore the quite different relational bases for interfirm contracting that underlies the Japanese model that has been adopted by Lucas's executives. Both as a group and within its operating units, the company has set out to establish the basis for a mutual governance of its joint activities with suppliers and customers. As recounted above, the culture of the region in which one of its major activities, auto components, is embedded makes for extreme suspicion among its would-be collaborators. Over the last century, both smaller suppliers and not-so-large assemblers have referred to the group as "Uncle Joe." Joseph Lucas was the founder, but clearly from the experiences of the Cold War came another more sinister meaning. Among the highly individualized small "jobbing" units of the West Midlands, Uncle Joe was seen as the Big Brother attempting to impose bureaucratic order while remaining aloof from the cut-and-thrust of EEF politics.

Strangely, one might suggest that the logic of action underlying Lucas's strategy remains today as predictable as that of Bosch — in spite of its apparent turnaround. The group's problems are expressed in the "total systems engineering" language of Ohno rather than, as formerly, in the language of Taylor and Bedeaux. There is the same implicit belief that if local employees and suppliers read the instructions and grasp the logic of them, they will accept and internalize both — or if they do not, it is through sheer cussedness. Although the group is expending more on training than most other British companies, it is almost all focused on internally devised systems engineering. At the strategic level, its further movement into aerospace and software engineering denotes a determination not only to "stick to its knitting," but also to appropriate fresh knowledge through buying the existing design capacities of acquired companies. For Lucas development engineers who have suffered from a perceived neglect of internal invention, this can sometimes be galling. The parallels with the group's response to wider crises in the 1920s and early 1930s are too evident to need emphasis.

Indeed, it is possible to interpret the histories of the two corporations in terms of what Lodge and Vogel (1987) have described as the contrasting typologies of "individualistic" and "communitarian" ideational systems. In later-developing countries such as the German states, comparisons with Britain and the United States, together with their own militarist history, have brought a greater awareness of a holism and interdependency within the hierarchy of their societies. This has caused them to maintain a communal structure for the recognition and sponsorship of sociotechnological change that incorporates groups possessing new knowledge and skills within a continuing frame of symbolic status. By contrast, Anglo-Saxon individualism demands that rights to scarce resources should be legitimized through the market and claimed as specific "properties" (Loveridge, 1983).

Such a frame of interpretation is all too evident in the analysis of new institutional economists and, indeed, in most models of organizational change. Innovation itself is often described as revolving around a specific predesigned project that has an initiator, champion, and sponsor in senior management. It is extremely difficult to unearth these factors in German and Japanese firms or to disentangle specific projects from a systemic evolution in the organization as a whole (unless the interviewee has been in an MBA program). It is precisely this systemic aspect to the frame of reference used by actors in the Württemberg context that comes across in the language in which particular innovations are described relative to the whole culture of the organization and its context. Instead of adopting the perspective of a particular task or function, the narrator describes the system and the place of the latter within it.

To trace this perspective to its psychological and institutional origins is beyond the scope of this chapter and the ability of the writer. Elsewhere (Loveridge, 1990b), I suggest that the frames of disciplinary logic taught in German education and training are much more "open" than those in traditional British education. (The use of so-called multidisciplinary study offers little opportunity for integration; see Bernstein, 1982.) What seems clear is that the history of state and organizational regulation in these later-developing countries has gelled with the socialization of different groups in a manner that has created what Durkheim ([1893] 1964) describes as "organic solidarity." This is *not* to say that there is any direct linearity between traditional value systems such as Confucianism, but rather that the division of labor within particular societies has acquired a moral significance that has been perpetuated through current modes of organizational governance.

More recently the anthropologist Mary Douglas (1982) has used the expression *grid* to describe constraints imposed by the collectivity on the individual. She describes the social *group* as providing an identity through incorporation of the individual. The interaction of imposed constraint with group identity produces behavioral outcomes such as those labeled in the illustration reproduced in the adapted form in Figure 3.1.

Figure 3.1. Organization Behaviors Resulting from Interaction Between Group Identity and External Constraint.

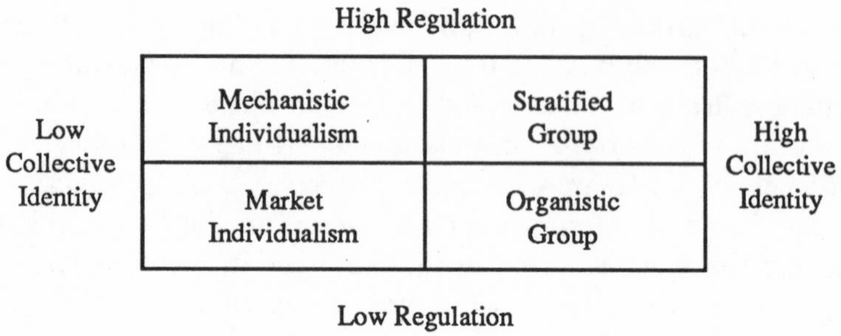

High Regulation

Low Collective Identity	Mechanistic Individualism	Stratified Group	High Collective Identity
	Market Individualism	Organistic Group	

Low Regulation

The Bosch hierarchy (Stratified Group) can be seen as being embedded in an occupational hierarchy that stretches far beyond the firm's boundaries. Underlying it is a moral acceptance of academic achievement as the means to social mobility, both within the internal market and in the external market, giving access to artisanal or professional self-employment. The existence of a shared knowledge paradigm (in the sense of an *episteme* or academic discipline) provides a foundation in depth that simply does not exist within the formally poorly educated employees of West Midlands firms. The very pragmatism that underlies the British approach to vocational education gives an essentially tacit, experiential, and highly localized quality to the design capability of the typical manufacturer. Hence, the fragmentation that was characteristic of eighteenth-century craft associations applied, and to a large extent still applies, to "learned societies" in modern management. This holds back both the rapid diffusion of knowledge and the "normalization" of best practice.

In the Lucas case, competition between individualized enterprises (Market Individualism) resulted in each work group becoming the basis for its own competitive advantage (or monopoly rent). The attempt at providing a tiered structure of supply along Japanese lines has been perceived as introducing an imposed regime (Mechanistic Individualism). A possible alternative might have been one that enabled change to derive from the work group in an organic fashion. By this is meant that in the manner of the successful electronic instrument manufacturers studied by Burns and Stalker (1961) in the 1950s, well-qualified professional or artisanal groups are allowed to create their own collective norms. Some local managers in the Lucas group are, in fact, adopting this approach successfully. However, it might seem that in the national context in which change was being attempted and in terms of the standards against which it has to be judged, the company's present configuration provides at least a mechanistic matching with its environment and is leading to increased commercial success.

Conclusions

The contrasting paradigms of global change presented by modernism and postmodernism appear to treat the nature of interorganizational relations in a wholly superficial and somewhat trivial manner. The juxtaposition also reflects a set of Anglo-American values that could be described as ethnocentric and of doubtful scientific validity. The macho language of most postmodernist texts contrasts with the sober, bureaucratically styled texts and addresses given by German and Japanese writers. It is sometimes difficult to believe that the latter are what the former are speaking of as "the competition."

One might, indeed, suggest that much of the interpretation of our times has been strongly influenced by the predominance of an Anglo-Saxon tradition of market individualism — of Locke and Adam Smith rather than Durkheim, perhaps? When the American scholars Miles and Snow (1986) write of the "switchboard corporation," they are using a metaphor of interfirm relationships that can be left hollow until temporarily filled for purely utilitarian purposes. This kind of instrumentalism is an aspect of modernism that has, of course, been subject to the fairly consistent criticism of psychologists and sociologists for many years. There is little in the observations of postmodernists such as Kanter (1990) to suggest that the anomie, or loss of self-direction, that often accompanies rapidly changing and contradictory instructions from above has been solved within cellular systems of "quasi-firms."

The model of Japanese production design as expounded by its Western advocates is often seen as freely transferable within a codified blueprint, with some adaptation to the objective circumstances of the recipient organization. (See, for example, Womack, Jones, and Roos, 1990.) Some social skills training may be required to ease installation of the model and to provide analysis of anthropological bolt-ons.

A more useful dichotomy, illustrated by the experiences of the two corporations described earlier, might be that used by two French philosophers, Deleuze and Guattari (1980). They make the distinction between behaviors that resemble the growth of rhizomes that send out shoots horizontally to entrap other rhizomes, and those resembling trees that put down local roots and create a substantial trunk with which to support branches. It is an old analogy, one used by the Tory philosopher Edmund Burke some two centuries ago. It might still offer lessons for contemporary government. To be fair to Piore and Sabel (1984) and to the advocates of "industrial districts," it might be said that they are describing tree planting. In successful communities, local authorities that offer "real goods" or provide collective services (Brusco, 1990) are providing an incentive for collective associations between local producers. Similarly, governments that insist that offshore investors should help enhance locally shared schemes of education and technology transfer are likely to attract rooting stocks rather than tumbleweeds looking for financial subsidies. It is significant that when Bosch chose the site for its first British manufacturing base two years ago, it did so on the basis of prior discussions with technical college staff across several regions rather than simply because of highway or railroad connections to markets.

PART TWO

Valuing Continuity

The uncovering of history's lessons and realization of threads of continuity in our experience give rise to choices. The chapters in this part are concerned with how one chooses which practice, idea, or interpretation to preserve. Each contributor sees this as an exercise in *valuing*. The message conveyed by all three chapters is that attention to continuity is, above all, a matter of caring for what is right; it is a virtuous agenda that transforms past sources of connectedness into possibilities for future ongoingness.

In Chapter Four, Schwartz demonstrates how attention to continuity creates choicepoints or dilemmas that can only be managed when there is consensus about the goal or purpose of the organized effort. He then shows that it is the nature of those that accounts for executive choices that are experienced either as continuous or disruptive. Organizational ends based on the dominant paradigm of economic imperialism, he argues, systematically erode those internal, intrinsically rewarding goods and goals that arise from a clear sense of one's *practice,* core task, or *raison d'être*. Valuing continuity leads to organizational adaptation (evolution) that is value driven from intrinsic beliefs about what is best, rather than to disruptive change that stems from instrumentally shaped goals based on a sole valuing of economic ends.

In Chapter Five, Salipante asserts that traditionality in organizations becomes a larger voice in determining what will be valued from the past, kept, and pursued in the future. Like Schwartz, he sees an external influence operating to denigrate those practices and values inherent in tradition. He contrasts the utility of traditionalism and rationalism in accounting for the continuation of an organization, and he poses a concept of *evaluative traditionality* as an archetype of an organization that embraces the valuing of time-tested practices along with strategic choice-making in order to experience "continuity-in-change." He illustrates pragmatic ways this is done via a case history of a well-known service organization.

In Chapter Six, Lynn extends the theme of valuing traditions in order to produce change to the Japanese experience. One of Japan's leading steelmakers is used to illustrate how holding on to "old" practices and values can actually enable major change to occur — in this case, a major strategic shift to new businesses and significant alteration of current product mix. His analysis focuses on how hiring, training, personnel, and decision processes that represent traditional values were used to assist in the steady assimilation of new people and ideas into this firm. Through recognizing that the organization had always placed primary importance on employees and managers as key stakeholders and that work relationships were the primary "bonding" agents in the organization, Lynn details how this major firm is bringing about constructive change. New ideas and practices are being introduced, but not at the expense of learned abilities, loyalties, and cohesion from the past.

Chapter Four

Attending to Continuity
and Organizational Goals

Barry Schwartz

I want to begin by telling you two stories. To understand the
first story, you need to know a little about softball, so let me
set the scene. Imagine a situation in which there is a runner
at first base and one out. A ground ball is hit to the pitcher.
The pitcher fields the ground ball and wheels around to second
base. The idea is to try for a double play by throwing to second
to force the runner from first, and then having the throw relayed
from second to first, in time to beat the batter. Typically, when
a ball is hit up the middle of the diamond, the second baseman
and the shortstop converge at second base. When the pitcher
fields the ball and turns to throw, the proper play is to throw
the ball to the shortstop. The shortstop is moving toward first
base, while the second baseman is moving away from it. So the
shortstop's momentum will carry this player in the direction that
the ball must be thrown, while the second baseman will have
to stop, pivot, and then throw. The throw from second to first
is much easier for the shortstop than for the second baseman.

That is all the softball you need to know to understand
my story. It was a gorgeous early fall morning, and I had just
begun a sabbatical in Cambridge, Massachusetts. I was playing,
as an invited guest, in a relaxed, friendly, mostly social, coed
softball game. It was a game in which the participants played

by the rules and, by and large, wanted to win. But the game was really an excuse for some postadolescent fooling around in the sunshine. The one thing about the game that was dead serious was that the women did not want to be patronized; they wanted a full measure of respect from the men as competitors.

I was pitching in this game, and the situation I just described arose; there was one out and a runner on first. A ground ball was hit to me. I fielded it cleanly and spun around to begin the try for a double play. Both the shortstop, a man, and the second baseman, a woman, were converging on second base to receive my throw. I wound up to throw, and then was stopped in my tracks. Who should I throw to? I knew, as I just told you, that the "right" play was to throw to the shortstop. But I hesitated. Would the woman understand that it was the right play? Or would she think that I was excluding her and throwing to the man, who was more likely to catch it and throw accurately on to first than she was? Would she think that I regarded her as an obstacle to be avoided rather than as a teammate? Did she know enough about the game to know what the "right" play was? Or was she so touchy that she would be offended anyway? Had she been involved in any previous incidents around the alleged mistreatment of women in our game? What would she think of me? Would she think I was an enemy of one of the major social movements of our time? Small wonder that I hesitated, wrapped up as I was in this existential and social crisis.

All of these thoughts washed over me in what could not have been more than half a second. And I never resolved them. To this day, I do not know what I should have done. What was the "right" play? Why had I been so indecisive? The more I thought about it, the less sure I was of the answer. Sure, I "knew" that the right play was to throw to the shortstop. But I slowly realized that the rightness of that choice depended on what I thought the game was that we were playing. If we were merely playing softball, then the shortstop should have gotten the throw. But we were playing more than softball. We were involved in a social movement, one that is struggling to eliminate certain well-established gender roles and replace them with a gender-neutral social orientation. And we were involved in a complex social interaction, in which the feelings and objectives of all participants were to be taken seriously. What is the right play in that kind of game?

I do not know what the right play is, and I do not know what the right play was. But let me tell you what I did. After agonizing about who to throw the ball to, I had to rush my throw. And of course I still did not know whether the second baseman or the shortstop should get the ball. So I solved the problem (unintentionally of course) by throwing it to *neither* of them. I threw it three feet over both of their heads into center field. No double play. No single play. And that is no way to play at all. I was confused about what to do, and I screwed up.

Now I want to tell you a second story, this time about an experiment I did several years ago to examine the effects of monetary incentives on the problem-solving behavior of college students (Schwartz, 1982, 1988). In a typical procedure, subjects are seated in front of a matrix of light bulbs, five across by five down. Beside them are two pushbuttons and a counter to keep track of their score. Periodically, the top left bulb in the matrix lights up, signaling the start of a trial. "This is a game," subjects are told. "By pushing the two buttons, you can change the position of the illuminated light in the matrix of lights. If you do it right, you get a point. What I want you to do is to figure out the rules of the game; figure out what you have to do to earn a point." A subject might first push the left button and observe that the light moves down one position. She might then push the right button and observe that the light moves across one position. Left, right, left, right. After four alternations, all the lights go out, and the subject gets a point. The next trial begins, and she pushes the buttons in exactly the same order, and again gains a point. She does the same thing, with the same result, on the third trial.

Thinking she has the game figured out, she calls over the experimenter. "You have to start on the left and alternate between left and right. Four alternations get you a point." "Wrong," says the experimenter, "try again." The subject realizes she has made a silly mistake. The experimenter wants to know what one has to do to get a point—what is *necessary*. All that she has discovered is one particular way to do it — what is *sufficient*. The way to find out what is necessary is to vary what one does on each trial, in systematic fashion. For example, to test whether it is necessary to alternate, starting on the left, one starts a trial on the right. The name of this game is *experimental science*. There is a phenomenon, the getting of points, and the task is to discover its causes. One goes about this task by formulating guesses or hypotheses and by doing experiments to test the hypotheses. The process one goes through in attempting to discover the rules of the game is precisely the one that scientists go through as they attempt to discover the rules of whatever "natural game" they are studying. And the process has two essential ingredients: formulation of hypotheses and tests of the hypotheses by systematic variation in experiment. Moreover, there is nothing about these processes that is unique to science. People engage in them frequently, if less systematically, in everyday life.

In our experiments, college students were asked to try to discover the rules of the game. When they succeeded in discovering a rule, it was changed, and the students did it again. They were given no instructions about how one might most effectively tackle the problem. Sometimes, the students were told that they would get a few cents for each point they earned in the process of discovering the rule. Sometimes they were told they would get a dollar for each rule they discovered. Sometimes, they were able to get a few cents for every point and a dollar bonus for every rule. Finally, sometimes no monetary rewards were available at all.

When students played the game, these varying conditions of reward made no difference at all. In all cases, students varied their responses from trial to trial with great efficiency. Almost every one of them discovered each of the rules, and they did so quite rapidly. The monetary payoffs failed to have any impact. But there is more to the story. Another group of students was exposed to the same set of problems with the same payoffs as the first set. What distinguished the two groups was that this second group had had prior experience playing the game. The prior experience was this: they were brought into the laboratory, shown the game, and told that every point they scored would earn them two cents. Nothing was said to them about discovering rules. They were then given 1,000 opportunities (trials) to play the game. Within the first 100 trials, each student developed a particular sequence of responses that succeeded in winning points. Once this sequence was established, it occurred in stereotyped fashion on about 90 percent of all trials. The little game and the payoff contingency had turned the students into the essential equivalent of assembly-line workers, engaged in the same task, done the same way, over and over again.

What happened then when these newly formed assembly-line workers were instructed to discover the rules? Compared to the first, inexperienced group, they were much less effective. They discovered fewer of them and took longer in discovering the rules when they were successful. And unlike the first group, what they did was powerfully influenced by the operative payoffs. They were especially ineffective at discovering rules if each point they got earned them money. Under these conditions, they seemed torn between varying what they did from trial to trial to gain information and repeating what they did on trial after trial to gain points and money. Thus, prior experience with monetary payoffs had negative effects on the problem-solving performance of (very bright) college students (see also Deci, 1975; Greene, Sternberg, and Lepper, 1976; Lepper and Greene, 1978; Lepper, Greene, and Nisbett, 1973).

Changing Goals

What's the point of these stories, and what do they have to do with organizational continuity? These stories speak to what I regard as the first question that must be addressed when we think about organizational continuity: in what does the continuity of organizations consist? My answer to this question is teleological: the continuity in organizations consists in the continuity of goals. With continuity of goals, maintaining organizational continuity is easy; without continuity of goals, it is virtually impossible. The conflict I experienced in the softball game was a conflict between goals — playing to win on the one hand, and contributing to a significant social movement on the other. These goals need not conflict, but in the particular instance I described, they did. If goals other than winning are introduced piecemeal—present in some games but not others; present in some players but not others—the game of softball will remain recognizable to those who played it the old-fashioned way. But if goals other than winning are introduced widely and systematically, the game will be fundamentally altered.

And the students in my experiment also experienced a conflict between goals—discovering true generalizations on the one hand, and maximizing financial gain on the other. If gain maximization is introduced piecemeal—present in some problem-solving activities but not others; present in some people but not others—then problem solving, and the social institution (science) that embodies it, will remain recognizable to those who did it the old-fashioned way. But if gain maximization is introduced widely and systematically, the game of science will be fundamentally altered.

So I chose these two stories to illustrate the central role of goals in defining and sustaining socially significant activities and the organizations that engage in these activities. But I chose these stories for another reason as well. Not only do they illustrate what the preservation of continuity requires, but they also illustrate the principal threats to continuity.

The softball game illustrates how continuity is threatened by broad social movements, like feminism, that suggest new goals. The social transformation that these movements demand may be good, but a consequence of this transformation will be a dramatic shifting of goals, a breakup of organizations, and a dislocation of individuals. After another generation of the influence of feminism, softball may be almost unrecognizable, and the people who were comfortable with it the way it used to be may find themselves without a game to play. We all might agree that this is a very small price to pay for a massive, positive social transformation. But the reason the price is small is that softball is so trivial. Organizational disintegration and individual dislocation more generally are not trivial. And obviously, softball is not the only game whose goals and structure are being challenged.

What *was* the right play in my softball game? Increasingly large numbers of people in modern America face questions like this one almost every day. And much more rides on the answers to the versions of this question people face in real life than just the completion of a double play. What kind of game is being a student? a doctor? a lawyer? a teacher? a parent? a spouse? a lover? a friend? an athlete? a corporate executive? What is the objective of these games? What are the rules? And what are the right plays? The world in which modern "enlightened, rational" people live is one in which the rules of each of these games are up for grabs.

Until fairly recently, the character of the various games we play was established by cultural traditions that changed slowly and gently when they changed at all. Each of the games had its own set of "goods," of standards. Our conduct in them was governed by traditional values that we acquired as we grew. While these traditional values were certainly not infallible, they often pointed us in the right direction. At the very least, they pointed us in *some* direction. By acquiring these traditions, and becoming members of the communities that lived them, we developed a cultural framework and a set of social ties that established the boundaries within which our individual life choices would be made.

This is no longer true. Communities, cultural traditions, and social ties grow weaker by the day, and as they weaken, so also do the boundaries on freedom of choice. Nowadays, everything is possible. Even in the game of softball there are complexities and options that were previously unimagined. And all this freedom and flexibility that is open to individuals is also open to organizations. What games the firm, the research institute, or the university will play and how it will play them is much more open to modification — even transformation — than it ever was before.

So what's the problem? What's wrong with having all this freedom to make our own games, with our own rules? What's wrong with a world where anything is possible? To begin to answer this question, I offer an old African proverb: "If a man does away with his traditional way of living and throws away his good customs, he had better first make certain that he has something of value to replace them."

The "something of value" that modern society has come up with to replace the constraint and guidance of tradition is the self-regulating, competitive market. The market is the institution that caters most directly to the goals of individual and organizational freedom of choice. People and organizations do whatever they want, and competition produces results that maximize or at least enhance social welfare. Reliance on the market is predicated on embracing the economist's views about what individuals and organizations want to achieve — the maximization of self-interest, normally understood to be economic interest.

What I am going to suggest in the remainder of this chapter is that this market-oriented, economic alternative to the traditional interpretation of goals and activities that governs the behavior of both individuals and organizations is not a solution to the problem of maintaining the continuity of organizations by maintaining the continuity of goals. Quite the contrary: it is actually part of the problem. That it is part of the problem is what my second story was intended to illustrate. In my experiments, when economic incentives were introduced into the problem-solving situation, they took control of the behavior of the students. Maximizing money rather than maximizing information became the goal that shaped and governed the students' activities. When the goals changed, the activities changed. So rather than maintaining continuity of motive and action, economic incentives destroyed it. My focus for the remainder of this chapter will be on how certain kinds of economic influences produce a change in individual, organizational, and institutional goals and thus threaten the continuity of organizations or institutions. The challenge faced by the modern executive, I will suggest, is to find a way to resist or overcome these economic influences rather than embracing them.

The Creation of New Means-Ends Relations and the Changing of Goals

As a psychologist, my approach to understanding the character of organizations and their goals is to look at the influences on goal formation and change in the individuals who make up the organizations. The hope is that an analysis at the microlevel of individual behavior rather than the macrolevel of economies, or industries, or even firms can be built into an account of what threatens continuity at a macrolevel. Let me then elaborate my claim that an embrace of economic incentives and market mechanisms threatens organizational goals and thus organizational continuity by discussing how goals change in individuals.

The part of experimental psychology known as behavior theory or reinforcement theory has focused historically on how instrumental behavior is controlled by its consequences. The study of how behavior is controlled by consequences has had built into it the presumption that means and ends — responses and payoffs — are both conceptually and empirically distinct. The relation between the particular response one requires an organism to make and the rewarding consequence of that response is *arbitrary*. It does not exist prior to the experimental intervention (for example, Herrnstein, 1974; Schwartz, 1989). The various means to reward are essentially interchangeable with one another, and they have no value apart from their relation to the consequences they produce. These kinds of arbitrary response-outcome relations are studied, principally with animals as experimental subjects (for example, rats pressing levers or pigeons pecking keys), because they are thought to be paradigmatic of the means-ends relations that characterize human behavior. Just as the lever-pressing rat can as well be trained to run down an alley for its food, the automobile assembly-line worker can perform anywhere on the line for his or her weekly wage. Which particular task is required is presumed, minor considerations aside, to be a matter of indifference to the worker, as long as the rate and quantity of payoff are held constant.

Some human activities do reflect the kinds of means-ends relation that characterizes laboratory studies of instrumental behavior. However, the relation between means and ends need not have this arbitrary form. For some activities, means and ends are interconnected. To see the point, consider the concrete example of a man who works as an automobile mechanic from nine to five each day and then goes home to pursue his hobby — restoration of antique cars to running order. On his job, fixing cars is purely instrumental. The weekly paycheck is the reward. He would not be fixing cars were it not for the paycheck, and he would just as soon do some other kind of work for an equivalent or greater paycheck. Thus his job is a means and his paycheck is an end, and there is no special relation between the means and the end that could not be duplicated by substituting some other job for his current one.

The situation is quite different when he gets home. Now, fixing cars is both means and end. While it is true that he does not tinker with cars just for the sake of tinkering—achieving the goal of a smooth-functioning automobile is an important influence on his activity—it is also true that he would not be satisfied with any old means of achieving that goal. He would not, for example, be satisfied with hiring someone else to restore the antique cars for him. The rewarding consequences of the activity are a part of the activity itself, and other kinds of activity are not interchangeable with it in the service of the same reward. Indeed, we might even say that "owning antique cars that run well" is not even properly a reward, for it will not reward any behavior except for "fixing antique cars." Similarly, "fixing antique cars" is not properly an instrumental response, since it will not be rewarded by any outcome except "having antique cars that run well."

The distinction between this man's job and his hobby should be familiar. Some people have jobs that are like this man's; they are simply means to an end, performed solely for the wage, that would be given up immediately if a bigger wage came along. Other people have jobs that are more like this man's hobby. While the wage is certainly significant, and without it people would not do the job (just as for the hobbyist, having a finished, working automobile is crucial, and without it, he would abandon his hobby), it is not everything. There are aspects of the job itself that make it more than just a means and that make people unwilling to substitute other jobs that pay just as well or better. So even though people work at these jobs at least in part for the wage, the jobs themselves are both means and end.

Whether activities will be purely instrumental or will possess some intrinsic value or connection to the ends they produce depends on how those activities are organized. And the way in which activities are organized is subject to historical and cultural change. Thus, activities that have intrinsic value, or that are characterized by a built-in relation between means and ends, can be turned into activities that are purely instrumental and arbitrary. As the goals that are served by an activity change, the character of the activity itself changes. Nowhere is this more clearly in evidence than in the history of the workplace.

The transition from feudalism to industrial capitalism is a long and complex one that cannot be reviewed here (Hobsbawm, 1964; Polanyi, 1944). I want to focus on the last stages of this transition — the emergence of the factory system and of wage labor. Prior to the development of the factory, workers typically engaged in a wide variety of different activities in the course of a day. Their work required flexibility and decision making. The rhythm and pace of their work changed with the seasons. In addition, the work they did was integrated into the rest of their daily activities. They did not leave home for the shop, work from nine to five, then return home to engage in personal pursuits. Indeed, the kind of work they did was largely regarded as an inalienable part of themselves. A blacksmith could no more turn himself into a cooper (if the market conditions were right) than he could turn himself into a woman. Workers did not hire themselves out to the highest bidder, or demand as wages what the traffic would bear. Instead, who they worked for, how they did the work, and what they were paid were largely determined by a network of customs and social relations that operated in local communities.

As factories began to develop, all of this changed. The work people did came to be completely dominated by the wages they received. And the reason that work came to be completely dominated by the wage is that custom, its principal competitor for control, had been systematically and intentionally eliminated. A central component of the final stages of development of the workplace, in its modern form, was a movement explicitly designed to eliminate custom as an influence on behavior. The movement was one of the earliest examples of what is now called *human engineering*. It went by the name of *scientific management* and its founder and leader was Frederick Winslow Taylor.

Taylor ([1911] 1967) argued that custom interfered with

efficiency and productivity. What industry needed was a set of techniques for controlling the behavior of the worker that was as effective as the techniques used for controlling the operation of machines. Accomplishing this control involved two distinct lines of human engineering. First, it was necessary to discover the rates and schedules of pay that resulted in maximal output (for example, Gilbreth, 1914). Second, it was necessary to break up customary ways of doing work and substitute for them minutely specialized and routinized tasks that could be accomplished mechanically and automatically. The idea was to strip work down to its simplest possible elements, to eliminate the need for judgment and intelligence, and to wrench work free of its customary past. With this done, there would be no possible source of influence on work except for the schedule of pay. And the schedule of pay was something the boss could control. Thus, work as pure means, as purely instrumental behavior, as utterly detachable from the self, is a relatively recent human invention. It is an invention that took all value out of work itself and located it instead in the wage, the consequence. And it is an invention that was abhorrent to most of the workers subjected to it. As Marglin (1976) has pointed out, bosses had enormous difficulty in harnessing the efforts of their workers. Workers chafed at the confining discipline of the factory. They malingered, they failed to appear, they quit altogether. Harnessing the worker was difficult, and for the successful boss, it was a singular achievement. But eventually, the problem of inducing workers to put up with the conditions of the factory disappeared. Eventually, what for one generation was the wrenching out of a complex network of customs and social relations was for another "only natural." So it was that scientific managers could see themselves as merely increasing the efficiency of work rather than transforming its very character (for more detailed discussion of this process and its implications, see Lacey and Schwartz, 1987; Schwartz and Lacey, 1982, 1988; Schwartz, Schuldenfrei, and Lacey, 1978).

The problem-solving experiment I mentioned toward the beginning of the chapter was meant to be a laboratory simulation of the historical transformation of the nature of work I just described. And the literature provides many other examples. In one particular demonstration (Lepper, Greene, and Nisbett, 1973), the experimental subjects were nursery school children. They were given the opportunity to draw with felt-tipped drawing pens, an activity they found quite delightful. After a period of observation, in which experimenters measured the amount of time the children spent playing with the pens, the children were taken into a separate room, where they were asked to draw pictures with the pens. Some of the children received "Good Player" awards for their drawings; others did not. A week later, back in the regular nursery school setting, the drawing pens were again made available, with no promise of reward. The children who had received awards previously were *less* likely than the others to draw with the pens at all. If they did draw, they spent less time at it than other children and drew pictures that were judged to be less complex, interesting, and creative. Without the prospect of further awards, their interest in drawing was only perfunctory.

This study, and my own research, are just two of many demonstrations of the negative effects of rewards (for example, Deci, 1975; Lepper and Greene, 1978). Taken together, these demonstrations indicate that exposure to extrinsic rewards can create efficient patterns of behavior that can be executed with effortless and mechanical precision, just like work on the assembly line. The structure of the task makes it possible for people to do the right thing, over and over again. Lapses of attention have no cost, because attention is not required. Lack of intelligence has no cost, because intelligence is not required. That this automization is achieved at the expense of other potential influences on the nature of the activity becomes apparent when the quality of drawings is examined, or when college students are later asked to solve complex problems or discover rules. College students without pretraining know what problem solving means and what it requires. They have been participating in a tradition of problem solving for years, and it is a relatively simple matter to plug new challenges into their traditional wisdom from previous ones. The pretrained students in the experiments I described at the beginning of the chapter are a part of this same tradition. But they have been induced, by their pretraining, to place this particular task outside it. The debilitating effect of this pretraining is modest. But one can imagine that if they were required to engage in this pretraining task for eight or more hours a day, day after day, week after week, year after year, the effect might be considerably more dramatic. And if everyone around them was engaged in a similarly repetitive activity, the effect might be more dramatic still. For instead of simply failing to locate this task in the problem-solving tradition, that tradition might erode and disappear all together. Adam Smith ([1776] 1937, pp. 734–735) captured this possibility most forcefully. He had this concern about the side effects of factory work: "The man whose life is spent in performing a few simple operations . . . has no occasion to exert his understanding, or to exercise his invention in finding out expedients for difficulties which never occur. He naturally loses, therefore, the habit of such exertion and generally becomes as stupid and ignorant as it is possible for a human creature to become." Exactly so.

Practices and Their Contamination

The research I described, along with my thumbnail sketch of the transformation of work, are examples of how activities that are valuable in themselves can be transformed into activities that are simply means to ends that could be attained in other ways. They are examples of how the goals of activities can be transformed, and along with them, the character of the activities themselves. To appreciate better the general character and significance of the transformations reflected in this work, we need a clearer idea of what it means for a domain of activity to be valuable in itself. What is it that participants strive for when they engage in activities that are not purely instrumental? This question has been illuminated by MacIntyre (1981) with his concept of a *practice*. Practices are certain forms of complex and coherent, socially based, cooperative human activities. Among their characteristics are these:

1. They establish their own standards of excellence, and indeed, are partly defined by those standards.

2. They are teleological, that is, goal directed. Each practice establishes a set of "goods" or ends that are internal or specific to it and inextricably connected to engaging in the practice itself. In other words, to be engaging in the practice is to be pursuing these internal goods.
3. They are organic. In the course of engaging in a practice, people change it, systematically extending both their own powers to achieve its goods and their conception of what its goods are.

Thus practices are established and developing social traditions, traditions that are kept on course by a conception of their purpose that is shared by the practitioners. And most important, the goals or purposes of practices are specific or peculiar to them. There is no common denominator of what is good, what is valuable, like utility maximization, by which all practices can be assessed. I can illustrate the concept of a practice, and at the same time shift the level of the discussion from individuals to institutions and organizations, by considering an example of a practice in some detail.

The collection of activities referred to as *science* is a practice. Sciences are certainly complex, social activities. They establish their own standards of excellence. They have a set of "goods," the pursuit of which partly defines them. And they develop. The goal of science is to discover generalizations that describe and explain the phenomena of nature. Different scientific disciplines develop traditions that provide guidance as to which generalizations are worth going after, which methods are best suited for going after them, and which standards should be used for determining whether one has succeeded. Not all people who do what looks like scientific work are engaged in the practice of science. People who do experiments to achieve impressive publication records are not engaged in the practice. The goods they seek — fame, wealth, status, promotion — are not internal to science. Science is just one means to those goods among many. It is certainly true that people who are pursuing such external goods may do good science; that is, they may contribute to the development of the practice. But they are not themselves practitioners. And if everyone engaged in science were to start pursuing these external goals, the practice of science would cease to exist. The core of the practice of science — the thread that keeps it going as a coherent and developing activity — lies in the actions of those whose goals are internal to the practice.

And these internal goals are not commensurable with other kinds of goals. The scientist does not choose from among a variety of market baskets, each containing some amount of truth and some amount of status and money, the one market basket that maximizes her or his preferences. One does not bargain away portions of truth for portions of something else, at least not if one is working within the practice of science. In the problem-solving experiments I described, some of the experimental subjects did precisely this. They bargained away truth, or more accurately, the best techniques for discovering truth, in return for money. For subjects who were pretrained to perform a particular task for monetary reward, the problem-solving task was not "pure" science. It was an amalgam of truth seeking and money seeking, of doing what will yield a general principle and doing what will yield points. These students struck a compromise between two competing masters when they faced the problem-solving task. Their compromise was not necessarily deliberate, but it was there nonetheless. They forsook traditional methods of doing good science that their unpretrained colleagues followed, so that they could earn more money.

One does not need our laboratory demonstrations to see this compromise between scientific and economic objectives. Economic considerations have been affecting the behavior of real scientists, doing real science, for years, and continue increasingly to do so. It is not good science to do the same experiment again and again — to repeat what works. Yet with research success, promotion, and the granting of tenure largely determined by rate of publication, many scientists do so. Each experiment is a minor variant on the preceding one, because such mechanical and unimaginative variation is the quickest road to print. It is not good science to decide what to study on the basis of what people are willing to pay for. Yet government agencies are able to manipulate fields of inquiry by shifting funding from one domain to another. It is not good science to keep one's results a secret, keeping others in the dark, or even intentionally misleading them. Yet in areas that are hot, scientists often do this, as a way of protecting claims to priority, even at the cost of scientific progress. Above all, it is not good science to lie — to misrepresent results willfully, or to invent results of experiments that were never conducted. Yet in the last several years, numerous examples of blatant falsification have been uncovered at major research institutions. This last perversion of science, presumably in the interest of self-aggrandizement, is especially crippling. Science must proceed on the presumption that its practitioners always tell the truth, even if they are not always successful at finding it. If this presumption were seriously undermined, science would grind to a halt. Either all experiments would have to be repeated by all interested parties, to make sure of the veracity of published reports, or monitors would have to be stationed in all laboratories. In the first case, science would stop being a collective, cooperative, and cumulative enterprise. In the second case, we would have to worry about how to monitor the monitors.

Spurred by the growing number of research partnerships between universities and industry, concerned scientists worry that it is just a matter of time before corporate interests start taking control of the university laboratory, dictating which problems are to be studied, who is to be hired to study them, what information is allowed to be made public when, and the like. At the very least, even if they do not dictate the direction of research or encourage distortion, corporate sponsors can be expected to exert substantial control over communication. It does them little good to foot the bill for research if everyone can gain access to its products, through the scientific journals, at the same time they do. If the practice of delaying or withholding publication becomes widespread enough, it will create substantial doubt among scientists about just how accurate and up to date the reports they see in their journals really are (see Schwartz, 1986, forthcoming, for further discussion of this and other examples).

A particularly vivid example of the difficulties for scientific practice that arise when science is penetrated by goals that

are not internal to science has surfaced in the last few years with
the commercialization of microbiology in general and genetic
engineering in particular. Recent advances in molecular genetics
have opened the way to a mass of potential practical applications. Though only a handful of these applications are presently
being used commercially, the potential for enormous profit is
so great that numerous companies have been formed, each in
hot pursuit of the brass genetic rings. A number of these companies have gone public, issuing stock, and they have as major
stockholders internationally prominent scientists. For the potential investor, the trick is to buy stock in one of these companies
before it makes a major breakthrough — to get in on the ground
floor. Once the breakthrough occurs, the stock will skyrocket
in price. Thus investors hang on every word about progress
toward successful application.

So imagine a scientist of world renown who is a director
of one of these companies, holding, say, 100,000 shares of stock.
He calls a press conference and announces that his company
has just made a significant scientific discovery, bringing application of genetic engineering a major step closer. He cannot,
of course, disclose the discovery in detail because of the intense
competition. Within a week of the press conference, the price
of company stock rises $30 a share. The scientist is now $3 million richer. There is nothing necessarily wrong with reaping a
personal profit from a discovery. But notice that in this illustration, the profit comes not from any actual discovery, but from
the scientist's *claim* that a discovery has been made. He presented
no evidence, but people believed him. Why?

To see why, imagine the president of General Motors calling a press conference to claim that his company is on the verge
of producing a car that gets seventy miles to a gallon of gas. What
would happen to the price of GM stock? We cannot say for sure,
but it is reasonable to suppose that such an announcement would
be greeted with substantial skepticism. People know what the
interests of the GM president are, and it is perfectly possible
that he would make such a grandiose claim to improve the position of his company, whether or not it represented a substantial exaggeration. Such exaggerations, if not out-and-out mis-

representations, are commonplace in the world of business. *Caveat emptor.*

What about the scientist? When he makes his announcement, is he wearing his scientist's hat (always tell the truth) or his board of directors' hat (always maximize profit)? It is because we assume he is wearing his scientist's hat that we take his announcement so seriously. But he can switch hats — and get very, very rich, very, very fast — long before anyone catches on. What is the poor scientist to do? Just a little exaggeration will make him and his company so much better off — give them capital with which to expand their research efforts. And who knows? The extra research effort may actually produce the breakthrough that the scientist already announced.

An isolated scientist who wears his scientist's hat when he speaks, but speaks words that serve his entrepreneurial interests, will not affect either the character of his practice or the public's perception of it. But certainly, if scientists start wearing both these hats in increasing numbers, and start making exaggerated or distorted claims about discoveries, they will eventually have no more credibility in the public eye than any other businesspeople. And as their credibility is undermined, so will the credibility of science in general. Science will become not a set of practices distinct from the economy and governed by noneconomic considerations, but a part of it. The goal of science will be profit maximization, just like that of any other industry.

Economic Influences on the Transformation of Goals

My example of the scientist as entrepreneur was intended to illustrate how economic considerations can penetrate practices and change their goals. The spread of economic calculations of interest or profit to practices that were once regarded as noneconomic has been referred to in the literature as *economic imperialism* (for example, Hirsch, 1976; Radnitzky and Bernholz, 1987; Schwartz, 1986, forthcoming). The term is sometimes used approvingly and sometimes not. It sometimes refers only to the application of the *tools* of economic analysis to domains that have traditionally been viewed as noneconomic (Radnitzky and Bernholz, 1987). At other times, it refers to the application of the *goals* of economic activity to domains that have traditionally been viewed as noneconomic, to the infusion of practices with the pursuit of external goods (Hirsch, 1976; Schwartz, 1986, forthcoming). Typically, those who use the term in the first sense are approving, while those who use it in the second sense are not.

I am using it in the second sense. The pursuit within practices of extrinsic, economic goods pushes the practices in directions they would not otherwise take, and in so doing, it transforms the traditions that comprise the practice and the organizations that participate in it. When practices are penetrated by economic considerations, practitioners are pushed to evaluate their activities by a common economic denominator, abandoning the ones that fall short and encouraging the ones that do not, without regard to the internal goods that each practice possesses uniquely. And when internal and external goods conflict, economic considerations move people or organizations in the direction of maximizing the latter, sometimes at the cost of eliminating the former.

The scenario I described for the institution of science is a sketch of what could happen to the practice of science if it came to be dominated by economic considerations. (Notice, please, the use of the word *dominated*, as opposed to, say, *influenced;* no one would be so naive as to suggest that science or anything else was or could ever be un*influenced* by economics.) This potential transformation is, of course, not unique to science. I would like to consider briefly two other examples: high-level athletics (since I began the chapter with a story about softball) and university education.

Economic encroachment into the world of sports has been going on for years. At the professional level, it has become a commonplace that sports are just businesses. Organizations buy teams to make money, or even to lose money so long as the losses bring tax advantages. They do not work to promote the pursuit of excellence in the sport; they work to promote the pursuit of profit. Schedules are determined, game sites and times established, and playing conditions arranged not to ensure that athletes will always have the opportunity to perform at the limits of their capacity, but to ensure maximal television audiences and the lucrative television contracts that they bring with them. Professional teams relocate at the first sign that there is additional profit to be made elsewhere, or threaten to do so as a way to extort their home cities into making concessions on stadium rental, parking facilities, and the like. An example of such extortion is near-bankrupt Philadelphia, where the city's professional basketball and hockey teams threatened to move across the river into New Jersey unless Philadelphia came across with a multimillion-dollar gift of land.

The athletes themselves, following the example set by their employers, sell their services to the highest bidder, without concern for team loyalty, continuity, or excellence. They long to be free agents and refuse to be bound by their contracts after an unusually productive season. They sell any product whose logo can fit on a tennis or golf shirt. They even sell their autographs. They have various performance bonuses written into their contracts that reward them for individual excellence rather than team success. These performance bonuses have interesting effects. First, they often manage to dissociate the individual player's interests from the team's interests. And second, they often manage to induce team management not to do everything it can to win, as, for example, when they "rest" a player near the end of a season who has a large incentive bonus for appearing in a certain number of games or for achieving a certain level in a significant statistical category.

At the amateur level, examples of abuse in big-time athletic programs are recounted daily in the newspapers. Football coaches out-earn college presidents, and football stars live by their own set of rules. Curricula are established that allow almost illiterate athletes to stay eligible for competition without being constrained to study, so that they can devote all of their time and energy to the sport in which they have been recruited to compete. Most recently, university athletic programs have been abandoning the athletic conferences to which they have had long-standing and rich traditional ties in pursuit of greener (more television revenue) pastures. Organized athletics have frequently been defended as builders of the strong character people will need to be upstanding and outstanding citizens of the larger society. The lessons learned on the playing fields are supposed to earn their keep on the battlefields and in the board rooms. If this defense is true, we can expect our future battlefields and board rooms to be populated only with mercenaries.

The fact that some people participate in the practice of sports largely to pursue external goods like money or fame need pose no threat to the integrity of the practice itself. So long as those goods do not come to dominate the activities of all (or most) of the participants in the practice, it can tolerate the external motives of a few. Many of those who participate in a practice in pursuit of external goods will eventually drop out, or be left behind, by those in pursuit of internal goods. However, if external goods *do* come to dominate a practice, it becomes vulnerable to corruption. For practices develop, and the direction that development takes will be determined by participants in the practice. Development that serves internal goods and development that serves external goods may be quite different and have strikingly different effects.

Sometimes developments in a practice are so striking that they require a fundamental reorganization of the practice—a change in the rules of the game. But what form the rule changes take will depend on what goods participants are trying to realize. Consider, for example, the game of basketball. The goods internal to basketball were once taken to involve adept dribbling and passing, accurate shooting, and above all, careful coordination among members of the team. It then developed that some very tall people with enough coordination to put the ball in the basket from close range started playing the game. The game turned into an exercise of muscle and height. One simply passed the ball to a tall player positioned near the basket, and that player shot. Now what had previously been taken to be the goods of the game became less and less important to success. To preserve these goods, the rules were changed. Players were only allowed to camp beneath the basket for brief periods of time. Most effective play still involved getting the ball to the big players near the basket, but now exquisite timing, planned movement, and sharp passing were required to do that effectively. The goods of the game had been preserved.

Contrast this rule change with another one, the introduction of a time limit within which a shot had to be taken. This rule was introduced to speed up the game, making it more appealing to spectators and thus more successful commercially. Its immediate effect was to diminish the opportunity for realizing the goods of basketball. With little time available for passing or coordinated team play, players just started launching shots from far away at their first opportunity. Eventually, skill levels developed so that the goods of the game were again realizable. But the point here is that the way a practice must change to maintain its pursuit of internal goods and the way it must change to maintain its pursuit of external goods need not coincide. And if the practice is controlled by people with external aims, it may be corrupted to the point where it ceases to be a practice. The most recent rule changes in professional football, designed to keep the length of games within three hours, illustrate the problem. Small nibbles were taken out of various aspects of the game, reducing the number of plays that were likely to occur in a game and the opportunities available to teams for strategic adjustments during a game. At the same time, the number of commercial opportunities per game was *increased.* This may be the way to enhance television audiences and team revenues, but it is certainly not the way to enhance the quality of play.

A story similar to my story about sports can be told about university education. For a large part of its history, the United States has had the luxury of regarding university education as an institution for the creation not just of skilled professionals, but of informed, responsible citizens. The educational revolution in this country has been the extension of this ideal of general education from the wealthy classes to the population as a whole. But this conception of university education is changing. The ever-escalating costs of university education, together with increasing competition among members of society for good jobs, the ticket to which is almost invariably a university education, have been changing the character of the university. With education so expensive and so closely tied to job entry, it is becoming an "investment" in one's future. The money spent on school is expected to be returned, *in kind,* and with interest, later on. It is easy to see how thinking of education as an economic investment can affect what people want out of education, and thus how they evaluate what they get. If enough people assess their education in these terms, what actually goes on in the college classroom will change. Colleges and universities will have to be sensitive to market demand; they will have to provide what students want, or the students will go elsewhere. To the claim that one cannot put a dollar value on having an educated citizenry comes the reply, of course one can. One simply looks at how much extra salary the education makes possible. Extra salary becomes the yardstick for evaluating the effectiveness of an educational institution.

Another face of this problem recently surfaced at my own institution, a very wealthy and expensive college that never seems to have enough money to do what it wants to do. A committee on which I served was trying to pare down the coming year's operating budget. We looked for ways to reduce support personnel, and questions arose as to whether the size of the development (fundraising) staff, which had mushroomed in the last decade, could be reduced. The head of development responded to this suggestion with the information that each dollar for development in the budget returned seven dollars in funding. This, of course, was an argument for making the development staff even larger. As the discussion progressed, the deep divide that developed was between those who thought that the size of the development staff should be a simple matter of cost-benefit calculation and those who thought that, financial benefits aside, massive efforts by a massive development staff changed the character of the institution, turning it into a place that always faced the outside world with an open hand rather than an open book.

The concept of a practice, and the distinction between internal and external goods exemplified in my discussion of science, of sports, and of education, help clarify what can happen when economic considerations penetrate and eventually dominate practices. When this happens, practices are pushed in directions they would not otherwise take, and the social traditions that comprise them are transformed. As the goals of practices shift from internal to external, the continuity of the practices is broken. To make the connection between the continuity of practices and the continuity of organizations, all we must realize is that the activities of organizations, no less than the activities of individuals, are embedded in practices. If the practices in which organizations participate are threatened with a change in goals, then the organizations themselves are threatened with a change in goals. It may not be possible for one laboratory to pursue the truth, for one pro team to pursue athletic excellence, or for one university to pursue general education in a context in which their fellow organizations are pursuing something else. Indeed, as the rules change within these practices to accommodate new, economic goals, continued pursuit of traditional goals may come to appear literally incoherent or nonsensical. So if it is true that the continuity of organizations consists in the continuity of goals, organizations that are worried about continuity must dedicate themselves to protecting the practices in which they participate.

Transformation of Goals and Economic Activity

My argument that economic imperialism threatens the distinctive goals and thus the distinctive character of many social practices and institutions may strike a responsive chord in those who are nostalgic for the good old days when science, sports, and education were not big business. But much of the work that is done on organizations is done on profit-making—or at least profit-seeking—firms, and this argument may seem largely irrelevant in connection with the character and organization of these firms. What, after all, can it mean to suggest that economic considerations are penetrating and dominating organizations whose goals are and have always been explicitly economic? Paradoxically, perhaps, I think that domination by economic goals has the same meaning for organizations that have traditionally operated inside the economy as it does for organizations that have traditionally operated outside it. That is, a certain kind of orientation toward economic activity—one that has become increasingly common in the last decade or so— threatens the distinctive character of many economic practices and institutions. This orientation is one that identifies the maximization of profit as the exclusive goal of all economic activity, elevating it above other possible goals, like productivity, efficiency, or quality. The economic historian Karl Polanyi (1944, p. 30) put it this way:

> The peculiarity of the civilization the collapse of which we have witnessed was precisely that it rested on economic foundations. Other societies and other civilizations, too, were limited by the material conditions of their existence — this is a common trait of all human life, indeed, of all life, whether religious or non-religious, materialist or spiritualist. All types of societies are limited by economic factors. Nineteenth century civilization alone was economic in a different and distinctive sense, for it chose to base itself on a motive only rarely acknowledged as valid in the history of human societies, and certainly never before raised to the level of a justification of action and behavior in everyday life, namely, gain. The self-regulating market system was uniquely derived from this principle.

Before I am misunderstood to be suggesting that in the "good old days" people engaged in economic activity out of an altruistic regard for their fellows, let me clarify. Where previously, even in the time Polanyi was writing about, the pursuit of profit was linked to the particular activities of production or commerce that individuals were engaged in, it is now detached from any particular activities and floats freely above them all. Where previously people might have defined themselves as manufacturers of cloth, furniture, or some other product who endeavored to make that activity profitable, now they would define themselves as pursuers of profit who happen to manufacture that product. It is just a difference in emphasis, but sometimes emphasis can make all the difference.

Think, for example, about a hypothetical steel company, operating, say, in 1950. The goal of that company is presumably to make money. Well, no, not quite. The goal of that company is to make money making steel. Activities in pursuit of that goal might include research and development of technological advances that improve production efficiency and perhaps create new products. They might include development of employee management policies that maintained a highly skilled, highly motivated workforce. They might include development of marketing strategies that would increase sales. And they might include the raising of capital for expansion. Each of these activities could be understood as efforts to improve and extend the practice of manufacturing and distributing steel. Making and selling steel are what this company does; they are part of the company's essence.

Now think about a hypothetical steel company operating in 1990. The goal of this company is to make money. Period. Activities in pursuit of this goal might include the ones I just mentioned, but they might also include closing down or selling plants and investing the proceeds of the sale in a Korean steel company. They might include buying stock in IBM. They might include investing in real estate or opening gambling casinos or fast-food restaurants. For this modern steel company, making and selling steel are simply a means, a contingency, a historical accident. They have nothing to do with the company's essence. Profit making, not steelmaking, is what defines this modern company.

The difference between these two hypothetical companies is reflected in the organization of many real ones. Over the last several years, control of many major corporations has shifted from people in the organization who are involved with production to people in the organization who are involved with finance (see Chandler, 1990). This shift in leadership reflects a shift in organizational goals. Production people know and worry about making things. Financial people know and worry about making money. For production people, capital assets are plant and equipment; for financial people, capital assets are cash. Production people move assets around so that the product can be made more efficiently. Financial people move assets around so that money can be made more efficiently.

This shift in emphasis has many consequences, several of which have economists worried about the long-term well-being of the U.S. economy. There is enormous concern about how the single-minded pursuit of profit leads to a kind of "short-termism" that has CEOs of large corporations selling the company's future for a profitable quarter. This short-term orientation is encouraged by the modern character of the stock market, where the majority of trading is done by institutional investors who control large blocks of stock that can be traded almost instantly as a function of the value of a parameter in a computer program. Institutional investors care only about the value of their portfolios, not about the long-term health of the companies whose shares they own. So the CEO is really under pressure to make the company look good on a quarter-by-quarter basis, in order to keep the institutional investors on board.

There is also enormous concern about merger and acquisition mania, especially about acquisitions in which the buyer has no expertise in the running of the business of the seller. On this issue, an illuminating, large-scale study of corporate mergers by Scherer and Ravenscraft (1987) indicated that, in general, these mergers resulted in increased efficiency and profit only when they were so-called vertical mergers, that is, when the acquiring company was already in the business that it was acquiring. So-called horizontal mergers tended to be unprofitable. Indeed, almost half of such acquisitions lost money and were eventually sold off. Those mergers that do result in increased efficiency and profit seem to derive their benefits largely from the dismissal of high-level, overcompensated management rather than from any significant change in processes of production or distribution of goods. Perhaps more telling, in a study of companies acquired in the mid 1980s, money spent on research and development decreased by almost 13 percent after the acquisition. This contrasts with an *increase* of more than 5 percent in spending on research and development by similar companies, at the same time, that had not been acquired (Scherer, 1989).

In a recent review of different historical and cultural patterns of industrial organization, Chandler (1990) summarizes some of these trends, which incidentally, while dominant in the

United States, are largely absent in Japan and Germany. Where previously in U.S. industrial history corporate expansion and diversification came by extending production processes that the company already had under control into new domains, in the last twenty years, U.S. corporate managers began to invest in facilities and enterprises in which they had absolutely no expertise. Along with this came a breakdown in communication between top-level and middle-level management, largely because the top-level managers knew about managing money but not about managing any of the specific activities with which the mid-level managers were concerned. These two developments, together with practices of asset allocation and assessment that made the most profitable arm of a corporation the standard of comparison against which all other arms of the corporation were judged, led to the development of a new business — the buying and selling of companies. All of a sudden, the people with controlling interests in companies had no interest in the activities of the companies they held and manipulated and exchanged them, losing no sleep over the long-term consequences of their transactions. As several commentators have observed, the institution that best represents the character of modern capitalism in the United States is not the factory, but the gambling casino. These are some of the consequences of the shift in emphasis from making steel for a profit to making a profit with steel.

I have suggested that these various organizational changes are the result of a kind of economic domination *within* the economy. But something else may be at least partly responsible as well. I have in mind the development of disciplines like "management science." The existence of these disciplines suggests that management is a skill — perhaps even a practice — that can be applied across all organizational domains. Principles of good management apply to any organization, and people who employ these principles will be good managers of any organization. Whether one is managing a steel company, a machine tool company, a textile company, an investment bank, or even a university is just a detail. The goals of good management, as well as the means for reaching those goals, transfer across organizations. It is not hard to see how people who believe that good managers can manage anything will be tempted to move the firms they manage into areas of production and sale with which they have no specific expertise or experience.

I do not know whether in fact principles of good management *can* be generalized across organizations. Disputing this presumption is not my aim. Instead, my intention is to suggest that the goals of good management may not be isomorphic with the goals of the organizations or practices that are being managed. For example, what one aspires to and does in attempting to create a well-managed steel plant may not be the same as what one aspires to and does in attempting to create a plant that produces steel of high quality at a competitive price. If this is true, when professional managers bring their generalized management goals to the firms they manage, they may be introducing significant changes in the goals of the organization. And by doing that, they may be undermining organizational continuity. If I am right about this, management science as an enterprise may constitute a threat to organizational continuity, and asking how principles of management science may be used to sustain continuity may be a little like asking how bribes can be used to create honest politicians.

Implications for Future Organizational Goals

This volume is concerned with the preservation of organizational continuity. I have suggested in this chapter that continuity of organizations requires continuity of goals. This poses a very significant challenge to modern organizations and to the individuals who run them. All around us, pressure is being applied to change. Technological change is required for organizations to maintain production efficiency. Marketing change is required for organizations to stay competitive in our newly global economy. Financial change is required for organizations to grow in an era of leveraged investment. And social change is required for organizations to keep pace with the demands and expectations of the larger society. Faced with all this relentless pressure to change, it is hard to imagine how traditional organizational goals can be maintained. Some kind of change seems inevitable.

It *is* inevitable. But let me distinguish between two different kinds of change, one of which contributes to the health of an organization, while the other contributes to its demise. When I first introduced MacIntyre's concept of a practice, I indicated that one of the central characteristics of practices is that they evolve. Both the means of achieving the goods of a practice and the character of the goods themselves are changed by participants in the practice. So practices develop. But they develop from inside. New goals and new means are organically and historically connected to the goals and means they replace. They are not imported from outside, by people engaged in different practices. So the key to managing organizations that are simultaneously continuous with their past and responsive to demands for change may be to protect those organizations from outside domination and allow the change to evolve from within. The key to maintaining organizational continuity may be to insist that organizations be constrained in what they seek and what they do by their past. Even this will be difficult in an age whose unofficial ideology is that "everything is possible." But whether or not it is difficult, I believe it is essential.

Chapter Five

Providing Continuity in Change: The Role of Tradition in Long-Term Adaptation

Paul F. Salipante, Jr.

Traditions and *traditionality* are terms receiving scant attention in organizational literature, as if they were elements and forms that had passed from the scene long ago. Being in the New World, we Americans tend to view traditions as insignificant elements of our society, as something found in more backward or class-bound social systems in other corners of the world. Incongruously, these negative views of traditions coexist with the burgeoning of literature on the nature and significance of organizational culture and on the importance of organizations being value driven. Literature's neglect of the roles of continuity and traditionality has encouraged organizational leaders to attempt the rapid development of new organizational cultures, seeking to align core values and beliefs with new organizational strategies. In such efforts, member commitment to past practices and beliefs is seen as inhibiting adaptation. Leaders think of continuity versus change.

This chapter considers the polar opposite view, that continuity *in* change, provided by reliance on organizational tradi-

Note: The author is indebted to Karen Goldman for her stimulating work on organizational tradition and wishes to thank Joel Becker, Bruce Fortado, Robert Wiseman, Timothy Wilmot, and Craig Wishart for their useful comments on an earlier draft.

tionality, can produce adaptation that is effective over a long time frame. Stimulated by study of a successful organization whose managers embraced traditionality (Golden, 1988), it questions whether tepid and frequent changes that look only to the immediate future, that treat not only costs but also past organizational practices as "sunk," are the appropriate way to make an organization adaptive. While a strategically rational view conceives of devotion to the past as impeding change, a neotraditional view (Golden and Salipante, 1990) focuses on the symbiotic relationship between the past and the future. The latter view encourages the reader to consider such questions as whether fast rates of change are preferable to slow rates, and whether substantial environmental changes force internal changes on an organization, if it is to survive.

To build a base for considering the role of traditionality in organizational change, we first consider the neglect and denigration of traditionality and organizational continuity, then explore some indications that traditionality can enhance organizational adaptivity. I draw on two surveys of organizational members to indicate that modern American organizations seem to rely on traditions with startling frequency and that a neotraditional view of organizations is justified. The core of the chapter then follows: By enumerating a number of the positive functions that traditional elements serve for organizations and their members, I argue that traditionality can effectively guide change in a way that ensures a coherence to organizational practices and member commitment to key organizational values and beliefs. The chapter concludes with several propositions concerning the balancing of rationality and traditionality.

Views of Traditionality and Organizational Functioning

Contemporary understanding of organizations is founded on an understanding of the transition from tradition to reason as the basis for organizational action. Weber (1947) produced a major shift in our views when he drew attention to the dominance of the rational and boundedly rational (March and Simon, 1958) perspectives, implying that well-functioning modern organizations were very different from their traditional forebears. While it is recognized that political and social processes, and individuals' limitations, cause deviations from the ideal bureaucratic model, modern organizational thought is firmly based on the assumption that organizations are rational, not traditional, systems.

Since the 1960s, the open-systems model of organizations (Thompson, 1967; Katz and Kahn, 1978) has provided a complementary foundation to that of rational bureaucracy, calling attention to organizational ability to adapt to changing, often turbulent, environments (Emery and Trist, 1965). Organizations are seen either as "muddling through" such changes or, prescriptively, as needing to strategically plan their long-term responses to them. Similarly, the flexibility gained by organic organizational forms is seen as aiding organizational adaptation (Burns and Stalker, 1961). Emphasis is on the rapidity of recognizing change in the environment and responding to the change in a rational, calculated fashion that formulates a new strategy (Andrews, 1980) and a structure aligned with it (Chandler, 1969).

While these basic concepts of strategic rationality underlie the dominant contemporary views of proper organizational functioning (Mintzberg and McHugh, 1985), their reality and the efficacy of their prescriptions have come under significant challenge. Investigators who have examined decision-making processes in organizations have disputed the concept of strategy as explicitly developed at top levels and passed down to individuals who then implement. Empirical research suggests that strategy is better understood as having strong emergent elements, with strategy-as-implemented reflecting an interplay between patterns of actions flowing upward in the organization and deliberate plans flowing downward (Burgelman, 1985; Mintzberg and McHugh, 1985). More radically, the idea that change is tied to leaders' strategic plans and to environmental threats has been questioned (March, 1981; Weick, 1976), with some authors maintaining that organizational change is largely uncontrolled (Hannan and Freeman, 1984).

An even more fundamental challenge to strategic rationality is offered by the organizational ecology school. An evolutionary theory of the firm sees firm behavior as coming more from its own past than as a result of rational decision-tree analysis

(Nelson and Winter, 1982). Each economic organization is characterized as possessing a particular set of competencies, embodied in organizational "routines" that provide regular and predictable patterns of behavior. If the organization has been successful through the execution of its routines, it risks failure in its market by each attempted change that departs from these routines. In a similar vein, Hannan and Freeman (1984) posit that organizational survival rests on the ability of organizations to provide reliability and accountability, leading them to conclude that organizations with high inertial forces will be favored and that attempts at reorganization will increase the likelihood of organizational death. These views of organizational routines and inertia open the door to valuing traditionality in modern organizations.

Evidence and Personal Construction of Traditionality

One reason that most writers have undervalued the efficacy of the past is that they have confused traditionality with the specific traditions found in pre-Weberian organizations. As Shils (1981) has emphasized, it is critical to note the distinction between particular traditions and traditionality. A particular traditional system of organization, founded in ignorance and ascribed status, has been confused with traditionality itself. Traditionality should be defined as independent of any one set of traditions. Its essence is simply the willing reception of practices, beliefs, and values from the past and their use in guiding current action.

With a clearer view of what constitutes traditionality, we can explore through fieldwork whether reliance on traditions is as unimportant as today's organizations seem to assume. We can also investigate organizational members' views toward their organizations' traditionality. This exploration of traditionality focuses only on managers and managerial-level staff members and their perceptions.

Traditionality and Adaptivity in One Firm

The currently dominant views of strategic rationality condition researchers studying successful organizations to expect to find adaptive processes and managerial decision making that is, at the least, described by managers in rational terms. Karen Golden (1988) reported just such expectations when she initiated research on managerial decision making related to human resource management at a large Fortune 500 manufacturing organization (hereafter labeled HAPCO). This organization outperformed its competitors financially during the 1980s, with several of the latter having gone bankrupt. Due to the strength of her expectations, several months of intensive on-site observation of managerial decisions and discussions were necessary before Golden realized that the key managers at HAPCO construed their actions traditionally. The managers were open in acknowledging their reliance on traditions, but the field researcher's expectations concerning the efficacy of rationally based innovation inhibited recognition of the cultural system supported by the managers (Golden and Salipante, 1990). Stability and persistence of behavior, grounded in organizational traditions, were of primary importance, not adaptation and rational arguments. Managers relied on certain traditions, such as avoiding reliance on government work, handed down from prior managers. This was so even at the strategic decision-making levels of the organization. Despite researchers' misgivings about the wisdom of the firm's reliance on traditions, during the two-year-long course of the field research HAPCO successfully weathered several environmental crises that damaged many of its competitors.

So, what does this one field investigation tell us about the superiority and ubiquity of strategic rationality over traditionality? Is HAPCO to be interpreted as merely an isolated aberration or, conversely, as the falsifying evidence leading to rejection of theory (Popper, 1968)? Given the dearth of investigation of organizational traditions, both of these interpretations are premature. It is preferable to see HAPCO's reliance on traditions, along with its long-standing growth and continuing success, as an anomaly (Kuhn, 1970). This calls for further conceptualizing and research into the following issues: (1) How can an organization built on the fundamentally different organizing principle of traditionality survive and prosper in threatening, changing environments? What functions does traditionality serve for the organization and its individual members? (2) Is organizational traditionality more common than organization theory would ever lead us to suspect?

Archetypes for Research

The intensive analysis of one firm, HAPCO, has provided some understanding of what traditionality can mean in a successful contemporary organization. This understanding is used here to create archetypes of traditionality and rationality, allowing investigation in other organizations of issues (1) and (2) above.

The archetype of organizational traditionality is founded in the essential elements Golden identified at HAPCO: appreciation of the past, reliance on past practices and the values and beliefs embedded in them as a guide to current action, and an emphasis on perceived loyalty of the individual to the organization. Traditionality encompasses all three levels of organizational culture identified by Schein (1985a), namely, artifacts, values, and underlying assumptions. However, traditionality goes beyond Schein's view of organizational culture in two ways. First, a system of traditionality requires a passing down of recognizable traditions over a period of at least two generations (Shils, 1981). It is fallacious to believe that traditional systems do not evolve and change (Gusfield, 1967), but they do possess a strong sense of historicity. Second, unlike several examples of organizational culture cited by Schein, traditionality involves an explicit recognition by its members of the organization's key assumptions, since these are part of the transmitted traditions.

In defining a concept, it is essential to specify what the concept is not (Osigweh, 1989). Traditionality can be contrasted with a rational/strategic organizational archetype that is built on the adaptivity stream of organization theory discussed earlier. For use in survey research, operational definitions of the traditionality and rational/strategic archetypes can be stated (Types A and B, respectively) as follows:

> *Type A organization:* This type of organization is guided by appreciation of practices and values that have been passed down through several generations

of leaders. When they deviate from these, organizational members are reminded by their managers and peers of the organization's important values and the correct way of doing things. Members are expected to be personally loyal to the organization and its leaders.

Type B organization: This type of organization is guided by rational assessment of the current situation. The efficacy of one or several alternative approaches is considered and critically analyzed until a satisfactory approach is found. The organization's leaders are concerned with changing the organization and its strategy in response to environmental shifts, and decisions are based on their fit with the strategy. Members are alert to job opportunities in other organizations.

Exploratory Surveys

Motivated primarily by curiosity about HAPCO's uniqueness, a brief survey was designed and administered to two convenience samples in educational settings. Their written responses and subsequent discussions generated insights that went well beyond the incidence of traditionality, by illustrating the nature of traditions and their meaning to respondents. Much of the remainder of this chapter is based on the survey responses.

The above descriptions of the two archetypes prefaced an open-ended survey that asked individuals to rate the degree to which their organization was Type A versus Type B, then to describe their organization's elements that corresponded with each type, as well as its core values and the individuals' own ideas on how they felt their organization should evolve. Respondents were also asked to rate the overall performance of their organization versus its performance five years before. The following two groups received the survey: (1) forty high-level managers (employed staff) in the autonomous local councils of Girl Scouts of the USA (hereafter, GSUSA), a nationwide nonprofit founded early in this century and staffed mostly by volunteers, and (2) thirty-two part-time graduate students, almost all working full time in for-profit organizations. The response rate for both groups was over 90 percent.

While no claim can be made that the survey produced responses representative of a broader set of organizations, the rated incidence of Type A (traditionality) elements was surprisingly high. Out of a total of 100 points allocated between the two types, the GSUSA managers' average rating for Type A was 45. For the heterogeneous (covering many different organizations) second group, the average rating was 49. This writer hoped that perhaps half of the respondents would rate their organizations as having significant Type A elements, so that they could describe those elements as they played out in their organizations. In fact, the vast majority rated the Type A elements at 25 points or higher, the threshold point on the questionnaire for being asked to describe these elements in their own organizations. Taken together, 58 percent of the two groups rated their organization as equally or more strongly Type A than Type B. The high incidence of traditional elements leads to further doubt concerning the premise of managerial rationality.

The Meaning of Traditionality. The highly rated incidence of Type A elements raises the question of what Type A and Type B meant to the organizational members as they filled out the surveys. The Type A description, as derived from the concepts of Shils and Golden, refers to a system of traditionality that governs the thoughts and behavior of organizational members. As a system, it was thought of as an integrated whole, yet many respondents depicted their organization as having significant elements of both Type A and Type B. For the heterogeneous sample, a few respondents' comments on how their organization functioned clearly indicated a system of traditionality, but most respondents' descriptions indicated a mixture of traditionality and rationality in some type of hybrid system. For the GSUSA sample, the author has enough additional information on its functioning (based on its policy, mission, and planning manuals and extended discussions with several of its managers) to believe that, as experienced by the vast majority of its volunteer members in the local units and those staff who interact most directly with volunteers, the system is one of traditionality. However, GSUSA has two parallel structures, and the comments of respondents indicated that the staff half of the structure contained significant (often dominant) rational elements concerned with planning and innovating. Given these parallel structures and their differing orientations, many local units seem to have a duality of traditionality and rationality.

While organizational systems of traditionality have received minimal attention, the role of traditional elements in dominantly or ostensibly rational organizations is even less understood. The reader is warned that, in the following discussion, traditional elements will be described in terms of their functioning in complete systems of traditionality, such as at HAPCO and the volunteer section of GSUSA, even when illustrative comments are drawn from respondents in organizations that mix traditionality and rationality.

Respondents' Constructions of Traditionality and Rationality. Respondents' descriptions of the traditional elements in their organizations indicated a mixture of evaluative views toward the presence of those elements. Slightly less than 40 percent of the GSUSA managers gave a generally negative connotation to the traditional elements, saying that they slowed needed change, led to the retention of inappropriate methods, and reflected volunteer leaders who were out of touch with the needs of today's girls. A group of equal size had a mixture of positive and negative views toward their traditional elements, while the remaining 25 percent had positive views. Positive connotations involved loyalty to the organization's values and mission, the strong spirit and commitment of organizational members, behavioral reinforcement of values, and realized expectations of moral behavior on the part of members.

The generally balanced view of the GSUSA sample toward traditionality was not repeated in the heterogeneous sample. Only 10 percent provided a positive connotation for traditionality, 30 percent a mixed connotation, and fully 65 percent a negative connotation. Labels attached to Type A included the following: paternalistic, "on automatic pilot," mechanistic, covert, parochial, static, and stagnant. The few positive connotations for traditional elements focused on being value driven. Several respondents emphasized the closed and autocratic quality of the traditional elements, implying that their organization's leaders were relying on traditions primarily to further their own personal ends.

Many comments from the heterogeneous sample strongly implied that the traditional elements they were describing were dysfunctional for their organizations. However, their own ratings of the change in their organization's performance over the previous five years did not reflect the supposed dysfunctional effects. Ratings of change in organizational performance were not related at all to the rated strength of traditional elements in the GSUSA sample and only slightly related (in the negative direction) in the heterogeneous sample. To state this result in another fashion, Type B organizations were just as likely to be rated as declining in performance as were Type A organizations. These samples provide more reason to question the premise that organizations must be dominantly rational and their leaders change oriented for the organizations to remain viable.

The differences between the two samples in the connotations attached to traditionality are notable and may reflect several important differences in the sample populations. The graduate students, while employed full time, generally were younger and had lower levels of responsibility and organizational status than the GSUSA managers. The former group was split roughly equally in terms of gender, while the latter group had very few males. The GSUSA managers had longer average tenure with their organization. Perhaps most important, few of the GSUSA managers had ever participated in degreed management education programs, while the graduate students were pursuing degrees either in business or organizational change. Formal management education emphasizes rationality and the need for rapid change so strongly that its recipients can be expected to develop highly jaundiced views of traditional elements in their organizations.

The more balanced views toward traditionality of the

GSUSA respondents relate to the nature of their organization and its long-established mission. Traditionality was seen as creating "loyalty to our values and mission," in the words of one respondent, while another saw the "values and traditions . . . as contemporary today as in 1912 [the year of GSUSA's founding]." These and other comments indicated the respondents' views on the utility of traditions for reinforcing among volunteers the values critical to the achievement of GSUSA's mission.

In the Girl Scout councils, traditionality is intertwined with its volunteer base. Reliance on and appreciation of traditions is driven by the continuity of the organization's mission and by the intergenerational commitment of its volunteers. Today's volunteers were the girls being served by the organization at an earlier point in their lives, and they carry with them fond memories of the organization's traditional practices. The volunteers' appreciation of these traditions is critical to the maintenance of traditionality.

Indeed, in a discussion following their responding to the survey, the council managers commented on the significance of the distance between their roles and those of the volunteers. Their point was that those who were supervising volunteers rated their organization as higher in traditionality. In contrast, the executive directors said that they rated their units as lower in traditionality. Their roles emphasized organizational planning and innovation, and they were attempting to impress on their councils an expanded element of the organization's mission that was being promulgated from the national level — service to girls of all backgrounds. They saw older volunteers as impeding the changes needed to accomplish the expanded mission. It is not surprising that role responsibility for change creates a stronger climate for rationality and a less favorable view of traditionality.

The particular descriptions that GSUSA managers provided of their organization's Type A and Type B elements indicated that they did not see traditionality and rationality as mutually exclusive. Because elements of both types could be found in one or the other sides of their parallel (staff and volunteer) organizational structure, managers could speak positively about both traditionality and rationality. As stated by one, "The balance between tradition and change must [be kept] or the organization's purpose and mission will change." Another GSUSA manager noted that the Girl Scouts had been too strongly gripped by tradition and that "an organizational value of responding to change has rescued the Girl Scouts from the doldrums it experienced fifteen to twenty years ago."

Functions of Traditionality

The positive connotations given to traditionality by many of the GSUSA managers, and a few of the graduate students, suggest the functional roles that traditions can serve for organizations and their members. To counter the negative views of organizational traditionality that our current theories produce, I will review a number of the functional aspects of traditionality. These aspects were suggested by Golden's observation of managers at HAPCO, written comments on the surveys, and discussions with survey respondents.

Functions for the Individual

Several years ago two management students were discussing family-owned businesses. One decried the second-class status of non-family members who were superior performers. The other, drawing on her experience, replied that some family members might not be so talented, but when the chips were down and times became tough, they could be counted on to remain and fight for the organization's survival. This remark stuck in the author's mind, becoming one stimulus for this chapter. Personal loyalty and commitment is one contribution of traditionality to organizational adaptivity. We cannot understand the functions of traditionality for organizational adaptivity without first understanding why managers are loyal and committed, and why they perpetuate their system of traditionality. What do members gain personally from traditionality that makes them loyal and committed?

Social Connectedness. A traditional system's spirit of kinship, evident at HAPCO by the social interaction of its managers outside the workplace and their description of the organization as a family and community, bonds the individual to others in the social system of the organization. In contrast, the bureaucratic ideal of impersonality calls for a denial of affiliation needs, for a separation of the "official" self from the personal self. Traditionality recognizes the personal and represents a system of social solidarity (Durkheim, [1893] 1947). One GSUSA respondent noted "a group of volunteers in their sixties and seventies who have been meeting and working together in [the organization] since their high school years." By allying social interaction with mission attainment, traditionality directly counters two of the components of work alienation identified in modern economic organizations—social isolation and self-estrangement (Kanungo, 1982). Unlike rationality, traditionality does not breed a separation of the work self from the outside-of-work self.

Moral Guidance. Through processes of selection and socialization, traditionality fosters social bonding with others who view the world with the same construction of reality, providing a counter to the anomie that comes from normlessness (Seeman, 1959). The economic rationality of many contemporary organizations creates ethical conflicts with personal values, such that managers feel they must occasionally set aside personal values and norms when operating in the organization. In a traditional system, members are less susceptible to normlessness, since traditions are closely intertwined with personal values. While a shallow commitment to newly developed values is often the most that can be accomplished in rational organizations, members of traditional systems associate with others having truly similar, and strongly held, personal values and beliefs. A system of traditionality is similar to religion in that it appears to its members as definitive, continuing, and endless. Members do not waffle since they know what is proper and improper. Through belief in the organization's established values and ways, issues become black and white, not gray.

At GSUSA, shared values stemmed from devotion to "the Movement." At HAPCO, similarity of values and beliefs was supported by the managers' common backgrounds, which made possible an alignment of personal values with those found in the workplace (Golden, 1988). With traditionality, shared values are not divorced from concrete experience; the practice of traditions, ranging from the daily use of certain meeting protocols at HAPCO to the ceremonies periodically dramatized at GSUSA, represent a behavioral enactment of the social system's values, reinforcing the values and guiding behavior so that it conforms to the values.

Pride, Appreciation, and Enjoyment. Members take pride in being part of an organization with an illustrious history. In an interview, a top-level executive explained that customers and suppliers would ask for his advice because of their respect for the executive's company and its ways of operating. Similarly, GSUSA managers took pride in their organization's historical and continuing status, being able to see their actions as helping fulfill the vision of the distinguished founder of the Girl Scouts.

Some traditions have a personal value in and of themselves. It is this quality of personal appreciation that separates the practice of traditionality from habit (Golden and Salipante, 1990). People enjoy performing the traditional practices. As one GSUSA manager—referring to some frustration in inducing volunteers to change their methods—put it, "Ways of delivering the program . . . have become ends in themselves." The comments of several GSUSA managers indicated that the greatest devotion to maintaining the traditional ways occurred in the volunteers' running of programs for the girls. Volunteer leaders enjoy the opportunity to lead, particularly when they can repeat for a new generation the practices that they themselves had received a generation earlier.

Confidence in Own Knowledge and Skills. Traditions increase the comfort and confidence of managers. As one manager reported in an interview, procedures and beliefs that earlier managers had passed down were understood to have passed the test of time. Managers observe the positive results associated with the traditional practices and experience them firsthand when viewing the efficacy of their own actions: "We did it our way, and it worked." Traditions reduce uncertainty about the correctness of decisions. The resulting confidence that managers display in their decisions, combined with other members' long-term assimilation of the organization's traditions, makes it easier for managers to gain the backing of others. Ease in gaining support reduces managers' anxiety.

Traditions also increase confidence for individuals promoted to higher levels of responsibility. Since continuity in practices and beliefs exists, individuals who were recipients of these in previous years already know how the organization wants them to function. This is especially valuable in an organization where a gap may occur in people's involvement with the organization. Similarly, it means that individuals making an investment in learning how to do their job can be more certain that they will be able to reap a return on the investment for many years — a particularly critical factor for volunteers who contribute part time to an organization, often over a period of decades.

Personal Welfare. In a traditional system, members believe that the social system and its leaders will provide personal protection. One graduate student recounted a meeting whose outcome the respondent described as "amazing." Taking place in a small firm where employees were very loyal to the president, the company's long-time members rejected the need for the organization to adopt a death benefit policy, saying "they would trust the president to take care of their families." There is similarity here to feudal fiefs, in which residents were protected by their lord in return for their loyalty and commitment to him and to the community (Tuchman, 1978).

Reviewing the personal benefits to be found in systems of organizational traditionality, we find a parallel between organizations based on traditionality and the small community social systems of earlier ages. In urban settings today, the magnitude of the population and its diversity of interests inhibit strong attachment of the individual to the broader society. In the midst of these settings, it is possible for traditionally oriented organizations to have a scale and form that offer a sense of community, a sense provided in earlier periods (and perhaps now in rural settings) by strongly integrated feudal and village social systems.

Functional Consequences for Organizations

Although most often described as dysfunctional by respondents concerned with organizational change, traditionality can play overlooked but important functional roles for the organization.

Strengthening Individual Commitment. As noted earlier, traditionality creates strong attachment and commitment of the individual to the organization. One GSUSA manager remarked on "experienced volunteers who have a strong commitment to the Girl Scout Way." Another said that one of the core values was loyalty to the national and local organizations and to the executive director. Since many of the personal benefits members receive are strongly linked to values and mission commitment, individuals are motivated to perform well. In the words of one manager, "By more clearly . . . showing how members benefit from adopting the Girl Scout Way, we instill good performance, development, and loyalty." By providing the personal, intrinsic satisfaction that comes from the enactment of certain (usually ceremonial) practices, traditions serve not only to attract and retain members but also to mobilize them toward its mission. Also, since members of a traditional system experience a social connectedness to other members and the organization, their loyalty and effort can be counted on in difficult times.

Transmitting Organizational Learning. Written policies and procedures are often ignored in organizations. This is especially true of statements from high organizational levels concerning unethical and illegal behavior (Waters, 1976). Traditions are transmitted and enforced by direct personal influence, being passed in a more meaningful pattern orally and experientially between people, rather than simply in the form of written policies and procedures that are often ignored.

Traditions are a means of ensuring that organizational

learning is embodied in actual practice. They serve as organizational programs (March and Simon, 1958) that guide individuals. Present organizational members do not have to understand the rationale for a traditional practice to be able to appreciate and use it. Its effect has simply stood the test of time. In a system of traditionality, members' appreciation of the past ensures that prior organizational learning will not be dismissed prematurely. In contrast, rationality has led to adoption of many practices that produce short-term gains at the expense of long-term societal costs, as will be discussed in a later section.

Facilitating Interpretation and Decision Making. Traditions that reflect the organization's core values create uniformity of practices across units of the organization as well as over time. The code of the Girl Scout movement is alive in all its regional councils, and the organization's ceremonies and standard program procedures create a commonality of understanding that allows managers from various regions to communicate and work together effectively. This was evident in the management education context that the author observed, but it also operates when council managers participate in national-level planning. People across the organization know how information and decisions were generated and how they are meant to be interpreted, which facilitates decision making and implementation.

Stimulating Ethical Behavior. Traditionality carries forward values established in the past, providing value premises (Simon, 1957) for members' decisions. Some of these value premises define what constitutes ethical and unethical behavior. For example, the story of its founder returning money to the government circulates today at HAPCO (Golden and Salipante, 1990).

Enhancing Networking and Investment in Individuals, Allowing Decentralized Control. One of the individual benefits of traditionality noted earlier was security in one's knowledge of organizational practices. The facilitating of individuals' accumulation of knowledge is critical to organizations that rotate members through many local units and stress broad, general knowledge of the organization (Aoki, 1988; Lynn, 1990). When practices vary greatly across units and change frequently, job rotation does not produce cumulative knowledge of current value.

Because of the continuity of traditional practices and their uniformity throughout the organization, as well as individuals' loyalty to remaining in the organization, many individuals will accumulate the knowledge needed for leadership. This is critical to an organization like GSUSA, which must rely on volunteers for actual program delivery, but it is clearly valuable to any organization, especially as organizations become flatter and more reliant on individual self-management.

Preventing Usurpation of Control. Relying on traditions can be a means of keeping control in the hands of a particular group (the volunteers, in the case of GSUSA) that would otherwise be dominated by others (employed staff). Knowledge of traditional practices and the values underlying them enables Girl Scout volunteer leaders to counter the control efforts of the change-minded staff. Power distance between staff and volunteers is minimized because of volunteers' expert knowledge (Mulder, 1976).

Traditionality's Functions in Adaptation

Since they have been conditioned by theories that emphasize environmental turbulence and the need for adaptive changes in strategy, structures, and culture, it is natural to expect that traditional organizations will be maladaptive. We would then anticipate that any organization whose current action is predicated on the following of traditions would be relatively ineffective in reacting to environmental threats. However, Golden's analysis of HAPCO revealed adaptive strengths. Also, the graduate student surveys indicated tendency toward maladaptive change in their rationally driven organizations.

Vigilance

Individuals were found to be involved in change at HAPCO (Golden, 1988). Living as they do in an economic system whose rhetoric emphasizes survival of the economically fit, even managers operating in a system of traditionality must attend to their organization's economic viability. By attending to their organization's survival, the managers are rational within the traditional perspective — that is, rational in the sense that their tradition-guided actions are congruent with their view of the reality of running a business, rather than the economic rationality of attempting to optimize economic outcomes.

To elaborate, the dominant view of business reality constructed by HAPCO managers is rather feudal, that of a hostile outside world against whom their organization (fief) must be protected (Tuchman, 1978). Managers told historical stories in which the forces of this world, including actors such as the government or unions, took particular actions against HAPCO that nearly resulted in its death (Golden and Salipante, 1990). Consequently, the leaders of a traditional organization like HAPCO are likely to create a mood of vigilance. They are steadily on the alert for any action on the part of outsiders (or the occasional maverick insider) that could threaten the system's survival. They celebrate as good and rational whatever promotes their organizational community and condemn whatever prevents the attainment of good for the organization. As a result, managers act to buffer the organization, defending it against negative forces. Their emotional commitment to the organization is significant, and they demand comparable loyalty and effort from other employees in coming to the organization's defense. In its defense, they tend to act in concert with their established traditions, since these traditions have stood the test of time by demonstrating their ability to help the organization survive. In sum, managers' vigilance concerning survival against outsiders makes them attuned to environmental threats and makes the organization's members ready and willing to take necessary protective action.

Loyalty, Voice, and Action

Compared to many bureaucracies, traditional systems such as HAPCO's suffer less of an agency problem. The strong integration of the individual and the organization in a traditional system reduces the incidence and severity of managerial action that is dominated by short-term concerns and self-interest. Individuals are more willing to subordinate immediate self-interest to the good of the organization. This subordination is especially likely when members see themselves as part of a movement, as at GSUSA. Not only are managers more committed to the organization's survival and mission attainment, but they see their own long-term interests as intertwined with the community that is their organization.

Individuals' strong commitment and loyalty in a system of traditionality discourages the use of exit and encourages the use of voice when the organization confronts a problem, which aids organizational recuperation (Hirschman, 1970). To the degree that the traditional organization follows the feudal ideal of protecting the members of its community, the security net for individuals permits them to take greater risks. Recuperative voice is then more likely to be exercised, as long as the voice is phrased in the context of protecting the organization.

The view of HAPCO managers that they were part of a family and that their careers rested with the company in the long term aided this recuperative advantage. When the organization is seen to be threatened and additional effort is needed, the intensity of managers' attachment to the organization ensures that they will put forth this effort. Unlike the usual situation in rational organizations that undergo crisis, the needed talent is not likely to exit but, rather, to remain and fight for the organization.

Maintenance of Mission

Traditionality discourages a turning away from the agreed-on mission of the organization, preventing adoption of a strategy that is inconsistent with the members' values and beliefs and the organization's structure and practices. This view is founded on a belief that equifinality holds with regard to strategy—that is, that several strategies are available that will enable the organization to cope with its environment, but that some of those strategies match better than others to the organization's long-standing mission and its inner strengths, as these have developed over the years.

An example was provided in one of the GSUSA survey responses. In one council, staff asked volunteers to add to a proposed new facility certain features that would meet girls' needs through currently popular activities, providing the facilities with some features commonly found in fitness centers. Volunteer leaders resisted these additions and decided that the facility would be designed to provide the traditional services. By not duplicating the offering of services available in other facilities, the unique image of the organization was maintained. A dilution and shift of its mission was avoided.

Slowing Change

From the preceding discussion, we can see that traditionality slows the rate of change, earning it the disparagement of change-oriented researchers and managers. But is slower change necessarily bad? Some simulations of organizational learning have shown that organizations that are the first to adapt reach lesser levels of effectiveness than those that adapt more slowly (March, 1986). Also, a number of the graduate students described their rationally dominated organizations as engaged in change that was too rapid, which appeared to one of them as "whimsical." As one respondent stated, the organization had "two reorganizations within a year, the second one undoing and contradicting the first." Another said that "values change too quickly for the organization to change," and someone else commented that "managers verbalize values about change even if they do not believe them." The problems suggested here involve not only the pace of change but also the substance of change.

Customizing Change

A common problem of organizational adaptation is tailoring change to the organization's social structure, tasks, and people (see Dalton, 1971). Traditionality demands the tailoring of change by inhibiting the adoption of practices that do not reflect the organization's values and beliefs, as illustrated by the preceding example involving the new facilities. When an organization has traditions that it closely follows, the substance of change is constrained to lie within practical bounds and the tailoring process is automatic. At GSUSA, for example, any new practice must be in accord with its most basic traditions — namely, its mission and values.

HAPCO employees "HAPCOized" — that is, customized — new approaches so that they fit the organization's traditions. When this was not done, proposals for change were vetoed by other managers (Golden, 1988). Note that the root of the term "*custom*ize" suggests aligning with tradition. Customizing integrates a new approach with the old; it makes it part of a coherent whole of organizational practices. Any new practice will be based on the template of an existing routine and supported by complementary activities that have been in operation for years (Nelson and Winter, 1982). Since the new fits with standard organizational practices, organizational members are more likely to understand and accept it. Thus, the process of customizing is extremely functional in buffering the organization and its members while they are adapting and in facilitating the proper use of the new practice.

A clue that organization is traditional and favors the customizing of change is found in its members' use of the term *Way*. The GSUSA manager's responses were full of references to the "Girl Scout Way." Similarly, employees of Hewlett Packard are reported to describe the essence of their organization as the "HP Way" (Von Werssowetz and Beer, 1985). Just as managers at HAPCO had to "HAPCOize" a change so that it appeared to fit with existing values and practices, the author was informed of an example of "HPizing." When Hewlett Packard considered the just-in-time inventory concept, it modified the concept to fit with existing organizational practices and gave it a name that was compatible with Hewlett Packard jargon. This linking of traditionality with the customizing of change has been overlooked in the literature on change.

Lengthening the Time Horizon

Is there an organizational parallel between concern with the past and concern with the future? A rational organization whose view is that the past is largely irrelevant has no "backward time horizon." This may explain why so few American organizations have a lengthy future time horizon. The reverse may also be operative, namely, that a short future time horizon encourages a focus on the present to the point of ignoring the past, of ignoring organizational learning. The survey responses noting frequent, whimsical change in rationally dominated organizations support these views. Such change totally ignores even recent organizational practices and history.

In contrast, traditional organizations *implicitly* emphasize the long-term future through their commitment to traditional practices and their desire to ensure the organization's survival. Is it an accident that Japanese organizations, embedded in a society that is tradition oriented, have longer time horizons and different objectives than most American business organizations?

Objectives other than profit maximization go hand in hand with a longer time horizon. At current discount rates, profit maximization requires no time horizon longer than about seven years. At HAPCO managers were concerned with objectives other than profit maximization, objectives closely linked to long-term survival (Golden and Salipante, 1990).

Traditionality creates within its members a concern for future generations. A notable example is the effort of the Cree Indians in northern Quebec (Gold, 1990) to preserve their current environment so that their traditional way of life will not be threatened in succeeding generations. The paradox is that through their regard for the past and its traditional ways, members of traditional systems look to the long-term future.

The Correct Traditions for Adaptation

Traditions can facilitate effective organizational change. However, not just any traditions will do. Having the correct traditions is critical. These must be traditions that reinforce the organization's most basic values and beliefs and that are suited to the organization's mission and environment. The adaptivity of an organization based on traditionality depends on the fortuitous evolution of traditions.

Typically, these traditions and their corresponding values and "worldview" are forged during the organization's early years. Stinchcombe (1965) argued that organizations were tuned to conditions existing at the time of their forging, implying that they would be ill-suited to newly evolving conditions. If an organization's traditions were developed during a time when the organization faced a relatively benign environment and much organizational slack existed, they may well be ill-suited to helping the organization cope with a more threatening economic or political situation. In contrast, traditions whose roots lay in response to crisis and organizational survival, as at HAPCO, may facilitate adaptation.

HAPCO's demonstrated ability to succeed in conditions that bankrupted some of its competitors may be traced to its weathering a crisis early in its history (Golden and Salipante, 1990). The conclusion of World War II (with its attendant profits and expansion for the organization) coincided with the death of HAPCO's founder. In responding to this crisis, the organization adopted a number of practices that were subsequently passed on as traditions. These practices included reducing reliance on the government, divisionalizing operations, and selecting loyal employees. These particular traditions, and the concern for organizational survival that was forged during its 1940s crisis, have served HAPCO well over the years. Similarly, Thomas Watson (1963; also Watson and Petre, 1990) credits adherence to a few long-standing basic beliefs as the most critical factor in IBM's success. The loyalty of its members, inherent in any truly traditional system, and the forging of survival-oriented traditions can provide systems of organizational traditionality with a hardiness that enables them to thrive in the presence of environmental shocks.

In sum, organizational systems of traditionality may possess advantages for survival that have been lost by modern bureaucracies whose leaders are anxious to create change due to the economic rationalities of restructurings, buyouts, and mergers. As experience and research are making increasingly clear, these approaches often lead to wholesale loss of valued talent and uncertainty and reduced effort from those who remain (Harshbarger, 1987; Schweiger and Ivancevich, 1985). As exemplified by HAPCO and many Japanese organizations, perhaps the long-term advantage rests not with rapid strategic change and organizational flexibility, but with reliance on systems of traditionality that slow and guide change and that encourage widespread employee commitment to the changes.

(Im)Balances of Traditionality and Rationality

Many factors, from the primacy of science and the obsession with progress that began with the period of Enlightenment (Shils, 1981) to recent organizational literature and managerial education, have supported a belief in the superiority of rationality in organizations. The result is a lack of appreciation for the foundations of an organization and for longer time frames. This is reflected in the actions of some new owners and executives at the strategic planning levels, who have made changes that ignore their organization's past.

Despite this emphasis on rationality, the investigations covered in this chapter suggest that rationality is not the sole organizing principle of contemporary organizations. While looking for rationality at HAPCO, we found traditionality. When managers were asked to describe their organization's practices and values, they revealed conceptually contradictory combinations of rationality and traditionality. In the most basic sense, these results are significant in showing that strong elements of traditionality are present in a number of organizations. Just as Gusfield (1967) demonstrated that tradition and modernity can interweave and be mutually supportive in producing change in broader social systems, I have argued that elements of traditionality are functional. Still, the results from the surveys raise some provocative questions about the mixing of the traditional with the rational. Are these conceptually distinct systems most functional in their pure forms? Since combinations of the two seem prevalent, do they possess advantages in terms of organizational adaptation? By probing these questions here, I argue that change and continuity need not be antagonistic phenomena and that there can and should be continuity *in* change.

By postulating that the Type A and Type B organizational elements are not mutually exclusive, we can conceptualize organizations as falling into one of four categories. Each category, depicted as one of the quadrants in Figure 5.1, represents a particular combination of the rationality and traditionality archetypes; for example, Quadrant I captures organizations high in both rationality and traditionality.

Figure 5.1. Combinations of Traditionality and Rationality.

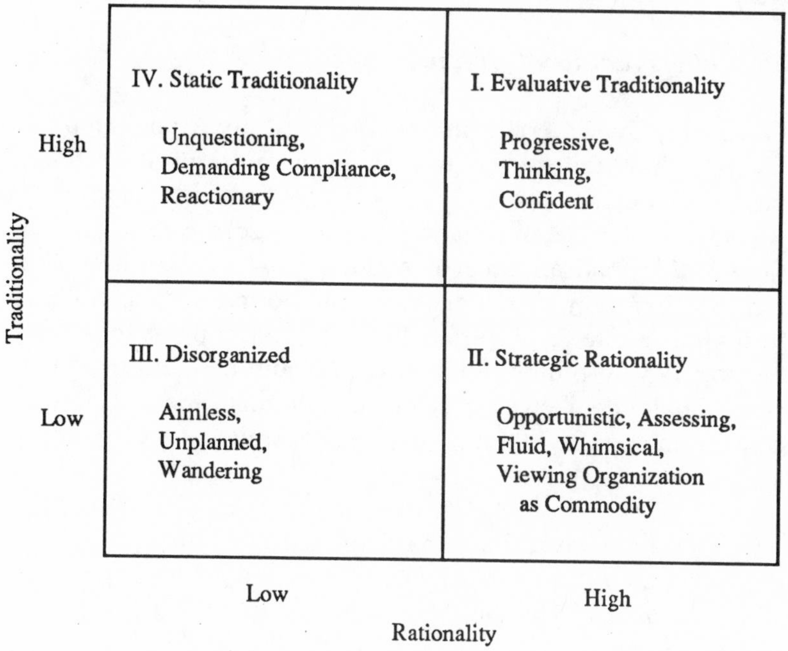

		Low Rationality	High Rationality
Traditionality	**High**	IV. Static Traditionality Unquestioning, Demanding Compliance, Reactionary	I. Evaluative Traditionality Progressive, Thinking, Confident
	Low	III. Disorganized Aimless, Unplanned, Wandering	II. Strategic Rationality Opportunistic, Assessing, Fluid, Whimsical, Viewing Organization as Commodity

Rationality

In considering these types of organizations, it will be useful to distinguish between two types of mistakes concerning adaptation. A Type 1 error of adaptation is the failure to change when appropriate. These errors have been the focus of organizational literature, to the neglect of Type 2 errors. A Type 2 error involves changing when one should not. Relatively little theoretical attention has been given to the consequences of poor judgments that result in change, perhaps because there is a value bias toward change and action and a perceived need to encourage innovation and risk taking. Often, the problem is seen as one of an implementation failure or a plan that was not fully developed, whereas the more basic problem may be that the magnitude and timing of the change were simply wrong. The value bias toward change is understandable when it results in experimentation and pilot programs, but when it results in untested, large-scale change efforts in the name of adaptation, the risks can be enormous. Type 2 errors of adaptation can be at least as detrimental as Type 1 errors.

Statically Traditional Organizations

Of course, Type 1 errors are common. Many American organizations have failed to change when, in hindsight, they should have. Such errors are likely to be associated with static traditionality, indicated in Quadrant IV of Figure 5.1. Organizations in this quadrant do evolve, but at slow rates. Andrew Pettigrew (1973) found managers in some organizations holding to inappropriate assumptions for periods as long as ten years. Managers who blindly follow the past and demand that their subordinates do likewise may indeed find that time and circumstances have passed them by. A rather straightforward proposition captures this view.

> P1a. Organizations characterized by static traditionality (Quadrant IV) are most subject to Type 1 errors of change.

This proposition is highly consistent with strategic rational views. We can move beyond it by recalling the functions of traditionality for adaptation — vigilance, loyalty and use of voice, maintenance of mission, slowing rates of change, customizing change, and lengthening the time horizon. In combination, these functions help traditional organizations maintain themselves with only evolutionary changes. When an organization's decision makers are confronted with the dilemma of choosing between possible Type 1 and Type 2 errors (to change or not to change), the most critical functions of traditionality are its effective transmission of organizational learning and its ensuring that effective past practices are continued. As noted earlier when we discussed the correct traditions for adaptation, the most valuable traditions are likely to be those forged during times of crisis. Organizations whose traditions have evolved over time, having been tempered by competition and past environmental shocks, can rely on those traditions as effective guides to current decisions. Their traditions have turned out to have survival value, and, in many instances, the organizations will barely suffer from failing to change or changing at a slow rate. In contrast, statically traditional organizations whose environments have not subjected them to shocks in the past may be poorly protected when an environmental jolt hits. Accordingly,

> P1b. Among statically traditional organizations Type 1 errors of change are less likely for those that evolved under competitive conditions.

As suggested by this proposition, reactionary systems are capable of long-term survival. Their age and probably larger size compared to younger competitor organizations provides them with market advantages that reduce their need to respond to all but the longest-term trends (Hannan and Freeman, 1984). If they have survived for many decades, their traditional practices and member loyalty provide protection from environmental shocks. Hence,

> P1c. Organizations characterized by static traditionality will suffer less from a given environmental shock than will strategically rational (Quadrant II) organizations.

An example from another sphere illustrates just how long term a statically traditional system's survival can be. Recently, agricultural scientists have begun to question modern farming methods designed to maximize crop yields. Concerned with the increasing resistance of insects to pesticides and the long-term environmental damage of these methods, they are developing the new concept of "sustainable agriculture" (Dover and Talbot, 1988). However, this concept turns out to be old, not new. The researchers are rediscovering the efficacy of several traditional farming methods, such as interplanting two crops simultaneously in the same field. Such methods have survived among the Amish and in a few other areas of the world (Crosson and Rosenberg, 1989; Ehrenfeld, 1987). The traditional social systems that have employed these practices have survived many cycles of environmental shocks (drought, pestilence) because of (not despite) their reactionary nature, and they have preserved practices that may now benefit wider populations.

To sum up, statically traditional organizations forged under harsh conditions can survive with only the most gradual of internal changes. When faced with an environmental shift or the common (sometimes, hasty) movement toward a newly accepted practice, such organizations may choose to remain with their traditional ways and yet be successful.

Dominantly Rational Organizations

Quadrant II represents strategically rational organizations that are low in traditionality. Shils (1981, p. 329) captures the unavoidable difficulty with the pure version of this form: "The fact is that our knowledge of future events is very poor and unreliable." It is easy to overlook this view because of its commonsense nature, yet it has the most critical implications for strategically rational organizations and for organizations trying to become so. As anyone who has engaged in attempting to develop multiyear plans can attest, high levels of uncertainty about important future events and trends exist. This brings out the most critical problem for strategic rationality: the requirement of knowing what the future holds, so one can adapt to it. Bounded rationality holds that human beings' limited ability to process information and the costs of search are the important limitations to rationality (March and Simon, 1958), but for strategic rationality the uncertainty of the future is the ultimate constraint.

Strategic rationality requires that decisions be made in the face of uncertainty, and so many decisions will inevitably be made whose premises will prove faulty. This implies

> P2. Organizations characterized as strategically rational (Quadrant II) are most subject to Type 2 errors of change.

Consider a painful example of the uncertainty of opportunistic rationality. In the 1980s, the banking industry — commonly viewed at the time as conservative and traditional — found that deregulation had opened the door to greater competition. The accepted wisdom was that financial institutions needed to become more dynamic and discard their old ways. Many attempted to move into Quadrant II, adopting new strategies and making substantial attempts at change. In what appeared at the time to be taking rational advantage of opportunities provided by deregulation, banks changed their traditional lending practices, investing heavily in commercial real estate. How difficult it was to forsee the costs that these institutions, and taxpayers, would eventually bear. Abandoning practices that had evolved and succeeded over many years constituted the discarding of organizational learning.

While theory has tended to ignore or miscategorize Type 2 errors, examples reported in the press abound. In the auto industry alone, many can be cited: the ill-timed restyling of the Jaguar sedan; American manufacturers shifting production heavily to smaller cars, only to have gas prices fall, then shifting back to larger cars just before fuel prices rose again; General Motors in the 1970s abandoning the traditional differentiation of its brands in order to rationalize production through common bodies and engines for all its lines; General Motors in the 1980s deciding to maximize profits by raising prices at the cost of reduced market share.

Evaluatively Traditional Organizations

These examples illustrate that abandoning traditions to take advantage of current opportunity or to adapt to expected change opens the organization to risk (see Friedman, 1989). Nelson and Winter's (1982, p. 400) view is that "a changing environment can force firms to risk their very survival on attempts to modify their routines." However, the decision to attempt a change is not forced on the organization, but a choice that its members make. In making this choice, members should attend not only to the uncertainty of the future but also to the possibility that the organization may be well tuned for survival. Changing one practice can put the entire system at risk. Moving from quadrant IV to Quadrant II is fraught with danger. An executive provided an example from his own experience in a personal conversation with me in October 1990. What follows is my paraphrase of his story:

> A machinery manufacturer had survived over the years despite the sensitivity of its industry to the business cycle. A larger company acquired the manufacturer, replacing the board of directors and some managers. When the economy took a downturn, the firm laid off many of its engineers and employees, as was common practice in many industries. As conditions improved, the firm failed to rebound effectively, and eventually the failing firm was sold. The reason was that effective manufacture of the firm's product required craft-like skills. Many of these skills were lost when layoffs were issued. In past recessions the firm had done whatever was necessary, including taking on high-skill subcontracting work, in order to retain its employees, even if this resulted in temporarily reduced profits. The manufacturer's managers had not been able to provide sufficient reason for the firm's tradition of retaining workers to convince the acquiring firm's executives. Only the departed board members, with the experience of guiding the firm for many years, sufficiently understood the efficacy of the tradition.

This example suggests the desirability of an evaluative form of traditionality. As shown in Quadrant I, this form of organization involves a duality of high traditionality and high rationality. Had the managers in the machinery company better understood the rationale underlying the retention of workers and seeking of outside work during recessions, they could have convinced their new owner to continue this traditional practice. The benefits of evaluative traditionality may be stated as follows:

> P3a. Organizations characterized by evaluative traditionality are (of the four organizational types) least subject to Type 1 and Type 2 errors of change and most likely to survive over the long term.

The most valuable knowledge possessed by a Quadrant I organization is an understanding of the functioning of its traditional practices, both in the general functions that have been explored earlier in this chapter and in the types of specific functions suggested by the no-layoffs practice in the machinery manufacturer example. By analyzing the failure of this manufacturer, we can make several important points. First, the distinction between static traditionality, strategic rationality, and evaluative traditionality will be most evident during periods of environmental shock, in the consideration they give to past practices and their revealed knowledge about the adaptive functioning of those practices. As Myer (1982) found, phenomena of this type can be so submerged in the organization's social fabric that environmental jolts are needed to reveal them. A second point from the no-layoffs example is that evaluative traditionality will be most valuable during environmental changes, when the hard choices about whether and how to change, and at what rate, are being confronted. A final point is that an understanding of the adaptive and survival functions of traditions may be best acquired by organizational members studying crisis periods in the firm's history. Indeed, the transmission of stories from times of crisis, as at HAPCO, is a reflection of such study and one potential indicator of evaluative traditionality.

Many of the examples given in the discussion of Proposition 2 involved organizations attempting to change strategically, only to find that their rate of responsiveness (in other words, their time constant of change) was too slow for the rate of environmental change. In the Jaguar example, a car company known for the beauty and timelessness of its styling changed the XJ6 sedan from a rounded style (the firm's styling trademark) to a slab-sided style. The latter was in vogue at the time the new style was designed, and the simplified body panels would make the car cheaper to manufacture. However, because of Jaguar's characteristic lag in bringing the new car into production, automobile styles had returned to rounded forms by the time of the car's introduction, and it was immediately judged to be both out of date and out of character. Such examples illustrate the need for temporal matching between organization and environment (Hannan and Freeman, 1984). An important part of evaluative traditionality, then, is knowing the organization's time constant of change. Similarly, as in the case of the Girl Scout volunteers who rejected fitness center–like facilities, evaluative traditionality preserves the long-term mission of the organization and the outputs and values that its clients identify with the organization. Consequently,

P3b. Evalutively traditional organizations will be less likely than other organizations to produce products or services that are not synchronized with environmental factors.

From the preceding discussion, we can summarize the types of knowledge valuable to evaluatively traditional organizations as understanding the adaptive mechanisms of the organization's traditional practices, comprehending the organization's time constant of change, and recognizing the elements of the organization's mission and values most appreciated by clients. In addition, an organization needs to be aware of the interdependencies among its various traditional practices and values. This is invaluable for the designing of *customized* changes that will interface with, rather than disrupt, established routines and competencies. Thus,

P3c. Changes introduced by evaluatively traditional organizations will be more likely to be both func-

tionally adaptive and well implemented by organizational members than changes introduced by
other organizations.

Structures for Evaluative Traditionality

What types of organizations are likely to be evaluatively traditional? GSUSA is a Quadrant I organization because of the
creation of a healthy tension between the rationally and change-
oriented staff and the traditionally oriented volunteers. The separation of the rational from the traditional in two parallel organizational structures allows each to maintain its own inner logic.
GSUSA's particular value of democratic decision making and
devotion throughout the organization to "the Movement" keep
in check destructive conflict between the two structures. The
result is an organization that moved some years ago from Quadrant IV to Quadrant I, becoming rejuvenated while maintaining its historical strengths.

GSUSA's parallel structures suggest two elements that
may more generally characterize evaluatively traditional organizations. The first element, for organizations whose internal
units are dominantly traditional, is the presence of individuals
having an outsider's perspective, with this perspective being
dominantly rational. At GSUSA, many of the employed staff
did not come up through the ranks of volunteers. In addition,
they received reinforcement of a strategically rational perspective from a vigorously pursued planning and change process
emanating from the GSUSA national office. As noted in the no-
layoffs example, an independent board of directors might provide an outsider's perspective. Another structural alternative used
in some local governmental units is a lay committee of informed
citizens. A second element that may characterize evaluative
traditionality is tension. At GSUSA, tension existed not only
across the parallel structure but also across hierarchical levels,
given lower-level employed staff's greater identification with
volunteers.

The combination of outsider's perspective and tension can
easily lead to inappropriate dominance of strategic rationality,
unless the outside perspective is moderated by a valuing of the

organization's mission and core beliefs. For example, contemplate the risks for a GSUSA council in having a high proportion of its board composed of males prominent in financial and manufacturing organizations.

The Essence of Evaluative Traditionality

Although evaluative traditionality involves the combination of two conceptually distinct archetypes, its central behavior is not difficult to identify. It can be likened to Supreme Court decision making. A current case is not treated as unique or only of short-term concern. Rather, it is measured against past learnings, as represented by precedent, and its implications for future cases are considered. In short, the Supeme Court applies a reasoning process that depends heavily on legal traditions. Similarly, an organization can benefit by measuring current decisions against the rationales underlying its traditional practices. By understanding that the organization's traditions are based on many past experiences that culled the good from the bad, managers will have greater confidence in standing by the traditions when it is appropriate to do so. When they do change, the modifications will be customized so that they blend effectively with the continuing traditions, providing continuity in change.

For organizations whose decision makers exhibit such evaluatively traditional behavior, strategic rationality alone provides too narrow a decison-making arena.

> P3d. Evaluatively traditional organizations will utilize a broader array of criteria in decision making involving adaptation than strategically rational organizations will.

As an illustration, ponder a problem in one of the most rational spheres, academia. Using the case of one specific organization, the problem may be put bluntly as follows: Should Wellesley College continue to refuse to become coeducational? The pros and cons involve so many uncertainties and value judgments that rationality alone provides no definite answer. Only by understanding the essence of its mission, appreciating its past practices, and abiding by its core values could the college's members and alumni decide on an appropriate and acceptable course of action.

An Action and Research Agenda

By finding that managers in a wide range of organizations construe some of their own and others' behavior as traditional, and by exploring the functionality of an organizational system that relies on and appreciates the past, we have seen that the view of organizations as organisms that should be in continuous and rapid adjustment to their environment is seriously flawed. Treating organizations as commodities that can be rapidly refurbished through organizational change ignores the most basic functions of organizational continuity. By moderating strategic rationality with essential knowledge of the organization's past practices and values, errors of adaptation can be better avoided and the often unique ways by which particular organizations function and contribute can be perpetuated.

More descriptive investigation of decision making in organizations is badly needed. Just as one asks whether HAPCO, with its successful reliance on traditions, is an aberration, Mintzberg and McHugh (1985) wondered whether the organization that they had intensively investigated (and that displayed emergent versus deliberate patterns of decision making) was an aberration. Are we to be continually surprised when the most intensive studies of single organizations reveal the importance of history and traditions in organizational functioning? Just as Gusfield's (1967) study of Indian society indicated that tradition and modernity are not mutually exclusive at the societal level and that traditions need not be weakened by modernization, proper study can reveal the complementary relationships among traditionality, rationality, and change at the organizational level. Organizational ideologies, traditions, and myths can be invisible to typical survey reseach methods (Myer, 1982), especially when researchers premise their investigations exclusively on strategic rationality. A broader perspective and diverse methods will be needed to open the door further to understanding organizational continuity.

Chapter Six

Valuing Tradition
While Changing:
The Japanese Experience

Leonard H. Lynn

A major reason the Japanese have been so successful, we think, is their continuing ability to maintain a strong and cohesive culture throughout their
entire country. Not only do individual businesses
have strong cultures, but the links among business,
the banking industry, and the government are also
cultural and also very powerful.
—Deal and Kennedy, 1982, p. 5

Do not assume that more culture or stronger culture is better. What is better depends on the stage
of evolution of the company and its current state
of adaptiveness.
—Schein, 1985a, p. 42

A 'strong' culture through implicit coordination
helps to further immediate and short-term performance, but, over the longer run, such a culture
tends to restrict the number of options available to
an organization. Since variety is needed to react
to and control an organization's environment, a
highly consistent, 'strong' culture may sometimes
inhibit this process."
—Denison, 1990, pp. 79–80

The Japanese environment provides a rich natural experiment in "strong" corporate cultures. Common Japanese employment and personnel practices fit together in a system that seems to a Westerner almost an idealtypic machine for the creation and sustaining of corporate culture. How are these corporate cultures managing in an increasingly turbulent environment, an environment that seems to require rapid change? Is the strength of their corporate cultures helping Japanese firms or hurting them? What does this say more generally about strong corporate cultures?

This chapter begins with a description of corporate culture and the efforts of a major Japanese steelmaker to ease out of an unpromising industry. It suggests that for better or worse, the strength of the company's culture has caused it to move far more slowly than might be considered acceptable in the United States. Then the chapter discusses the reasons this and other Japanese firms have come to have such strong cultures. These involve certain aspects of the Japanese employment system, such as the mechanisms of recruitment and socialization commonly used in Japanese business. Finally, the chapter draws on the experiences of the Japanese steelmaker and of Japanese business more generally to discuss the meaning of corporate culture and how it affects continuity and change.

Changing a Strong Corporate Culture

As Kawasaki, Japan's third largest integrated steelmaker, entered the 1980s, the overwhelming share of its sales was accounted for by steel products. Most of the rest was in engineering services such as the building of iron and steel plants outside Japan. The early 1980s were bad years for steelmakers, even Japanese steelmakers. In 1982, Japanese crude steel production dropped below 100 million tons for the first time in eleven years. Production dropped even further in 1983. Although production passed the 100-million-ton mark again in 1984 and 1985, it still remained five or six million tons below the levels of 1979 and 1980. In 1986 and 1987, production once again fell below 100 million tons (Japan Iron and Steel Federation, 1990).

In this environment, Kawasaki saw its sales remain stagnant at 1.2 and 1.3 trillion yen in 1982 and 1983, respectively, then edging down to 0.9 trillion yen in 1987 and 1988 before partially recovering to 1.1 trillion yen in the fiscal year that ended in March 1990. Profits dropped from around 90 billion yen annually in 1980 and 1981 to much lower levels in the mid 1980s and even a loss of 7 billion yen in 1987, before recovering in 1989 and 1990. Because of the growing competition of nearby low-wage countries such as Taiwan and Korea with advanced new steel plants, there seems little reason to be optimistic about the longer-term prospects of the Japanese steel industry.

Given similar, though more severe problems, U.S. firms drastically reduced employment and moved aggressively to enter new industries. In just six years (1979–1985), the U.S. Steel Corporation, for example, reduced its dependence on steel from 70 to 30 percent of sales (changing its name to USX in the process). National Intergroup moved almost entirely out of the steel industry (Lynn, 1988).

Management at Kawasaki Steel also decided that diversification would be desirable. The process by which this was done and progress toward it, however, have been far slower and more deliberate than in the United States. In April 1983, two ad hoc committees were set up to study diversification strategies (Newsletter, July/August 1984). In April 1985, Kawasaki drafted its *Vision for the Year 2000,* a long-term plan commemorating the fiftieth anniversary of the establishment of the company—an event to be celebrated in 2000. The *Vision* projected that in the year 2000, some 40 percent of the company's sales would be outside the steel industry (Yamaguchi, 1989). In June 1985, shareholders approved an amendment to Kawasaki's corporate charter to permit the company to engage in a wider range of businesses, including real estate, nonferrous metals, ceramics, and electronic materials (Newsletter, July/August 1985).

The company engaged in a flurry of highly visible activity. It bought several small firms in a variety of high-technology industries and entered into strategic alliances with others. These included foreign and domestic firms in the semiconductor, telecommunications, electronics, information services, and other industries.

New units (again most of them quite small in terms of staffing) were set up within Kawasaki to handle new lines of business. The corporate research laboratories were reorganized to strengthen research in the new areas. Given Kawasaki's tradition of permanent employment, it was not easy to staff these new units. Some of the staffing was done by retraining steel specialists, and new employees were also assigned to the new units. Inevitably, however, it was necessary to hire outsiders, a sharp break from past practices. This was not done in a wholesale manner. Of forty-four people in the LSI Department in 1988, only seventeen were people with experience at established semiconductor producers. Of the seventy researchers at the LSI Research Center in 1989, only a quarter had been hired from outside. Half were new employees who had joined the company directly out of the university within the last three years, and the rest former steel specialists (Yamaguchi, 1989). By 1990, an article in a company magazine reported that Kawasaki had hired 102 "career employees" (those with previous employment at other companies, universities, and government agencies). While this number may not seem like many in a company of Kawasaki's size, as will be suggested below it seems to have been felt as something of a shock.

Several steps were taken to oversee an orderly evolution in the identity of the company in the face of these changes. In early 1986, a program was inaugurated to change Kawasaki's "tonnage-oriented culture," and in November of that year, Kawasaki established a Corporate Identity (CI) Committee under an executive vice president. A major reason for the committee was to transform Kawasaki from a "steel culture company" into a "multicultural company." It was hoped that this restructuring of Kawasaki's corporate identity would make it easier for the company to get the human resources it needed to diversify.

In 1988, Kawasaki announced a new management philosophy and code of conduct. Along with this came a new high-fashion advertising campaign in both print and broadcast media. The advertisements were designed to shock and to promote a new image of Kawasaki as an "interesting company." One hope was that this would help attract new graduates who are a little different from those who entered Kawasaki in the past. In one part of the campaign, several leading Japanese designers produced dresses made out of stainless steel foil. In another, Kawasaki showed a video featuring a popular rock group surrounded by an elephant, llama, and other wild animals.

In view of all these activities, it is somewhat surprising that the percentage of Kawasaki's sales accounted for by steel changed little in the period 1985–1990. In 1985, it was some 80.8 percent; in the first half of fiscal 1990, it was 81.3 percent. Most of the rest came from steel plant engineering services and the manufacture of chemicals made from the by-products of integrated steel production. In 1988, new business accounted for only 12 billion yen out of total sales of more than one trillion yen. In 1990, the company president said the company had never expected that the new business activities would contribute significantly to sales within the next ten years or so. The goal for the first five years of the fifteen-year diversification strategy was, he indicated, to increase Kawasaki's efficiency as a steelmaker (Kawasaki Steel Bulletin, July/August 1990).

The rationale was that the small-scale activities in new industries would be nurtured to positions of strength. By the year 2000, LSI technology is to account for 10 percent of corporate sales, new materials another 5 percent, and information and communications a further 6.5 percent. The chemicals division of the company is to expand into new high-technology products to account for 8 percent of sales (the division now makes up about 4 percent of company sales).

Is this a reasonable way to diversify out of a troubled industry? Isn't this diversification taking an unreasonably long time? Only time will tell us the answers to these questions, but a look at Kawasaki's corporate culture can tell us why this approach to diversification may have been the only one possible for Kawasaki.

Kawasaki might be thought of as a "steelmaker's steelmaker." The company was begun as a spinoff of Kawasaki Heavy Industries under Nishiyama Yataro after World War II. Nishiyama, the major "hero" in corporate lore, was a prizewinning steel engineer himself. He instilled a strong steelmaking technology culture. In the 1950s and 1960s the company had a spartan image. The office buildings were plainer than those of the other major steelmakers. When journalists asked Nishiyama why the director's meeting room was not air-conditioned, he reportedly said, "Because the blast furnace shops aren't." Kawasaki, according to stock manuals in the 1950s, was the *nobushi* (mountain samurai) of steelmakers — plain, somewhat unsophisticated, and mission oriented (Lynn, 1982).

In one of the most widely written-about episodes in postwar Japanese business history, Nishiyama led Kawasaki in building Japan's first postwar integrated iron and steel works. This project was strongly opposed by the Bank of Japan. Nishiyama is commonly portrayed as having made this "gamble" based on his sound intuition about the possibilities of new steel production technologies. As a result, Kawasaki Steel overcame the "bean counting" mentality of the Japanese establishment to initiate the dramatic postwar growth of the Japanese iron and steel industry (Lynn, 1982; Yonekura, 1990).

Nishiyama was the CEO of Kawasaki Steel until his health failed in 1966. His successors have all been metallurgical engineers. A majority of the board members have engineering degrees. Thus, the primary orientation has been toward steel production, not finance, not marketing (it tends to sell in large lots to trading companies and other large customers), not the acquisition of raw materials, and not basic research. The scale of production has been gigantic, centering on two giant integrated steel works. Large-scale coordinating efforts have been essential. Perhaps as a result, the company has been somewhat bureaucratic. When a new president was named in 1990, that man (like his predecessors) was a metallurgical engineer who had joined the old Kawasaki Heavy Industries, Ltd. after graduation and followed Nishiyama as the steelmaking division became independent.

It is easy to see that Kawasaki's powerful corporate culture, despite its strong grounding in technology, may not be well suited to new industries, which have tended to be dominated by small, flexibly organized groups closely linked to basic research and to markets. U.S. firms with strong cultures that are judged to be inappropriate for changing conditions sometimes change their cultures. This usually happens through personnel changes (Sapienza, 1985; Dyer, 1985; Lorsch, 1985). Outside directors may force a change in top management. Top management may make changes in their subordinates.

The strategy of having outside directors replace top management is not a real option at major Japanese firms. These companies have few if any outside directors, and involuntary top-management turnovers are so rare as to be suggestive of scandal (Abegglen and Stalk, 1985). In 1989, Kawasaki's board included thirty-six members. All were officers in the company. Indeed, all but three had worked at Kawasaki for some thirty years or longer. The other three had come from important outside organizations — the Ministry of International Trade and Industry, Dai-ichi Kangyo Bank, and Nippon Telephone and Telegraph — but are now Kawasaki Steel executives (Japan Ministry of Finance, 1989).

Personnel changes are difficult in Japanese firms, though the case of Kawasaki suggests that getting rid of personnel is much easier than getting new people to replace them. Although Kawasaki continued to hire new university graduates throughout the 1980s, it reduced its overall employment from 37,000 at the beginning of the decade to just over 18,000 in early 1990. The ways in which employment was so drastically reduced are suggestive of how "lifetime employment" functions in a crisis. Early on the cuts were made by traditional mechanisms. Of the cut in the workforce of roughly 6,000 before 1985, roughly half was achieved through attrition, the rest by transferring employees to some thirty Kawasaki affiliates (descriptions of this process do not indicate how the affiliates were able to absorb so many new workers). In 1987, a two-year plan to shed another 5,000 workers was drawn up. At this point, however, it was no longer possible to gain significant reductions through attrition and transfers to affiliates. The next measures taken involved creating new companies and also "lending" employees to unrelated firms. When this was done, the recipient firm would generally pay less than Kawasaki had paid, so Kawasaki would make up the pay difference. Often the work former steelworkers were sent to do had little to do with their previous experience. Company publications mention, for example, employees who were sent to do cleaning work at Narita International Airport and others who were sent to work at a sake brewing company. In these ways, Kawasaki met the expectation of lifetime employment, while still attaining substantial reductions in its workforce. All of this led to substantial improvements in productivity in the steel division.

As was noted earlier, new employees were brought in to staff some of the positions in the new businesses. This was seen as a radical action within Kawasaki. The March 1989 issue of Kawasaki's company magazine, *Kawatetsu Mansuri,* gave the results of a survey administered to the 102 new "career" employees. The entry of these people was seen as both a shock and an opportunity for the company. As the company magazine put it, "For some time it has been said that human resources are becoming more fluid. At first this was only a phenomenon in a few industries and occupations, but now the movement of people within different industries has become accepted as a common scene. This company is no exception. Indeed, we are breaking out of the framework of stability symbolized by "steel" and beginning to welcome a wide variety of human resources. This is, so to speak, an example of a harbinger: the mix of human resource in the new business areas can be thought of as a model (p. 5).

From a U.S. perspective, one wonders what all the fuss is about. On the face of it, the hiring of 102 new employees in a company of 18,000 would not seem such a major event. Moreover, this hiring was not done all at one time; some of the 102 in the survey are identified as having joined the company as long ago as 1984. In other words, within a period of about five years, the group of midcareer hires was only about equal in number to the new university graduates hired each year. Beyond this, about half of the new hires were in the new High Technology Laboratory and another third were in the new information/telecommunications and electronics industries. In short, over a period of about five years, only about twenty new hires were scattered among the traditional business operations of the company.

The largest percentage of the midcareer hires (41 percent) previously worked for firms in the electronics industry. The next largest group (21 percent) were previously with universities and research laboratories. Most of the rest were from firms in the chemical, precision instruments, petroleum, shipbuilding, machinery, and nonferrous metals industries. Most (54 percent) were in their thirties when they joined Kawasaki, though 23 percent were in their forties, 20 percent in their twenties, and 3 percent in their fifties.

The survey reflected some signs of strain on the part of the midcareer hires. More than 40 percent did not bother to respond to the questionnaire. Of those who did, fairly large numbers reported coming into the company with somewhat negative images (19 percent said they had thought of Kawasaki as being constrained and restricted, 15 percent thought of it as a conservative company—multiple responses were allowed, so these may have been the same people). On the other hand, 42 percent had an image of the company as moving into new lines of business and 22 percent identified the company with its traditional mountain samurai image. When asked if their image of the company had changed since they started working there, 25 percent said it had improved, but 24 percent said it had worsened. The biggest complaint seemed to be about "red tape" in the company. About a third of the respondents said they were dissatisfied with work in their current workplace. Some complained about not fitting in (though many were concentrated in areas where there were also large numbers of other midcareer hires).

To understand why larger numbers of new employees could not be brought in to Kawasaki and why those who did come in had difficulty gaining acceptance, it is necessary to review the general characteristics of the Japanese employment system and then to take up the ways in which Japanese employees are socialized in the culture at major firms.

The Japanese Employment System

The Japanese employment system is popularly characterized by its "three sacred treasures," lifetime or permanent employment (*shushin koyo*), seniority-based promotion (*nenko*), and enterprise unionism. This characterization has been traced back to James Abbeglen's classic study *The Japanese Factory* (1958) and to a subsequent elaboration of these themes by Japanese business leaders such as Takeshi Sakurada, a former president of Nikkeiren (the Japanese Federation of Employers' Associations) (Shimada, 1983). The essence of this overall stereotypic image has not been strongly challenged, though specialists have argued about the origins of this system, its appropriateness for modern or postmodern economies, how extensively it is actually used, how strongly committed Japanese firms are to it, whether aspects of the system could or should be transferred to the United States, and what the actual content of each of the three treasures is. (For overviews of the Japanese employment system, see Abbeglen, 1958; Abbeglen and Stalk, 1985; Clark, 1979; Cole, 1971, 1979; Dore, 1973; Dunphy, 1987; Inohara, 1990; Okochi, Karsh, and Levine, 1974; Shimada, 1983.)

An early assumption that the sacred treasures grew out of Japanese cultural tradition was quickly challenged by scholars who pointed out that none of the treasures was characteristic of the Japanese employment system during Japan's early industrialization. Indeed, the system did not fully develop into its present form until the 1950s (Taira, 1962; Cole, 1979; Gordon, 1985). A question still hotly debated is whether the three treasures are uniquely rooted in Japanese culture or are an effective response to the needs of business in the current economic environment (Marsh and Mannari, 1988). A possibility is that it may be both. Thus, Robert Cole (1979) suggests that Japanese managers may draw on tradition in creating organizational forms that meet current needs. Aoki (1988) speculates that aspects of the Japanese cultural tradition such as small-group values may have played a role in shaping Japanese organizational practices, again noting how in some environments these practices have enhanced the competitiveness of Japanese organizations.

Whatever its origins and present-day linkages to Japanese culture, Lincoln and Kalleberg (1990) characterize the Japanese employment system as a form of "welfare corporatism," a commitment-maximizing organizational form. This form is not uniquely Japanese, but it is far more common in Japan than in the United States. It does not result in high levels of worker satisfaction (as numerous comparative surveys of employees in the United States and Japan show), but it reduces alienation and enhances commitment. Welfare corporatism comprises

> permanent employment guarantees that reduce turnover and increase the worker's investment in the firm; organizational structures such as tall job hierarchies and proliferating work units which break up occupational and class loyalties while encouraging the formation of organization-wide cohesive bonds; programs for relieving the fragmentation and monotony of jobs and tasks through rotation and enlargement that increase the intrinsic rewards of working and build identification with the organization as a whole; mechanisms for fostering employee participation in decision-making without the formal guarantees or high-level access that might threaten management control; a legal structure of formalized rights and obligations that confer corporate citizenship on employees and avert reliance on alienating personal forms of supervisory domination; and the trappings of strong organizational culture — ritual, ceremony, symbolism, and the like — along with a potpourri of tangible welfare benefits including family subsidies, education programs, housing, and health benefits [Lincoln and Kalleberg, 1990, pp. 248–249].

It is not difficult to see how such a system could create strong corporate cultures. In a study of strong-culture firms in the United States, Pascale (1985) found that seven techniques were used (though few firms used all seven): (1) careful selection processes (which rely in part on deselection by inappropriate candidates); (2) humility-inducing experiences; (3) "in the trenches training," which often entails step-by-step promotions; (4) careful attention given to systems for measuring operational results and rewarding individual performance; (5) rigorous adherence to the firm's transcendent values so as to develop a "family feeling" that reconciles the personal sacrifices individuals must make for the organization; (6) the use of folklore and stories; and (7) having consistent role models, which may come in part from stability. While major Japanese firms do not emphasize rewards for individual performance, they have been notable for using all the other techniques, in some cases to a degree that would not be possible in the United States.

Selection Processes

In a lifetime employment system, the stakes in hiring are immense for companies. One handbook for new graduates points out that over his career an employee represents a cost to the company of about 350 million yen (some $2.8 million at the current exchange rate of 125 yen to $1) (Hitotsubashi Shoten, 1984). Even though, as we saw at Kawasaki, there are more mechanisms for getting rid of undesirable employees under the Japanese "permanent" employment system than most Americans might imagine (also see Aoki, 1988), these devices themselves (for example transferring employees to affiliates or encouraging older employees to take early retirements) cost money. They are also costly in terms of their implications for other employees of how strong a commitment the firm is making to its employees and the disruptions caused in strong-culture companies by misfits. The problem is aggravated by the fact that the new hires do not have an employment history that might help predict future behavior and the additional problem that in most years the demand for new graduates exceeds the supply.

In *The House of Nomura* (1990), Albert Alletzhauser describes the recruiting process at Nomura Securities, Japan's (and the world's) largest securities firm. He says that most of Nomura's recruiting is completed by September, even though universities do not allow recruiters to visit campus this early. The process begins early in the summer, with younger Nomura salesmen being sent to find the best prospects from their alma mater.

Prospective candidates are invited over the telephone to meet a company representative at a coffee shop and then are taken to a hall with hundreds of other prospects. Nomura has reportedly taken prize prospects from the elite Tokyo University to Hawaii as part of the company's recruiting effort. After three interviews, Nomura may commit itself by giving a pledge of employment (*naitei*) to the prospect. Graduates of the Tokyo University may have three or four pledges to choose between. Alletzhauser describes episodes in which Nomura recruiters had extreme reactions against prospects who chose other firms: in one case throwing cold noodle sauce at a prospect, in another intervening to have the pledge offered one prospect by another firm withdrawn. As Alletzhauser describes it, the recruitment of women is different. Here the preference is not for elite university graduates, but rather for women who are attractive, single, and obedient. Two-year graduates are preferred. These women are said to become good marriage prospects for Nomura salesmen — particularly because they come to understand the company culture so well in the years they work at Nomura that they become more supportive of their husbands. Forty percent of Nomura men marry Nomura women.

The recruiting of engineering graduates is also somewhat different (Lynn, Piehler, and Zahray, 1988). Here university professors play a major role. A professor in an electrical engineering department at a major national university explained to the author that the first step in the process is for a company to decide how many graduates from this particular university it wants to hire. The engineering faculty placement office would then allocate these slots to the various professors in charge of research laboratories (to each of which are attached undergraduate students). The professor then gives one recommendation to each student, matching the performance of the student to the prestige of the company, taking into account the professor's opinion of how well the student would do at that particular company. The professor indicated that he was reluctant to recommend that his students take a job at companies that he had no experience with, even in the case of well-known companies.

The formal recruiting process typically involves both interviews and written exams. A survey of firms listed on Japan's major stock exchanges found that 71 percent used written exams for general managers and 68 percent used them for technical graduates (Joho Shisutemu Senta, 1988). The written exams cover a very broad range of topics. One handbook for new graduates seeking employment in the machinery industry gives sample questions testing the recruit's general knowledge, his ability in Japanese and English, and his knowledge of mathematics and science. The general-knowledge questions are remarkably broad in their content. One multiple-choice question asks the student to associate key concepts with such writers as Hobbs, Fromm, Weber, Rousseau, and Locke. Another asks what mechanisms the U.S. government has imposed to prevent the dumping of steel. Still another asks the recruit to identify the United Nations Secretary General who succeeded Kurt Waldheim. Other questions ask about geography, music, literature, golf tournaments, and the definitions of an array of sports terms (Hitotsubashi Shoten, 1984).

Despite the comprehensiveness of the written exams, there is a sense that these are insufficient to evaluate potential employees. As a result, most companies also interview candidates. A guide for new graduates seeking employment in the Japanese machinery industry says that firms vary in the number of interviews given potential recruits, but that the general range is from two to seven. The examiners include, aside from those in the personnel department who prepare the interview, young employees who have been with the firm four or five years, assistant section managers, section managers, the head of personnel, directors, and the company president. These people rank the interviewee on a scale of A to E based on company rules. The contents of the interview together with the results of the first interview are passed from the first examiner to the second examiner. They may point out instances where the interviewee gave different answers to the same question.

Four types of interview exams are used: individual interviews, group interviews, group discussions, and "living together" interviews. Individual interviews are the most common. Here the interviewee is invited to a designated room. He bows, enters the room, goes to the indicated seat, bows again, gives his university's name, his own name, and his interviewee number, and finally sits down. He will have filled out an interview card with answers to questions that may give the examiners a starting point for their questions. The examiners will ask introductory questions to help the interviewee relax before the real interview begins. The end of the interview is announced. As indicated, the interviewee stands up to withdraw. He bows after standing and then again before leaving the room. The whole interview may last from ten to thirty minutes. Group interviews are used to make it easy to compare various candidates. They are longer than the individual interviews, lasting some fifteen minutes to one hour. In the group discussion interviews, typically the topic is written on a piece of paper. The candidates are given ten minutes to think over the topic. Each is then given two or three minutes to give his opinion on the topic. The discussion leader is chosen from among the interviewees. The discussion begins. The examiners do not take part in the discussion but merely observe. The group includes five to nine interviewees and lasts thirty to sixty minutes. Some topics that have been used include the special characteristics of the candidate's generation, the kind of work that motivates people, the Japanese as "economic animals," and how a person should use his or her spare time. Many companies invite the interviewees to stay with examiners for two or three days. During this period, individual interviews, group interviews, discussions, and physical exams may take place. Some firms use only the individual interview; others use it in combination with one of the other types of interviews. A few firms use only group interviews.

While there is a good deal of variation between companies, the content of individual interviews includes the following areas:

1. *Motivation:* Why do you want to work in this industry? For this company? What other companies do you think you would like to work for? Where else have you taken tests? What do you know about this company and its industry? What do you think are the strong points and weak points of this company? What will you do if we do not hire you? Do you know anyone who works here?

2.   *Work:* What is your reason for choosing this line of work? What would you do if you disagreed with orders from your boss? What do you think about overtime and weekend work?
3.   *University life:* Why did you choose your university and major? What did you like and dislike about university life? What were your most and least useful subjects?
4.   *Personal life:* Where does your father work? What do you do with your friends? Do you drink? How is your health? How do you spend your free time? What are the strengths and weaknesses of your character? Do you disagree with your father on anything in particular? What interesting books have you read recently (Hitotsubashi Shoten, 1984)?

Naturally, while the companies are intensively studying prospective recruits, the recruits are also studying the companies. Their investment too is very high. But the costs of gathering information are perhaps lower than in the United States. Aside from word of mouth, advice from university counselors, and other such sources of information, Japanese new graduates have access to an overwhelming literature on industries and major companies. To give a few examples: In 1990 one publisher, Kyoikusha, had books on twenty-three industries in its current series, plus books on twenty-nine other industries still available from series published in the past two or three years. These books sell for $7 or $8 each. Nikkei Sangyo also has a series of industry descriptions; in a recent year, these were available on twenty-one different industries. Toyo Keizai, Daiyamondo, and other publishers also publish industry descriptions—all of which are widely available in bookstores at moderate cost. Other companies publish books on specific companies. Some years ago, Eichosha had 100 books on individual companies in its Japanese Enterprise series. These sold for $9 or $10 each. Toyo Keizai has published a series of autobiographies by such business leaders as Inayama Yoshihiro, the long-time CEO of Nippon Steel. As of 1982, the Nihon Keizai Shimbun series "My Personal History" had recorded the autobiographies of about 140 business leaders. Major bookstores in Tokyo have tables covered with newly published books on corporate strategies, personnel practices, or events at various influential companies. Recently comic books have even been published on episodes in the histories of various companies such as Honda and Sony. Publishers churn out other books on both business leaders and companies, often with subsidies from companies to put a particular spin on corporate images because of concerns about recruiting or for other reasons.

Some publishers have found a niche publishing books for new graduates seeking employment in one industry or another. Kyodo Shuppan had nineteen books covering industries in its 1989 employment data reader series. Hitotsubashi Shoten also publishes an Industry Examination Guide Series for a range of industries. These books give an overview on the focal industry, then detailed descriptions of the leading firms.

Kyodo Shuppan advises the job seeker to pay particular attention to eight points in selecting a company: its growth potential, stability, future prospects, corporate culture, viewpoints of top management, technological strength, marketing strength, and "fit" for the job hunter. It helps guide the job seeker by providing the sorts of information that would be in an investment manual, with help in interpreting these data according to the eight points. These books also give information of special concern to prospective recruits that would be very difficult to get at all in the United States. Kyodo Shuppan's 1989 description of Asahi Chemical Industries, for example, tells the reader that the company has 15,541 employees with an average age of 37.5 (13,898 of them male). The average male worker is 38.5, has been with the company 16.4 years, and earns 297,412 yen per month (plus about 5.2 months bonus). New university graduate employees were paid 161,900 yen per month in 1986. Working hours are 9:00 to 6:00 at the head office (7:30 to 4:30 at the plants), five days a week. Employees get four days off for New Year's, start with ten days annual vacation, and can ultimately get twenty days annual vacation. The retirement age is sixty. The various benefits are listed. The training for new employees is outlined. A description says that merit is emphasized over seniority in promotions. After eight years, a new university graduate can expect to reach his first managerial rank.

After eleven years, the average graduate will be an assistant section manager, after seventeen years a section manager, and after twenty-two years a division manager. Affiliated companies where people may be transferred are listed. The prospective recruit is told that the average age of the company's thirty-four corporate officers is sixty, and fourteen of them graduated from Tokyo University. The book reports how many graduates the company hired from each university in recent years. There is also a description of Asahi Chemical's corporate culture: it is one of challenge and intensity, where the enthusiasm for a project may be so great that people forget about weekends. This contrasts sharply with the description of the culture at other chemical companies. The guide says that at Mitsubishi Chemicals, for example, "The starting point is always 'respect for people.' In practice, to attain this spirit the company has implemented a system for overseas study and other programs for the development of individual employee ability."

In brief, then, several distinctive aspects of the recruiting process by major Japanese firms help ensure that company employees will be highly amenable to socialization in the corporate culture. Most recruiting is of employees coming directly out of school. This process is conducted by specialists within the firm (there is no independent hiring by separate divisions). Both recruiter and recruitee collect considerable information on the other, and such information is relatively easy to obtain.

Control of Socialization

Japanese firms have long been noted for their efforts to instill the corporate culture in their employees. Some of the techniques, while not unusual in the West, seem to be carried to greater levels of intensity in Japan. Here we will focus on two dimensions of socialization in the Japanese firm. One relates to the specific career planning for cohorts of employees passing through the lifetime employment. The other relates to generalized symbolic activities that impart and reinforce the corporate culture.

A number of observers suggest that personnel departments are substantially more important in Japanese firms than in their

U.S. counterparts. Surveys done in 1962 (cited in Cole, 1971, p. 168) and 1970 (cited in Inohara, 1990) found that about 2 percent of all employees in Japanese firms are in personnel departments, compared to fewer than 1 percent in U.S. firms. Pucik (1984) found Japanese personnel departments to be larger specifically in the automobile industry and Westney and Sakakibara (1986) in the computer industry. Rohlen (1974) says personnel departments have higher status in Japan than in the United States. Inohara's (1990) description of personnel departments in Japanese firms is consistent with this claim. Inohara notes, for example, that in the largest firms the personnel managers will typically be on the board of directors.

The larger size and higher status of Japanese personnel departments is associated with their wider range of activities and greater centrality. In major Japanese firms, personnel departments are the central agency in all personnel matters: recruiting, job assignment, training, promotion, discipline and separation, salary administration, working conditions, welfare, and labor relations. While individual line managers may make recommendations and be consulted, Inohara says it is the personnel managers who make final decisions in these matters. Thus there is a concentration of power over careers in the hands of personnel managers in Japan. Beyond this, the power of the firms over careers in Japan seems stronger than in the United States. In a survey of engineering careers in the United States and Japan, Lynn, Piehler, and Zahray (1988) asked large samples of U.S. and Japanese engineers what their most important reasons had been for taking their current positions. Nearly 70 percent of the Japanese said the most important reason was that they had been assigned to it by their firm — only 12.4 percent of the Americans gave this response.

Inohara characterizes Japanese personnel departments as embodying the corporate philosophy. In many companies, new employees are put under the general supervision of the personnel department for the three to twelve months before permanent assignments are made. This period is often one of intense initial socialization — a task presumably made easier by the fact that the new employees come to the firm directly out of school.

Alletzhauser (1990) describes the process at Nomura Securities. After a rallying speech by the CEO, the new employees are sent to branches, where they are given a desk, a telephone, and a mentor. There is a month of what Alletzhauser characterizes as humiliation: work that largely consists of making cold calls. This provides an important lesson to the new graduates from elite universities about their dependence on lesser humans. The new employees live apart from broader society in a company dormitory. After this month, there are three years of "combined training." This takes place at a training center, where they cook their own food. There are lectures, often until two or three in the morning, on finance, economics, taxes. The new employees are indoctrinated to feel superior to salesmen at other leading securities firms. In his classic study of a Japanese bank, Rohlen (1974) describes further aspects of spiritual education (*seishin kyoiku*), including such activities as raking leaves, singing, keeping diaries that are reviewed by trainers, taking part in a marathon, and offering services without explanation to the bemused citizens of a mountain village. Training practices of this sort are not restricted to university graduates. At Toyota, for example, new high school graduates are placed in a dormitory for single men, where they are given an "older brother" one or two years older. This "mentor" helps socialize the new graduates both on and off the job (Lu, 1987).

After this initial socialization, employees enter a lifetime of career development programs (known as CDP in Japanese) (see, for example, Ryohei, 1988). This includes a systematic rotation of employees through certain positions within the firm and training sessions around the time of promotions and other major changes. Lynn, Piehler, and Zahray (1988) found in their engineering sample that though Americans stayed longer in a position within the firm the older they got, this was not true of the Japanese. Indeed, their data are consistent with a notion of strategic development rotation: nearly half the Japanese sample had been transferred to R&D as part of their training, but only about one-sixth of the Americans; more than a third of the Japanese had spent time in production, but fewer than a fifth of the Americans.

Hitachi managers reportedly receive training within one or two years of taking a managerial position. Hitachi's four Institutes of Management Development now train about 5,000 people annually. Most undergo one- or two-week programs in groups of eighteen to twenty. The training has five objectives: (1) to give managers a clear sense of Hitachi management concepts — for example, of the founding maxims of "harmony, sincerity, and pioneering spirit"; (2) to cultivate the entrepreneurial spirit; (3) to broaden the awareness and insight of managers; (4) to unify the sense of direction of Hitachi managers "so that Hitachi Group companies may have a common, cohesive outlook"; and (5) to improve overall business management. Top management is involved in the sessions. The president attends the course for division manager and higher employees, and vice presidents attend the courses for section managers. Presidents of Hitachi Group companies serve as instructors, and board members also attend. About 70 percent of the instructors in these programs are from Hitachi. A Hitachi executive explains: "This is because of a desire to receive education while maintaining traditions, exchanging business know-hows, etc." (Tanaka, 1989, p. 14).

Many writers have commented on the symbolic paraphernalia used by Japanese firms to reinforce the corporate culture. Much of this is to reinforce corporate values. While the use of corporate philosophy is common in American firms (Deal and Kennedy, 1982), it seems unlikely that efforts to inculcate these values in employees go as far there as they do at many Japanese companies. Kono (1984), for example, notes how at all Matsushita Electric sites, meetings take place every morning at which the company song is sung and the company's "seven spirits" are recited. The song dedicates Matsushita to building a new Japan and sending Matsushita products to the people of the world like "water gushing from a fountain" (Inohara, 1990, p. 18). The company creed expresses the aspiration of improving people's social life and making home electric appliances as cheap and plentiful as water. These are the seven spirits: "Matsushita service through industry; Fairness and faithfulness; Harmony and co-operation; Struggle for betterment; Courtesy and humility;

Adaptation and assimilation; and Gratitude" (Kono, 1984, pp. 62–63).

Kono contrasts the corporate philosophy embodied in these sentiments at Matsushita with those of another firm in the electrical appliance industry, Hitachi. While Matsushita emphasizes supplying goods to consumers in Japan and around the world, Hitachi's company creed stresses technology and the national interest. Kono notes that Hitachi has not done as well in consumer markets as Matsushita.

A common means of creating and sustaining culture is the use of heroes. This is widely done in Japan, Western images of faceless Japanese salary men notwithstanding. As was noted earlier, autobiographies of prominent business leaders are common. Companies often sponsor the publication of books in which a late business leader is remembered. Lu (1987) describes a perhaps extreme form of organizational memory of a "hero," that of the Seibu Group (which include major real estate firms, hotel chains, and railways). According to Lu, Seibu Group employees have assembled at the grave of Yasujiro Tsutsumi, Seibu's founder, on each anniversary of his death since 1965. A few employees come to the grave at around 5:00 and maintain a vigil until 8:30 the next morning. They sweep the gravesite and ring a temple bell (Lu, 1987).

Employees also remember those who have gone before them in the company in other ways. Some Japanese companies, particularly those based in the Osaka area, even have memorials for their deceased employees. The president of Asahi Beer, for example, reports on company results twice a year at the memorial. A survey of Asahi employees found five out of six wanted to be enshrined with co-employees. Besides Asahi Breweries, such major firms as Kubota, Matsushita, Sharp, Nissan, Komatsu, and Kirin maintain memorials for deceased employees (Brauchli, 1989).

Again, although some Western firms such as Bell Telephone and Standard Oil have developed elaborate company histories, the emphasis on company histories rarely goes as far as it commonly does in Japan. In carrying out a study of technology transfer in the steel industry, for instance, I collected several examples in that industry. The fiftieth-anniversary history of Nippon Kokan (there were also earlier histories at roughly ten-year intervals) is a monumental effort. The book comes to nearly 1,100 large-format pages. It includes photographs of everyone who was ever a corporate officer; tables of sales, profits, and so on, for every six-month period in company history; lists of every ship launched at its shipyards; detailed chronologies of major events in every division and every plant of the company; and former corporate charters and organization charts. All of this is elegantly bound in silk, with some overlay pages made of rice paper.

Nippon Kokan's history is not unusual. Kawasaki Steel produced a comparable volume for its twenty-five-year history. Other voluminous histories of steel firms have been produced by Nippon Steel, Sumitomo Metals, and Kobe Steel. Some of these histories have reminiscences from older employees. On occasion, there may be a few pages of discussion by retired executives telling inside stories and episodes that were instrumental in the development of the firm. Often these discussions (which may be facilitated with sake) are remarkably uninhibited. Enough volumes of company history have been produced that one bookstore near the campus of Tokyo University specializes in them.

Conclusions and Implications

Some of the earlier writers on corporate culture, particularly those oriented toward practitioners (Deal and Kennedy, 1982; Peters and Waterman, 1982) stressed the advantages of strong corporate cultures for competitiveness. This view came to be challenged, particularly in more academically oriented publications, by authors who argued that strong corporate cultures can block necessary changes and thus be dysfunctional, especially in more turbulent environments (Wilkins and Ouchi, 1983; Schein, 1985a; Denison, 1990). In such cases, the prescribed solution is personnel changes. If top management is too closely identified with the dysfunctional culture, outside directors should change top management. Management should bring in large numbers of new people to dilute and overthrow the dominant culture (see, for example, Lorsch, 1985).

At Kawasaki Steel, as we have seen, a wholesale change in top management would be virtually impossible unless problems arose that were severe enough to threaten the short-term survival of the company. Bringing in large numbers of new people also seems very difficult. Given the strength of the company's culture and its apparent incompatibility with the most promising paths toward diversification, it is perhaps not surprising that progress toward diversification has seemed glacial. The company recognized early in the 1980s that it should increasingly reduce its dependency on steel. It announced a strategy in 1985, but a cynic might see the "strategy" as doing little more than disguising a refusal to change with a few symbolic gestures. Indeed, the first five-year plan in this strategy concentrated not on the entry into new industries, but rather on cost cutting in the steel industry. To be sure, new units were set up in the company, acquisitions were made in a variety of target industries, and a few mid career employees were hired. But none of these activities amounted to much, given the size of the company. Perhaps not surprisingly, the company was as dependent on the steel industry for sales in 1990 as it had been in 1985.

Another interpretation is possible, however. By focusing its attention on the steel division, top management gained time for the company to change. The drastic cuts in workforce in the steel plants were coupled with a reorganization of production at the company's major iron and steel works. The result was substantial economies. As a consequence, in 1988 and again in 1989 Kawasaki Steel enjoyed record profits. Management has said it expects the new businesses to require at least ten years to become significant contributors to the company. This might simply be an excuse for a lack of progress, but it might also be seen as a reasonable way for a strong-culture corporation to bring about change. During this ten years, three things are happening:

1. Strong efforts are being made to diversify the corporate culture through company publications, television commercials, and so on. This may improve the acceptance of new types of people in the company by those who were socialized into the old culture.

2. The media and other recruiting tools are being used to entice new graduates into the company who differ somewhat from those in the past. In ten years or so, many of these will be in the lower and lower-middle ranks of management.

3. Cadres of more senior midcareer people are being brought into the new businesses and into R&D and other functions of the company. As these people gain increasing acceptance by other Kawasaki employees over the years and reach higher levels of management, they may provide a cadre to run the new businesses and integrate them into Kawasaki.

And, of course, the efforts to increase the competitive position of the steel industry are consistent with the company's plan to maintain some 60 percent of its sales in steel. The acquisition of large numbers of smaller companies in a variety of industries may be an effective way to test on a pilot basis the compatibility of various ventures with the evolving Kawasaki Steel corporate culture.

Only time will tell whether or not the Kawasaki approach results in a successful diversification of the company, but a few points might be made. One issue concerns who can best judge the extent to which a company should leave an industry in search of new opportunities rather than more intensively exploiting remaining opportunities in the old industry. A management that is expert in the old industry presumably is best qualified to evaluate new possibilities in that industry, but at the same time it has a vested interest in avoiding or postponing change. As Dyer (1985) observes, changes in corporate culture have power implications. Alternatively, outside pressures (such as from shareholders) may tempt the current management to diversify in a precipitous manner. Jobs are likely to be at stake. The result may be an inadequate exploitation of opportunities in the current industry or a quick jump into industries in which the organization has little to offer.

At Kawasaki, there is little pressure for precipitous diversification. But is there adequate pressure for the level of diversification the company will require? And what are the sources of this pressure? The answers to these questions probably lie in the Japanese employment and managerial systems. To the degree there is a consensus within Kawasaki that the company must diversify by the year 2000 or else face a cloudy future, decision makers at all levels in the company have reason to support diversification. Most will still be working for the company after the turn of the century. To the degree there are strong emotional ties to the company, management as well has strong incentives to work for diversification. The strong-culture corporation, after all, is something more than just a workplace. And if the pace of change is relatively slow and controlled, the political costs are somewhat reduced for many of the actors. I am not arguing, of course, that all strong-culture corporations will thrive if they are simply left alone. Individuals in positions of power may lack the vision to see what is in the corporation's longer-term interests. The transformation required may mandate more than gradual changes. The case of Kawasaki does suggest, however, that strong-culture corporations may have a wider range of adaptability than might be assumed from the literature.

Some writers have examined the relationship between corporate culture and national culture (for example, Hofstede, Neuijen, Ohayv, and Sanders, 1990). Without plunging into a discussion of the relationship between the concept of culture at the national and organizational levels, I might note that institutional arrangements found in different countries can make a difference. First, it is unlikely that any American corporation could achieve a corporate culture as strong as Kawasaki's. In Japan, an infrastructure for the mutual interchange of information exists that allows effective selection and self-deselection. Opportunities outside the firm, once one has "joined" a firm, are more severely constrained in Japan. Attitudes toward midcareer entrants are different and less of a market exists for them in Japan. Finally, Japanese management tends to be more sheltered from shareholders (and, for that matter, from most other "stakeholders" aside from employees and managers) (see Abegglen and Stalk, 1985).

More generally, whatever mechanisms are in the tool kit of those who want to create strong corporate cultures in U.S.

firms, these mechanisms are present in far more powerful forms in Japanese organizations. Indeed, in Japan companies seem to provide an environment close to Goffman's notion of total institutions. Like Western prisons, military training programs, mental hospitals, and monasteries, the idealtypic Japanese company seems remarkably isolated and in control of its members. Individuals entering these firms are stripped of roles they previously held through training and rigorous dress codes. The new "self" developed through this and other processes is reinforced by long work hours (2,100 compared to 1,900 in the United States) and a tendency to spend off-duty time with co-workers. In their study of U.S. and Japanese engineers, Lynn, Piehler, and Zahray (1988) found that Japanese engineers over the age of thirty spent an average of 3.2 hours of off-duty time with co-workers, compared to 1.6 hours for Americans.

This suggests another conceptual issue. What actually do we mean by "strong" corporate cultures? One operationalization of corporate culture strength is the inverse in the variance in values and practices of organizational members (Hofstede, Neuijen, Ohayv, and Sanders, 1990). The idea is that homogeneity of values and practices is the essence of corporate culture strength. Others have described strong corporate cultures as ones where values and norms are consistent with corporate goals (for example, Deal and Kennedy, 1982; Peters and Waterman, 1982). The Japanese experience shows that another aspect of the concept of strength deals with how deeply organizational values and norms are inculcated in members.

A final point suggested by this chapter is that a study of the Japanese experience has considerable potential for contributing to our understanding of organizational cultures and how they evolve. As exemplified here, Japanese organizations take some of the notions of corporate culture to an extreme seldom experienced in the United States. Yet their ability to adapt and compete globally provides what are for Americans in some respects novel and provocative lessons in managing large systems change.

PART THREE

Developing Continuity

The more we pay attention to continuity and value lessons from the past, the more we experience the often-paradoxical nature of group and organizational life. The four chapters in this part all address *how* we can create processes that encompass seemingly bipolar, or contradictory, realities: continuity-in-innovation, stable change, vital stability, stable mobility, changing sameness, change for the preservation of continuity, and so on. In their various prescriptions, each author calls on us to honestly and enthusiastically face the reality that life in organizations is one of both continuity *and* change, and to treat the apparent tension between the two as a force that is creative and life giving.

In Chapter Seven, Klein and Farris question our typical view of the means-ends relationship in bringing about organizational continuity. Rather than imposing sameness of means to achieve ends, they argue for a system that ensures continuity of ends and flexibility of means. It is the consistency of goals or purpose, across leadership levels over time, that produces continuity. They introduce guidelines for managerial roles, structural linkages, and decision processes to ensure that habit (constancy of means) does not block innovation and that adaptability to the environment (flexibility of ends) does not produce undue disruption or chaos. Their prescriptions result in a complex managerial role. Their ideal leaders are captains of ends

195

(control) and catalysts for means (empower). The resulting tension or conflict between these is seen as a constructive force in the overall coordination of means versus ends in the organization.

In Chapter Eight, Quinn, Spreitzer, and Hart continue to explore the leader's role in managing continuity. They view continuity as having to do with the experience of "bothness" with respect to issues that are typically seen as bipolar or opposite, such as stability-change or people-task. The research they report on here examines the behavioral complexity required of managers in dealing with continuity in organizations. They focus on two areas: productive teamwork, which calls on the manager to be good at *tough love,* and practical revitalization, which requires the manager to be skilled at *practical visioning.* They challenge us to view skills that were previously seen as separate instead of as parts of a whole.

In Chapter Nine, Evans explores the duality of change and continuity in organizational life and suggests systems and structural methods to increase the "constructive tension" between the two. *Layering* and *decision architecture* are presented as lessons from studies of how adults manage continuity-change choice-points in the maturation process. These concepts are applied to organizational settings in order to achieve a *dynamic balance* between continuity and change, centralization and decentralization, loose versus tight controls, and so on. He argues in favor of embracing the continuity-change duality as a vital source of tension or difference that, if treated well, is life giving. It is also a reminder that continuity management does not lead to sameness or comfort all the time.

Finally, in Chapter Ten, Bartol examines another duality: continuity and innovation. Her question is, "How can organizations pursue an appropriate degree of continuity and yet promote the necessary amount of innovation for success?" She sees pay and reward systems as critical mechanisms for promoting both innovation and continuity. After a thorough review of the effects of different pay and recognition systems on creativity, she calls for systems that combine the connectedness of past-to-present (historical) performance with present-to-future concerns such as plans, visions, and so on. This approach promotes "incremental innovation" within a context of continuity.

Chapter Seven

Developing Leadership for Continuity and Change: Matters of Ends and Means

Jonathan I. Klein, George F. Farris

Organizational scientists and practitioners alike have long subordinated the need for organizational continuity to the need and strategies for organizational change. Perhaps this reflects an assumption that the importance of organizational continuity is too obvious to require analysis. Alternatively, organizational change by definition represents the sort of discontinuity that captures the attention of both organizational analysts and newscast audiences. Change is also consistent with a cultural preference for action and novelty. As a result, organizational change has been elevated to the status of a virtual discipline: organizational development. By contrast, no such discipline exists for the study and optimization of organizational continuity.

Nevertheless, continuity is firmly embedded in the very definition of the organization. This is reflected, for example, in the recognition that organizational structure has been "imprinted" by societal conditions (Stinchcombe, 1965); it is also reflected in the belief that organizing is an ongoing social process (Weick, 1969). Interpreted from a functional standpoint, continuity characterizes the organization because it meets many of the organization's needs.

Note: The authors gratefully acknowledge inspiration and support for this research from the Graduate School of Management at Rutgers University and the Weatherhead School of Management at Case Western Reserve University.

The Functions of Organizational Continuity

Organizational continuity is functional for several reasons. It involves fidelity to an area of competence, or a willingness to "stick to the knitting" (Peters and Waterman, 1982), qualities that enhance organizational effectiveness because they deploy the organization's skills to best effect, enlist commitment from its members, and provide a benchmark for evaluating individual and organizational performance. Continuity is also reflected in the organization's "memory" (Galbraith, 1977), which permits retention of past lessons and therefore organizational learning (Klein, 1989). As a result, one of the gravest threats to the continued survival of the organization characterized by a "work hard, play hard" corporate culture is posed by the departure of older members, who represent repositories of such learning (Deal and Kennedy, 1982). Finally, continuity meets employees' various individual needs, including security, certainty, and perhaps symbolic immortality. Evidence that continuity fulfills important needs includes individual resistance to change, as noted by theorists from Freud to Starbuck, Greve, and Hedberg (1978). For all these reasons, continuity or constancy represents a significant criterion for effective leadership (Bennis, 1985), as well as for successful performance in general. As a result, only at our peril do we ignore those who resist organizational change and the reasons for their resistance (Klein, 1966).

Organizational literature, then, has recognized rather than overlooked the importance of continuity relative to change, but only implicitly or ambivalently. Recently, some authors have begun to address explicitly the relationship between continuity and change, for example, by suggesting that a key part of the CEO's job is to achieve balance between the two (Jonas, Fry, and Srivastva, 1990). The purpose of this chapter is to demonstrate the compatibility rather than mutual exclusivity of continuity and change. We show how the two can be integrated by identifying the respective domains within which each is appropriate and by developing specific leadership strategies for doing so.

The Utility Principle of Leadership

Jonas, Fry, and Srivastva (1990, p. 42) suggest that "continuity is expressed through the organizational culture, which essentially consists of the core strengths, core technologies, and core logic of the firm." To this list we can add the core beliefs and values that define corporate culture (Deal and Kennedy, 1982). In contrast, transition entails more effective ways of getting from point A to point B. Thus, continuity is prescribed for "core" aspects of the organization, and change for better "ways" of doing things.

This conceptualization implies that effective leadership requires *continuity regarding ends and flexibility regarding means.* This rests in turn on the "equifinality" principle (Von Bertalanffy, 1950), which states that "a system can reach the same final state from differing initial conditions and by a variety of paths" (Katz and Kahn, 1966, pp. 25–26). The selection of path is ideally dictated by its utility in reaching the desired "final state"; hence, this principle is called the *utility principle of leadership.* The utility principle holds that continuity is justified not as habit or inertia but only as an instrumental means to an end; change, on the other hand, is justified only as an instrumental end to more overarching ends, not simply for its own sake.

Problems in Applying the Utility Principle

Complications in applying the utility principle to leadership practice appear to arise from several sources.

Means as Determinants of Ends. One apparent complication stems from the fact that organizational means often suggest ends and, from a functional standpoint, *ought* to, as well. A classic example involves the "goal displacement" at the National Foundation for Infantile Paralysis after the Salk vaccine was discovered. The foundation shifted its priority from fighting polio to fighting disease in general in order to exploit its fundraising capacity — a means that appeared to dictate a choice of ends. However, organizational survival represents an end (Scott, 1981) ultimately advanced by goal displacement. Consistent with this are emergent subgoals (for example, fighting all disease) that reflect the utility principle after all.

Organizational Focus on Means. The function of means as a source of organizational self-concept and self-esteem — that is, as a source of the "core strengths" and "core technologies" that contribute to organizational culture — also suggests that means are an apparent determinant of ends. While this function assigns a high priority to means, it does not in itself assign *causality* to means. On the contrary, it identifies a strong culture as an end advanced by positive valence for the organization's unique capabilities and members' recognition of them, which in turn represent means to strategic ends. In sum, an organization's means are certainly important, but recognizing their importance represents a means to an even more overarching end.

The "Means-End" Ethic. The recommendation that ends dictate means certainly differs from the assertion that a desirable end justifies *any* means. Indeed, recognizing the distinction between these two premises eliminates the "means-end" ethic (Steiner and Steiner, 1988) as a basis for objection to the utility principle.

The Means-End Decision Chain. Finally, the "means-end chain" that describes decision making in organizations (March and Simon, 1958) presents perhaps the greatest complication. In this chain, each decision outcome represents an end that also represents a means to a more overarching end; at the same time, each means represents an end in relation to a more microscopic means. Based on the utility principle, each decision outcome — as both an end and a means — appears to warrant *both* continuity and change. For example, a job profile for an in-house advertising copywriter that specifies prior experience with a limited product type may be retained as an end in itself, to satisfy the personnel department's need for continuous hiring criteria, or it may be varied as a means to a strategic change in different product mix. Clearly needed, therefore, is a heuristic for identifying each decision as either a means or an end.

We propose a *telescope principle* to represent such a heuristic. This captures the idea that, like a telescope, decisions ideally emerge with increasing narrowness. Specifically, the telescope principle states that the order in which objectives should be addressed is dictated by the inclusiveness of the organizational processes they directly affect. Thus, the organization evaluates each "end" for retention, or continuity, only after it has favorably evaluated and retained the end that affects the organizational process immediately more inclusive. To pursue the preceding example, maintaining a job profile for a specialized advertising copywriter clearly depends on strategic planners' maintaining a product mix. This evaluation process first targets the objectives affecting the organization as a whole, then objectives affecting successively narrower organizational processes. Unfavorable evaluation of any objective invalidates *all* narrower ones because they are ultimately instrumental to it. Most dramatically, invalidation of the most overarching organizational objectives automatically invalidates all others. For this reason, any organization must be flexible, particularly within a turbulent environment.

Prescribing a decision-making sequence in an order dictated by the inclusiveness of affected process is certainly intuitive. Yet it is necessitated by the alternative, "nonrational," and demonstrably widespread preference for prioritization of means over ends (for example, Cohen, March, and Olsen, 1972). The counterproductiveness of this preference is underscored by the definition of organizational management to include a *planning* function (Certo, 1986). This in turn presupposes directedness toward goals or ends. Mindful of a mandate for prioritizing ends over means, then, we now turn to the use of the utility and telescope principles in operationalizing this relationship. The task requires us to identify specific organizational means and ends. For the sake of generalizability, we must first generically delineate the "means-end chain" to the widest possible range of organizations.

The "Decision Telescope"

Scholars usually group issues concerning decisions in organizations in categories that represent an organizational "decision

telescope." This involves a sequence dictated by decreasing inclusiveness or increasing specificity of organizational processes
affected by the decisions. Such categories include, in order, (1)
the organization's "major mission" or overarching objectives; (2)
the production and marketing strategy for carrying out the major
mission; (3) the internal structures and processes (that is, policy,
rules, methods, and procedures) for implementing strategy; (4)
selection, evaluation, reward, and career development methods
for promoting short- and long-term task performance by the employees who occupy and contribute to such structures and processes, respectively; and (5) employee task performance itself.
To apply the utility and telescope principles, one must establish continuity at each category level only after verifying that
decision outcomes are instrumental in achieving objectives identified at the preceding level.

Leadership Principles for Continuity and Change

Both the utility and telescope principles are applied specifically
through a series of leadership principles for continuity and
change. These principles require effective leadership of four
types: (1) system, (2) organization, (3) people, and (4) tasks.
The four levels correspond to the dimensions of leadership identified by Farris (1989). Farris originally presented them as end-
points of two perpendicular axes that depicted his "TOPS" model
of leadership. (TOPS is an acronym consisting of the first letter from each dimension, reading clockwise from the "9:00" position in Figure 7.1.) Although the bulk of the literature has focused on people and tasks, Farris (1989) demonstrated the
importance of the system and organization dimensions to leadership in research and development. In the following discussion,
we will present and interrelate all four types of leadership by
applying the utility principle to each.

> *The system principle:* continuity regarding the major mis-
> sion and flexibility regarding the strategy for fulfilling it

> - *The open-system principle:* continuity regarding the or-
>   ganization's function in society and flexibility regarding
>   strategic goals to be achieved in fulfilling it

Figure 7.1. Farris's "TOPS" Model of Leadership.

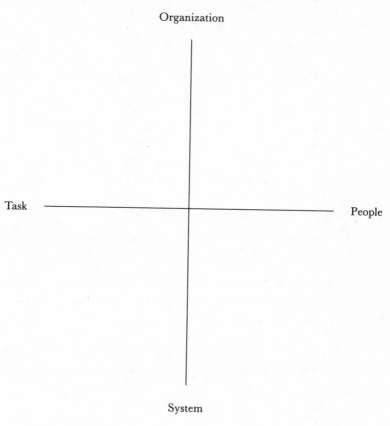

Organization

Task

People

System

Source: Farris, 1989.

- *The rational-system principle:* continuity regarding the organization's core beliefs and values and flexibility regarding ways of expressing and promoting them

The organization principle: continuity regarding strategy and flexibility regarding organizational structures and processes for implementing it, which are reflected, respectively, in

- *The structure principle*
- *The process principle*

The people principle: continuity regarding organizational structures and processes and flexibility regarding the management of human resources that comprise and contribute to them, respectively

- *The assignment principle:* continuity regarding people and flexibility regarding their assignment to positions
- *The evaluation principle:* continuity regarding performance standards and flexibility regarding their achievement
- *The reward principle:* continuity regarding amount of reward relative to performance and flexibility regarding type
- *The career development principle:* continuity regarding employee career development and flexibility regarding career path

The task principle: continuity regarding the management of human resources and flexibility regarding the supervision of tasks

In the following paragraphs, we present a justification for each principle. Later we take up specific issues the principles raise and touch on leadership strategies individuals can use in applying the principles.

The System Principle of Leadership

Continuity in regard to the organization's major mission is essential because it helps align organizational objectives with long-term societal ones. Organizational objectives are in turn made feasible by their alignment with the objectives of the individual members responsible for achieving them.

The system principle is subdivided into the open- and rational-system principles to apply a distinction proposed by Scott (1981). The organization can effect both environmental adaptation and the internal rationalization to achieve it by applying the following open- and rational-system principles of leadership, respectively.

The Open-System Principle. Continuity regarding the major mission permits the organization to fulfill its long-term societal function. In exchange, the organization receives vital resources. Additionally, the organization's major mission reflects its primary area of competence, which if properly defined and continuously exploited is compatible with the varied goods and services required to meet multiple and changing societal needs. IBM, for example, is no less at home in the present computer industry than it was in the earlier typewriter industry, having identified its mission as the production of business machines. Thus, continuity regarding the organization's major mission is not merely *compatible with* but also *requires* and *enhances* flexibility regarding specific strategic goals that must be achieved in fulfilling that mission.

The Rational-System Principle. Continuity regarding the major mission presupposes continuity regarding the organization's core beliefs and values. The latter optimizes organizational effectiveness by (1) guiding the strategic management needed to pursue it, (2) providing a benchmark for evaluating it, (3) justifying the cooperation needed to achieve it, and (4) enabling the organizational change to maintain such effectiveness in the face of environmental change by minimizing its disruptiveness. To reiterate an earlier point, then, organizational *continuity is instrumental to change.*

The Organization Principle

The organization principle is subdivided into the structure and process principles.

The Structure Principle. Ostensibly, structures are organizationally rational, created and maintained to achieve organizational objectives. In actuality, they are "occupationally rational," in that they are instrumental to and maintained to advance individual objectives and are irrelevant, perhaps even hostile, to organizational objectives. It is easy to see why. Structures are composed of positions, positions provide resources, and resources are taken for granted (Pfeffer, 1981) because they are committed to various uses, and salient needs require new resources. Moreover, an incumbent's vested interest in maintaining a position is bound to exceed others' interest in altering it. Finally, as an "expert" regarding the position, the incumbent is able to defend its retention with a high degree of credibility. An incumbent sales manager, for example, is likely to defend his or her position against needed organizational redesign as a source of commission income that is committed to various obligations (for example, a home mortgage, an auto loan), and additional purchases (such as a second car) become feasible and attractive.

In sum, occupational rationality is likely to be pursued to the neglect and perhaps detriment of organizational rationality. To better link the two and advance strategic goals, we recommend that the structure principle of leadership, or flexibility regarding structure, be applied. Specifically, this can be done by decoupling incumbency from resource acquisition, ample opportunities for which might instead be generalized across all employees. Examples include an organizationwide emphasis on and rewards for "innovativeness" regardless of the rank at which it is displayed.

The organization may also advance strategic goals and subordinate occupational goals by using ad hoc organizational structures among which a person rotates and authority and responsibilities vary. Advantages include flexibility, gaining of experience, and a reduced need to optimize one's position within a formal hierarchy. Also recommended to deemphasize hierarchy are formal position descriptions that differ qualitatively rather than quantitatively, reflect team rather than individual functions, and are supplemented by the use of informal roles and networks (Farris, 1981).

The Process Principle. As a number of observers have noted, there are many reasons that policies, rules, methods, and procedures become ends unto themselves rather than organizationally rational means to strategy ends. Bureaucratic dependence on subordinates produces "bureaupathic" overreliance on rules, inflexibility, and overemphasis on authority (Thompson, 1961). Subordinates in turn may use rules to express "bureautic" suspiciousness. Rules are inappropriately prioritized because of cognitive reversal of means and ends (Merton, 1957), conformity (Blau, 1955), and vested interest in the positions and responsibilities they justify (Gouldner, 1954). Possible results include divisiveness, conflict, immobility, and system destruction.

To "rationalize" intraorganizational processes, we recommend that organizations (1) clarify strategic objectives to which the processes are purportedly instrumental, (2) continuously evaluate such instrumentality, and (3) modify it when needed to ensure its legitimacy. Organizations should take care in modifying rules so that no one mistakes flexibility in formulating them for flexibility in enforcing them or for lack of importance attached to them. Organizations can prevent such confusion by identifying flexibility as a norm (that is, "continuous change") and thus indicative of planning rather than second-guessing or shortsightedness, which might understandably invite skepticism and resistance.

The People Principle

The people principle is subdivided into four subprinciples.

The Assignment Principle. The success of many Japanese companies (and lack of the same for many of their American counterparts) reveals the importance of commitment to employees. For the most part, Japanese organizations retain and reassign their employees where needed rather than replace them.

Commitment to employees is functional because it allows them to reciprocate since they are at minimal risk for failing to explore options elsewhere. This in turn minimizes the company's risk of squandering time and effort in long-term employee development. Organizational commitment to and from employees therefore represents a self-perpetuating social process.

Benefits of employee loyalty to the company include purposiveness, energy, and initiative. Benefits of flexibility in task assignment include retention of experience with and knowledge of the organization; exploitation of learning from previous mistakes; short-term employee stimulation; long-term development of generalists with a broad, companywide perspective and sensitivity to the needs and problems of others; and consistency of job assignments with employee preferences and self-evaluated abilities. Replacing employees, on the other hand, incurs costs of recruitment, selection, training, suboptimal start-up performance, and dysfunctional effects on both the motivation of termination "survivors" and the cohesiveness of the work groups they comprise.

To be sure, a policy of replacing employees may also benefit the organization with sensitivity to the environment and the employees with encouragement to maximize open-market value. However, the organization may achieve the former by being flexible in assigning employees, while obviating the need for the latter by retaining them. Arguably, then, the benefits of applying the utility principle vastly outweigh the costs.

The Evaluation Principle. Standards for evaluating task performance should be continuous across both time and personnel to maximize work motivation that is greatest for goals whose difficulty is maintained rather than relaxed (Locke, 1976) and to effect the reward equity (Adams, 1968) of those who have already attained such standards. On the other hand, tolerance for failure to achieve performance standards should exist to encourage the risk-seeking behavior essential to creativity and innovation, without relaxing the standards themselves. In addition, failure itself reveals lessons that employees should learn. This represents a key benefit of retaining and teaching rather than dismissing employees who make mistakes (Klein, 1989). This point was dramatized by IBM chairman Thomas Watson when he summoned to his office a young executive who had lost $10 million of the company's money in a risky business venture. To the young man's offer to resign, Watson replied, "You can't be serious. We just spent ten million dollars educating you" (Bennis, 1985).

Flexibility regarding the achievement of task performance standards is reflected in the employee's full and demonstrably beneficial participation in the design of performance appraisal instruments and procedures and in the discussion of performance feedback (Latham and Wexley, 1981).

The Reward Principle. Equity also demands continuity across time and personnel regarding the amount of reward relative to a given level of performance. At the same time, individual needs and preferences vary; therefore, the subjective value of a reward also varies. Organizations may address variable individual needs by being flexible about *types* of reward. They might, for instance, initiate cafeteria pay plans. Single employees, for example, may prefer deferred compensation to meet relatively low current expenses and in anticipation of higher (for example, family or retirement) costs later on; married employees with higher expenses may prefer greater current liquidity.

The Career Development Principle. Continuity in regard to human beings presupposes a long-term developmental view of people rather than simply a short-term utilitarian view. This represents the *practical imperative* (Steiner and Steiner, 1988) inspired by Immanuel Kant's admonition in *Foundations of the Metaphysics of Morals* to "act so that you treat humanity, whether in your own person or that of another, always as an end and never as a means only." The practical imperative is expressed in efforts to help employees attain career objectives, which in turn are served by a highly individuated sequence of formal positions and informal roles. These "career paths" can vary among the "linear," "transitory," "spiral," or "steady-state" types (Driver, 1980).

Based on the practical imperative, employee development is justified as an end unto itself. Clearly, however, it also represents a means to organizational ends because it is likely to maximize employee job satisfaction, commitment, and competence, all to the organization's benefit.

The Task Principle

"One best way" expresses the principle underlying early "classical" approaches to management. These include Henri Fayol's *fourteen principles* of management, on the macroscopic or administrative level of analysis, and Frederick Taylor's *scientific management,* on the microscopic or task level. Such approaches were discredited largely because they neglected the multiplicity of task means to ends, variable individual ability to make effective use of prescribed means, and nonphysical (for example, psychological and social) determinants of task performance. Addressing these considerations and antithetical to classical management is the task principle of leadership.

On the basis of both the task principle and equity theory (Adams, 1968), we recommend continuity across employees regarding the difficulty of task objective relative to compensation for achieving it. Flexibility is recommended in regard to employee methods for achieving the task objective. Such flexibility is ideally demonstrated by delegating authority and responsibility for task planning, design, evaluation, and—if needed— follow-up modification rather than simply implementation. These are all elements of job enrichment. Their benefits to employee productivity and satisfaction have been amply demonstrated (Herzberg, 1966).

Practical Implications

The utility principle may be applied by designing organizational structures and processes to include responsibilities and procedures for doing so.

Organizational Structure and the Utility Principle

Positions assigned design responsibilities can be divided into the *captain* and *catalyst* leadership classifications identified by Farris (1989). Within each leadership category, a catalyst maintains flexibility by continuously evaluating the means or *instrumentation* needed to achieve ends or *application* and by proposing their continuity or change as needed. The catalyst simultaneously serves as the captain within the next, less inclusive category, effecting continuity or change by articulating ongoing or new objectives (see Figure 7.2).

Captain and catalyst responsibilities are folded into one position to (1) promote ongoing analysis rather than mere advocacy of current practice, (2) ensure that this analysis considers

Figure 7.2. Leadership Roles Assigned to Four Employees
(A, B, C, and D), by Leadership Category.

Leadership Role

		Captain (Administrative Function)	Catalyst (Planning Function)
	Environment		D
	System	D	C
Leadership	Organization	C	B
Category	People	B	A
	Task	A	A

level of consistency not only with application in the next leadership category but also with instrumentation in the same category,
and (3) realize the demonstrated benefits of participative management by institutionalizing it.

Organizational Process and the Utility Principle

Administration within each leadership category is the captain's
responsibility and represents an element of a broader, organizationwide *implementation* function; traditional hierarchical departments and managers may assign responsibility for and supervision of this function. The captain is referred to formally as
the department administrator and in this capacity reports to supervisory personnel within the functional area.

A separate organizationwide function is *planning*. The purpose of planning is to evaluate consistency among activities at
various leadership levels. The planning function is assigned to
the catalyst, who is therefore identified as the department planner. In this capacity (rather than as the administrator at the
next, less inclusive leadership category), the planner reports to

an organizational planning officer and staff. Structurally, then, implementation and planning comprise permanent elements of a matrix organizational design (see Figure 7.3). Procedurally, planning is carried out within structures and levels through "means-end" or "instrument" audits and on an organizationwide basis at periodic meetings of the planning committee, which consists of all catalysts. Like a zero-based budget, current practice is retained only if the findings of the instrument audit and evaluation by the planning committee justify it.

Responsibilities of contributors to the planning function and the issues or "tensions" they must resolve (see Table 7.1), are specified in the following two sections.

Planning Within the Leadership Categories: Captains and Catalysts

System Planning

Open-System Planning. The open-system "catalyst" (typically the CEO or another upper manager) performs a planning function that includes identifying environmental goals and needs, evaluating their consistency with organizational strategic goals, and changing the latter as needed to match the former.

The success of strategy is traditionally predicated on accommodation of the environment. An alternative, "strategic-choice" view assigns discretion to the organization rather than causality to the environment. The first view is likely to be operationalized in a conservative, highly analytical strategy, and the second in a proactive and aggressive strategy. One tension reflected in strategic planning, then, counterpoises *environmental determinism and strategic choice.*

The strategic or organizational planner must also determine whether negative environmental feedback reflects a strategy's inappropriateness or simply novelty and lack of proven efficacy. To do this, the planner must identify the point at which a strategy has had enough time to demonstrate its effectiveness. Overemphasis on continuity risks "escalation of commitment" (Staw, 1981) beyond the point at which it represents a "rational"

Figure 7.3. A Matrix Organizational Design for Implementation and Planning Functions.

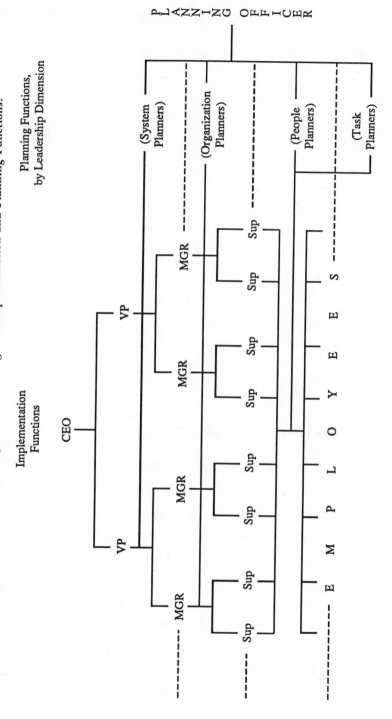

Table 7.1. Issues to Be Addressed Within Each Leadership Category.

Leadership category	Key issues
Institution	Goal specificity versus abstractness
System	Environmental determinism versus strategic choice
	Efficiency versus effectiveness
Organization	
Structure	Certainty versus mobility
Process	Utility versus consistency
People	
Short term	Individuality versus cooperation
Long term	Short- versus long-term productivity
Task	Control versus autonomy

expenditure of resources. Overemphasis on flexibility, on the other hand, risks insufficient commitment to produce definitive results. A key tension confronting the open-system catalyst, then, counterpoises *efficiency and effectiveness.*

Rational-System Planning. The open-system catalyst also serves as a rational-system captain, fulfilling an administrative function by articulating old or new organizational objectives. This person thus effects organizational continuity or change, depending on the decisions he or she made as an open-system catalyst.

Where needed, then, the rational-system captain functions as a key organizational change agent, effecting change overtly, through justification, clarification, and consensus building. The rational-system captain also does this covertly, as a "manager of meaning" (Weick, 1969), through manipulation of the organization's symbols—for example, through such rituals as ceremonies for appointing new officers. As noted earlier, change is effected best if it is nondisruptive. It can be made so if the captain presents it within the context of long-term continuity, specifically, by articulating abiding organizational beliefs and values with which change is consistent and by identifying long-term organizational objectives to which change is instrumental. To achieve the former, we recommend flexibility in articulating beliefs that favor and values that include utility and responsibility to society. To achieve this, we recommend deliberately managed goal displacement: presentation of the organization's long-term objectives in a manner that is sufficiently abstract to accommodate changes in its short-term objectives.

Articulating an abstract organizational objective also accommodates the multiple and varied personal objectives of members (Barnard, 1938) whose services and commitment will be required in the long term. Members have varied objectives for two reasons. First, skill differences are required by the division of labor that is fundamental to organizations and that requires variable training, experience, and personal traits. Second, the transactional nature of employment (Barnard, 1938) reflects different individual and organizational objectives.

Thus, an abstract objective serves useful organizational functions. On the other hand, the organization's major mission should be sufficiently specific to prevent a more specialized competitor from appropriating its environmental niche. Law firms, for instance, tend to specialize in such areas as divorce, personal injury, and entertainment to carve out an adequate niche in an increasingly competitive industry. A key tension confronting the rational-system captain, then, is *specificity versus abstraction* of the organization's purpose.

Organization Planning

Structures. Job responsibilities and interrelationships are ill-defined in an organically designed organization and well defined in a mechanistic one. Research findings (Burns and Stalker, 1961) have long recommended a mechanistic structure for the certainty presented by a static environment and an organic structure for the responsiveness demanded by a dynamic environment. Hence, the tension inherent in designing an organization for continuity and change is between *certainty and mobility*.

Processes. Policy is intended to articulate and implement a strategic plan internally. Rules, methods, and procedures represent programs or "routines" that are meant to translate such policy into specific behaviors. These should be flexible enough to accommodate policy changes and to permit sufficient employee discretion to produce self-fulfilling benefits from initiative and creativity. On the other hand, overly flexible behavioral programs are costly, difficult to promulgate, and inimical to the credibility of both the programs themselves and those responsible for administering them. The key issue in the organization leadership category, then, counterpoises *utility and consistency.*

People Planning

The primary tasks in the people leadership category are in the short term to promote and in the long term to develop behaviors, programmatic or otherwise, that are needed for organizational effectiveness.

The Short Term. Behaviors reflect personal characteristics that are made to vary across members by the organization's need to diversify. Such traits call for flexibility in assigning individuals to tasks, evaluating their task performance, and rewarding desired performance. The employee can ensure such flexibility by participating in job and reward system design and performance feedback — strategies for workplace democratization and interactive performance evaluation, with the benefits noted earlier (Latham and Wexley, 1981).

On the other hand, organizations are defined as cooperative systems (Barnard, 1938) in which standards must be roughly equivalent across employees to establish collective rather than individual rewards for performance as well as equity. Japanese management techniques have demonstrated the importance of collective rewards. Equity maximizes the coordination needed to manage employees' interdependence. In sum, the issue of prime importance in the people leadership category is *individuality versus cooperation.*

The Long Term. Both the organization and the employee have a vested interest in short-term performance: the organization needs immediate productivity, while the employee needs immediate compensation. Thus, long-term career development imposes costs on the organization — in management and employee time — and on the employee — in management support and goodwill. The employee's potentially heightened wage demands or departure to a higher bidder imposes additional costs on the organization; the perhaps minimal demand for skills outside the organization in which they were developed imposes additional costs on the employee.

The organization can help resolve both problems by demonstrating commitment to the employee — by applying the assignment principle prescribed for the people leadership category. Moreover, the current value of a more skilled employee to the organization far exceeds that of an undeveloped one. And certainly the employee can also expect to benefit from added personal value from long-term development. Thus, a key tension in the short term in the people leadership category is between the employee's *short-term productivity and long-term development.*

Compared to the organization as a whole, the employee has a high potential return on personal career development. Therefore, it is the employee who is responsible for ensuring sufficient management flexibility to facilitate a chosen career path. Fulfillment of the catalyst role in the people leadership category explicitly underscores the employee's ultimate responsibility for his or her own career development and choice.

Task Planning

Supervisory authoritativeness or directiveness is justified by (1) lack of subordinate "maturity" (Vroom and Yetton, 1973) or self-management skill, (2) the supervisor's unique management skill, and (3) the need to apply it to the coordination of subordinate tasks. Democratic or participative management, in contrast, is justified by the self-fulfilling effect of a positive self-evaluation on subordinate maturity and by its benefits to the development of employee self-management skills. An employee is managed participatively in an enriched job position, the benefits of which to employee productivity and satisfaction have been noted elsewhere in this chapter and in the literature (Herzberg, 1966). The choice between authoritative and participative management therefore reduces to a choice between *control and autonomy*. In short, we recommend the management style of autonomy, consistent with the venerable Theory Y (MacGregor, 1960), because of the self-fulfilling development of employee characteristics already assumed in adopting it.

In an enriched job position, the employee is responsible not only for execution but also for the planning assigned to the catalyst and the goal setting and evaluation assigned to the captain. For this reason, the employee ideally functions in the task leadership category as both a captain and a catalyst.

Analysis and Resolution of Tensions Within Leadership Categories

The tensions at each leadership level represent the conflict recently recognized as an inevitable concomitant of intraorganizational diversity and thus as virtually definitional to organizations. This recognition contributes to the resolution of conflict by attributing it to structure, thereby depersonalizing it. A key purpose of the present discussion is to facilitate the resolution of intraorganizational conflict by identifying its sources in structural dynamics toward continuity and change.

Conceptualizing the leadership function to include articulation of means and ends is highly reminiscent of the path-goal model of leadership originally proposed by House and Mitchell (1974). Specifically, delegation of responsibility for establishing means reflects *consideration* (that is, the "path" component of leadership), while retention of responsibility for articulating ends reflects *initiating structure* (that is, the "goal" aspect of leadership).

Thus, the utility principle is consistent with a model of leadership for which there is persuasive empirical support (Miner, 1980). Moreover, this principle is justified not simply by the obvious benefits but also by the microscopic determinants of organizational effectiveness — the path-goal instrumentalities that motivate individual behavior. Finally, this framework contributes a conceptualization of each decision outcome as both a goal in one leadership category and a path in the next, more inclusive one; with this comes the recognition that leadership enhances organizational effectiveness as a potential linchpin across organizational structures essential to their coordination.

A caveat is called for. Because "telescoping" assigns priority to decisions based on inclusiveness of affected process, it appears to require a traditional, hierarchical organizational structure. However, it should be clear at this point that implementation of the utility principle represents a virtual blueprint for workplace democracy. Specifically, it calls for those who are affected by organizational structures and processes to take responsibility for planning them. In the next section, we present recommended procedures for workplace democratization.

Planning Across the Organization: The Planning Committee

The organization can ensure the "telescoping" of decisions across leadership categories through a periodic "telescope" audit that reviews, integrates, evaluates, and if needed supplements or modifies findings from various instrument audits. The telescope audit is conducted at meetings of the organizational planning committee. Guidelines for conducting such audits include the following:

1. Participants include all department planners.
2. The purpose of the audit should be explicitly identified as articulation within and among leadership levels.
3. The planning officer serves as the facilitator, not supervisor, responsible for ensuring the integrity of the analytical process rather than determining its content or outcome.
4. There is no differentiation among other participants regarding authority or responsibility during the audit. All participants fulfill equivalent roles.
5. The focus is a *problem* focus, and the orientation is problem resolution rather than assignment of blame.
6. Decision-making procedures should be designed to preclude dysfunctional effects from organizational rules and role,

group process, and political motives. Recommended procedures include the familiar nominal and Delphi decision-
making techniques.

7. Decisions should be arrived at consensually to compel par-
    ticipants to attend to mutual needs and concerns and build
    universal support for large-scale and otherwise difficult or-
    ganizational design undertakings.

The telescope audit should not only result in consistency
among organizational means and ends but, more broadly, in
the establishment of organizational analysis and design as an
ongoing, widely involving, and well-informed activity.

Theoretical Implications

We have proposed the utility principle to change the relationship between means and ends in organizations that are popularly characterized as "rationalizing" rather than rational (for
example, Weick, 1969; Cohen, March, and Olsen, 1972). Rationalization is arguably functional to a certain extent because
it reflects an absence of prior purpose, which might otherwise
constrain organizational action, innovation, and self-discovery.
Nevertheless, rationalization ultimately produces purpose, imposing no fewer constraints on organizational action than does
"rationality." Moreover, by its emergent nature, rationalization
reflects occupationally rather than organizationally rational vest-
ing of interests. Proposing the utility principle, therefore, implicitly characterizes rationalization as a problem and represents
an effort to address it. Theoretically, one may view the utility
principle as the normative side of the coin; the other, descriptive side presents theories of organizational rationalization.

Empirical Implications

We can summarize the utility principle as both the normative
theory and the research hypothesis that organizational effectiveness requires a continuity of ends to be determined in a "tele-
scoped" sequence. Observers from the various specializations

associated with each leadership level of the organization (for example, human resource management and so on) may longitudinally measure goal *consistency* across leadership levels to determine goal *continuity*. Organizational effectiveness may be operationalized "ecologically" as satisfaction of key stakeholders (Miles, 1980), as measured by questionnaire or interview assessments.

The organization may also evaluate the utility principle in a laboratory setting by assigning to "employees" a task that is (1) sufficiently complex to require some organizational differentiation and integration and an alignment of means and ends across processes of variable inclusiveness and (2) multistage, to reveal continuity or change over time. Finally, in both laboratory and field settings, the organization may use path analysis to establish the "telescoping" of means and ends.

Conclusion

We strongly urge organizational scientists and practitioners to recognize that organizational effectiveness demands continuity as well as change. Although such recognition is justified by the implicit importance of continuity in organizational theory and practice, it is conspicuously absent from the explicit offerings of the organizational field. Absent as well among such offerings and thus an additional focus of this chapter are leadership strategies for choosing between and — where appropriate — optimizing either continuity or change. We conclude by cautioning that it is enlightened, proactive, and reasoned leadership, not the press of unplanned events, that dictates the appropriate choice between continuity and change.

Chapter Eight

Integrating the Extremes: Crucial Skills for Managerial Effectiveness

*Robert E. Quinn, Gretchen M. Spreitzer,
Stuart L. Hart*

Scientists tend to create theoretical categories. The categories may range from abstract concepts to operationalized variables. The purpose of such categories is to focus attention, facilitate analysis, and aid in communication. These theoretical categories, however, often tend to be constructed under assumptions of bipolarity. In fact, Bobko (1985) argues that implicit assumptions of bipolarity or high differentiation are at the heart of nearly all of the theory construction and all the analysis that takes place in the managerial sciences. He points out that "answers are assumed to be right or wrong, organizations are assumed to be highly structured or loosely structured, tasks are seen to be creative or routine" (p. 99).

However, while essential for some purposes, the bipolar employment of theoretical categories may hinder the process of discovery. This may be particularly true when a behavior in nature reflects two highly differentiated theoretical categories. Indeed, research has shown that many creative breakthroughs involve the conceptualization of a process in which two highly discrepant categories are interrelating or interpenetrating in some surprising way (Rothenberg, 1979). While differentiating between categories may be more natural than thinking about the integration of categories, such thinking may prove generative. Some have argued, for example, that relaxing the assumptions of bipolarity in the theory-building process can result in constructs that are integrative and nondualistic, and that the generation of such constructs can enhance our understanding of many complex processes (Hampden-Turner, 1981; Bobko, 1985).

The purpose of this chapter is to challenge the assumptions of bipolarity in the field of managerial leadership. First, we introduce the notion of *interpenetration* (that is, the dynamic integration of bipolarities) and provide examples from both psychology and organizational studies. Second, we introduce and describe two types of interpenetration in managerial leadership: the instrumental-latent interpenetration (tough love) and the integrative-adaptive interpenetration (practical vision). Both concepts are operationalized and issues of measurement are discussed. Finally, we explore implications for theory and practice.

Traditional Categories in Managerial Leadership

The conceptual literature on managerial leadership is permeated with categories that are presented in a bipolar fashion. McGregor (1960), for example, suggests that people operate under assumptions of Theory X or Theory Y. Zaleznik (1977) argues that individuals are either managers or leaders. Burns (1978) contends that leaders are either transactional or transformational. Taggart and Robey (1981) posit that managers are either left-brained or right-brained. Likewise, the extensive empirical literature is summarized by such categories as autocratic or democratic, directive or participative, task oriented or relations oriented, and initiating structure or consideration (Bass, 1981). Such differentiations, as pointed out earlier, are useful in focusing attention, creating meaning, and communicating. Moreover, they lend themselves to theory building, measurement, and rigorous analysis. These differentiations, however, can be problematic in at least two ways: they tend to generate implicit value judgments and carry a bias toward a static orientation. Each of these problems is discussed further below.

First, categorical differentiations give rise to implicit value judgments. For example, the first element in each of the bipolarities discussed above (Theory X, transactional, left-brained, auto-cratic, directive, task oriented, initiating structure) tends to be associated with such notions as orderliness, control, rationality, direction, and procedure. In contrast, the second element in each bipolarity (Theory Y, transformational, right-brained, demo-cratic, participative, relations oriented, consideration) tends to be associated with such notions as looseness, flexibility, spon-taneity, trust, and development. Because people often inherently value one of these general orientations over another, they may unconsciously define one side of the bipolarity in a negative fashion and the other in a positive fashion (Hampden-Turner, 1981). As a result, they often fail to see the strengths and weak-nesses associated with both sides of the bipolarity. Hence in the leadership examples given earlier, the order/control/stability ele-ments tend to be seen as "traditional" management and the flex-ibility/spontaneity/development elements tend to be viewed as "enlightened" management. In such cases, one side of the bipolar-ity comes to be seen, assumed, or even formally defined as "bet-ter" than the other. Consequently, the analytical power of the "negative" category is lessened and the capacity to observe any creative tension that may exist between bipolarities tends to be-come lost (Hampden-Turner, 1981; Bobko, 1985).

Even if the positive-negative valuation is controlled, by establishing a clearly positive definition at each end of the bi-polarity, a second problem can emerge. Because of the bipolar structure, the differences between the categories tend to become heightened. The interpretation of the relationship between the bipolar elements is viewed from a static, rather than dynamic, perspective. Situations are seen as either flexible or controlled, spontaneous or planned—never simultaneously both. As a result, the creative tensions and developmental tendencies that occur when bipolar concepts are integrated become hidden from the view of the observer.

The notion of interpenetration of bipolar concepts helps overcome the problems inherent in positive-negative valuations and a static orientation bias. Interpenetration is the dynamic process by which bipolar concepts become integrated. It is de-scribed below.

The Notion of Interpenetration

Interpenetration is an interesting and challenging concept. It suggests two differentiated forces or elements acting on one another in such a way that the two become part of one larger system. Where penetration suggests the dominance of one force, interpenetration suggests two strong forces or elements acting together. The idea is not entirely new. The notion of interpenetrating cultures, for example, is common in anthropology and is related to an interest in the relationship of oppositional elements in that field (Maybury-Lewis and Almagor, 1989). Moreover, in the hard sciences, it is increasingly recognized that growing systems are driven by interpenetrations (Gleick, 1987, p. 198).

In our own field, the work of Munch (1981, 1982) is particularly insightful. He reviews the role of interpenetration in Parsonian theory, arguing that few theorists understand the evolutionary nature of Parsons and that most sociologists mistakenly accept the assertions of a Parsonian order bias. Here we draw on Munch, not because we agree or disagree with his interpretation of Parsons, but because of his articulation of the notion of interpenetration.

According to Munch, the notion of interpenetration reflects the influence of Kantian transcendental philosophy on the thinking of Parsons. At the heart of Parsonian analysis are two general sets of bipolarity assumptions: orderliness and the absence of orderliness. From the juxtaposition of these oppositions, Parsons eventually develops a framework of four categories. One pair of categories contrasts instrumental and latent concerns (goal attainment versus relationships); the other contrasts integrative and adaptive concerns (stability versus change). According to Munch (1982, p. 776), these four polar differentiations are necessary in order to "analytically detach subsystems . . . from the concrete manifold of reality." With these polar differentiations in place, Parsons could analyze "subsystems as pure 'ideal types' while also studying the nature and extent of their interpenetration" (Munch, 1982, p. 773). As Munch (1981, p. 734) explains:

The fundamental theorem here is not the old doctrine of differentiation, according to which systems can increase their capacities through a process of functional differentiation, but the theorem of interpenetration, according to which only a process which allows both the greatest unfolding of the internal laws of a subsystem and the greatest amount of interpenetration with other subsystems can produce a new level of development for the subsystems and the system as a whole. *This new level of development is as much the result of the tension between the subsystems as it is the result of their unity. The interpenetration of subsystems unifies opposites and raises the threshold level of tension which the systems can accommodate while still retaining their identity and unity* [emphasis added].

According to Munch's (1981, 1982) argument, then, interpenetration is a key to understanding processes of development and higher levels of complexity. It reflects the crossing of analytic categories and the presence of creative energy. When interpenetration is consciously observed and conceptualized, the new conceptualization often recognizes the *simultaneous* operation of opposites. During interpenetration, a new system emerges from the integration of the two original differentiated systems. Consequently, as the new system emerges, the original independent systems become subsystems in a developmental process. As parts of the new system, the subsystems, individually, are able to reach new levels of performance (Russell and Branch, 1979; Halberstam, 1981). In this way, interpenetration is the process through which the potential of any system is turned into reality.

Consider an example of an interpenetration between a home and visiting team in a basketball game. Professional players often describe great games as having "magic" or inherent beauty (Russell and Branch, 1979). This attribution has nothing to do with winning or losing but with the level and quality of play (Halberstam, 1981). The level of play is typically attributed to the synergy between the two opposing teams. When players describe this synergy, they point out that individuals on both teams become inspired and fully extend themselves. Each team becomes highly cohesive, and the creative play by one team lifts the play of the other. While still distinct entities, the two teams begin to stimulate each other to higher and higher levels of performance and become joined elements in a larger, more dynamic system. The crowd, stimulated by the new level of development, also becomes part of the new system and begins to reinforce the evolution that is taking place. The observer of such an event may experience the interpenetration of the home team with the visiting team and the consequent emergence of the new and larger system; however, the observer is unlikely to have the conceptual or linguistic tools to provide a lucid description.

The Observation of Interpenetration

The comprehension of any process of interpenetration requires a complex view of polar categories, of how the categories become one, and of how new qualities emerge that reflect both of the original categories. Such comprehension means understanding both the original categories and the more complex and dynamic transformational processes by which they have become integrated. The discovery of interpenetration in a given situation usually proves to be a major breakthrough in terms of theoretical insight. For example, Munch (1981, p. 712) suggests that "only by developing such zones of interpenetration is it possible to synthesize the results of differentiated subsystems into a unified whole which would possess its own specific character and which would have more power to illuminate the world than either an undifferentiated unity or the sum of the particular subsystems themselves."

The comprehension of polarities and of interpenetration does indeed have considerable power to "illuminate the world." Rothenberg (1979), in fact, found this kind of conceptualization at the heart of many major creative breakthroughs and called it "janusian thinking" — that is, the capacity to see the operation of simultaneous opposites. However, it remains incomprehensible unless one challenges the traditional either-or assumptions and develops constructs to reflect a new and more holistic frame.

Given the above need for more holistic frames, it is useful to think about the development of theoretical or operationalized constructs of interpenetration. By removing the either-or perspective from traditional bipolarities, interesting new notions may emerge. Bobko (1985) provides an example from psychology.

Traditionally the personality constructs of masculinity and femininity were viewed as bipolar opposites on the same measurement scale. Eventually the assumed negative relationship was theoretically questioned and empirically examined. It was found that in most cases the two constructs were positively related. This finding led to the development of separate measures and the emergence of a new construct: androgyny. Androgyny refers to the strong presence of both masculinity and femininity — that is, interpenetration of two contrasting concepts of masculinity and femininity. When it first began to be discussed, androgyny seemed a strange notion for which many people had no empirical referent. Now, given its operationalization, not only are measures of the construct regularly utilized in psychology, but the term tends to be a part of our general vocabulary. In the next section, we move toward developing constructs of interpenetration in the field of managerial leadership.

Managerial Leadership:
The Instrumental-Latent Interpenetration

In the study of managerial leadership, the development of constructs similar to androgyny may be possible. As discussed earlier, many of the bipolar elements inherent in theories of managerial leadership are measured by instruments that force an either-or approach (Bass, 1981). Such measurement reflects a bias that blinds one to the more complex associations that may actually exist. Consideration and initiation of structure, for example, in the Leader Behavior Questionnaire LDBQ (Hemphill and Coons, 1957) are orthogonal factors, assumed to be uncorrelated. Yet in a review of studies using the LDBQ, Schriesheim, House, and Kerr (1976) found that in eleven of thirteen studies, positive correlations between measures were reported. In fact, the median correlation was .45. Given the high correlation between such instrumental (task) and latent (people) concerns, why has there not been more attention to their relationship? With the exception of Blake and Mouton's (1985) notion of the "9–9 manager" (a concept generally ignored by empiricists), the relationship has been overlooked. The explanation may have to do with the general incapacity to observe interpenetration at a concrete level. Hence, an illustration of interpenetration at the level of managerial leadership may be helpful.

Consider the first scene of the movie *Patton*. In this scene, Patton gives a speech to his unseasoned troops as they are about to enter the war. In the speech, Patton conveys an unmistakably clear statement of his expectations and objectives. If a typical observer of the film were asked to explain why the speech is so effective, the observer might use words like expertise, authority, goal clarity, power, distance, and intimidation. These are characteristics that tend to be associated with traditional managerial assumptions of order and control. At the surface level, these assumptions are indeed manifest. A deeper analysis, however, shows a simultaneous demonstration of characteristics associated with the opposing latent (people) notions of development, caring, and relationships.

While Patton clearly uses symbols of power and expertise (an American flag, ivory-handled pistols, a swagger stick, medals, music, and so on) that differentiate him from his troops, he simultaneously uses language and metaphor (profanity, stories reflecting and resolving their innermost fears, and so forth) that convey closeness, identity, and understanding of their feelings. While maintaining distance and an instrumental focus, he is simultaneously sensitive and responsive to their most central fears and helps them to address their anxieties about dying and showing cowardice. While simultaneously directing and caring for his men, he lifts and empowers them. In this way, Patton illustrates an interpenetration between latent (people) and instrumental (task) concerns.

This example shows that it is possible to bring about an interpenetration of opposing theoretical categories by simultaneously tending to both. Awareness of this behavioral complexity in the actor increases the cognitive complexity of the observer (Quinn, 1988). This awareness, plus the appropriate skills, could lead to increased behavioral complexity in the observer and perhaps the capacity for interpenetrations. While the typical observer might initially explain Patton's performance in terms of expertise, authority, goal clarity, power, distance, and intimidation, if made consciously aware that Patton is simultaneously demonstrating a series of behaviors from distinctly different theoretical categories, the observer is also likely to view managerial leadership from a fresh and more complex point of view. Nevertheless, the observer would still have few, if any, conceptional or linguistic tools for conveying the new awareness. As seen with the construct of androgyny, the development of such tools is critical for enhancing awareness of the potential for interpenetrations.

Managerial Leadership:
The Integrative-Adaptive Interpenetration

Like the instrumental-latent differentiation, which has received extensive attention in the organizational sciences, the differentiation between stability and change has also been widely discussed (for example, Greiner, 1972; Miller and Friesen, 1980; Tushman and Anderson, 1986; Peters, 1987; Kanter, 1988). Indeed, Gouldner (1954) differentiated the entire field of organizational analysis into two contrasting models: the equilibrium-preserving "rational model" and the developmental "natural-systems model." In a key paper, he pointed out the need to integrate the two models into a larger, more comprehensive perspective but offered little guidance on how the task might be accomplished.

Focusing on inherent problems in administrative leadership, Aram (1976) also considered the conflicting demands of stability and change. Reviewing a number of leadership studies, he clarified this differentiation between stability and change and concluded that a dominant emphasis on either traditional norms or new directions is likely to undermine the stature of a leader. In a somewhat prophetic statement, he argued that

> All organizations and groups are normative systems that have traditions, values, and stable, time-honored procedures, and today's society is anything but placid in the degree of social, economic, techno-logical, and political change. The dilemma of ad-hering to changing organizational norms, if not widely present now, is likely to become a familiar experience of organizational leadership. Managers will more and more be required to meet the twin requirements for change and stability, to be both symbol of time honored traditions and change agent for the future. In managing groups, administrators will increasingly be called upon to balance, inte-grate, or combine their organizational responsibil-ities with personal needs for stable work relation-ships. The impact of these forces is likely to be left to managers as a direct function of the general rate of national and global change [p. 118].

From a current vantage point, it appears that Aram is quite correct. Today, with the emergence of a global economy and ever more intense levels of competition, the need for orga-nizational change and innovation is clear. With such an increas-ing emphasis, however, the need for continuity in organizational experience is also becoming increasingly clear (Weick, 1990). Itami (1987) characterized these competing demands as the need for "dynamic fit" or the need for simultaneous order and chaos in effective organizations. In a recent study, for example, Jonas, Fry, and Srivastva (1990, p. 45) concluded that today's CEOs are increasingly aware of the need to "holographically" and "si-multaneously" accomplish the multiple objectives of bringing change and maintaining order: "Part of the role of the CEO is to simultaneously embody the status quo and to question it. As custodian of the firm's history, he or she strives to define the strengths of the enterprise by acting as a force for stability and an expression of its culture. Equally concerned with the future, he or she regularly asks the frame-breaking question, challenges organizational norms, and plays the maverick to stimulate creativity and innovation." Clearly not all executives do both. Many individual leaders are primarily concerned with *either* change *or* the preservation of the status quo. The observations in the study just cited, however, suggest that some executives understand the importance of doing both. Unfortunately, as with the latent-instrumental interpretation, few, if any, conceptual or linguistic tools exist for conveying this integration. Hence, the development of such tools is critical for enhancing awareness of the potential for interpenetrations.

The Need for Two Constructs of Interpenetration in Managerial Leadership

Quinn (1988) has described both the differentiation between stability and change and the differentiation between task and person. He explains how managerial leaders face contrasting expectations in their work roles and operationalizes these contrasting expectations through the differentiation of eight leadership roles. These eight leadership roles can be logically aggregated into four organizational functions and two general orientations, as shown in Figure 8.1. In this way, the roles are viewed as complementary and thereby provide a logical framework of managerial leadership.

Quinn (1988), however, does not adhere to the theoretical logic demonstrated in Figure 8.1. Rather, he focuses on the cross-functional contrasts between the roles. Consider, for example, the generally contrasting expectations of caring for people versus pursuing task completion. In caring for people, a managerial leader is expected to be a mentor and facilitator, to maintain caring relationships, to manage conflict, and to develop consensus, commitment, and morale. In pursuing the completion of a task, the managerial leader is expected to be a director and producer, to clearly initiate structure, and to stimulate productivity. The managerial leader is expected to manage these contrasting expectations by being sensitive and caring, on the one hand, and by being decisive and productive on the other.

Figure 8.1. Managerial Leadership: A Logical Framework.

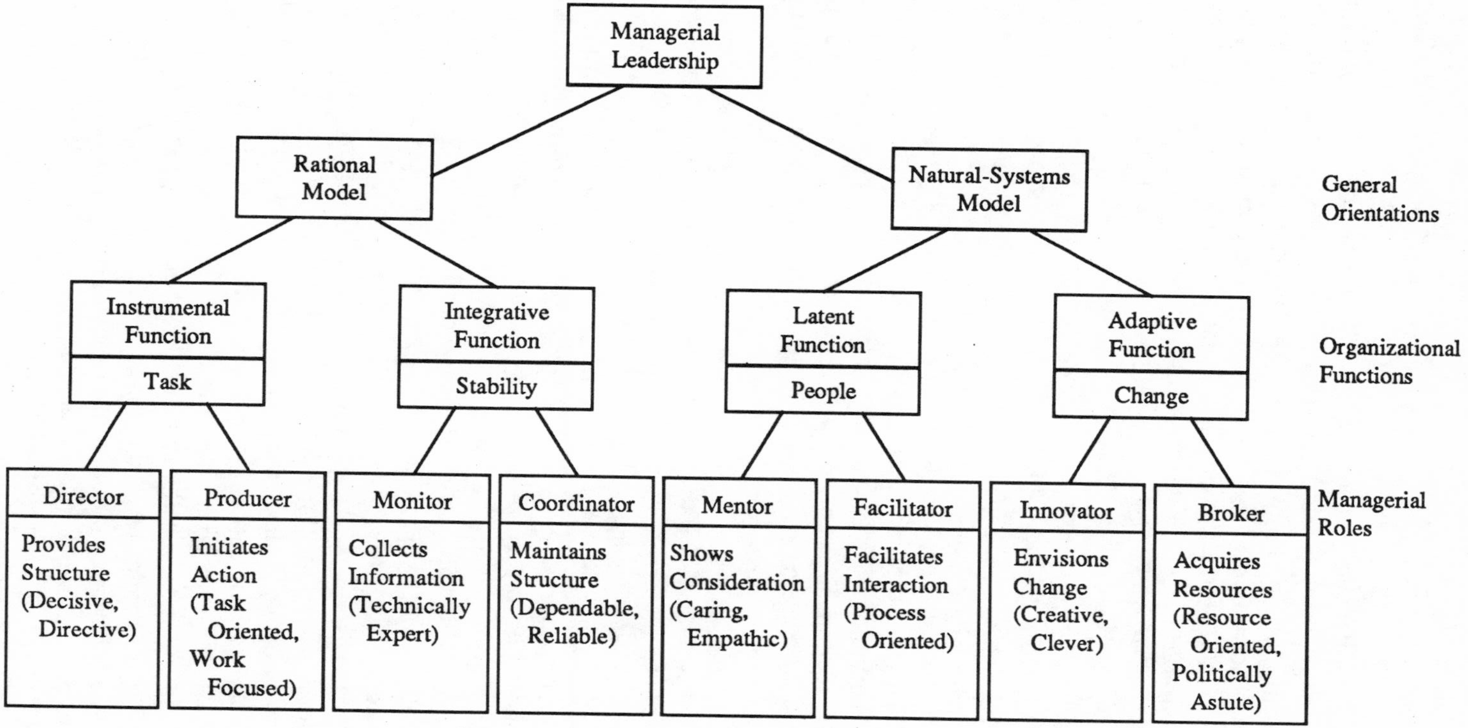

Likewise, the managerial leader is expected to manage the competing tensions between stability and change. In maintaining order, a managerial leader is expected to be a monitor and coordinator. Here the individual is expected to have detailed expertise about the internal functioning of the system and to maintain the existing structures. In contrast, in bringing change and adaptation, a managerial leader is expected to be an innovator and a broker. Here the individual is expected to envision new ideas and to influentially persuade superiors and/or outsiders to accept and support the changes by providing the necessary resources. The two sets of demands suggest the need to be knowledgeable, loyal, and credible, on the one hand, and creative, clever, and persuasive, on the other. Taken together, they suggest the need for a level of cognitive and behavioral complexity that allows for a managerial leader to transcend the paradoxical tension (Quinn and Cameron, 1988). Thus, constructs to reflect these two managerial leadership interpenetrations need to be developed.

Here we offer two new constructs that may assist in the development of a more complex understanding of managerial leadership: tough love and practical vision. These two constructs are depicted visually in Figure 8.2.

Tough love reflects the dynamic tension between task accomplishment and group cohesion. The two forces, which are shown on the vertical and horizontal axes of the top diagram in Figure 8.2, are in continuous interaction. When accomplishment is high and cohesion is low, conflict tends to emerge. When cohesion is high and accomplishment is low, collusion tends to occur. The interpenetration between accomplishment and cohesion is labeled tough love. To create this new system or interpenetration, the leader must attend to both task and people and do so simultaneously. Such a leader, like Patton, must be able to reach out and support people, while also demanding the best they can give, must see that the interests of each individual and the overall values of the group are mutually reinforcing, and must reward both individual productivity and cohesive accomplishment. For a description of actual organizations that accomplish this interpenetration, see Kiefer and Senge (1984) and Harrison (1983).

The second interpenetration depicted in Figure 8.2 is *practical vision*. It recognizes that organizational responsiveness is the result of a continuous dynamic between stability and inno-

Figure 8.2. Two Constructs of Interpenetration.

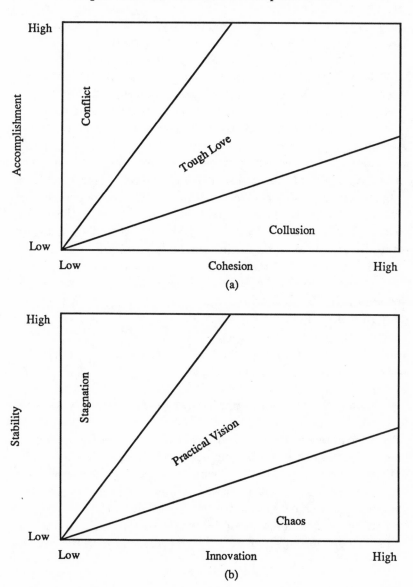

vation. When stability is high and innovation is low, the organization faces the danger of becoming unresponsive and stagnant. In contrast, when stability is low and innovation is high, the organization faces the danger of disintegration through chaos. When both stability and innovation are high, a new system or interpenetration may occur. Here stability reinforces innovation and innovation reinforces stability. The result is the experience of organizational continuity *and* growth.

During this interpenetration, at the individual level, individuals have a sense of security in their alignment with and commitment to the organization. This is accomplished by a managerial leader who builds credit by conforming to the norms of the group and then draws from and builds on that credit by introducing ever larger changes (Hollander, 1958; Merei, 1958). Such a leader is also likely to create a sense of commitment to a meaningful and motivational strategic intent. Here the existing structures and processes become a means by which change can occur because the organization member understands and accepts the mission and vision of the organization. In this way, stability and innovation begin to stimulate one another. To create such a mindset, a managerial leader must be both visionary and credible. Such a managerial leader must solve short-term problems in the unit while maintaining a long-term perspective in terms of organizational vision, must develop structures and plans while being open and responsive to new opportunities, and must maintain both a technical-operational and a strategic-political orientation.

Managerial Leadership: A Paradoxical Perspective

With the above constructs of interpenetration, we can introduce a new framework of managerial leadership (see Figure 8.3). The hierarchical relationship between the roles and the functions is unchanged. The diagram, however, does not join the traditionally complementary functions but instead unites the oppositional functions (that is, instrumental-latent and integrative-adaptive). This integration of oppositional functions results in the two interpenetrations: tough love and practical vision.

Figure 8.3. Managerial Leadership: A Paradoxical Framework.

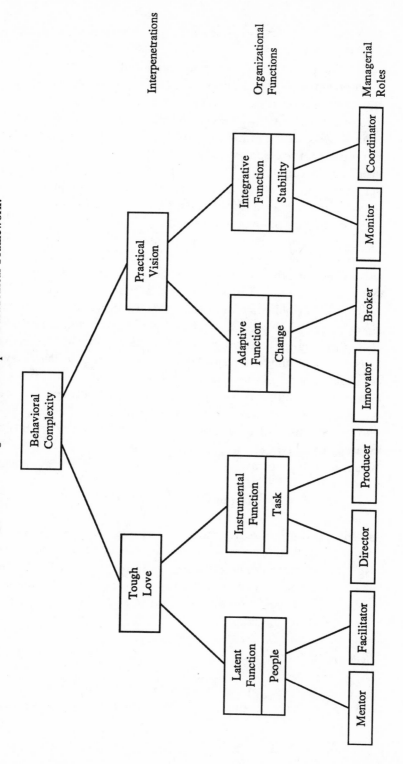

The paradoxical framework in Figure 8.3 contrasts with the logical framework in Figure 8.1. Figure 8.1 shows a hierarchy of distinct categories, a clear set of conceptualizations or ideal types. These may be well suited to the task of traditional analysis. According to Munch (1981, 1982), however, such ideal types inhibit the discovery of interpenetrations or second-order processes brought about by the interplay of oppositional categories. Interpenetration, as we have seen, requires a high degree of complexity in our thinking and seldom occurs in the social sciences. Figure 8.3 expands our thinking because it distorts the hierarchical logic illustrated in Figure 8.1 by joining not the complementary functions but the oppositional functions. This is done by introducing the two proposed interpenetrations into the diagram. Figure 8.3 suggests that some cognitively complex managerial leaders may exist who perceive their organizations not only as logical structures but also as dynamic processes that fully engage contradiction and conflict. Consequently, by masterfully managing the processes in counterintuitive ways, managerial leaders may be able to create new systems that will continually vitalize the organization. Such managers are behaviorally complex. Behavioral complexity includes cognitive complexity and is the ability to act out a cognitively complex strategy by playing multiple, even competing, roles in a highly integrated and complementary way.

Exploring Tough Love and Practical Vision

In this section, we are interested in an initial exploration of these two types of interpenetration. Our questions include the following: (1) What are the behaviors associated with tough love and practical vision? (2) Are tough love and practical vision related to managerial performance? We develop some hypotheses in the pages that follow.

Behavioral Correlates

As noted earlier, Jonas, Fry, and Srivastva (1990) report that today's CEOs see the management of competing values as crucial to their success as executives. They suggest that "the executive experience is more holographic than linear, more concerned with accomplishing multiple objectives simultaneously than discrete objectives sequentially" (p. 45). We extend these arguments to managers in general. In today's fast-changing environment, the ability to manage competing values is considered a critical competence for effective managerial practice (Cameron, Freeman, and Mishra, 1991). Managers skilled in tough love and practical vision, by definition, should exhibit high versatility. Tough love should require managers with the capacity to build cohesion, stimulate productivity, or create an interpenetration between the two. Practical vision should require managers who exhibit stabilizing behaviors, innovating behaviors, or both simultaneously. In short, such managers must be versatile and have more capacity to react effectively to a changing environment. This suggests the following hypothesis:

> H1. The interpenetrating constructs of practical vi-
> sion and tough love exist and can be validly
> and reliably measured.

Managerial Performance

Given their higher level of versatility, we would expect managers with capability in either tough love or practical vision to be highly effective. Indeed, the managers themselves, like their subordinates, peers, and superiors, should see such behavioral capability as relating strongly to high performance. This leads to the following general hypotheses:

> H2. Managers exhibiting the competence of tough
> love will be associated with high performance.
> H3. Managers exhibiting the competence of prac-
> tical vision will be associated with high per-
> formance.

Two aspects of performance are of particular importance — charisma and depth of change. In other words, interpenetration should affect the extent to which managers are perceived as charismatic and committed to deep, "second-order" change within the organization. Hypotheses are developed for each of these elements below.

Charisma. While the literature on charismatic leadership tends to emphasize inspiration, vision, and change (Bass, 1985), it has been shown that successful charismatics must also maintain credibility around the vision they present and be able to implement and manage that vision (Nadler and Tushman, 1990). To make changes, individuals must be provided with a sense of security and stability to enable them to take risks and attempt new behaviors. By definition, the practical visionary is engaged in efforts directed at both change and stability. We expect, then, that managers demonstrating such capability will be viewed as highly charismatic.

Charismatic leaders have an action orientation; they like to be in charge and to make things happen (Conger, 1989). At the same time, however, they must also build trust and commitment (Conger and Kanungo, 1987). Charismatic leaders must push for new standards of exertion while also showing concern. They build cohesive norms that reflect higher standards. We expect, then, that managers demonstrating capacity for tough love will also be viewed as highly charismatic. Thus, we hypothesize that

> H4. Managers exhibiting the competence of practical vision will be perceived to be highly charismatic.
>
> H5. Managers exhibiting the competence of tough love will be perceived to be highly charismatic.

Depth of Change. Second-order change is deep change. It tends to challenge the status quo. It can be described as multidimensional, multilevel, discontinuous, revolutionary, and irreversible (Levy, 1987). Kanter (1988) suggests that radical innovation (essentially second-order change) requires both a vision for change *and* a sense of stability and the continuity of people. A vision without continuity and stability tends to produce few results. By definition, a practical vision requires individuals who embrace change, who choose to break from the status quo, yet who are able to maintain a sense of stability and security for others as change occurs. Given that they are able to provide stability and coordination in the face of uncertainty, they may be more able and willing to undertake deeper, second-order changes.

In a similar way, we suggest that managers demonstrating tough love capability are also likely to attempt deeper, second-order change. Tough love produces high standards of performance and stimulates the development of new norms that support those standards. Such managers, with their goal-focused action orientation and their people skills, may also be more able and willing to engage second-order change. Thus it is hypothesized that

> H6. Managers exhibiting the competence of practical vision will tend toward second-order change efforts and have more successful change outcomes.
>
> H7. Managers exhibiting the competence of tough love will tend toward second-order change efforts and have more successful change outcomes.

An initial attempt to investigate each of the seven hypotheses follows.

Managerial Leadership and the Problem of Measurement

The two interpenetrations provide a somewhat radical twist to our normal thinking about organizations and managerial leadership. As a result, they are particularly troublesome as we consider the problem of measurement. In addition to providing a theoretical conceptualization of practical vision and tough love, in this chapter we are also concerned with developing reliable and valid measures for these constructs. As was illustrated through the androgyny example, the measurement of the interpenetration of masculinity and femininity substantially hastened the process by which the new concept became legitimated in the field.

Validation is typically assessed through the convergence of independent procedures (Campbell and Fiske, 1959). Validity is enhanced through substantial agreement among independent measures of a given phenomenon. We develop and discuss three independent scales of both tough love and practical vision in the following paragraphs.

Methodology

Three independent measures of our two interpenetrations and several measures of perceived managerial performance were used to construct a survey instrument given to a sample of middle managers to help us explore the validity of the new constructs and of our hypotheses, discussed earlier.

Sample

The sample population used in measuring the new interpenetrations consisted of 522 middle managers from a Fortune 10 company who attended an executive education program at the University of Michigan's School of Business Administration. Sample-selection processes within the company followed a near-random process; thus, the 522 managers formed a representative sample of the organization's middle-management population, which is approximately 3,000 in total. These managers were 94 percent male, with a median age of about forty-five years and a mean of fifteen years of company service. They were equally representative of each function in the organization. Approximately ten people (including the manager himself or herself and a number of superiors, peers, and subordinates) assessed each of the managers in the sample. Instruments were mailed to the managers six weeks prior to their attendance in the program. The managers' co-workers were instructed to return their assessments directly to the university. In this way, confidentiality was ensured and protected. (To remain consistent with the essay style of this volume, certain data supporting this empirical study have been omitted. For details pertaining to scale construction, reliability, and the construct validity of the measures and findings reported here, the reader is urged to contact the authors at the School of Business Administration, University of Michigan, Ann Arbor, Mich. 48109–1234.)

Measures

To test the hypotheses developed above, it was necessary to develop measures of both the interpenetrations — practical vision and tough love — as well as of managerial performance.

Measures of Interpenetration. We constructed three separate measures of both practical vision and tough love. Two originated from using the competing-values framework of leadership (Quinn, 1988). This framework is depicted in the following list:

> *Integrative (stability) function* (monitoring and coordinating)
>> Monitors compliance with rules
>> Compares records and reports to detect discrepancies
>> Avoids slip-ups by carefully monitoring details
>> Keeps track of what goes on inside of the unit
> *Adaptive (change) function* (brokering and innovating)
>> Exerts upward influence in the organization
>> Experiments with new concepts and procedures
>> Influences decisions made at higher levels
>> Persuasively sells new ideas to higher-ups
> *Latent (people) function* (mentoring and facilitating)
>> Encourages participative decision making in the group
>> Shows concern for the needs of subordinates
>> Shows empathy and concern in dealing with subordinates
>> Treats each individual in a sensitive, caring way
> *Instrumental (task) function* (producing and directing)
>> Continually clarifies the unit's purpose
>> Makes the unit's role very clear
>> Clarifies the unit's priorities and directions

The framework specifies four complementary approaches to managerial leadership and contrasts the adaptive or change-oriented functions (brokering and innovating) with the integrative or stability-oriented functions (monitoring and coordinating). It also contrasts the instrumental or task functions (producing and directing) with the latent or people functions (mentoring and facilitating). The validity of using this framework to operationalize four complementary measures of managerial behavior — that is, change, stability, people, and task orientations — has been shown elsewhere (Quinn, Denison, and Hooijberg, 1990). By partitioning the sample scores on each of the four scales in the list into high, medium, and low categories and then combining the stability and change (or people and task) scores to get high-high, high-low, low-high, and low-low groupings, a measure of interpenetration (high-high cases) could be assigned for both. We refer to these as the *partitioned* measures. We created a second set of measures for practical vision and tough love by using a formulation developed by Bobko and Schwartz (1984) for integrating bipolar concepts. They developed an equation for constructing an index of integrative balance between two contrasting dimensions — for example, stability versus change or people versus task. Their formulation distinguishes individuals who are high and balanced across contrasting dimensions from those who are either low or unbalanced across the dimensions. Scale scores from the two sets of bipolar functional orientations in the preceding list (stability with change and people with task) were thus converted to interpenetration scores. We refer to these as the *Bobko* measures.

A third measure of both practical vision and tough love was a scale composed of items shown in the following list that assess the extent to which individuals exhibit simultaneously contrasting leadership behaviors:

> *Tough love* (integrative stability and adaptive change functions)
>
> Works to have an alignment of individual and group values so that the unit is a team
> Sees that each group member has a clear role to play

and that each member also feels like a crucial part of
a cohesive team

Is sensitive to the concerns of others but also has high standards of performance for those others

Reaches out to support people while also demanding the
best they can give

Sees that the interests of each individual and overall values
of the group are mutually reinforcing

Practical vision (instrumental task and latent people functions)

Has an expert's understanding of the system's inner workings and a prophet's vision of what the system could
become

Solves short-term problems in the unit while maintaining a long-term perspective on where the organization
is going

Develops structures and plans while being open and responsive to new opportunities

Tends to be as comfortable in analyzing day-to-day details
as he or she is in conceptualizing exciting new ideas

Has both a technical-operational and a strategic-political
orientation

Organizes and structures things while also remaining responsive to changing conditions and situations

Here we hypothesized that two factors emerge, each containing six items. We submitted the items to a confirmatory factor
analysis. After dropping one item, we confirmed the two factors. A scale was created from each factor. We refer to these
scales as the *factored* measures of interpenetration.

Measures of Managerial Performance. Given the diverse jobs
represented across the sample of middle managers, no common
objective measures of effectiveness were available. Therefore,
we used several measures of perceived performance (Luthans,
Welsh, and Taylor, 1988). First, we employed a measure of
perceived overall performance; this measure was originally

reported by Quinn, Faerman, and Dixit (1988) and was in a semantic differential format. High scores on this measure indicated perceived overall performance, a judgment made about all managers and critical to political support (Turner, 1960; Landy, Barnes-Farell, Vance, and Steel, 1980; Quinn, Faerman, and Dixit, 1988). The five individual items reflected overall effectiveness judgments in terms of performance standards, overall success, comparison to peers, performance as a role model, and overall effectiveness as a manager.

The measure of charisma was adapted from a factor originally reported in Bass (1985). Six items were modified to a semantic differential format. They reflected the capacity to impact feelings, raise optimism, create a belief that obstacles can be overcome, inspire, raise effort level, and excite through vision.

As described above, second-order change is deep, multifaceted change. We used a scale composed of three individual items (assessing a focus on discontinuous change, a new paradigm, and irreversible change) to measure second-order change attempts. The individual measures were taken from Levy (1987).

We used five scales to assess the outcomes of the change efforts. These five scales were developed from a series of structured interviews with a different sample of middle managers from the same organization. In the interviews, the managers were asked to describe a change in their unit that they personally initiated. Then they were asked about the scope and extent of their change attempt and the types of outcomes that resulted from the initiative. We developed the individual items from the answers the managers provided on these questions. We factor analyzed the individual outcome measures, and five outcome factors emerged. Scales were created for each factor. The outcome scales include improved communication, improved organizational outcomes, new vision, improved morale, and process improvement. Table 8.1 provides the overall mean for each scale as well as the individual items comprising the scales.

Through an examination of the mean of each of the outcome scales and from discussions with respondents about the

Table 8.1. Outcomes of Change Initiatives:
Factors and Mean Scores.

Overall sample mean	Factor
4.16	Increased communication
	Increased communication between levels
	Increased communication between functions
4.00	Improved organizational outcomes
	Improvement in product quality
	Enhanced bottom line
3.89	New vision
	Developed new ways of thinking about change and innovation
	Set precedents for future action
	The initiative became a model for future change efforts
3.89	Improved morale
	Better morale of work group
3.28	Process improvement
	Reduction in complexity
	Simplification of process
	Reduction in need for overtime
	Shortened cycle time

meaning of these outcomes, we learned that some outcomes are fairly typical of most change efforts. For example, both improved communication and enhanced organizational outcomes had means of 4 or above on a 5-point scale. These outcomes were highly general and were described by respondents as easy to claim. Process improvement, on the other hand, had a much lower mean—only 3.28 on a 5-point scale. Individuals described this type of outcome as the deepest and most substantive type of change outcome—that is, as system change. The remaining two outcomes, new vision and improved morale, had average means (that is, 3.89) and were described as moderate changes in the discussions with respondents. Thus, from the examination of the means and qualitative findings, we noted that the five outcome scales seemed to be on a continuum from minor, highly typical change outcomes to deeper, more substantive, system changes.

Analysis and Results

In analyses not reported here, we confirmed the construct validity and reliability of the three interpenetrating constructs of practical vision and tough love, which provided support for Hypothesis 1. Because the Bobko measures have a number of methodological strengths and since reasonable convergent validity between the three measures of interpenetration existed, we used the Bobko measures in the subsequent analyses. The results were similar, though not quite as significantly predictive, when the analyses were run with either the partitioned measures or the factored measures. To assess Hypotheses 2 to 7, we examined the correlations between the Bobko measures of both practical vision and tough love and the dependent variables specified in the hypotheses (see Table 8.2). Significant, positive correlations will indicate support for the specified relationships between variables.

In support of Hypothesis 2, the practical vision scale was found to be significantly and positively correlated to managerial performance assessments by the managers' subordinates, peers, and superiors. It was not, however, significantly correlated to self-perceptions of managerial performance.

In support of Hypothesis 3, tough love was found to be significantly and positively correlated to managerial performance assessments by the managers' subordinates, peers, and superiors. It was not, however, significantly correlated to self-perceptions of managerial performance.

In support of Hypothesis 4, the correlations between practical vision and self- and peer assessments of charisma were found to be positive and significant at the .01 level. Subordinate assessments of charisma were found to be positive and significant at the .001 level, and assessments of charisma by the managers' superiors was positive and significant at the .05 level.

In support of Hypothesis 5, the correlations between tough love and subordinate and peer assessments of charisma were positive and significant at the .001 and .01 levels, respectively. As with practical vision, assessments of charisma by the managers' superiors was also positive and significant at the .05 level.

Table 8.2. Correlations of Hypothesized Relationships.

	Practical vision	Tough love
Managerial performance		
Managerial Performance (Self-assessment)	.04	.05
Managerial Performance (Subordinates' assessment)	.59[a]	.61[a]
Managerial Performance (Peers' assessment)	.20[a]	.27[a]
Managerial Performance (Superiors' assessment)	.21[a]	.23[a]
Charisma		
Charisma (Self-assessment)	.14[b]	.04
Charisma (Subordinates' assessment)	.52[a]	.56[a]
Charisma (Peers' assessment)	.15[b]	.21[b]
Charisma (Superiors' assessment)	.13[c]	.13[c]
Second-order change		
Second-order change	.40[a]	.13
Change outcomes		
Improved communication	.00	−.05
Improved organizational outcomes	.14	−.01
New vision	.11	.05
Improved morale	−.12	−.10
Process improvement	.32[b]	.26[c]

[a]Correlation significant at $p < .001$ level.
[b]Correlation significant at $p < .01$ level.
[c]Correlation significant at $p < .05$ level.

The correlation with self-assessments of charisma, however, was not significant.

In support of Hypothesis 6, positive and significant relationships (at the .01 level) were found between practical vision and second-order change. Of the five outcome scales, only the deepest change outcome, process improvement, was significantly related to practical vision.

Partial support was also found for Hypothesis 7. Hypothesis 7 posited that managers exhibiting tough love capability will attempt more second-order changes and will have successful change outcomes. No relationship was found between tough love and second-order change attempts. However, tough love was found to be related to the specific outcome of process improvement.

Discussion

The results presented here suggest strongly that practical vision and tough love contribute to effective managerial performance. They suggest behavioral complexity; that is, high-performing managers must have the ability to integrate the competing tensions between stability and change and between task and person. These managers must be able to be change masters, to be innovators, to be entrepreneurs, and to be transformational leaders, but at the same time, they must provide stability, security, and a sense of equilibrium to a changing system. Similarly, these managers must be instrumental, bottom-line focused, while at the same time concerned about the development and nurturing of their people. Thus, both practical vision and tough love become important concepts for understanding high-performing managerial behavior.

Interestingly, the results are strongest for subordinate, peer, and superior assessments of managers' behavior, yet self-assessments of practical vision and tough love generally show little relationship to perceived effectiveness. A possible explanation of this phenomenon is that such "master" managers are humble and show greater concern for organizational success than for personal success. A more likely explanation, however, pertains to the structure of reward systems. Since our dependent variables were either global in nature (effectiveness) or concerned with empowerment and transformation (charisma and second-order change), there is little relationship between these measures and the criteria used for performance appraisal and rewards in the company (for example, meeting objectives, performing to standard). The self-assessments may reflect benchmarking against these more formal criteria, and the message is that tough love and practical vision are not capabilities and behaviors that are formally rewarded within the organization.

Finally, while both interpenetrations were generally associated with all the outcomes, practical vision showed a particularly strong relationship to second-order change, whereas tough love was not significantly correlated with this outcome. Practical vision obviously seems to relate more to the paradigm and strategy of the overall organization than does tough love, which focuses more directly on the immediate work experience. By developing outcome measures that focus at different levels of organizational performance (for example, individual, work team, department, program, division, corporation), it may be possible to identify other significant differences between the two interpenetrations. Thus, while tough love and practical vision both seem to contribute strongly to effectiveness as operationalized here, each capability may produce rather different sets of positive outcomes for the organization.

Implications for Theory and Management

We have introduced the concept of interpenetration—that is, the integration of bipolar concepts. This concept provides us with a new, more complex way of looking at the world. It challenges our deeply ingrained either-or assumptions by suggesting a both-and perspective. Managers can be both transformational and transactional. Organizations can be both mechanistic and organic. Tasks can be both creative and routine.

This type of both-and thinking expands our horizons about the way we think about the world. The observation of interpenetration aids in the conceptualization of new phenomena. In this chapter, the observation of the process of interpenetration of the seemingly opposing concepts of stability and change and of opposing concepts of task and person results in the development of two new constructs: practical vision and tough love.

Given the need to manage competing values and paradoxes in today's increasingly complex and rapidly changing environment, the process of interpenetration and the concepts of practical vision and tough love have important implications for managerial performance. However, most existing models of management emphasize not only either-or thinking but also a static view of management—the attainment of "fit" or "consistency" among the various elements of the organization (Peters and Waterman, 1982; Galbraith and Kazanjian, 1986). While it may be possible to achieve "strategic alignment" in a stable environment, today's high-velocity competitive reality renders such thinking dangerously inadequate. This has been reflected in recent writings that advocate "thriving on chaos"—the need for perpetual change and innovation (Peters, 1987). The results of this study suggest that both schools of thought are correct: there is a need for both stability and change, people and task, order and chaos. This paradox is perhaps captured best by Itami's (1987) concept of "dynamic fit," which holds that the role of management in today's world is to both create and destroy balance. Management must work hard to send consistent messages and align organizational strategies, systems, and processes in order to achieve high performance; inconsistencies and mixed signals spell doom to any work organization. However, management must never allow the organization to settle into complacency. As soon as "balance" is achieved, it must be destroyed. The organization must be challenged to acquire new competencies so that it might be positioned for the future. For an organization to achieve "dynamic fit," capability must be developed deep within the company. Top managers cannot destroy balance without a knowledgeable and capable cadre of middle managers.

Many companies are beginning to recognize the critical role of middle managers. At one Fortune 100 company, for example, the middle-managerial development program frames managerial leadership as the ability to manage competing values and implicitly emphasizes the importance of acknowledging paradox and interpenetration for growth and survival in a turbulent world. We suspect that the concept of interpenetration will be indispensable to effectiveness in the years ahead and that managers and scholars alike will ignore it at their own peril.

Chapter Nine

Balancing Continuity and Change: The Constructive Tension in Individual and Organizational Development

Paul A. L. Evans

Change and continuity represent a fundamental duality in both individual and organizational development. By duality, we mean that one without the other leads to degeneration and pathology. Continuity without change leads initially to isolation and stagnation, and ultimately to unwanted change in the shape of crisis. Change without continuity leads to devitalizing stress, and the change itself turns out to be illusory and shallow. Understanding the interplay of change and continuity is one way of struggling to understand the dynamics of individual and organizational life, the vitality of social systems.

How can this duality be resolved? How can such a duality be balanced? This is the theme of this chapter, which draws inductively on observations from two streams of research. The first concerns individual development (adult development processes, notably the balancing of the demands of professional and private life during the life cycle). The second focuses on organizational development processes, particularly within complex multinational corporations in highly competitive environments. The underlying argument is that the change-continuity duality cannot be resolved unless we recognize that it mirrors the wider dualities in human nature and social organization.

The Dualities in Individual and Organizational Development

Let me begin by introducing these two areas of inquiry and explaining how the concept of duality emerged from each.

Balancing the Demands of Professional and Private Life

The awareness of the dualities in life dynamics emerged initially in a series of studies aimed at understanding the relationship between professional and private life (Evans and Bartolomé, 1979, 1986; Bartolomé and Evans, 1980). An initial survey of 522 managers showed that 45 percent of them felt that their lifestyles were unbalanced, a percentage that remained stable in later surveys covering 14,600 predominantly male managers in most regions of the Western world. A major explanation for this high degree of dissatisfaction was the widespread degree of job "misfit": if a person did not fit with the job requirements in the sense of competencies, needs, and motives, and deeper attitudes and values, the stresses would "spill over" into life outside work, compromising the quality of private life.

However, the phenomenon was not linear: good matching of personality and job did not guarantee a healthy private life. People who fitted extremely well with their jobs ran the risk of becoming prisoners of their own psychological success. Their energies would often be channeled entirely into the world of work, family life would become a haven for recharging batteries, and they would neglect investment in their family and leisure lives.

It was here that my awareness of the dualities in social psychological dynamics started. While a poorly functioning professional life leads to imbalance since it drains energies from other domains of life, an extremely healthy professional life may similarly lead to imbalance. Dynamic balance is a question of developing a *minimum* degree of fit, satisfaction, fulfillment in a particular life arena, not a maximum degree (as Hedberg, Nystrom, and Starbuck [1976] have observed with respect to organizations). Maximizing leads to pathology — also in the literal sense of the term. Over the years, we have been collecting pension statistics that suggest that the life expectancy for late-career "prisoners of success" (individuals who have maximized their working lives) is often between ten and twenty-four months of retirement (Evans and Bartolomé, 1979).

Thus healthy adult development demands a *minimum* degree of change and a *minimum* degree of continuity. If people are confronted with too much change, they risk a degenerative pathology. An example is what we labeled the *international executive syndrome*. This is the case of the executive who accepts a challenging post abroad, despite the reluctance of the family. The stresses of new professional challenge, of learning a new language and becoming familiar with a new culture, mean that the manager has little surplus energy to invest in private life. If that private life is unstable, it too becomes a source of stress. The cumulative stress may be such that the person finds it difficult to cope with these work and family demands, leading to a degenerative vicious circle and ultimate failure in professional adaptation, marriage, or both.

Conversely, too much continuity leads to pathology. The studies of Katz and Van Maanen (1976) on job satisfaction confirmed what most of us know, that people tend to get bored with their jobs after a five- to seven-year period. (More specifically, Katz and Van Maanen found that the relationship between job satisfaction and the properties of motivating jobs as hypothesized by Hackman and Oldham [1980] declines sharply between the fourth and seventh year in a position.) Excessive continuity leads to frustration, absence of fulfillment, and downright boredom. Our studies of professional and private life found that people renew themselves either by changing job or company, or by looking for compensatory challenge in other arenas of life. Their hobbies, for example, become their careers, and their attitude toward work shifts from an intrinsic to an instrumental orientation.

Indeed, I have come to suspect that there is a five- to seven-year cycle in life. Individual differences left aside, people tend to get bored with jobs during this period, as mentioned above. Professors who do not renew their jobs via the sabbatical (by long-standing tradition every five to seven years) run the risk of going stale. And the seven-year itch in marriage also exists, as we discovered when researching divorce statistics (Evans and Bartolomé, 1979). While a marriage is most likely to break up in its first year, the other peaks in the divorce statistics are found after seven, thirteen, and twenty-three years of marriage—reflecting a rough seven-year cycle. Additionally, housing and loan agencies tell me that people are most likely to change houses with which they are quite content around the seventh year, as if they feel an urge to renew their life-styles. There appears to be fertile ground for rigorous research on this issue.

Balancing Dualities in Organizational Development

Some years later, the same phenomenon surfaced in a very different area of inquiry. When concluding a series of studies on human resources management in international firms, I observed that healthy organization development also appears to involve striking a balance between dualities, some of which are listed in Table 9.1 (Evans and Doz, 1989; Evans, 1991). Almost all

Table 9.1. Some Common Dualities Confronting Organizations.

competition	— partnership
differentiation	— integration
loose	— tight
control	— entrepreneurship
planned	— opportunistic
formal	— informal
vision	— reality
decentralization	— centralization
business logic	— technical logic
analysis	— intuition
delegation	— control
individuality	— teamwork
action	— reflection
change	— continuity
professional	— generalist
top-down	— bottom-up
tolerance	— forthrightness
flexibility	— focus
accountability	— interdependency

(if not all) qualities of an organization (or a human being) have a complementary opposite quality, and excessive focus on one pole of a duality ultimately leads an organization into stagnation and decline (undue continuity), while the corrective swing to the opposite pole leads to disruptive and discontinuous crisis (excessive change). Thus excessive focus on *planning* can reduce the capacity to respond to *opportunities,* while unplanned opportunism rarely yields long-term results. Excessive *formality* (systems, structures, procedures) comes at the expense of innovation, while excessive focus on *informality* (open paths of communication, reliance on project groups and networks, flexibility in budgets) may enhance innovation but at the expense of the organization's ability to capitalize profitably on breakthroughs. We saw one $5 billion corporation carried away by a grandiose vision for the future which was not rooted in reality. For two years, top management waited for the middle to deliver the reality, while middle management waited for the top to tell them what to do. *Vision* that is not grounded in reality is dangerous, but attachment to *reality* without a vision of what might be possible is stultifying.

Change and continuity constitute a duality that is at the heart of organizational governance and development processes. Genuine change in the sense of qualitative or transformational change in the system (as opposed to change in the outputs alone) paradoxically involves continuity in the implementation of that change. Let me provide two examples.

An essential element of governance is succession management. In one major multinational corporation that I studied, key executive appointments fostered a culture of "too much change and not enough implementation." The practice was to move the CEOs of the affiliate companies every two to three years, and indeed remaining in a post for more than three years was equivalent to failure labeling. This had led to "zigzag" management. The game had become one of starting a new change or improvement program in the affiliate (quality management, cost reduction, or whatever), getting it to the glamorous point of early implementation, and then riding the wave of acclaim into the next post. The grind of implementation would be left to the successor, who had no interest in this unrewarding task. He or she would turn to a new improvement program, repeating the cycle.

A second example is seen in a study we undertook of major strategic turnarounds, which showed that a recurrent problem is the loss of momentum and continuity after the initial success of the change (Farquhar, Evans, and Tawedey, 1989). The continuity that transformation requires can be illustrated by Volvo's experience. Volvo's CEO, Pehr Gyllenhammer, began a process of organizational transformation in the late 1960s — the public symbols became the humanized and high-technology auto plant at Kalmar and subsequent factories, and the devolution of headquarters (staff were cut from 1,800 to 50 persons). But one of Gyllenhammer's right-hand men said the following to me in 1986: "If Pehr Gyllenhammer had quit or retired even in the late 1970s, Volvo's culture would have quickly slid back to where it was in the 1960s. It is only now that he could retire if he wished to, fifteen years after those changes were set in motion. For it has taken that time for a new generation of middle managers to come up in the new Volvo into positions of responsibility. The only Volvo that they have known is the new Volvo, and so the changes have been institutionalized."

Similarly, I heard Jack Welsh speaking in 1989 of the changes he has brought about at General Electric in the following vein: "We started in 1981, and today we've achieved about 30 percent of what has to be done."

The Emerging Duality Paradigm

The assumption that healthy development involves the balancing of opposites is clearly seen throughout personality theory and psychotherapy. Carl Jung, whose work laid the foundations for personality theory, viewed dualities as the core of human existence. The tension between opposites is what gives life its meaning, and all psychic energy is the result of the seesawing tension between dualities. Personal wholeness or unity (what Jung called *antinomy*) is only possible via the coexistence of opposites. Smith and Berg (1987) show how dualities (or *paradoxical*

thought) are central to the work of other schools of psychotherapy — Adler, Frankl, Freud, Perls, and Rank.

The awareness of dualities in organization appears to be
of more recent origin, where the concept appeared during the
1980s under different labels: dilemma, paradox, or competing
values. While the idea of balance is not new, the notion of duality surfaced in the *loose-tight* paradox that Peters and Waterman (1982) described.

Undertaking an empirical analysis of the criteria used by
organizational researchers to assess organizational effectiveness,
Quinn and Rohrbaugh (1983) found that dualities in the shape
of "competing values" underlay these conceptualizations of organizational effectiveness. Cameron and Quinn (1988) went on
to suggest that mastering paradox is essential in managing organizational change and transformation.

Hampden-Turner (1990) argues that the essence of organizational learning and development is the ability to resolve
dilemmas that appear in changing forms: economies of scale
and of flexibility, broad markets and niche markets, short-term
pressures for profits and longer-term strategic considerations,
to name only a few. For Hampden-Turner and Baden-Fuller,
strategy becomes the process of reconciling opposites rather than
the conventional notion of choosing between alternative courses
of action. In a study of three appliance firms, they identified
nine dilemmas confronting these enterprises and measured their
ability to resolve these dualities (Hampden-Turner and Baden-
Fuller, 1989). They showed how the ability to resolve each dilemma facilitates the resolution of other dualities and leads in
turn to positive financial performance. Thus, the resolution of
dualities creates either virtuous, positive loops of organizational
performance or vicious circles of degenerating performance.

Similarly, Pascale (1990) suggests that the tension or dynamic synthesis between contradictory opposites is the engine
of self-renewal and long-term organizational effectiveness. He
traces the history of companies such as General Electric, Ford,
Honda, and Hewlett Packard, showing how some of these firms
have alternated between periods of polarized stagnation (for example, an excessive focus on decentralization) and crisis-driven

reorientation to the other pole (for instance, excessive financial control). Some enterprises such as Honda are successfully building a synthesis of opposites and harnessing the dynamism of creative tension.

It has been argued elsewhere that this duality perspective is an emerging paradigm for applied organizational theory (Evans and Doz, 1989). For the last twenty years, management thought and practice has been dominated by the "fit" or contingency paradigm, with its values of coherence and consistency and its underlying prescription of paying attention to matching processes. Conventional notions of strategic management, human resource management, sociotechnical theory, and the like are rooted in that "fit" paradigm that has proven to be increasingly inadequate in guiding management and organization in a more dynamic, competitive era. The example of that inadequacy at issue here is managing change and continuity. The fit of either to the immediate situation is likely to result in an imbalance that leads to stagnation (undue continuity) or description and crisis (undue change).

Building Dynamic Balance

What are the generic ways in which dualities can be dynamically balanced or resolved in the process of development? My assumption is that dynamic balance can only be achieved by striking a balance between change and continuity. In this sense, change-continuity constitutes a metaduality that is fundamental to our understanding of developmental processes. *Dynamic balance* is defined by the relationship between change and continuity. As we have implied, change without attention to continuity is *not* dynamic balance, and neither is continuity without change.

Conceptually, a duality can be dynamically balanced in one of two ways. First, dualities can be balanced over time by shifting attention asymmetrically from one pole to the other. Periods of change alternate with periods of continuity. Historically, this is seen in the shifting focus of organizational attention to the "hard" and "soft" aspects of management since the

Industrial Revolution (Ouchi, 1989), or in the seesawing concern with decentralization (local responsiveness) and centralization (corporate integration) during the last fifty years (Prahalad and Doz, 1987). However, these pendulum swings become more frequent as the environment becomes turbulent and complex, and it then becomes necessary to anticipate the later swing to the opposing polarity and "to build the future into the present." This we call *sequencing*.

Second, a duality can be managed by building its complexity into the organization (consider the law of requisite variety, which maintains that the complexity of a social system must reflect the complexity of its environment). This means that change and continuity are fused in the process of dualistic development rather than alternated. A state of creative tension is developed — change within continuity and continuity within change.

This can in turn be achieved in two ways. The duality can be built into the cultural fabric of the firm, a method I call *layering* since it involves building the new on top of the old. Alternatively, a duality can be resolved through the management of decision-making processes, what I call *decision architecture*. The classic notion of matrix is an example. Effective decision architecture and layering cause constructive tension to be built into the organization, though if ineffective, that tension may become conflictual and destructive.

These mechanisms for balancing a duality are not independent. Sequencing may over time lead to layering, especially if it is accompanied by appropriate decision architecture. Layering is unlikely to be effective unless it involves decision architecture.

Sequencing

Sequencing is the natural way in which dualities are experienced, as captured by the pendulum metaphor. Let me take the organizational level of analysis to outline this. Environmental forces lead developmental attention to be focused on one pole of a duality, and adaptive responses are learned or discovered. If these continue to be successful responses, they will become internalized or institutionalized as success factors. However, to the extent that this happens, the other pole of the duality is neglected, exposing the organism to weakness. Awareness of that weakness leads initially to efforts to resolve the problem via increased application of the success formula. This fails and engenders a crisis. The crisis focuses the attention of the organism on the opposite pole of the duality, leading to the discovery of new adaptive responses and a new success formula. So the cycle repeats itself. Typically, sequencing occurs spontaneously through such cycles of crisis change/evolutionary continuity/crisis change as described by Greiner (1972) and by Tushman, Newman, and Romanelli (1986). However, today the turbulence of the environment leads to the shortening of the cycle time. Organizations that used to undergo a major strategic or structural shift every twenty-five years, as described by Chandler (1969), may now experience a strategic change every three to five years. The seesaw of the pendulum gets shorter, to the point where we experience swinging fashions, as graphically described in a 1986 *Business Week* cover story, "Business Fads: What's In-and-Out."

When these swings become rapid or when the side effects of the crisis may endanger the survival of the organism, deliberate or planned sequencing becomes necessary. This involves recognizing the likely patterns of change and evolution in the future — and building the future into the present. The management processes of today are designed not only with today's operating plan in mind, but also with an eye to the inevitability of a future transition. In this way, the transition becomes a smooth process rather than a disruptive, painful, and costly crisis.

As we will see, when recognized and managed appropriately, planned sequencing leads to a *helix-type process of progressive development* in the organism (as opposed to pendulum cycles), where the poles of the duality are gradually layered into the organism in successive cycles (see Figure 9.1). In this helix process, the forces of change and continuity become fused in an ongoing process of development. Let me provide some examples drawn from research on adult and organizational developmental processes.

Figure 9.1. The Helix-Type Process of Sequenced Development.

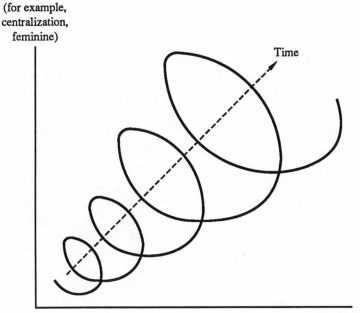

Duality Pole 1
(for example,
centralization,
feminine)

Time

Duality Pole 2
(for example,
decentralization,
masculine)

Source: Adapted from Rapoport and Rapoport, 1980; Hampden-Turner, 1990.

Sequencing in Individual Development. Sigmund Freud saw life as a struggle between dualities, one of them being the pair of love and work. Most researchers who have studied the process of adult development have come to recognize the validity behind this (Kanter, 1977; Levinson and others, 1978). While work is associated with the working career and love with marriage and parenting, this is a simplification. Many people find their deepest relationships with working colleagues, and work and active leisure are conceptually similar (Evans and Bartolomé, 1979).

Our studies of adult development processes over the life cycle showed that people balance this duality by means of sequencing (Evans and Bartolomé, 1979, 1984; also Evans and Bartolomé, 1981, 1986). Their developmental attention shifts from one arena of life to another, and these shifts in preoccupation define stages in adult development.

The idea that sequenced preoccupations define age-related stages in life development is shared by Levinson and others (1978). Each of these authors' life phases is characterized by a particular developmental focus, the resolution of which engenders a transition, leading to a next stage where developmental attention will focus on the opposite pole that has previously been neglected. When the individual fails to resolve a developmental preoccupation at a particular life phase, the transition may take the form of crisis (for example, the midlife crisis).

The origins of this sequenced concept of life development go back to Carl Jung and were first popularized in the work of Erik Erikson (1968). However, Klinger (1977) provides the clearest theoretical statement of sequenced preoccupations in life. The core of Klinger's (1977, pp. 53, 54) theory of psychological functioning is that "people are sensitized to those cues in their environment that relate to their current concerns. . . . One travels through one's world of stimulation ignoring most of it, processing primarily those features of it that fit into one or more current concerns." At a particular stage in life, the current concern will be a specific pole of a developmental duality.

Until recently, most people launched a series of different "careers" in the short space of ten years, between the ages of twenty and thirty: a work career and active leisure interests, and a marital and a parenting career as well as social friendships. Yet it is impossible to cope with all these developmental tasks at the same time. People undertake this consciously or unconsciously through sequenced development.

In the 1970s, the typical sequenced pattern that we observed empirically in adult male managers was as follows. In their mid twenties to mid thirties, the prime focus of attention was on launching the working career. These younger managers were less sensitive to conflict, tension, and unhappiness in their relationships with their spouses; their self-image and self-esteem were more wrapped up in professional life. This preoccupation is reflected in the fact that career success leads at this stage to renewed striving for further success (polarized focus on that pole of the love-work duality). Career failure also leads to renewed striving (Schneider and Hall, 1972); only at later stages does career failure lead to decreased work motivation. In our sample, where managers were sensitive to the parenting role, it was more to the pain and trauma of childrearing than to the joys of sharing in the development of the children. However, there was typically a shift in developmental preoccupation among managers in their mid thirties to early forties. Attention now focused more on private life. "Am I really fulfilled in my marriage?" This question would often spark a process that we called "the renegotiation of the marriage." In the words of one such manager, "How do I spend my weekends? With my boat and friends, despite the fact that my wife and children hate sailing? Or with the family? That's far more of a dilemma than anything I experience at work."

The important point here is that the transition is more likely to take the shape of crisis to the extent that the future has not been built into the present (that is, the need for sequenced rebalancing has not been anticipated). If the preoccupation with the work career has been excessive and polarized at the previous stage, the transition is likely to be painful. For example, we observed that some younger managers who experience marital or family problems subjugate these tensions by "escaping back into the world of work." This behavior in turn aggravates the tensions, leading ultimately to premature crisis rather than transition. A growing number of individuals seem to be aware of this sequencing, leading them to decide to postpone marriage and parenting until such time as their work careers are established.

Transition may also be difficult if the life development task in the previous stage has not been adequately resolved. If the work career has not been satisfactorily launched or "anchored" (to use the term of Schein, 1978), developmental attention will be diffused across two life tasks, compromising the chances of success in either.

The preceding description is only an illustration of sequencing dynamics. The precise pattern of sequencing reflects social norms rather than human nature. The typical pattern for women may be different from that of men, and the content of the pattern is certainly changing since our late-1970s data.

The process of sequencing applies to personality development as well as to coping with the love-work duality. Levinson and others (1978) show how the midlife transition can best be conceptualized as the task of rebalancing polarities. Building on the earlier insights of Jung, Levinson's longitudinal study of forty men showed that the early years of adulthood are characterized by polarized development on salient dualities: masculine as opposed to feminine, attachment as opposed to separateness, young as opposed to old. The task in the midlife transition is that of facing up to the shadow side of the duality and achieving generativity (to employ Erikson's [1968] term) via the integration of duality. That integration is analogous to the concept of layering that we will turn to later. Through helix-type development, successful sequencing leads ultimately to layered integration (Rapoport and Rapoport, 1980).

Sequencing in Organizational Development. As mentioned earlier, organizations develop naturally through alternating cycles of crisis and evolution. Sequencing implies that although the precise content and timing of future shifts may be uncertain and unplannable, it is quite predictable that the future will require a focus on the opposite and complementary pole of attention. In this sense, the future can be prepared by building it into the present, thereby ensuring transition rather than crisis. Let us provide some examples to illustrate this.

A first example is the development of Apple Computers (Evans and Farquhar, 1989). The interesting question about Apple is not why it has grown in fifteen years to become a $6 billion enterprise. The more interesting question is why it has *survived* in an industry where there are only twenty survivors out of more than 200 entrants. This leads to two relevant examples of sequencing.

In the volatile microcomputer industry, predicting and anticipating competitor reactions, technological changes, and the like is difficult. But certain dualistic cycles are quite predictable. One is that every successful upturn will be followed by a downturn. If the downturn in the cycle has not been anticipated at the time of growth, if the organization has been mesmerized and polarized by the excitement of expansion, the downturn may well force the company into a crisis of survival (takeover or liquidation).

During its early years, Apple learned to build the future downturn into its present growth. After some years of heady expansion, the entry of IBM into the personal computer market led to the first major downturn and crisis. Survival was touch-and-go, ensured only by major layoffs and the successful development of the MacIntosh. From that trauma, Apple Computers learned a lesson that guaranteed its survival in successive future downturns. During periods of growth, it put aside a "rainy day" cash fund of $500 million that would guarantee that it could manage in the troughs as well as at the peaks.

Furthermore, Steve Jobs, whose technical brilliance had led to the early success of the firm, anticipated early that personal computers would become a marketing commodity. He successfully initiated a sequenced change in the culture of the firm that was symbolized by the recruitment of John Sculley from Pepsi Cola. This was a case of sequencing rather than layering, since the shift to marketing was to some extent at the expense of technical excellence.

The recent wave of downsizing in the United States provides a negative example of poor sequencing. As Hampden-Turner (1990, p. 71) points out, "What is fashionably called 'restructuring' is the butchery that follows five to ten years of folly." A decade of successful growth had led many firms into complacent habits of poor management, where latent problems were ignored as long as profits were coming in. Finally, the productivity and competitive squeeze from foreign competition led to a radical swing in the opposing direction. In many U.S. firms, we experienced wave upon wave of downsizing, restructuring, and layoffs. That in turn now appears to be generating a new problem for the 1990s. The good old-fashioned loyalty and long-term commitment of employees is replaced by a short-term and cynical "everyone-for-themselves" mentality in an increasingly contingent workforce. Under these circumstances, as anyone versed in the human capital school of economics will point out, investment in staff training and development makes poor business sense (employees will jump ship, and it is competitors who will benefit from the investment). This reinforces short-term action to cope with increasing competition, and the next crisis builds up.

The management of large-scale projects is a more concrete and positive example of planned sequencing. It is now well known that the leadership and structure of a project at one stage in its development are not necessarily effective at its next stage. The requirements at the research stage of a project to develop a new aircraft differ from those at the prototype engineering stage, which differ in turn from those at the production stage (Galbraith, 1972). To facilitate a smooth flow in project development (thereby avoiding the excesses of either continuity or change), the engineering manager who will assume leadership in the prototype phase should be a member of the initial research team, which is led at that stage by a more entrepreneurial individual. Indeed, massive projects such as building an oil refinery go through some six differentiated stages over ten years, each requiring a different team, with the final team being those persons who will actually run the refinery. In-company research at a major oil corporation showed that it was profitable to include key members from all future teams, including the ultimate operating team, in the initial design group. People would be phased out rather than phased in. In this way, change is built into continuity, while continuity in change is ensured.

The necessity for sequencing is clear in project management, since the notion of sequenced evolution is part of the concept of a project. But I am suggesting that businesses themselves should be seen as projects, which leads to another example— that of the development of the IBM personal computer (Evans and Doz, 1989). IBM had twice failed in projects to develop the PC in its constraining mainstream environment. As is well known, this succeeded only when the PC project was spun off as a separate business unit, with relaxed checks and controls and a certain autonomy over hiring and procedures. But the reluctance of IBM to relax all controls proved inadvertently to be essential to success in the next stage of PC development, namely the integration of the PC project business unit and its new technology into the mainstream of IBM as part of a network for data processing. If such a venture unit is allowed *total* freedom over budgets, salaries, and personnel practices (as opposed to the minimal freedom that is necessary), the later problems of integration may be horrendous. Key technical and managerial staff, hired from the outside or accustomed to high autonomy and generous bonuses, may choose to quit the firm. In the IBM case, the policies and controls of the mother firm were relaxed rather than abandoned at the venture stage; IBM personnel practices in particular were still applied. Consequently, the reintegration was accomplished over a four-year period without major crisis. Autonomy has to be balanced with the awareness of predictable later needs for control.

Dualistic sequencing has typically been the lesson of happenstance rather than foresight, as the IBM example shows. This is seen in a last example, based on the centralization-decentralization duality. I recently studied retrospectively the seven-year history of two affiliates in a multinational group, one in Britain and the other in Germany. Prior to the 1980s, both companies had tightly integrated and centralized organizations. However, the price of such structures was slow decision making, bureaucratic rigidity, and excessive costs. In 1982, both decided to reorganize along the lines of decentralized business units and to reduce layers of management by devolving headquarters staff to these business units.

However, there was an important difference in their approaches. The British company allowed full devolution. The newly created business units were allowed to move into offices that were sometimes far from the headquarters in London but much closer to their main customers, and far cheaper than expensive London property. However, the German company had recently invested in an expensive Frankfurt main office. Their business units were allowed autonomy with a "but": they could not move out of the central headquarters building. For several years, this was a major bone of contention for the German business unit managers.

In the longer term, which company would be most successful? Most managers predict that it would be the British firm, whose approach is more thorough and coherent when evaluated by the conventional canons of "fit/consistency" theory. And indeed, short-term implementation was more speedy in Britain. However, in 1988 the failing performance of the British company led to a major review.

An important point to note here is that the results of second-order change—for example, via dualistic layering—may take some time to become apparent. Some evidence for this claim is found in a study of organizational change in eighty Finnish banks (Santalainen and Hunt, 1988). Three years after a results-oriented organizational development program, there was no observed difference in performance measures between banks that implemented this program through strategic changes as opposed to mere operational changes (first-order change). However, after six years, the former banks were significantly higher on organizational performance measures than the latter. The operational changes wear off (no continuity), whereas strategic change leads to qualitative change in the system itself.

To return to the dilemma of the British company, the review concluded that the top-management team had lost control over the company. The integrated bureaucracy had been replaced by decentralized feudal kingdoms jealously guarding their prerogatives, and the interdependencies that had been the basis for the previous integrated structure were not being managed. One evil (extreme decentralization) had been substituted for another evil (extreme centralization). In contrast, the German firm was a high performer despite a competitive market. While the business unit managers felt accountable for their units, the interdependencies between business units were being managed through corridor exchanges in the central building. These included coordination toward common customers, drawing on each other's expertise rather than reinventing the wheel, swapping personnel where necessary, and multiple forms of "you-scratch-my-back-and-I-scratch-yours" behavior. Via chance rather than foresight, the needs for integration had been allowed for in the process of decentralization.

This German firm embodies what I call the layered organization, where the properties of the future are layered on top of the properties of the past. Indeed, successful sequencing leads to dualistic layering. Let us move on to this second mechanism for resolving a duality.

Layering

Layering involves developing new capabilities and qualities in the personality of the individual or the culture of the firm *while reinforcing its past strengths*. New, complementary capabilities are layered on top of the existing capabilities, leading to a new cultural identity. The organism thereby becomes more multidimensional and more capable of handling complexity.

A note on terminology may be appropriate. The term *layering* is unfashionable; after all, are many firms not trying to *reduce* the number of layers in the organization? However, the term is used deliberately not only because it is descriptively accurate. It is a reminder of the dangers of hierarchical "delayering." If layers of an organization are removed without ensuring that the purpose behind these layers is met in other ways, we can expect to see those layers returning in the future.

If we keep in mind the concept of layering, Laurent's (1989, p. 84) observations about the process of organizational change are most relevant:

> Managing organizational change has little to do with shifting from state A to state B, it has more to do with transforming state A to state B [where $B = A + A'$], which is very different. A process of transformation requires equal attention to be given to understanding the past, assessing the present, and envisaging the future.
>
> Our linear conception of time in the western world needs to be enriched by the eastern circular conception. A spiral is a more accurate imagery of change than a straight line. Spirals remind us of the historical nature of evolution where previous

states are progressively transformed into new states. Straight lines may feed the illusion that the past can be left behind, encouraging a "*fuite en avant*" pathology.

Thus in terms of change, layering paradoxically implies very high change and very high continuity (though this is only a paradox for those who do not comprehend the duality paradigm). Layering implies high change in the sense that the layering of the new on the old implies qualitative transformation rather than quantitative change, second-order or double-loop change rather than first-order change (to use the terms of Levy and Merry, 1986). On the other hand, layering implies high continuity first in the sense that past strengths and capabilities are valued rather than rejected, and second in that working through the process of transformation requires great continuity.

Layered development may be the progressive result of iterations of successful sequencing in the spiral or helix process that was described earlier. Or it may be the result of deliberate learning, innovation, and transformation. Let me again provide examples drawn from the domains of individual and organizational development.

Layering in Individual Career Development. The process of sequenced development in different arenas of life, as described earlier, may if successful lead to generativity (Erikson's term effectively summarizes the resulting layered and integrated state). The individual's perspective on work and career is different by virtue of successful development in private life, and vice versa. Vaillant's (1977) longitudinal study of Harvard elites captures this. But let me provide a different example, applying the concept of layering to career development.

The process of career development is typically conceptualized in terms of different stages (Hall, 1976). In the first career stage, the person explores himself or herself and the world of opportunities, leading to the crystallization of a career self-concept (Schein, 1978). The second stage is one of establishment and advancement within that chosen career path, and the third stage is characterized by growth, maintenance, or stagnation in the career identity. This traditional career concept is focused and unidimensional; growth and development are linear and upward in direction.

Contrast this with the concept of the *layered career* (Evans, 1990). (The concept of the layered career was inspired by Driver's [1980] parallel concept of the spiral career.) Here the individual does not pursue a single career but a series of different and complementary careers (in the plural). For a person initially trained as an engineer, the first series of jobs may be for seven years in an engineering career. However, involvement in a customer service project leads the individual to get interested in sales work, leading to a career transition into the sales department. Some years later, he or she shifts to a full-time parenting career to raise small children and then is attracted into a role as a strategy consultant working with engineering companies. By this time, the person has started to develop powerful layers of individual competence. This involves deep familiarity with engineering that has been updated and transformed through the sales career experience, complemented by a sense for mentoring nurtured in the parenting role and now by strategic skills. One day, he or she is headhunted into a job as divisional general manager of an engineering company that is trying to develop a market orientation. Through sequencing, this person has gradually built up layers of distinctive competence. Each career change has increased breadth of competence. However, since most changes reinforce, build upon, and transform previous competencies, the depth that is the product of continuity also emerges.

Layering in Organizational Development. This leads to a parallel organizational example, taken from the case of decentralization within the German company that was mentioned earlier. The example also illustrates in microcosm the process of transformation that dualistic development involves.

At this company, the company controller strongly resisted the idea of decentralization to segmented business units on the grounds that it would lead to a loss of control. This fear stemmed from his belief that a decentralized controller would be viewed as a spy unless that person were a credible member of the local management team. Most of the corporate controllers had functional backgrounds and did not possess this credibility; thus, he argued that decentralization would lead to a loss of corporate control. (Note that the objections of this controller reflect the insight that decentralization is one side of a duality, the other being integration or control. Typically, however, such objections would be branded as "resistance to change"!)

The controller was overruled, but he decided to stick to his principles in the implementation of the decentralized organization. He went to the ranks of the newly created marketing business units to find marketeers who had a talent for financial control and who were looking for a career shift. He gave himself two years to find and train these persons to become decentralized controllers while he found other jobs for his former staff. In fact, he largely achieved this task within a year.

Seven years later, he commented that he knows no company in Germany that has such outstanding real control with so few people and so little bureaucracy, thanks to this layering. The marketing background of the controllers means that they are respected members of the local management teams, while their jobs and their relationship with him and his small team of corporate specialists ensure a dynamic balance between corporate and local interests.

If the controller had not stuck to his principles (principles that were clarified by the hot debate prior to reorganization), this transformation probably would not have been achieved. Functional controllers would have been tolerated as spies, leading to a loss of control and perhaps ultimately to a swing of the pendulum back to some version of the previous integrated organization.

Since layering focuses on the cultural facet of the organization, management and human resource development are particularly important tools. Pascale (1990) provides us with a good example from Honda. To maintain Honda's leadership in automotive engineering and design, R&D, Engineering, and Manufacturing were spun off as *separate* companies with their own presidents. Yet a variety of human resource development mechanisms are used to ensure the layering that is necessary for their collaboration. Design engineers have to spend 25 percent of their time at trade exhibitions and dealer shows to keep in touch with market requirements, and all other Honda managers must exchange jobs annually for two weeks with someone in another function. Some succession paths are explicitly prescribed: the president of the R&D company will be the successor as CEO of Honda. This guarantees layered perspectives in two ways. First, ambitious managers in other Honda companies know that R&D is the key function. Second, the president of R&D will avoid engaging in functional empire building, since this executive would otherwise inherit these problems when moving into the CEO position.

As the preceding examples suggest, layering is a particularly important mechanism for balancing the dual forces of centralization and decentralization. Given the significance of this duality in the organization of multinational firms, it has received more attention than any other (see Prahalad and Doz, 1987; Bartlett and Ghoshal, 1989). The initial step is to recognize that international integration (centralization) and local responsiveness (decentralization) is a duality rather than an either-or choice. If the heritage of the firm is one of decentralization, the challenge is *not* that of changing to a more centralized organization; the challenge is "How can we 'layer' an appropriate degree of integration on top of this decentralized organization while respecting the local responsiveness that separate units require?"

Viewing organization development as a process of layering encourages transformation that respects the past and links it to the future. Here, indeed, is one way of operationalizing the second-order change concepts of organizational learning and innovation. The questions that drive transformation and learning are dualistic, layered questions. The issue is not "How can we reduce our costs?" but "How can we maintain our reputation for quality and high-value added, but at the lowest possible cost?" "How can we improve productivity and reduce bureaucracy, while maintaining the loyalty, staff commitment, and respect for the individual that we have built up?" "How can we loosen the organization so as to generate more innovation, while maintaining the tightness and efficiency that are necessary to commercialize those innovations profitably?"

Decision Architecture

The third way of resolving or dynamically balancing dualities is decision architecture. Once again, this is not a separate mechanism. Effective decision architecture facilitates sequencing and layering; without it, the organization cannot cope with the higher-order complexity of a dualistic world.

Decision architecture refers to the way information is processed and decisions are reached. All dualities involve tension between opposites, and managing tension is the heart of decision architecture. The problem with continuity is that it is free from tension; the problem with change is that it may generate excessive tension. Decision architecture balances these two extremes.

Effective decision architecture leads to *creative tension,* fostering ongoing learning, transformation, and innovation. The hallmarks of ineffective decision architecture are those of excessive continuity (paralysis, complacency, sterile conflict, compromise) or of excessive change (anarchy, crisis, rampant emotional conflict, radical pendulum swings).

Since decision architecture refers to a collectivity, our examples here are drawn from organizational rather than individual development. At the level of individual development, the analogous processes would be those that are conducive to harnessing the tensions of life into constructive growth rather than neurosis and pathology. (See Smith and Berg, 1987, for this discussion at the individual level. As they point out, individual or group development has to confront the paradox that while the *existence* of conflict and opposition is threatening for a person or a group's life, the *absence* of these same forces is also a serious threat.)

Let me provide four examples of effective decision architecture: multifocalism and reconciliation, complementarity in team decision making, attention to procedural justice, and the use of constructive tension.

Multifocalism and Reconciliation. Unless multiple perspectives are brought to bear in decision making, a strong risk of unidimensional decisions exists. Ensuring this multifocalism is a feature of the *nemawashi* process of decision negotiation in Japan, where a low-level manager typically has the responsibility for managing the decision process as opposed to the decision content. The analogy in Western firms is "buy-in" decision processes exercised by companies such as Digital Equipment and Shell. Multifocal organizations tend to view themselves in terms of networks of relationships as well as hierarchies.

Multifocalism lies behind ongoing developments in information and measurement systems, as well as planning and budgeting processes. Take horizontal business planning, for example. Each business unit develops its plan, but top management has specified the strategic interdependencies between business units (who should collaborate with whom). Each business plan is not consolidated by top management but circulated to other interdependent business units. Meetings or task forces are set up to resolve conflicts or exploit synergies, initiating changes and improvements. It is only if these conflicts cannot be resolved that the matter goes up the conventional hierarchy, since it then raises a question of principle, strategy, or basic structure.

Reconciliation is the other pole of multifocalism. Unreconciled multifocalism can lead to paralysis and a breakdown in communication. In the preceding example, multifocalism is guided in two ways. First, the key interdependencies are specified by top management; it is not everyone who should consult with everyone else. Second, the hierarchy acts as a court of contention management, ensuring that unresolved conflicts are diagnosed and dealt with, probably with respect to their second-order change implications (see Evans and Doz, 1989, for a more extended analysis of multifocalism and reconciliation).

Complementarity in Team Decision Making. Another element of decision architecture involves making sure that balance exists within decision-making teams. This goes beyond conventional issues of ensuring balance between technical and functional inputs.

Research suggests that high-performing project or management teams possess different but complementary skills in the repertoires of their members. A Cambridge University researcher, R. Meredith Belbin (1981), spent a decade studying the composition of winning and losing teams, using performance on a business game as the dependent variable. With the aid of psychometric testing, he identified eight complementary *team roles,* and he gave these popular labels such as *shaper, coordinator, company worker, team worker,* and *monitor-evaluator.* Most people are only comfortable playing one to four of these roles.

Belbin discovered that if team members could collectively only play a few of these roles, the performance of the team would be poor. Teams without the critical eye of the monitor-evaluator had a tendency to get carried away by their enthusiasms. The driving task leadership of the shaper, challenging complacency and pushing for high achievement, could frustrate colleagues unless it was complemented by the process leadership of the coordinator and the interpersonal sensitivity of the team worker. High-performing groups were those where there was strong diversity of roles within the team and yet high complementarity between the roles of group members.

Procedural Justice. In organizations, especially multinational corporations, decisions have to be taken where individual and subsystem interests must be balanced with overall long-term corporate interests. A strong sense of "community," of identification with the continuity of the organization, is necessary to ensure the willingness for individual sacrifice and change. The empirical research of Kim and Mauborgne (1991) into the process of strategic decision making in multinationals suggests that procedural justice is an essential element of decision architecture, fostering the long-term sense of community that balances short-term imperatives.

The concept of procedural justice, rooted in studies of the psychology of justice, maintains that people react to decision outcomes not only in terms of the perceived fairness of outcomes for themselves (distributive justice) but also in terms of the fairness of the procedures by which those decisions were reached. Kim studied procedural justice in strategic decision making in 142 subsidiaries of nineteen multinational corporations. He showed that the perception of just process was positively related not only to outcome satisfaction but to longer-term organizational community variables: organizational commitment, trust in head office management, and social harmony between headquarters and subsidiary management. This suggests that procedural justice is an important element of decision architecture in dualistic organizations, providing a way of balancing individual and organizational interests.

Constructive Tension. As Nonaka (1988) has pointed out, management theories have evolved around the question of how to maintain order (continuity). Disorder (change, fluctuation) should be eliminated by systems (planning, budgeting, and control). The quintessence here is the Weberian concept of bureaucracy where disorder is eliminated.

As the environment became more turbulent, the search for static systems to cope with disorder gave way to "fit" theory (dealing with disorder through matching processes, as explained in Evans, 1991). Today, the degree of change is such that we must go one step further and build the capacity to harness and exploit disorder (change) into our organizations. The key here is creating the architecture of organization so as to foster constructive or creative tension. Change and disorder need to be continually managed through micro processes rather than via macro crises of organizational upheaval and reorganization.

The origins of the concept of constructive tension can be found in the concept of matrix management that gained ground in the 1970s. Matrix structures represented the first widespread attempt to channel the dualities of organization. However, structure is a cumbersome tool, and the disadvantages of dual reporting systems sometimes outweighed their advantages. Matrix structures are giving way to a host of more flexible mechanisms to manage constructive tension. Indeed, "matrix" should be seen as a frame of mind rather than as a structure (Bartlett and Ghoshal, 1990).

The examples of constructive tension are legion since they are to be found in so many emerging practices of management and organization. Nonaka (1988) provides an excellent account, as does Pascale (1990). Many of these practices are paradoxical, if seen with yesterday's orderly paradigm, since they involve the balancing of opposites.

- The Japanese culture is more hierarchical and sensitive to authority than in the West. However, constructive tension at Honda is managed through sessions where subordinates can openly but politely challenge their bosses and the status quo (Nonaka, 1988). Intel has a similar practice. In some Western firms, upward appraisal via attitude surveys work against the hierarchical reality that top management rarely knows what the middle of the organization thinks.
- Project teams, ad hoc task forces, and quality circles all have roles in creatively stimulating and channeling conflict. New breakthroughs at both Honda and Volvo have come from project teams of critical young professionals drawn from different parts of the firm. They had been given the assignment of making a radical breakthrough in design, and in both cases their first efforts were rejected as being insufficiently radical.
- Job rotation and mobility encourage constructive tension, as does the recruitment of outsiders or "hybrids" (people who left the company and are rehired). Outsiders are more likely to challenge the status quo and to bring with them new experiences. Nonaka (1988) notes that Epsom encourages designers to spend 70 percent of their time on their main jobs and 30 percent of their time in marketing or their minor functions.
- Disorder and variety are amplified rather than reduced, either by creating crises or by raising standards (Nonaka, 1988). At Honda, creative tension may be induced by halving the best-case time for a product development cycle, or by shooting for a 30 percent improvement in plant productivity rather than a more reasonable 3 percent increase.
- Experimentation — the trial-and-error process of trying things out on a small scale — is encouraged. The failures are forgotten, while the formal hierarchy and systems reinforce and build on the successes.
- Despite the availability of resources, budgets for development projects may be kept deliberately tight so as to encourage creative thinking and "How can we do more with less" breakthroughs. Ericsson, the Swedish telecom multinational, recently banned hiring in personnel departments

throughout the world despite increased workload. But they invested in networking these personnel departments so that they could cope by drawing on one another's complementary expertise, thereby encouraging the development of a new mode of organization.

- Dual appointments may build constructive tension into individual roles. Responsibility for international personnel at the Swedish group Alfa-Laval has been assigned to the British personnel manager in London. At Digital Equipment, the role of serving European financial institutions has been attributed to the London general managers and not someone at the Geneva headquarters. Product managers at Shell U.K. have the responsibility for corporate functions in the company. And there are numerous other examples as the concept of global centers of competence spreads in application.

- Challenging but equivocal goals and visions may become stimuli to constructive tension and experimentation, as embodied in the concept of strategic intent (Hamel and Prahalad, 1989).

- Partnerships may foster creative tension, taking a wide variety of shapes and forms: developmental partnerships with customers or suppliers; ventures with educational and research institutions; and spinning off service functions to become independent satellite firms in supply, training, and engineering functions.

All of these mechanisms, if appropriately used, build constructive tension into the organization. They harness change creatively as a part of everyday life — as stimulation, fun, excitement — rather than as an episodic, periodic threat that descends from the environment via top management in the shape of devastating destruction of the status quo. Change and continuity become fused in a constant process of organizational development.

However, there is a danger of pendulum reaction. Such mechanisms need to be balanced with mechanisms that embody more traditional order. Networks should not replace hierarchies; they should merely complement them. Creative tension should not substitute for focused goal-oriented behavior and systems; they should counterbalance their negative features.

Conclusions

Let me summarize the basic observations behind this chapter with three conclusions. First, change and continuity constitute a duality, in fact one of the essential dualities of life. Change without attention to continuity is superficial, destining us to dwell in the illusory world of first-order change when the cycles of the past return to haunt us in the future. Continuity without change is stagnant; the paradox is that it destines us ultimately for crisis. How to balance one with the other is the source of vitality, in individual as well as organizational life. In this sense, duality theory is one step along the road to an understanding of the *dynamics* of social systems.

We see this in two very different avenues of inquiry, at very different levels of analysis — individual development and organizational development. What emerges is the observation that the change-continuity duality can only be resolved (1) if we recognize that it mirrors the wider dualities in human nature and social organization, and (2) if we focus less on trying to bring about change or to maintain continuity and more on trying to develop *dynamic balance* between these dualities.

Second, the change-continuity duality turns out to be a metaduality in that it defines the central notion in duality theory, that of dynamic balance. Dynamic balance implies the balancing of change and continuity — building continuity into change, and change into continuity. It implies the rationality of minimizing rather than maximizing, seeking to maintain minimum thresholds on the poles of development within social systems.

Specifically, this can be attained in one of two ways: either by smoothing the seesaw of alternating attention through building the future pole into the present (*sequencing*), or through building dynamic balance into the fabric of the organism, be it an individual's personality or an organization's culture (*layering* and *decision architecture*). This leads to the three mechanisms of dynamic balance that have been discussed and illustrated in this chapter.

Finally, these concepts and ideas reinvoke the importance of the task of "organizational development" (Evans, 1989). While no one would deny that individuals must develop, the task of organizational development needs attention — not in its former sense of "planned organizational change," but in a new sense of building creative tension into the fabric of the firm. Duality theory provides a new roadmap for this challenge of organizational development.

Chapter Ten

Rewarding Continuity and Innovation: Strategies for Effective Pay Systems

Kathryn M. Bartol

Lincoln Electric Company, a Cleveland-based, ninety-three-year-old manufacturer of welding machines and motors, is well known for its stellar employees, who outproduce their counterparts in rival firms by a factor of two or three. Part of the company's secret is a reward system that provides strong incentives to work efficiently and effectively. Among other things, large bonuses are based on both individual and company performance. Every six months, each employee is evaluated on four criteria: output, quality, dependability, and idea generation and cooperation. The company long has had a policy of no layoffs, a critical element in encouraging employees to innovate and operate efficiently (Posner, 1988). Another legendary company with a reputation for innovation, 3M, also makes judicious use of its reward system to help foster innovation. One approach involves giving special awards for extraordinary accomplishments. Another focuses on allocating middle managers' bonuses partially on the degree to which their divisions generate at least 25 percent of their revenue each year on products that did not exist five years earlier (Johnson, 1986; Knowlton, 1988). Both Lincoln Electric and 3M have been in business for a considerable period of time, have achieved continual prominence in their industries, and are well known for effectively rewarding their workers. The two companies constitute examples of organizations that have used their compensation systems to help reinforce both continuity and innovation.

In examining in greater depth the prospects for using pay systems as mechanisms for promoting continuity and innovation, this chapter first explores the nature of the continuity and innovation concepts and considers their strategic implications. Then it assesses the potential role of pay systems in promoting innovation while preserving continuity. Next, the chapter investigates various major methods of allocating pay and evaluates their usefulness for fostering innovation. Finally, a section takes a preliminary look at the prospects for combining compensation approaches to achieve differential amounts of innovation while also fostering the necessary levels of continuity in the operating and innovating parts of organizations.

The Nature of Continuity and Innovation

Srivastva defines continuity as "the connectedness over time among organizational efforts and a sense of ongoingness that links the past to the present and the present to future hopes and ideals" (letter of invitation to the Case Western Reserve University Continuity Symposium, June 6, 1990). This definition recognizes that fulfillment of organizational goals depends on appropriately harnessing and coordinating organizational energies, providing a feeling of stability that is rooted in knowledge of past and present events, and sharing a vision of the future.

Innovation, on the other hand, is the application of a new idea to improve a process, product, or service (Kanter, 1983). Because of its focus on the new, innovation in one sense represents discontinuity; yet continuity is also a critical factor in the innovation process.

There are several reasons why continuity plays an important role in innovation. One reason is that the process of innovation itself implies some continuity across the main stages or phases. Although there are a number of different delineations of the main stages or phases in the innovation process, they tend to be reasonably similar (Amabile, 1988; Maidique,

1980; Zaltman, Duncan, and Holbek, 1973). For instance, with innovation, there is usually an initial stage where there is some recognition of a problem or opportunity. The second stage typically involves diagnosis and preparation, including the gathering of information and resources. The third stage is idea generation, whereby a new idea emerges that appears to have promise. The fourth stage normally involves validating that the idea is a viable one. The fifth stage focuses on implementing the new idea. The sixth and final stage typically encompasses monitoring the results. Hence, some continuity is required in order to progress through the various stages in the innovation process, since each stage depends heavily on the preceding stage.

Other major reasons for the importance of continuity in the process of innovation are related to three basic ingredients identified by Amabile (1983) as necessary for individuals to successfully engage in creativity and innovation. For one thing, individuals need domain-relevant skills. Such skills are associated with expertise in the relevant field and include related technical skills or artistic ability, talent in the area, and factual knowledge. Therefore, the domain-relevant skills associated with creative ideas represent continuity in that they are heavily embedded in knowledge of both the past and the present. Another important ingredient in creativity and innovation is creativity-relevant skills. Such skills include a cognitive style or method of thinking that is oriented to exploring new directions, knowledge of approaches that can be used for generating novel ideas, and a work style (such as persistence and high energy) that is conducive to developing creative ideas. Again, creativity-relevant skills depend to a large extent on continuity because they are made up of skills, knowledge, and work habits acquired over a period of time. Finally, creativity and innovation require ongoing task motivation, yet another dimension where continuity is needed because creativity depends on the ability to persist over time.

While continuity is an important aspect of the innovation process, an excessive amount of emphasis on the past and present aspects of continuity could work to preserve the status quo and preclude significant organizational innovation. The likely relationship between the degree of emphasis on the past and present versus the future from a continuity point of view and the probable impact on the extent of innovation is depicted in Figure 10.1. As Figure 10.1 shows, innovation can range from maintaining the status quo (virtually no innovation) to small, incremental improvements (such as a new feature added to a videocassette recorder) to radical new breakthroughs (such as laser technology).

Figure 10.1. Impact of Continuity on Innovation.

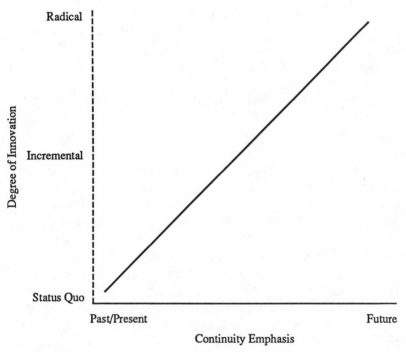

While radical innovations can be important to the strategic success of organizations, incremental innovations also can make valuable contributions (Port, 1989). For example, the recent success of quality efforts at many major corporations, including Motorola, Xerox, and Corning, relies in large part on multiple new ideas, many of which constitute small improvements.

Collectively these improvements have a major impact through supporting important strategic directions. Essentially, one could argue that organizations have difficulty developing and sustaining a competitive advantage without engaging in considerable innovation. In fact, continuity itself may depend on innovation, since it is likely to be impossible for an organization to survive over time without engaging in the adaptive behaviors associated with at least incremental innovation. How then can organizations promote the necessary amount of innovation for strategic success without unduly disrupting organizational continuity? Although it is certainly not the only means, this chapter argues that one potential mechanism for helping to promote appropriate levels of innovation is the effective use of an organization's pay system. Pay systems, then, can be a critical strategic factor in organizations (Carroll, 1987; Milkovich, 1988).

The Role of Pay Systems in Promoting Innovation

The relationship between rewards, particularly monetary rewards, and innovation is to some extent controversial. While a number of writers on innovation mention the importance of monetary rewards in promoting innovation, few empirical studies have directly addressed the issue. In one study of innovations within the semiconductor industry, Abbey and Dickson (1983) found that perceptions of a link between performance and rewards was significantly related to success in the various phases of innovation, including the early stages and the later implementation stage. The level of reward, though, was important only to success in the initial phase, suggesting that providing substantial rewards may be particularly important in encouraging risk taking during the critical early stages of the innovation process. In a study of new ventures in Fortune 500 corporations, Klavens, Shanley, and Evan (1985) found that venture success was related to bonuses tied directly to venture performance, but was unrelated to compensation that was not performance-based. More indirect or nonmonetary rewards such as improved career potential and opportunities to engage in other promising new ventures also were factors related to venture success. Thus there is some evidence that direct monetary rewards, as well as more indirect forms of rewards (such as promotions), can be important factors in promoting innovation in organizations.

On the other hand, based on her research on creativity, Amabile (1988) argues that individuals are likely to be most creative during the crucial idea-generation stage when they are motivated by intrinsic factors, such as interest, enjoyment, satisfaction, and the challenge of the work itself. In fact, in several experiments Amabile, Hennessey, and Grossman (1986) found that explicitly contracting with individuals to receive a reward for completing an activity had a negative impact on their creativity in completing the task. In contrast, providing no reward or a reward that was not contingent on completing the task did not adversely influence the creativity of the task outcomes. One possible explanation is that emphasis on the extrinsic reward caused individuals to focus on the reward rather than on the task. Amabile (1988) calls this phenomenon the *hydraulic effect,* whereby intrinsic motivation decreases as extrinsic motivation increases. As a result, Amabile warns about the dangers of overemphasizing the extrinsic rewards in attempting to foster creativity and innovation. Interestingly, in the one experiment by Amabile, Hennessey, and Grossman (1986) that involved monetary rewards, subjects who were told to perform a task for which they would be paid were relatively more creative than subjects who were allowed to choose whether they wanted to perform the task for a payment or than subjects who received no monetary reward at all. Hence, there may be subtle differences associated with how tasks and payments are presented. These results do suggest that individuals may indeed be creative when directed to perform certain tasks for which they will receive a reward, a common situation in organizational settings where there are tasks that must be completed.

At the same time, Amabile (1988) acknowledges that extrinsic motivation has a potentially important role in organizations. For one thing, many tasks in organizations do not require significant amounts of creativity. Instead they involve more routine or algorithmic problem solving that potentially can be completed successfully even though an individual is mainly motivated by extrinsic factors (McGraw, 1978). For another thing, even where innovation is important, there is evidence that extrinsic motivation may be particularly helpful in motivating individuals to persist during the rather laborious diagnosis/preparation and validation stages. Still another potential role of extrinsic motivation may be enhancing the creative inclinations of those who already have high intrinsic motivation for the task. In this instance, the effects of intrinsic and extrinsic motivation may be additive. In fact, Amabile speculates that what she calls the hydraulic effect may apply mainly to individuals who initially have only a moderate level of intrinsic motivation for the task. Thus, there still may be significant potential to use reward systems to enhance the motivation of those most likely to be creative — those with high intrinsic motivation for the task. Such enhancements may be possible even during the critical idea-generation stage, in which strong emphasis on intrinsic motivation seems to be most important because of the heuristic problem solving that is required (McGraw, 1978). Finally, Amabile argues that reward systems require a balancing act, whereby innovation is rewarded, but not by tying rewards to such specific actions that the system undermines the willingness to try out new ideas and take risks. Thus, while Amabile's findings help to highlight the importance of task-related intrinsic motivation in fostering creativity and innovation, she also acknowledges the potential importance of extrinsic motivation in promoting innovation.

One caution in attempting to apply Amabile's (1988) findings regarding the potential detrimental effects of extrinsic rewards on creativity is that her experiments may not be totally generalizable to organizations. One major reason is that many of her experiments involve children engaging in one-time activities, rather than adults working in actual job situations where both intrinsic and extrinsic outcomes are likely to be not only desired, but also *expected*. Another major reason for caution about generalizability is that her experiments have typically used situations in which individuals act alone without being embedded in an organizational context. Thus the potential internal equity issues that so often affect individuals' interpretations of reward systems within organizations were not salient and, hence, could not influence the outcomes (Wallace and Fay, 1988).

Yet inequities in reward systems can undermine the process of innovation. For example, in her work in innovation, Kanter (1988) relates the plight of a new venture manager for a major instruments manufacturing company, who had been working on a start-up business for six months. He was offered a promotion that would advance him several levels, making him the manager of 6,000 people in a major established division instead of the manager of fifteen people involved in the start-up. The promotion would provide substantially greater extrinsic rewards. After considerable deliberation, the new venture manager decided to take the promotion because it was clear that, if he turned it down, he might have to wait a considerable time for an equivalent opportunity. In later assessing the situation, the manager noted: "The corporation was set up to reward the person running a stable $200 million business more than some-one growing a business from zero to $10 million to $200 million, which is much, much harder." Nevertheless, he said that he "felt torn." Unfortunately, the new venture failed, in large part because of changing managers at a crucial period. Kanter (1988, p. 195) notes the irony: "Creating *change* required *stability*—continuity of people especially during the information-rich, knowledge-intensive development stage." Thus, equity issues and related reward systems can potentially have major impacts on both innovation and the necessary levels of continuity. This means that Amabile's findings may well understate the importance of extrinsic rewards in promoting innovation in organizations. At the same time, a number of researchers on innovation note the ease with which it is possible for organizational reward systems to unwittingly reinforce mainly the status quo (Tushman and Nadler, 1986; Kanter, 1988).

Pay Systems as Influences on Continuity and Innovation

Although researchers frequently allude to the potential influences of pay on continuity and innovation, they have made few attempts to assess the comparative usefulness of pay methods in maintaining the necessary continuity while simultaneously promoting the needed levels of innovation. In the context of this chapter, the term *pay method* is used in a generic sense to connote a specific means for determining how pay should be allocated. In contrast, the term *pay system* is used to designate the specific pay method or composite of methods formally adopted by an organization for distributing pay to organizational members. Thus, an organization can use one or more pay methods in devising its pay system and may also have different pay systems for different categories of organizational members, such as nonexempt and exempt employees.

Pay methods can be differentiated according to one of three main bases for determining the allocation of pay: characteristics of the job, performance or outcomes, or characteristics of the person (Mahoney, 1989; Lawler, 1990). This section explores the degree to which major pay methods within these three categories are likely to aid in promoting innovation. Overall assessments are made in terms of the extent to which the methods are likely to reinforce the status quo, encourage incremental innovation, or promote radical innovation. These assessments are summarized in Table 10.1. Since the impacts of various pay methods and systems on innovation have generally not been the subject of empirical research, many of these assessments are necessarily speculative.

**Table 10.1. Extent to Which Pay Methods
Are Likely to Encourage Various Degrees of Innovation.**

	Degrees of Innovation		
Pay Method	*Status Quo Retention*	*Incremental Innovation*	*Radical Innovation*
Hourly wage/salary	Likely	Possible	Unlikely
Merit pay	Likely	Possible	Unlikely
Piece-rate incentives	Likely	Possible	Unlikely
Individual bonus plans	Likely	Possible	Possible
Profit sharing	Somewhat unlikely	Likely	Possible
Gainsharing	Unlikely	Likely	Possible
Special awards	Unlikely	Likely	Likely
Skill-based pay	Somewhat unlikely	Likely	Possible

Pay Based on Job Characteristics

The predominant basis for pay in U.S. industry is the job held by an individual. Mahoney (1989) argues that the emphasis on pay according to the job grew out of the development of the factory system and mass production. The parallel emergence of scientific management highlighted the prospects for long-linked technology based on sequential sets of tasks. These sets of tasks could then be grouped into standardized jobs, facilitating the selection, training, and motivation of workers. Thus, mass production began to displace the customized production of goods by skilled craftspeople, making the prior compensation according to output more difficult.

To determine appropriate pay for various sets of tasks that now were standardized production links, job evaluation methods began to be used. Job evaluation became a means to determine the relative worth of jobs for compensation purposes precisely because it does not require direct measures of output to grade jobs for pay purposes. Basic pay began to take the form of an hourly wage rate or an annual salary.

The most popular method of job evaluation currently in use by U.S. companies is some variation of the point-factor method of job evaluation (American Compensation Association, 1989). Briefly, the point-factor method involves identifying several compensable factors (such as working conditions, problem-solving ability, knowledge required, and accountability), developing numerical scales indicating degrees for each factor, and determining weights to reflect the relative worth of each factor (Lawler, 1986; Milkovich and Newman, 1990). Then job analysis and job descriptions are developed and used as a basis for assigning points to each job, so that each job in the organization has points indicating its relative worth compared with other internal jobs. A representative group of jobs is usually next compared with pay for similar jobs in the marketplace to develop a hierachy of pay. Typically, pay scales are then developed for internal jobs with similar points.

Proponents of job evaluation argue that it clarifies the value placed on basic job requirements, indicates how increased job skills can lead to higher-paying jobs, helps managers be objective in outlining and making changes in job tasks, and signals the types of skills that are most important to strategic directions (Candrilli and Armagast, 1987; Plachy, 1987). On the other hand, the primary emphasis on job evaluation in determining compensation has been strongly criticized in recent years by Lawler (1986, 1990). Among other things, Lawler argues that allocating pay based on job evaluation systems promotes a bureaucratic management style because it places strong emphasis on job descriptions, facilitates performance appraisals that are tied to the job as the focus of worth to the organization, and fosters organizational control of the work to be done by job incumbents. In the process, he contends, job evaluation systems implicitly (and perhaps unwittingly) specify what is not to be done by the job incumbent, a stance that can be problematic if management wishes to foster an orientation whereby individuals engage in whatever activities are necessary to effectively handle situations and complete work. Another problem with job evaluation systems, according to Lawler, is that they can overly orient organizational members toward doing what is necessary to move up to the next rung, a factor that can operate to the detriment of effective performance in the current job. Hence job evaluation systems may help undermine the intrinsic motivation associated with a job rather than facilitate the potential supplementary enhancement of motivation through extrinsic means.

To the extent that Lawler's criticisms are valid, the related wage rates and salary levels associated with paying according to job characteristics also may tend to overemphasize the present aspects of continuity to the point of maintaining the status quo. While incremental innovation may be possible, there appears to be little in an hourly or salaried pay system by itself to encourage the risk taking associated with making innovative changes. The same logic applied to radical innovations suggests that a pay system based on job characteristics is unlikely to encourage radical innovations. One prospect for encouraging innovation might be to include innovation as a compensable factor and an important part of job descriptions — at least where significant innovation is desirable. In any event, pay based on job characteristics alone appears likely to mainly reinforce the status quo.

In many cases, though, pay according to job characteristics is combined with another pay method (Mahoney, 1989). As a combination, pay according to job characteristics may afford job incumbents the means of satisfying basic needs, so that it is more feasible to become concerned with growth needs. It is growth needs that are most likely to be associated with intrinsic motivation and related concerns for innovation (Alderfer, 1972). In considering possible combinations, another major means of allocating pay is based on outcomes.

Pay Based on Outcomes

A variety of methods exist for allocating pay according to outcomes. In some cases, the pay approaches are somewhat traditional, in the sense that they have been used extensively by organizations for many years. In other cases, the approaches are considered more nontraditional because they have only recently been introduced as mainstream methods of pay. This section first explores more traditional pay methods based on outcomes, including merit pay and piece-rate incentive plans, before turning to more nontraditional methods, including profit sharing, gainsharing, bonus plans, and special awards (Mahoney, 1989).

Merit Pay Plans. One common method of pay in many organizations is supplementing pay based on job characteristics by awarding additional annual payments that are based on individual performance. A survey of Fortune 1000 companies found that 96 percent had merit pay plans, and 31 percent of the responding companies reported that merit pay covered all employees (Lawler, Ledford, and Mohrman, 1989). Yet there is some doubt about the motivating effects of merit pay plans as they have been implemented in many organizations. One reason is that performance often is not measured adequately, leaving awards of merit pay to the subjective judgment of supervisors. Another reason for concern about the motivational effectiveness of merit pay plans is that merit increases typically are incorporated into base pay each year, so that they become, in effect, annuities that allow individuals to be paid over many years for their high performance in a given year. One implication is that individuals can be relatively highly paid because of high performance in prior years, even if their current performance is less than stellar. Such conditions have engendered skepticism about whether pay is, in fact, tied to performance in many organizations and about the current extrinsic motivating potential of such plans (Wallace and Fay, 1988; Mahoney, 1989; Lawler, 1990; Milkovich and Newman, 1990). From the point of view of the ability of such plans to promote innovation, merit pay plans, at least as they are often practiced in organizations, seem more likely to reinforce the status quo rather than to help motivate individuals to make incremental or radical improvements.

Piece-Rate Incentive Plans. As mentioned previously in conjunction with the discussion of pay based on job characteristics, individual incentive plans have a long tradition (Mahoney, 1989). Frederick Taylor introduced his well-known piece-rate pay system for production workers as part of his pioneering ideas on scientific management. During the 1920s and 1930s, the use of piece-rate incentive plans expanded rapidly (Lawler, 1971), but the trend toward the specialization of tasks made outcomes more difficult to measure and gradually caused a shift toward job-based hourly pay for much of production work (Mahoney, 1989). Individual incentives tended to be retained in areas like sales, where individual output is relatively easy to measure. To some extent, individual incentive plans continue to be used in production work, mainly in situations in which individual outcomes can be identified without difficulty.

However, there is some evidence that piece-rate incentive plans can be problematic (Lawler, 1990). For one thing, they sometimes channel employee energies into efforts to beat the system by attempting to set production standards relatively low so that they can gain the maximum pay with the least amount of effort. For another, such incentives can create dissension in the organization by causing individuals who are not on incentive plans to resent those who are. Thus, cooperation and information sharing among groups like sales and sales support can be undermined. Another potential problem is that individual incentive plans can limit the focus of workers to strictly what is measured and rewarded, causing neglect of related areas. As a result of these problems, Lawler argues that incentive plans have a place where the work is relatively simple, repetitive, stable, easily measured, and can be done relatively independently. Under such conditions, the potential for extrinsic motivation provided by piece-rate incentives may be particularly important. Even so, it still may be difficult to change standards as necessary, although heavy involvement of workers in task forces revising such standards may help. Thus, from the point of view of continuity and innovation, piece-rate-type systems are likely to largely reinforce the status quo or to provide impetus for mainly incremental innovations that increase the financial gains of the individual at the expense of the organization.

Profit-Sharing Plans. Although profit-sharing plans originated at some point during the first half of the nineteenth century, they are considered to be a nontraditional form of payment because, until recently, they have been utilized to a much lesser degree than have more traditional methods, such as job-based pay (Hammer, 1988; Mahoney, 1989). According to one estimate, there are about 350,000 profit-sharing plans in existence in the United States (Doyle, 1983). With profit-sharing plans, a portion of profits is distributed to organizational members, either through current payments or on a deferred basis (often at retirement). Because of tax considerations, about 80 percent of organizations with profit-sharing plans defer payments, while about 20 percent have plans whereby some profit shares are paid out on a current basis and the rest are deferred (Milkovich and Newman, 1990). Since much of the income tends to be deferred, there is some doubt about the ability of profit sharing to motivate workers. In fact, Wallace and Fay (1988) basically categorize deferred plans as a benefit and consider only plans that make at least annual cash payments as methods of pay for performance (outcomes).

One advantage of profit-sharing plans is that organizations generally have mechanisms in place to measure profits, and, therefore, such programs can be relatively easy to implement.

Another advantage is that the profit sharing applies to entire profit centers and can be used in units or organizations of different sizes. On the other hand, as size increases, organizational members tend to have more difficulty visualizing a clear relationship between their performance and profit levels. Still, with profit-sharing plans, organizational members may make at least some additional efforts at incremental improvements. One reason is that organizational profit-sharing plans often allow for greater employee participation and increased latitude in matters relating to their jobs. Thus, greater possibilities for intrinsic motivation coexist with the definite possibility of additional extrinsic rewards resulting from such efforts. Yet another reason why profit sharing may foster incremental innovation is that the existence of the profit-sharing plan focuses additional attention on profit-related issues, perhaps influencing employees to take actions that will help improve the bottom line. At the same time, profit-sharing plans appear unlikely to provide sufficient inducements to motivate the risk taking associated with radical innovations.

Gainsharing. Another nontraditional pay method based on outcomes is gainsharing. A gainsharing plan is an organizational system for distributing to organization members part of the gains associated with organizationwide improvements in productivity, cost reductions, quality, or some other criterion with financially important implications (Miller and Schuster, 1987). Most often, gainsharing also includes efforts to enhance employee involvement, since many of the improvements depend on the ideas and efforts of organizational members working alone and/or as a group. Although gainsharing in the form of the Scanlon plan can be traced back to the late 1930s, the notion of sharing the benefits of organizational improvements has been gaining in popularity in recent years. Reasons for the accelerating interest in gainsharing include the search for means of increasing productivity in the face of growing foreign competition, recognition that gainsharing plans may be useful methods of reinforcing the need for organizational change, pressure from unions for more objective means of distributing pay to workers, increasing dissatisfaction with the subjectivity associated with merit pay plans, and growing recognition that encouraging teamwork may have a greater impact on productivity than fostering individual efforts through reward systems (Welbourne and Gomez-Mejia, 1988). Whereas profit-sharing plans attempt to focus member attention on factors affecting net profits, gainsharing programs are oriented to more narrow criteria that are ultimately linked to increases in productivity.

Three of the most widely known gainsharing approaches are Scanlon, Rucker, and Improshare. With the Scanlon plan, bonuses are typically based on the ratio of labor costs to sales value of production, although more complex formulas are used in some applications of Scanlon plans (Graham-Moore, 1990). The Rucker plan relies on a ratio of value added (sales minus materials and supplies) to payroll expenses. Improshare (*im*proved *pro*ductivity through *shar*ing) relies on a relatively simple approach of developing production standards and providing bonuses for improvements over the standards.

While the three approaches use somewhat different formulas for bonus determination, they also differ in their provisions for worker involvement. The Scanlon plan places the heaviest emphasis on worker involvement through production committees that are expected to encourage new-idea development in organizational members and evaluate suggestions submitted. A screening committee oversees the work of the production committees, operates as an appeals mechanism for rejected suggestions, evaluates suggestions that fall within the jurisdictions of more than one production committee, and reviews calculations for the monthly bonuses that are paid out by the plan (Miller and Schuster, 1987). The Rucker approach also stresses worker involvement but does not provide the elaborate provisions incorporated in Scanlon plans. In contrast, Improshare does not explicitly provide for worker involvement. Proponents do, however, consider participation to be a likely outcome of Improshare plans, based on the premise that exceeding set standards typically requires the increased cooperation of organizational members (Welbourne and Gomez-Mejia, 1988). Since gainsharing plans focus on specific targets that are well within the purview of workers to affect, involve improvements over historical levels of performance, and usually require at least some problem solving among group members, gainsharing plans have the potential to encourage both intrinsic and extrinsic motivation and to lead to at least incremental innovation (Mahoney, 1989). Such pay methods, however, do not appear to provide sufficient rewards to reinforce the risk taking that is inherent in the process of radical innovation.

Nontraditional Bonus Plans. Although bonus programs themselves have existed for some time, recently bonuses (other than bonus-related gainsharing plans) are receiving new attention as an alternative to merit pay plans. The basic idea is to provide rewards for performance in the form of bonuses that are not added to base wage or salary levels. Instead the bonuses are awarded as one-time payments intended as rewards for performance during the previous year (or possibly some other time period). Of course, base wages and salaries are still adjusted to respond to changes in the labor market, but such changes are handled separately from bonuses.

One advantage of such bonuses is that they can increase prospects for more clearly differentiating between market adjustments and pay for performance, a distinction that is often lost under traditional merit pay plans (Mahoney, 1989). A second advantage is that bonus approaches can be fairly flexible, since bonuses can be awarded based on individual, unit, or organizational performance as well as some combination. For example, the awarding of a bonus might depend not only on individual performance, but also on the performance of a team or work unit. A third major advantage of bonuses is that the criteria can be shifted as necessary to encourage support of changes in strategic direction. Yet another potential advantage is that bonuses can be combined with base wages or salary levels that are somewhat below the market (McNutt, 1990). This arrangement places some base pay at risk, but it also allows individuals to receive rewards that are substantially above the market when goals are exceeded. One attempt to use the pay-at-risk principle in a compensation plan for Du Pont's fiber business was discontinued after two years because of strong discontent among employees. The employees had at first gained from the arrangement but assailed the plan when they faced a likely loss in 1990 during a business downturn (Koenig, 1990).

Because nontraditional bonus methods can be geared to reward significant improvements in performance, they appear to have the potential to reinforce incremental innovation. Where large bonuses are available for significant improvements, radical innovations also may be possible. However, as they currently exist in most organizations, bonus systems provide various gradations of goal levels with accelerated amounts of bonus for reaching more than 100 percent of goals. Unfortunately, radical innovations may introduce the risk of not receiving a bonus at all if the innovation fails, even though such innovations may offer the prospect of a substantial additional bonus related to greatly surpassing goals if the innovation succeeds. As a result, bonuses do not appear to be strong reinforcers of radical innovations, but they possibly could be structured to encourage more radical innovation. One way might be to provide one level of bonus for pursuing promising new directions and another for successfully developing and implementing a major innovation.

Special Awards. Another nontraditional method of pay is the special award. Special awards are payments given when an individual or group achieves some major and somewhat extraordinary accomplishment. As Lawler (1990) points out, ordinary merit plan budgets are normally neither big enough nor flexible enough to allow for a major award for stellar accomplishments and, hence, usually are inadequate for this purpose. Furthermore, the timing of merit pay often is not in synchronization with recognizing extraordinary accomplishments. An added issue is that the normal performance appraisal system may not be geared adequately to identifying and recognizing extraordinary performance. As a remedy, Lawler suggests a separate process that is, in essence, an internal Nobel Prize–type award process. A number of organizations, such as IBM, Amoco, and 3M, have special awards for research and development personnel, who are often in a position to generate radical breakthroughs.

Possibilities exist for using such awards to reward both incremental and radical innovations. For example, American Express has a program to reward exceptional performance through "Great Performers" awards that exceed $5,000 (Lawler, 1990). With such awards, the recognition aspect may actually be more important to some individuals than the monetary award per se, but the monetary amount can provide a crucial signal that the organization places significant value on the accomplishment.

Pay Based on the Person

A third major approach to the allocation of pay is based on the person. This nontraditional approach is relatively new and currently centers mainly around the concept of skill-based pay. Skill-based pay is a method whereby organizational members are paid according to the range, depth, and types of skills that they are capable of using. One recent study of Fortune 1000 firms found that about 40 percent had some type of skill-based pay plan covering at least some employees (Lawler, Ledford, and Mohrman, 1989). Potential advantages sometimes cited for skill-based pay systems are higher motivation, greater pay satisfaction, increased perceptions of self-worth, more effective problem solving, and higher organizational commitment (Tosi and Tosi, 1986; Gupta, Schweizer, and Jenkins, 1987; Lawler, Ledford, and Mohrman, 1989). Potential disadvantages include increased wage and training costs, difficulties of doing market pricing to determine appropriate pay (because other organizations may not have people with the same mix of skills), somewhat greater complexity of administration than a job-based system, and potential resistance from some employees who fear they will have difficulty learning new skills.

Skill-based pay methods tend to be used in organizations that are emphasizing high involvement through relatively flat structures and mechanisms like self-managing teams. For the most part, skill-based pay also is utilized mainly in blue-collar manufacturing jobs, although the pay method is increasingly used in a variety of other contexts (O'Dell, 1987). To the extent that such plans encourage employees to acquire greater skill depth and breadth, as well as possibly acquire more vertical managerial skills, such employees may be in a better position to recognize possible areas for at least incremental innovation and implementation of improvements. Still, while the pay method may encourage individuals to acquire more skills, it is not clear that the pay method reinforces actually using them. Nevertheless, in building the domain-relevant skills associated with creativity, skill-based pay may ultimately be useful in promoting incremental innovation. Such skill building may also enhance intrinsic motivation and reinforce horizontal communication channels across jobs — additional means of encouraging innovation (Kanter, 1988). Thus, skill-based pay may be useful in promoting at least incremental innovation.

Combining Pay Methods to Achieve Continuity and Innovation

Given the variety of pay methods available, it may be possible to combine such methods to create pay systems that foster appropriate degrees of continuity and innovation. In exploring this prospect, it is useful to first consider the notion of operating and innovating parts of an organization, before turning to issues of appropriate pay systems.

Operating and Innovating Parts of Organizations

Galbraith (1982) argues that most existing organizations are geared to performing similar tasks efficiently on a recurring basis. For example, an organization might produce the millionth calculator, process the millionth order, or serve the millionth pizza. Because their focus is on performing assigned tasks well, most organizations are not particularly adept at doing new things for the first time. Consequently, Galbraith contends that separate innovating units are often needed to increase the likelihood that the necessary levels of innovation will occur. Thus, he speaks of the operating and innovating parts of the organization. The less the culture of the organization supports innovation, the greater the necessity for separate units, particularly for radical innovations.

Galbraith (1982) calls separate innovating units *reservations*. Reservations can take the form of relatively permanent units like research and development, market development, process technology, or product development. They can also be temporary, as when members of the operating organization are assigned to teams charged with initially developing a new program, process, or product. In the case of temporary units, the members typically help transfer the new idea to the operating organization before resuming their operating responsibilities. Unfortunately, there is a differentiation paradox associated with reservations and innovation. The more the innovation effort is differentiated or separated from the operating part of the organization, the greater the likelihood of producing a significant innovation, but the less the likelihood of successfully transferring the innovation to the operating organization. In a sense, the operating organization represents mainly past and present aspects of continuity, without which the organization would likely falter. On the other hand, the reservations provide sources of major innovations, without which the organization would likely face difficulties due to insufficient adaptability to maintain future continuity.

Research on innovation in organizations also suggests that three important roles are involved: idea champion, sponsor, and orchestrator (Galbraith, 1982; Pearson, 1988). An idea champion is an individual who generates a new idea or believes in the value of the new idea and supports it in the face of numerous potential obstacles. Such individuals often are entrepreneurs, inventors, creative individuals, or risk takers. Since they often hold positions that are relatively low in the organizational hierarchy, they frequently experience difficulty pursuing their ideas without the help of a sponsor. A sponsor, on the other hand, is a middle manager who recognizes the organizational significance of an idea, helps to obtain the necessary funding to continue development of the innovation, and facilitates actual implementation of the new idea. The third important role is the orchestrator, a high-level manager who articulates the need for innovation, provides funding for innovating activities, creates incentives for middle managers to sponsor innovating ideas, and protects idea people. Orchestrators are critical because innovations, by their very nature, disturb existing conditions and may generate resistance among individuals with a vested interest in maintaining the status quo. In the absence of a strong orchestrator, resistors are likely to succeed. The orchestrator is usually the CEO; heads of major divisions also may act as orchestrators. Thus, the orchestrator, in particular, presides over both operating and innovating parts of the organization and, in that role, must foster continuity in terms of the past and present as well as encourage innovation aimed at future survival and competitive advantage. Sponsors to a lesser extent also can help aid continuity and change. One prime tool at the disposal of orchestrators and sponsors is the reward system.

The Reward System Component

Galbraith (1982) maintains that reward systems are an important component in the process of promoting innovation, as well as a critical element in motivating individuals in the operating sector of the organization to maintain the basic ongoing activities that are key to continuity. He argues that the reward systems used in the operating organization need to be adjusted for the innovating organization. The extent of the adjustment depends on how innovative the operating organization tends to be relative to the innovating organization. Yet Galbraith notes that, if the reward systems become too disparate, equity problems may result. Feelings of inequity may arise among members of the operating organization, who may feel that the difficulties and risks that they face in implementing ideas developed by the innovating organizations are inadequately recognized. On the other hand, members of the innovating organization may believe that the heavy risks associated with initiating and developing innovations, particularly radical ones, deserve concomitant rewards. Among Galbraith's suggestions for rewarding members of the innovating organization are special recognitions, such as the IBM fellows program (under which the fellows can work on projects of their choice for five years), the Carlton Award (a type of internal Nobel Prize) at 3M, one-time cash awards, and percentage awards based on profits or savings associated with the innovation.

Little is known about just how disparate rewards can be before they actually do create equity difficulties across the operating and innovating sectors of the organizations. Given current trends toward worker involvement (Lawler, Ledford, and Mohrman, 1989), many of the forms of nontraditional pay probably have better prospects than more traditional methods for promoting at least incremental innovation without disrupting continuity even in the operating sectors of the organization. At the same time, nontraditional approaches can be combined with special awards, not only for extraordinary innovations by the innovating sectors of the organization, but also for particularly significant innovations by the operating parts of the organization. Clearly additional research needs to be aimed at assessing the efficacy of using pay systems as means of promoting innovation in organizations. Evidence to date, though, suggests that managers can use pay systems to help shift the focus of continuity management from an overemphasis on the past and present to adequate adaptability for the future.

Conclusion

The Leadership Agenda:
Affirming Continuity to
Manage Change

Suresh Srivastva, Craig G. Wishart

Changes that occur in organizational life are most often a consequence of seemingly rational decisions made by leadership to adapt to the changes in their environment. This view to understanding organizational change is often rooted in a mechanistic perception of organized systems, in which structure and process can be readily corrected for more efficient production. Unfortunately, we have seen that this process of change is disruptive, since it is often enacted at the cost of the organizational history, tradition, and culture. For the members of the organization, these changes are like a tornado that uproots them from their grounding, forcing them to continually adapt to the new order of operation. They must rebuild a place for themselves and a culture for their organization out of the waste left behind by this destruction. But change does not have to lead to these consequences.

Our major premise here is that attention to continuity, as elaborated so eloquently by the contributors to this volume, frees us from a view of change that has become habitual and opens up new possibilities not only for appreciating the complex nature of change but also for actively engaging with others in our daily organizational lives to create the future while preserving the best of the past. After reviewing some of the main

307

themes presented in the preceding chapters, we turn to the major point of this volume: reframing the concepts of change and continuity to better enable executives and leaders to develop and renew their organizations.

The turbulence of the environment can and should be weathered without the loss of past human creation and knowledge, as in Salipante's "traditionally evaluative" examples in Chapter Five and in the steel company described by Lynn in Chapter Six. Since all that we know of human existence is built on the knowledge of past experiences and discoveries, every new idea is founded on the thoughts of old. Yet when we lose sight of this connectedness, we are bound to experience discontinuity in the process of change. As organizations adapt to their ever-changing and turbulent environment, they experience continuity when they affirm their history, traditions, culture, knowledge, and language as the sources of human activity that support organizational processes. With *preservation as a driving force*, continuity makes possible the aesthetic appreciation of organizational life. The meaning of past human experience, whether in the context of one-on-one working relationships or at the level of organizational linkages and interrelations with larger communal, regional, and social elements (as voiced by Loveridge in Chapter Three), is continually revisited and made a living part of present knowledge and future possibilities. The roots of organizational life are purposely preserved, not denied. Since preservation is a basic requirement for the survival of an organism or an organization, all efforts and activities that support preservation are at the service of continuity of the organism or organization. Historical inquiry becomes a powerful method to enhance continuity in organizational life. When we know where we have been and appreciate the meaningful choices we have made, we experience the present with a richer, fuller understanding and can more lucidly perceive where it is we ought to be going.

Unlike the conventional view of change, which is driven by the negation of the past, encouraging the dissolution of antiquated processes and planned, orderly movement toward a future state, the concept of continuity embraces the development of a future based on past and present experiences and understanding. Thus we see changing as being in the service of managing continuity. Continuity reinforces the basic commitment of organizational leadership to create the future by picking up the past, supporting it, and attending to what could be. In Chapter Seven, Klein and Farris described this basic commitment as attention to continuity of goals first, allowing for flexibility in means to follow. In this sense, managing continuity is a process of valuing and envisioning. It is value driven in that we choose from among past, proven practices those we wish to continue and at the same time envision what ought to be or what we ought to become. It is a concept that opens our awareness and urges us to attend to the possibilities and potentialities of our future.

Attention to continuity urges us to freely discuss what we do and do not know or understand, thereby creating dialogue around the exposition of meaning and understanding of organizational life. Without this dialogue, we cannot create the necessary shared meaning that enables us to collectively cope with the paradoxical dilemmas confronted in our everyday life and social systems. Perhaps the most basic of these paradoxes was introduced so cogently by Bateson in Chapter One: that our everyday lives are, at the same time, continuous and discontinuous. Organization leaders cannot individually manage these kinds of ambiguities and inconsistencies inherent in living organized systems. Attempts to control our environments or predict the future are fruitless. Uncertainty is the essence of our existential condition. As Gergen convincingly showed in Chapter Two, the only control we exercise in organizations is rooted in the *collective* choices and decisions that we make in response to the paradoxes and ambiguities we face. In organized systems, these choices must be the consequence of shared social construction and the understanding derived therein for members' existence to have meaning. Therefore, our leaders can and must construe the world of the organization in such a way that attracts and enables collective action (Jonas, Fry, and Srivastva, 1990). We can only develop or transmit the expressed meaning underlying the organizational rituals, traditions, and customs if our values are exposed and meaning is derived through consensus. This entails a search for our "practice," something that Schwartz called for in Chapter Four, and careful attention to that which we reward in day-to-day work life, as Bartol substantiated in Chapter Ten. Thus, the shared understanding and collaborative action that result from *discovering and affirming continuity* allow organizations to more deliberately and effectively manage paradox and ambiguity.

The assumptions behind the traditional dialectical relationship between continuity and change are a consequence of the prevailing functionalist paradigm and its concomitant empirical methodologies. An alternative, integrative approach is called for. In Chapter Eight, Quinn, Spreitzer, and Hart offered such an approach by emphasizing the *interpenetration* of continuity and change. For Salipante in Chapter Five and Evans in Chapter Nine, this integration had the sound of continuity-in-change. For us, it is more like change-in-continuity, where change strategies are seen to be at the service of the preservation and continuity of organizational process, life, structure, and health.

Traditional Conceptions of Continuity and Change

Current approaches to change in organizational life often start with the assumption that change is a one-sided process involving the destruction and replacement of the past with radically different ways of knowing and acting. As organizations struggle to survive during a period in which technological innovations are advancing at an unprecedented pace, they are discovering their environments to be increasingly hostile. Because competitive survival rests on the organization's ability to adapt its organizational processes and strategies, members are faced with continuous internal organizational change as they attempt to meet the demands of their rapidly changing external contexts. As a consequence, organization practitioners have become preoccupied with strategies of change that often fail to affirm the valuable contribution of the organization's past experience. Arguing that the present organizational processes and strategies are only relevant to the present conditions, organizations assume that the future requires innovative change. At the root of this argument is a conception of change that requires that the connection with the past be severed, effecting a kind of death of the old and birth of the new that lacks any referent to the old identity. In this view, retaining continuity in organizational life is correlated with the tenacious commitment to an antiquated course of action that inevitably leads to stagnation, the development of pathological mechanisms, and destruction. Indeed, our extreme distaste for these outcomes seems to have blinded many of today's executives to the seemingly irrational path they have chosen. As Machiavelli puts it in *The Prince* ([1532] 1964, pp. 43, 45), "It must be considered that there is nothing more difficult to carry out, nor more doubtful of success, nor more dangerous to handle, than to initiate a new order of things." Many organizational leaders seem to have taken this advice more as a dare than as a warning.

Organizational change and continuity have been pitted against each other in a dialectical relationship of extremes. Continuity is assumed to be antithetical to the goals of change. It would be helpful to examine the theoretical foundations of this apparent paradox. Poole and Van De Ven (1989) indicated that the development of dialectical, paradoxical theories is often the consequence of our contemporary methodologies that overemphasize internal consistency and attempt to avoid contradictory assumptions. We bound our analyses to enhance the apparent precision of our findings. Because this approach constrains the breadth and depth of our inquiry, the ambiguity and inconsistency of organizations are largely left unacknowledged. Consequently, we seldom develop cohesive and comprehensive theories that embrace paradox. We pursue an argument to its logical extreme rather than confront contradiction and seek more holistic understanding.

The present orientation to the dynamics of change may be a self-fulfilling consequence of widespread acceptance of the "bounded rationality" that March and Simon (1958) and others have posited as the nature of social systems. In this view, organizations are seen as rationally based systems that seek to establish homeostatic equilibrium through internal adaptive processes, yet inevitably fail because of the limitations of human rationality. Much of this and other organizational theory has been rooted in Parsons's (1949) structural-functionalist paradigm, which envisions organizations as rational, purposive, goal-directed entities with cultural roles, norms, and habits that are systematically adapted to the environment to procure internal stability. Parsons claims that organizations have two primary methods of adjusting to the environment. They may either reestablish an equilibrium by maintaining their current structure in the face of changes or undergo structural change by differentiating, specifying, and segmenting their system in response to environmental changes. The concomitant empirical methods of inquiry seek to identify and explain these predictable systematic patterns of organizational dynamics. Through the discovery of conceptual patterns of behavior, it is believed that predictability and control over organizational dynamics are enhanced. However, this paradigm generates mechanistic constructs of organizational culture and change that deny the creative potentiality of organizational life. It constrains our understanding of human intention and choice. For instance, Barrett and Srivastva (1991, p. 234) assert that "our romance with finding transhistorical principles and enduring patterns of behavior has blocked us from realizing the primary goal of science: making human *action* and *interaction* intelligible and understandable. In our efforts to *explain why,* we have been limited in *understanding how.* In a search for general patterns and structures, we have lost sight of the world of contingencies, choices, and dilemmas that do not fall into structural patterns. Human beings are simply not reducible to static properties. Human events are meaningful because of the possibility inherent in choiceful action, not because of inevitability."

Our notions of change become myopic when we attend only to the things that fit the primary assumptions and principles of this structural-functionalist paradigm and disregard other possibilities. When inquiry focuses on explaining the maintenance structures of organizations as a way to control and predict, the historical development of organizational life is largely ignored. The "givenness" of the current order of organizational life is assumed to be primordial, and survival therefore must rest on progressive, if not revolutionary, change. This destructive form of revolutionary change is widespread. Our political history has shown that it is a natural consequence of oppressive reified regimes, from which we rebel to make a clean break from past methods of organizing. Likewise, when organizational processes, structures, and cultures are allowed to become an objectified reality that is no longer perceived to be the product of human intention but is a closed, predetermined fact that is external to human creation, the existing order becomes the object of an oppressive, dehumanizing force that must be challenged and deconstructed. When faced with this condition, organization members seek radical change as a reactive response, disassociating themselves from the identity of the past order. The destruction of the past offers them illusory freedom from their alienation and empowers them with a sense of creative ownership of the new order. Because the functionalist paradigm elicits such predetermined, dehumanized views of organizational reality, the conventional view of change has been embodied in this radical, deconstructive element. But this psychic ownership is born at the cost of continuity. The learnings and experiences of the past become lost remains of an ancient culture.

Since this functionalist paradigm seeks to explain the present in terms of rational, clearly defined, and ordered structures, it essentially ignores or excludes the possible, meaningful contribution of the past in the continual creation of organizational life. Because the actions of organizations are assumed to be objectively predetermined and systematic, the historical contingencies and choices faced in order for them to have existed to the present are neglected. Consequently, the portrayal of organizational culture is limited, if not rejected, by the inadequate comprehension of the living historical foundations of organizational life. Barrett and Srivastva (1991, p. 235) question the degree to which human intention and action can be captured, let alone measured, by empirical constructs: "Human events and choices, such as decisions regarding how to organize, have meaning because of the possibility inherent in the choices, the variety of options and interpretations available, and not because of the dictates of necessity of some enduring pattern or structure."

An Integrative Conception of Continuity and Change

If we explore the dynamic tension between these two apparently opposing constructs, a more integrative perspective emerges that reveals that *change is always at the service of continuity.* We arrived at this proposition by first exploring the definition of *continuity.* The terms *uninterrupted connection, succession,* and *union* were not all that revealing. But the phrase "to hold together" deepened our understanding. Continuity does not entail a static or regressive condition, as previously suggested. For something to be continuous, it must be evolving. Continuity connotes a dynamic process of holding together, or, in other words, preserving connection throughout change. *Organizational continuity may therefore be defined as a process that unifies and links the past to the present and the present to the future, creating a sense of connectedness through transition over time.*

This alternative description of continuity led us to also reexamine the conception of change discussed earlier, which implied a radical and essential shift away from the current state, often incurred at the loss of the original identity. A conception of change that is more relevant to the present construct of continuity may be simply a form of alteration or modification, not a revolutionary deconstruction. This idea of organizational change entails a developmental, transformational, and renewal process. Through this process, connectedness with the past is maintained. Though change entails modification, there still exists something, the essence, that endures. Studies on organizational adaptation and evolution support this approach to organizational change (Singh, House, and Tucker, 1986; Boeker, 1989). These studies stress the important role of the organization's founding principles in effecting the form and course of future organizational change. Boeker (1989) claims that the circumstances surrounding the organization's founding imprint on the early patterns of organizing and affect the range and scope of change strategies considered in the future. He notes that it is not a question of whether organizations are characterized by inertial or adaptive tendencies, but to what extent the organization's initial strategy is more or less open to and capable of adjusting to change in the future. These studies indicate that there exists an important connectedness to the organization's historical foundations in the way it goes about changing. They direct our attention to an idea of evolutionary development as opposed to revolutionary change.

The existence of evolutionary development and renewal compels us to reassess the basic assumptions behind the concept of change. Change is inevitable and is necessary for organizational survival. Yet what is the driving force behind organizational change? One could argue that adaptive structural change is a necessary, planned response to environmental changes in order for the organization to progress and function most effectively in its identification and achievement of goals. But efficiency, progress, and goal attainment are the potential products of change, not the basic purpose of change. At the root of this process of adaptive change is the preservation of the organization, the continuation of the organization's life. As the organization interacts with the environment over time, it evolves in an attempt to preserve continuity, to retain the essence of its founding principles. Essentially, *strategies of change are simply instruments for the preservation and continuity of organizational process, life, structure, and health.* Machiavelli again provides enlightenment. In *The Prince* ([1532] 1964), he provides an example of change. Machiavelli emphasizes the need for change to preserve the power of the monarch of Florence. Though he describes how a monarch may successfully acquire territories and govern most effectively, the underlying goal is the retention of power and authority: the essential nature of monarchies.

Organizational continuity is a process of transformation, which builds on the past by identifying the things that need to be nurtured and enhancing and beautifying them. This construct of continuity does not seek "sameness" in organizational life but urges us to search, value, and develop those attributes and principles that define the organization as a dynamic, living social system. The question arises as to where and how we identify this amorphous essence of organizational life. If we assume that organizations are a social construction, evolving through human intention and choice, then the past principles of organizing will be transmitted through and embodied in the present culture (see, for example, Chapters Two and Four in this volume). Continuity is the forum through which the past is linked to the present and the future is envisioned. Attempts to define and bound this concept of organizational culture are often conflicting and confusing. But Schein (1985b, p. 9) provides a useful definition; he says culture is "a pattern of basic assumptions—invented, discovered, or developed by a given group as it learns to cope with its problems of external adaptation and internal integration—that has worked well enough to be considered valid and, therefore, to be taught to new members as the correct way to perceive, think, and feel in relation to other problems." Culture is thus a set of key assumptions and beliefs based on past and present shared experiences and learned responses as the organization faces the problems of survival. Often these guiding principles are explained and passed on in the form of reified traditions that have no connection with the human events, choices, and meanings that were part of their creation. Truly understanding the meaning and purpose of these principles requires that we engage in historical inquiry that makes us aware of how the past choices and decisions are continued and how they become a living part of the present culture. Culture is not a static product but is the result of a dynamic and evolving learning process. Barrett and Srivastva (1991, p. 236) describe a mode of historical inquiry into organizational culture that preserves continuity by de-reifying past knowledge and recreating the tacit meaning of the past, so that we may better understand and comprehend how it is shaping the present experience: "Understanding human cosmogony is an attempt to frame the future from learnings of the past so the *present can be understood*. We need to direct our efforts not toward explaining how something functions, but understanding how and under what conditions something was created, the choices considered and not taken as well as the paths chosen, the conjectures, the possibilities, the accidental and unintended. Historical awareness is thus empowering because it enhances and deepens understanding of the present."

Robert Frost's poem "The Road Not Taken" serves as a poignant example of the meaning brought forth through historical awareness. It is a personal anecdote, describing the existential dilemma people face in the journey through life. We must make so many choices and decisions as we travel. Our lives take on meaning as we recount the possibilities available and the paths we have chosen. Without this awareness, our lives may appear to be a collection of rambling events. But we take ownership of our lives and understand the present when we examine the alternatives considered. We are the creators of our present existence through the choices we have made.

> Two roads diverged in a yellow wood,
> And sorry I could not travel both
> And be one traveler, long I stood
> And looked down one as far as I could
> To where it bent in the undergrowth;
>
> Then took the other, as just as fair,
> And having perhaps the better claim,
> Because it was grassy and wanted wear;
> Though as for that the passing there
> Had worn them really about the same,
>
> And both that morning equally lay
> In leaves no step had trodden black.
> Oh, I kept the first for another day!
> Yet knowing how way leads on to way,
> I doubted if I should ever come back.
>
> I shall be telling this with a sigh
> Somewhere ages and ages hence:
> Two roads diverged in a wood, and I —
> I took the one less traveled by,
> And that has made all the difference
> [Frost, 1961, p. 131. Reprinted with permission.]

Yet the perception and experience of continuity often evade us. So often we perceive the individual events in our lives to be repetitive, regressive, or even chaotic and beyond our control. Somehow our behaviors appear to be contradictory. We may recognize no coherent pattern. But life does not unfold in a linear unidirected procession of interconnected events and experiences. Our life journey is a fluid, dynamic process of changing. Though the experiences of life and the choices we make may take us on many different courses, apparently deviating from some planned, preestablished path, our lives are not, as such, discontinuous. Often we are only looking at the most visible, overt descriptions. This level of comprehension is not decipherable, because of the variety of subjective interpretations we may impose on events. We may then delve deeper beneath our espoused values and beliefs to decipher some rational connectedness of events. But, once again we are faced with contradiction, because what we consciously know we "ought" to do is not always "what" we do. Additionally, our values have the propensity to undergo transformations. A given value may not continue to work reliably as a solution to the problems we face in our travels. Therefore, we must look deeper into the basic assumptions that guide our behaviors. We should examine those preconscious, intrinsic assumptions that make any other behaviors inconceivable. It is at this root level of comprehension that the continuity in the choices and decisions we have made in our lives exists. It is at this root level, according to Schein (1985b), that we discover the essence of organizational culture. *Historical inquiry into the foundations of human choices and creativity elicits continuity in organizational life.*

The question then arises as to how the fundamental principles are founded and transmitted to the organization members. It has been widely suggested that executives shape the organizational culture and provide the sense of continuity through their vision and actions. In particular, the organization founders are initially responsible for inculcating in the culture the basic assumptions underlying their vision for organizing. Of the many mechanisms available to leaders, simply consistent attention, in the form of rewards (see, for example, Chapter Ten) or everyday talk (Jonas, Fry, and Srivastva, 1990), is a most potent method to convey their basic principles. Additionally, critical incidents are an invaluable source for learning and transmission.

The manner in which the leader responds sends a clear signal to the subordinates. As the culture evolves, these incidents act as guideposts for deciphering the appropriate beliefs, values, and behavior. The critical incidents become beacons in the organization's history that are frequently referenced as members struggle to find solutions to problems in the future.

These fundamental principles of the culture are transmitted to the present and future generations of members by the organization's leadership. Executives, in particular, are the custodians of culture that ensure continuity in organizational life, inculcating the learnings of the past and present so that they may remain an ever-present living part of the future. But most important, the leadership must construe the world of the organization in such a way that attracts and enables collective action. For this reason, historical inquiry is an invaluable contribution to the evolution of culture. "All definitions of culture involve the concept of shared solutions, shared understandings, and consensus" (Schein, 1985b, p. 149). Through historical inquiry, the custodians of culture develop new shared understandings of the present.

The practice of "new manager assimilation" in General Electric's lighting business is a useful example of how an organization can both re-own the past and share understanding and experience fuller meaning in the present. It is commonly known at GE that successful upper- and middle-level managers move to different assignments every eighteen months to two years. For an organization of over ten thousand, that could represent a high degree of turnover and disruption. In addition, those managers wish to make a unique and visible contribution during their short tenure in the job, in order to remain successful in the eyes of their superiors (and therefore mobile). The result, from a staff or department member's perspective, might be continual new agendas, modifications, and additional work. Instead, the organization has recognized the threat of undue disruption and established a structured routine for new managers who inherit "old" staffs or departments. This ritual is called new manager assimilation. It is a half- or full-day meeting, often facilitated by a third party, in which the staff members, whose experience embodies the ongoing practices, values, concerns, and hopes of the workplace, teach the incoming manager about those issues. Their beliefs and expectations are given a full hearing before the new manager is invited to respond and introduce an agenda. By allowing the staff a strong voice at a time when it is typical for a new manager to dominate the dialogue, the forum signifies to everyone that continuity is represented by staff who are less likely to move or transfer than the managers. Yet the outcome of the assimilation exercise is the melding of past practices and values with the new leader's vision in a way that allows improvement, development, and renewal to occur. History, as interpreted by the staff, becomes the context for new ideas and opportunities elicited by the new leader. Disruption is minimized, while commitment to continuing change is fostered. When repeated throughout a system of this size (no upper-level manager is exempt), the assimilation practice shows that change (manager promotion or transfer) actually creates the opportunity to affirm continuity and, at the same time, create the future.

Continuity as an Affirmative Approach to Shaping the Future

Emphasizing change as servicing organizational continuity is an affirmative approach that empowers organized social systems rather than constraining and limiting them. Unlike March and Simon's (1958) proposition that social systems are boundedly rational and therefore limited in their potential to effectively organize and deal with complexity, this paradigm emphasizes the unlimited potentialities and possibilities unleashed through human creation. Rather than focusing on negating problem-solving strategies that yield simple, superficial solutions as an endpoint, identifying and affirming those life-generating forces that are the essence of organizing confirms the members' unique needs. The result is a heightened awareness of their condition and an invitation to envision alternative propositions without fear, because a sense of continuity with the past is the basis for transformation. Since this approach draws attention to the creation of possibilities, it has the potential to generate greater depths of enlightened awareness. For instance, Cooperrider and Srivastva's (1987) research into appreciative inquiry explores this alternative strategy for change. Viewing social existence as a mystery and a miracle that is always open to multiple comprehensions, the authors assert that we may generate knowledge and understanding of the unique qualities of human behavior by affirming and thereby illuminating the factors and forces in organizing that serve to nourish the human spirit.

The inherent value of continuity is its potential to circumvent our natural tendency to resist change. Resistance to organizational change is transformed by acknowledging and affirming the continuity with past ways of knowing. Organization members' resistance to change can prevent them from affecting a change in organizational strategies until their poor performance forces them to take a radically different, discontinuous course of action in a last-ditch attempt to survive. As Staw's (1981) research indicates, their commitment to a course of action can escalate and inhibit the discussion of strategic change possibilities. The consequential decisions to change are often too little and too late and can be destructive to the organization.

This psychological propensity to resist change is a well-known characteristic of human contradiction (Diamond, 1986). Consciously or unconsciously, we exhibit dual behavioral characteristics. We possess the tendency to be change oriented, because life experience urges us to learn about and change ourselves and our worldview as we continue to grow. But this process is met with our seemingly antithetical tendency to protect ourselves against the risk of change. This apparent paradox is conveyed in a symbolic representation of change in Chinese culture. This symbol represents the "crisis of change" with two characters. The upper character represents "danger," while the lower one conveys "hidden opportunity." Because of this duality, change creates feelings of discomfort that evoke varying levels of anxiety and insecurity, which often compel us to maintain the status quo and resist learning. We have developed various modes of defense to avoid anxiety and maintain security that often result in compulsive, repetitive, self-defeating behaviors. But what is it about the process of change that fundamentally threatens us? The painful and confusing events of maturation have taught us that the unknown is not always fortuitous and can be quite frightening. We emerge from infancy with a matured curiosity that emphasizes caution. We naturally begin to take comfort in and are drawn toward those things that are known, that offer us some sense of familiarity and groundedness in the midst of the chaos of our environment. Therefore, we perceive change as threatening, for when something changes, we suddenly become vulnerable. We are no longer in control of that part of our world. What was once sure becomes unsure. We are faced with risks and are forced to develop skills and learn coping strategies in order to adapt to uncertain conditions. Our world paradigm appears to lose its sense of continuity. Consequently, we fear the destructive forces of change and prefer to hold on to what is known and sure and deny the need for change until no other options exist.

This resistance to and fear of organizational change is especially prevalent when technological innovations are introduced into organizational life. The need for changing organizational process through the adoption of technological innovations is often sold to organization members by focusing on what is wrong or inadequate about their present ways of knowing. Their nascent anxieties are evoked by this disconfirming and negating strategy. It threatens to disrupt their world construct and elicits self-protective, defensive processes that distort and narrow their thinking and limit learning. When the sociocultural system of an organization is forced to adapt to rapid changes in the technical system, rearranging itself around external innovations, the organization members are abruptly faced with the perception that they lack control over their environment. Their immediate ways of knowing and behaving are no longer valid. To cope with the turbulent environment, they are forced to learn and adapt to the new ways. This framework of change necessarily invokes defensive responses. Change is a threatening reality that strips the members of the sense of security that they can perform effectively.

But when this framework of change is reversed, bringing that which was background to the foreground, the social system becomes the focus of attention and the idea of change is much less threatening. Technological innovations are adapted to meet the growing needs of the organization members to know and develop adaptive skills.

Organizational performance is enhanced because change is a transformational process that is imbued with a sense of continuation or connectedness. The actions and course of the organization's future are rooted in and build on the effective strategies and meaningful learnings of the past and present experience. Technical innovations become tools to be utilized by the members to improve their performance. Because the technical innovations are adapted to meet members' needs, their perception of control over their environment is enhanced. Though change is always accompanied by anxiety, the degree of threat and defensiveness may be lessened by focusing on the qualities of change that affirm the past.

Nonetheless, organizations must change over time to adapt to the conditions of the environment. The more readily, openly, and consciously an organization experiments with its organizational processes, the more it is capable of discovering and preserving continuity through the retention of its essential nature, its soul. When an organization resists change in an effort to maintain equilibrium in spite of environmental demands, or focuses its change strategies on overcoming resistance, it risks bifurcation and loss of its core values, principles, and history. On some level, an organization must change to cope with environmental changes. Though an organization may appear to maintain its current methods of organizing and responding to the environment, it may unwittingly compromise its founding principles and destroy its soul. For instance, if an American corporation is determined to retain its market niche by maintaining the lowest consumer prices regardless of inflated production costs and competition, it may be forced to compromise business ethics and individual integrity through the exploitation of a Third World labor force. Though the corporation appears to have maintained internal stability, it has fundamentally changed. It has compromised the founding principles and changed the soul of the corporation. But the issue is not that adaptation is the key to the retention or loss of the organization's soul. For an organization may adapt and retain its core values, or it may adapt and lose its core values. For instance, Johnson & Johnson attempted to expand into the health care market to increase revenues, enhance competitive positioning, and benefit shareholders. But in this process of adaptation, the corporation extended itself beyond its knowledge base into a field that did not fit with its basic principles of organizing. Because the leadership lost sight of these founding principles, this venture into health care did not share the history and soul of Johnson & Johnson and failure was inevitable. Yet when the same Johnson & Johnson responded to the Tylenol poisoning crisis, it did effectively adapt and retained its core values. In this critical incident, the leadership reexamined and affirmed the primary assumptions underlying the organization's values, integrity, and business ethics by deciding to first remove the product from the market and then to invest in a new packaging method. Though the corporation incurred a substantial financial loss or short-term investment cost, the leadership affirmed the principles of the organization's culture and strengthened the continuity of its relationship with the consumer. The key point is that continuity can be preserved when organizations are malleable in their responses to their environment, but only when a concerted effort is made to make the founding principles of the past an integral part of the present and future actions. Then the soul of the organization will endure.

In the Conclusion, we have attempted to enunciate the nature of organizational continuity as an alternative paradigm to the structural-functionalist theories. Through a humanistic mode of inquiry into organizational dynamics, we have tried to explore the need to understand and affirm the meanings underlying the choiceful actions of an organization's developmental history.

The message that emerges is that continuity *is* the driving force behind strategies of organizational change. Through historical inquiry into the foundations of human choices in the creation of organized social systems, organizations are capable of creating shared understanding and meaning for their members while adapting more effectively to their changing environments. As the custodians of culture, organization leaders preserve continuity by reaffirming the learnings of the past and present so that they may remain an integral part of the future.

References

Abbey, A., and Dickson, J. "R&D Work Climate and Innovation in Semiconductors." *Academy of Management Journal,* 1983, *26,* 362–368.

Abegglen, J. *The Japanese Factory: Aspects of Its Social Organization.* New York: Free Press, 1958.

Abegglen, J., and Stalk, G. *Kaisha: The Japanese Corporation.* New York: Basic Books, 1985.

Abernathy, W., Clark, K., and Kantrow, A. *Industrial Renaissance.* New York: Basic Books, 1983.

Adams, J. S. "A Framework for the Study of Modes of Resolving Inconsistency." In R. P. Abelson and others (eds.), *Theories of Cognitive Inconsistency: A Sourcebook.* Chicago: Rand McNally, 1968.

Aglietta, M. *A Theory of Capitalist Regulation.* London: New Left Books, 1979.

Alderfer, C. *Existence, Relatedness, and Growth: Human Needs in Organizational Settings.* New York: Free Press, 1972.

Alderfer, C. "Organization Development." *Annual Review of Psychology,* 1977, *28,* 197–223.

Alletzhauser, A. *The House of Nomura.* New York: Arcade, 1990.

Amabile, T. *The Social Psychology of Creativity.* New York: Springer-Verlag, 1983.

Amabile, T. "A Model of Creativity and Innovation in Organizations." *Research in Organizational Behavior,* 1988, *10,* 123–167.

Amabile, T., Hennessey, B., and Grossman, B. "Social Influences on Creativity: The Effects of Contracted-for Reward." *Journal of Personality and Social Psychology,* 1986, *50,* 14–23.

American Compensation Association. "Quantitative, Point-Factor System Is Most Popular." *ACA News,* Sept. 1989, p. 9.

Andrews, K. *The Concept of Corporate Strategy.* Homewood, Ill.: Irwin, 1980.

Aoki, M. *Information, Incentives, and Bargaining in the Japanese Economy.* New York: Cambridge University Press, 1988.

Aram, J. *Dilemmas of Administrative Behavior.* Englewood Cliffs, N.J.: Prentice-Hall, 1976.

Baez, J. *And a Voice to Sing With.* New York: Summit Books, 1987.

Barnard, C. *The Functions of the Executive.* Cambridge, Mass.: Harvard University Press, 1938.

Barrett, F., and Srivastva, S. "History as a Mode of Inquiry in Organizational Life: A Role for Human Cosmogony." *Human Relations,* 1991, *44,* 231–254.

Barrows, S. B. *Mayflower Madam.* New York: Arbor House, 1986.

Bartlett, C., and Ghoshal, G. "Matrix Management: Not a Structure, a Frame of Mind." *Harvard Business Review,* 1990, *68*(4), 138–146.

Bartlett, C., and Ghoshal, S. *Managing Across Borders: The Transnational Solution.* London: Hutchinson, 1989.

Bartolomé, F., and Evans, P. "Must Success Cost So Much?" *Harvard Business Review,* 1980, *58*(2), 137–148.

Bass, B. *Stogdill's Handbook of Leadership.* New York: Free Press, 1981.

Bass, B. *Leadership and Performance Beyond Expectations.* New York: Free Press, 1985.

Bateson, G., and Bateson, M. *Angels Fear: Towards an Epistemology of the Sacred.* New York: Macmillan, 1987.

Bateson, M. *Composing a Life.* New York: Atlantic Monthly Press, 1989.

Bateson, M. *Our Own Metaphor.* New York: Smithsonian Press, 1991.

Baudrillard, J. *In the Shadow of Silent Majorities — or the End of the Social.* New York: Senortexte, 1983.

Bauman, Z. *Legislators and Interpreters.* Ithaca, N.Y.: Cornell University Press, 1987.

Beckhard, R. *Organization Development: Strategies and Models.* Reading, Mass.: Addison-Wesley, 1969.

Beckhard, R., and Harris, R. *Organization Transitions: Managing Complex Change.* Reading, Mass.: Addison-Wesley, 1977.

Beer, M., Eisenstat, R., and Spector, B. "Why Change Programs Don't Produce Change." *Harvard Business Review,* 1990, *68*(6), 158–166.

Belbin, R. M. *Management Teams: Why They Succeed or Fail.* London: Heinemann, 1981.

Belenky, M., Clinchy, B., Goldberger, N., and Tarule, J. *Women's Ways of Knowing.* New York: Basic Books, 1986.

Bell, D. *The Coming of the Post-Industrial Society.* New York: Basic Books, 1976.

Bennis, W. *Leaders.* New York: HarperCollins, 1985.

Bennis, W., Benne, K., and Chin, R. *The Planning of Change.* New York: Holt, Rinehart & Winston, 1976.

Bernstein, B. *Class, Codes, and Control.* London: Routledge, 1982.

Best, M. *The New Competition.* Oxford, England: Polity Press, 1990.

Blake, R., and Mouton, J. *The Managerial Grid III.* Houston, Tex.: Gulf, 1985.

Blau, P. *The Dynamics of Bureaucracy.* Chicago: University of Chicago Press, 1955.

Bobko, P. "Removing Assumptions of Bipolarity: Towards Variation and Circularity." *Academy of Management Review,* 1985, *19,* 99–108.

Bobko, P., and Schwartz, J. "A Metric for Integrating Theoretically Related But Statistically Uncorrelated Constructs." *Journal of Personality Assessment,* 1984, *48,* 11–16.

Boeker, W. "Strategic Change: The Effects of Founding and History." *Academy of Management Journal,* 1989, *32,* 489–515.

Bouwen, R., and Fry, R. "An Agenda for Managing Organizational Development and Innovation in the 1990s." In M. Lambrecht (ed.), *Corporate Revival.* Belgium: Leuven University Press, 1988.

Brauchli, M. "Japanese Companies Keep Employees Together — Even the Dearly Departed." *Wall Street Journal,* July 10, 1989, p. A6.

Briggs, J., and Peat, F. *Turbulent Mirror.* New York: Harper-Collins, 1989.

Brownmiller, S. *Against Our Will: Men, Women, and Rape.* New York: Simon & Schuster, 1975.

Brusco, S. "Small Firms and the Provision of Real Services." Paper presented at the International Conference on Industrial Districts and Economic Regeneration, Geneva, Oct. 18–19, 1990.

Burgelman, R. *Inside Corporate Innovation.* New York: Free Press, 1985.

Burke, C. "Report from Paris: Women's Writing and the Women's Movement." *Signs,* 1978, *3,* 844.

Burns, J. *Leadership.* New York: HarperCollins, 1978.

Burns, T., and Stalker, G. *The Management of Innovation.* London: Tavistock, 1961.

"Business Fads—What's In-and-Out." *Business Week,* Jan. 20, 1986, pp. 52–55.

Cameron, K, Freeman, S., and Mishra, A. "Organizational Downsizing and Redesign." Unpublished paper, School of Business Administration, University of Michigan, 1991.

Cameron, K., and Quinn, R. "Organizational Paradox and Transformation." In R. Quinn and K. Cameron (eds.), *Paradox and Transformation: Toward a Theory of Change in Organizations and Management.* New York: Ballinger, 1988.

Campbell, D., and Fiske, D. "Convergent and Discriminant Validation by the Multitrait-Multimethod Matrix." *Psychological Bulletin,* 1959, *56,* 81–105.

Campbell, J. *The Hero with a Thousand Faces.* New York: Pantheon, 1956.

Campbell, J. *Myths to Live by.* New York: Viking Penguin, 1972.

Candrilli, A., and Armagast, R. "The Case of Effective Point-Factor Job Evaluation, Viewpoint 2." *Personnel,* Apr. 1987, pp. 33–36.

Carroll, S. "Business Strategies and Compensation Systems." In D. Balkin and L. Gomez-Mejia (eds.), *New Perspectives in Compensation.* Englewood Cliffs, N.J.: Prentice-Hall, 1987.

Certo, S. C. *Principles of Modern Management.* Dubuque, Iowa: William C. Brown, 1986.

Chaillou, B. "Definition et typologie de la sous-traitance." *Revue Economique*, 1977, *2*(28), 262–285.

Chandler, A. *Strategy and Structure*. Cambridge, Mass.: MIT Press, 1969.

Chandler, A. *Scale and Scope: The Dynamics of Industrial Capitalism*. Cambridge, Mass.: Harvard University Press, 1990.

Cheng, N. *Life and Death in Shanghai*. New York: Viking Penguin, 1986.

Child, J., and Loveridge, R. *Information Technology in Europe*. Oxford, England: Blackwell, 1990.

Chin, R., and Benne, K. "General Strategies for Effecting Changes in Human Systems." In W. Bennis, K. Benne, and R. Chin, (eds.), *The Planning of Change*. New York: Holt, Rinehart & Winston, 1976.

Chodorow, N. *The Reproduction of Mothering: Psychoanalysis and the Sociology of Gender*. Berkeley: University of California Press, 1978.

Clark, R. *The Japanese Company*. New Haven, Conn.: Yale University Press, 1979.

Clegg, S. *Modern Organisations*. London: Sage, 1990.

Cohen, M., March, J., and Olsen, J. "The Garbage Can Model of Organizational Choice." *Administrative Science Quarterly*, 1972, *17*, 1–25.

Cole, R. *Japanese Blue Collar: The Changing Tradition*. Berkeley: University of California Press, 1971.

Cole, R. *Work, Mobility, and Participation: A Comparative Study of American and Japanese Industry*. Berkeley: University of California Press, 1979.

Conger, J. A. *The Charismatic Leader: Beyond the Mystique of Exceptional Leadership*. San Francisco: Jossey-Bass, 1989.

Conger, J., and Kanungo, R. "Towards a Behavioral Theory of Charismatic Leadership in Organizational Settings." *Academy of Management Review*, 1987, *12*, 637–647.

Cooperrider, D. L. "Appreciative Inquiry in Organizational Life." In W. Pasmore and R. Woodman (eds.), *Research in Organizational Change and Development*. Vol. 1. Greenwich, Conn.: JAI Press, 1987.

Cooperrider, D. L. "Positive Image, Positive Action: The Affirmative Basis of Organizing." In S. Srivastva, D. L. Cooperrider, and Associates, *Appreciative Management and Leadership: The Power of Positive Thought and Action in Organizations.* San Francisco: Jossey-Bass, 1990.

Cooperrider, D., and Srivastva, S. "Appreciative Inquiry in Organizational Life." *Research in Organizational Change and Development,* 1987, *1,* 129–169.

Crosson, P., and Rosenberg, N. "Strategies for Agriculture." *Scientific American,* Sept. 1989, pp. 128–132.

Dalton, G. "Motivation and Control." In G. Dalton and P. Lawrence (eds.), *Motivation and Control in Organizations.* Homewood, Ill.: Irwin, 1971.

Damanpour, F., and Evan, W. "Organizational Innovation and Performance: The Problem of 'Organizational Lag.'" *Administrative Science Quarterly,* 1984, *29,* 392–409.

Deal, T., and Kennedy, A. *Corporate Cultures: The Rites and Rituals of Corporate Life.* Reading, Mass.: Addison-Wesley, 1982.

Deci, E. *Intrinsic Motivation.* New York: Plenum, 1975.

Deleuze, G., and Guattari, F. *Capitalisme et schizophrénie.* Vol. 2. Paris: Editions de Minuit, 1980.

de Man, P. "Autobiography as De-Facement." *Modern Language Notes,* 1979, *94,* 920.

Deming, W. *Quality, Productivity, and Competitive Position.* Cambridge, Mass.: MIT Press, 1982.

Denison, D. *Corporate Culture and Organizational Effectiveness.* New York: Wiley, 1990.

Diamond, M. "Resistance to Change: A Psychoanalytic Critique of Argyris and Schön's Contributions to Organization Theory and Intervention." *Journal of Management Studies,* 1986, *23,* 543–562.

Dinnerstein, D. *The Mermaid and the Minotaur.* New York: HarperCollins, 1976.

Dore, R. *British Factory — Japanese Factory.* Berkeley: University of California Press, 1973.

Douglas, M. *In Active Voice.* London: Routledge, 1982.

Dover, M., and Talbot, L. "Feeding the Earth: An Agroecological Solution." *Technology Review,* 1988, *91,* 26–35.

Doyle, R. *Gainsharing and Productivity.* New York: AMACOM, 1983.

Doz, Y. *Strategic Management in Multinational Companies.* Elmsford, N.Y.: Pergamon Press, 1986.

Driver, M. "Career Concepts and Organizational Change." In C. B. Derr (ed.), *Work, Family, and the Career.* New York: Praeger, 1980.

Dunphy, D. "Convergence/Divergence: A Temporal Review of the Japanese Enterprise and Its Management." *Academy of Management Review,* 1987, *12*(3), 445–459.

DuPlessis, R. *Writing Beyond the Ending.* Bloomington: University of Indiana Press, 1985.

Durkheim, E. *The Division of Labor in Society.* Glencoe, Ill.: Free Press, 1947. (G. Simpson, trans. Originally published 1893.)

Durkheim, E. *The Division of Labour in Society.* London: Macmillan, 1964. (Originally published 1893.)

Dyas, G., and Thanheiser, H. *The Emerging European Enterprise.* London: Macmillan, 1976.

Dyer, W. "The Cycle of Cultural Evolution in Organizations." In R. H. Kilmann, M. J. Saxton, R. Serpa, and Associates, *Gaining Control of the Corporate Culture.* San Francisco: Jossey-Bass, 1985.

Edwards, R. *Contested Terrain.* London: Heinemann, 1979.

Ehrenfeld, D. "Beyond the Farming Crisis." *Technology Review,* 1987, *90,* 46–56.

Elger, T., and Fairbrother, P. "Inflexible Flexibility." Paper presented at the annual conference of the British Sociological Association, Apr. 3, 1990.

Ellerbee, L. *And So It Goes: Adventures in Television.* New York: Putnam, 1986.

Emery, F., and Trist, E. "The Causal Texture of Organizational Environments." *Human Relations,* 1965, *18,* 21–32.

Erikson, E. *Identity: Youth and Crisis.* New York: W.W.Norton, 1968.

Evans, P. "Organizational Development in the Transnational Enterprise." In R. Woodman and W. Pasmore (eds.), *Research in Organizational Change and Development.* Vol. 3. Greenwich, Conn.: JAI Press, 1989.

Evans, P. "International Management Development and the Balance Between Generalism and Professionalism." *Personnel Management,* 1990, *7,* 46–50.

Evans, P. "Duality Theory: New Directions for Human Resource and Organizational Management." In C. Lattmann and B. Staffelbach (eds.), *Die Personalfunktion der Unternehmung im Spannungsfeld von Humanität und Wirtschaftlicher Rationalität.* Heidelberg, Germany: Physica-Verlag, 1991.

Evans, P., and Bartolomé, F. "Professional Lives Versus Private Lives: Shifting Patterns of Managerial Commitment." *Organizational Dynamics,* 1979, *7,* 2–29.

Evans, P., and Bartolomé, F. *Must Success Cost So Much?* New York: Basic Books, 1981.

Evans, P., and Bartolomé, F. "The Changing Pictures of the Relationship Between Career and Family." *Journal of Occupational Behavior,* 1984, *5,* 9–21.

Evans, P., and Bartolomé, F. "The Dynamics of Work-Family Relationships in Managerial Lives." *International Review of Applied Psychology,* 1986, *35,* 371–395.

Evans, P., and Doz, Y. "The Dualistic Organization." In P. Evans, Y. Doz, and A. Laurent (eds.), *Human Resource Management in International Firms: Change, Globalization, Innovation.* London: Macmillan, 1989.

Evans, P., and Farquhar, A. "Apple Computer Europe." In F. Foulkes and R. Livernash (eds.), *Human Resource Management: Cases and Texts.* Englewood Cliffs, N.J.: Prentice-Hall, 1989.

Evans, P., Lank, E., and Farquhar, A. "Managing Human Resources in the International Firm: Lessons from Practice." In P. Evans, Y. Doz, and A. Laurent (eds.), *Human Resource Management in International Firms: Change, Globalization, Innovation.* London: Macmillan, 1989.

Farquhar, A., Evans, P., and Tawedey, K. "Lessons from Practice in Managing Organizational Change." In P. Evans, Y. Doz, and A. Laurent (eds.), *Human Resource Management in International Firms: Change, Globalization, Innovation.* London: Macmillan, 1989.

Farris, G. "Groups and the Informal Organization." In R. Payne and C. Cooper (eds.), *Groups at Work.* New York: Wiley, 1981.

Farris, G. "Effective Leadership in Research and Development." Paper presented at the ORSA/TIMS Joint National Meeting, New York, Oct. 1989.

Faucheaux, C., Amato, G., and Laurent, A. "Organizational Development and Change." *Annual Review of Psychology,* 1982, *33,* 343–370.

Felson, R. "Ambiguity and Bias in Self-Concept." *Social Psychology Quarterly,* 1981, *44,* 64–69.

Feynman, R. P. "Surely You're Joking, Mr. Feynman!" New York: Bantam Books, 1986.

Flaherty, J., and Dusek, J. "An Investigation of the Relationship Between Psychological Androgyny and Components of Self-Concept." *Journal of Personality and Social Psychology,* 1981, *44,* 64–69.

Franklin, J. "Characteristics of Successful and Unsuccessful Organization Development." *Journal of Applied Behavioral Sciences,* 1976, *12*(4), 471–492.

Friedlander, F., and Brown, L. "Organization Development." *Annual Review of Psychology,* 1974, *25,* 313–341.

Friedman, R. A. "Interaction Norms as Carriers of Organizational Culture." *Journal of Contemporary Psychology,* 1989, *18*(1), 3–29.

Frone, M., Adams, J., Rice, R., and Instone-Noonan, D. "Halo Error: A Field Study Comparison of Self and Subordinate Evaluations of Leadership Process and Leader Effectiveness." *Personality and Social Psychology Bulletin,* 1986, *12*(4), 454–461.

Frost, R. *Complete Poems of Robert Frost.* New York: Holt, Rinehart & Winston, 1961.

Frye, N. *Anatomy of Criticism.* Princeton, N.J.: Princeton University Press, 1957.

Galbraith, J. *Designing Complex Organizations.* Reading, Mass.: Addison-Wesley, 1972.

Galbraith, J. *Organizational Design.* Reading, Mass.: Addison-Wesley, 1977.

Galbraith, J. "Designing the Innovating Organization." *Organizational Dynamics,* 1982, *10,* 5–25.

Galbraith, J., and Kazanjian, R. *Strategy Implementation.* St. Paul, Minn.: West, 1986.

Gallie, T. *Philosophy and Historical Understanding.* London: Chatto and Windus, 1968.

Gardner, J. *Self-Renewal: The Individual and the Innovative Society.* New York: W.W.Norton, 1981.

Gergen, K. "The Social Constructionist Movement in Modern Psychology." *American Psychologist,* 1985, *40,* 266–275.

Gergen, K. *The Saturated Self.* New York: Basic Books, 1991.

Gergen, K. "Organizational Theory in the Postmodern Era." In M. Reed and M. Hughes (eds.), *Rethinking Organization.* London: Sage, forthcoming.

Gergen, K., and Gergen, M. "Narrative of the Self." In K. Schiebe and T. Sarbin (eds.), *Studies in Social Identity.* New York: Praeger, 1983.

Gergen, K., and Gergen, M. "Narrative Form and the Construction of Psychological Science." In T. R. Sarbin (ed.), *Narrative Psychology: The Storied Nature of Human Conduct.* New York: Praeger, 1986.

Gergen, K., and Gergen, M. "Narrative and the Self as Relationship." In L. Berkowitz (ed.), *Advances in Experimental and Social Psychology.* San Diego, Calif.: Academic Press, 1988.

Gergen, M. "Talking About Menopause: A Dialogic Analysis." In L. Thomas (ed.), *Research on Adulthood and Aging: The Human Sciences Approach.* Albany, N.Y.: SUNY Press, 1989.

Gergen, M. "Life Stories: Pieces of a Dream." In G. Rosenwald and R. Ochberg (eds.), *Telling Lives.* New Haven, Conn.: Yale University Press, forthcoming.

Getty, J. P. *As I See It: An Autobiography of J. Paul Getty.* New York: Berkley Books, 1986.

Giddens, A. *The Consequences of Modernity.* Oxford, England: Polity Press, 1990.

Gilbreth, L. *The Psychology of Management.* New York: Sturgis and Walton, 1914.

Gilligan, C. *In a Different Voice: Psychological Theory and Women's Development.* Cambridge, Mass.: Harvard University Press, 1982.

Gispen, K. *New Profession, Old Order: Engineers and German Society, 1815–1914.* Cambridge, England: Cambridge University Press, 1990.

Gleick, J. *Chaos: Making a New Science.* New York: Viking Penguin, 1987.

Goffman, E. *Asylums.* New York: Anchor Books, 1961.

Gold, A. "Quebec Indians Ponder the True Cost of Electricity." *New York Times,* Oct. 12, 1990, p. A10.

Golden, K. *Human Resource Management in a Traditional Organization.* Unpublished doctoral dissertation, Weatherhead School of Management, Case Western Reserve University, 1988.

Golden, K., and Salipante, P. "Tradition as a Cultural System." Unpublished paper, Emory University, Atlanta, Ga., 1990.

Golding, A. *The Semi-Conductor Industry in Britain and the United States.* Unpublished doctoral dissertation, Science Policy Research Unit, University of Sussex, England, 1972.

Golembiewski, R., Billingsley, K., and Yeager, S. "Measuring Change and Persistence in Human Affairs: Types of Change Generated by OD Designs." *Journal of Applied Behavioral Sciences,* 1975, *12,* 133–157.

Gordon, A. *The Evolution of Labor Relations in Japan: Heavy Industry, 1853–1955.* Cambridge, Mass.: Harvard University Press, 1985.

Gouldner, A. *Patterns of Industrial Bureaucracy.* New York: Free Press, 1954.

Graham-Moore, B. "Review of the Literature." In B. Graham-Moore and T. Ross (eds.), *Gainsharing: Plans for Improving Performance.* Washington, D.C.: Bureau of National Affairs, 1990.

Greene, D., Sternberg, B., and Lepper, M. "Overjustification in a Token Economy." *Journal of Personality and Social Psychology,* 1976, *34,* 1219–1234.

Greiner, L. "Patterns of Organization Change." *Harvard Business Review,* 1967, *45,* 119–128.

Greiner, L. "Evolution and Revolution as Organizations Grow." *Harvard Business Review,* 1972, *50,* 37–46.

Griffin, S. *Rape: The Power of Consciousness.* San Francisco: HarperCollins, 1979.

Gupta, N., Schweizer, T., and Jenkins, G. "Pay for Knowledge Compensation Plans: Hypotheses and Survey Results." *Monthly Labor Review,* 1987, *110*(10), 40–43.

Gusfield, J. "Tradition and Modernity: Misplaced Polarities in the Study of Social Change." *American Journal of Sociology,* 1967, *72*(4), 351–362.

Hackman, J., and Oldham, G. *Work Redesign.* Reading, Mass.: Addison-Wesley, 1980.

Halberstam, R. *The Breaks of the Game.* New York: Knopf, 1981.

Hall, D. *Careers in Organizations.* Glenville, Ill.: Scott, Foresman, 1976.

Hamel, G., and Prahalad, C. K. "Strategic Intent." *Harvard Business Review,* 1989, *67,* 63–76.

Hammer, T. "New Developments in Profit Sharing, Gain-Sharing, and Employee Ownership." In J. P. Campbell, R. J. Campbell, and Associates, *Productivity in Organizations: New Perspectives from Industrial and Organizational Psychology.* San Francisco: Jossey-Bass, 1988.

Hampden-Turner, C. *Maps of the Mind.* New York: Macmillan, 1981.

Hampden-Turner, C. *Charting the Corporate Mind.* New York: Free Press, 1990.

Hampden-Turner, C., and Baden-Fuller, C. W. "Strategic Choice and the Management of Dilemma: Lessons for the Domestic Appliance Industry." Unpublished paper, Business School, University of London, 1989.

Hannan, M., and Freeman, J. "Structural Inertia and Organizational Change." *American Sociological Review,* 1984, *49,* 149–164.

Hardy, B. "Towards a Poetics of Fiction: An Approach Through Narrative." *Novel,* 1968, *2,* 5–14.

Harrison, R. "Strategies for a New Age." *Human Resource Management,* 1983, *22,* 209–235.

Harshbarger, D. "Takeover: A Tale of Loss, Change, and Growth." *Academy of Management Executive,* 1987, *1,* 127–138.

Hartsock, N. *Money, Sex, and Power: Toward a Feminist Historical Materialism.* White Plains, N.Y.: Longman, 1983.

Haus, R. *Katalog zu der Jubiaums.* Stuttgart: Robert Bosch Haus, 1986.

Hedberg, B., Nystrom, P., and Starbuck, W. "Camping on Seasaws: Prescriptions for a Self-Designing Organization." *Administrative Science Quarterly,* 1976, *21.*

Helper, S. "Comparative Supplier Relations in the U.S. and Japanese Auto Industries: An Exit/Voice Approach." *Business and Economic History,* 1990.

Hemphill, J., and Coons, A. "Development of the Leader Behavior Development Questionnaire." In R. Stogdill and A.

Coons (eds.), *Leaders' Behavior: Its Descriptions and Measurement.* Columbus: Ohio State University Press, 1957.

Herrigel, G. "The Politics of Large Firm Relations with Industrial Districts." Paper presented at a workshop titled "Networks: On the Socio-Economics of Inter-Firm Cooperation," Social Science Center, Free University of Berlin, June 1990.

Herrnstein, R. "Nature as Nurture: Behaviorism and the Instinct Doctrine." *Behaviorism,* 1974, *1,* 23–52.

Herzberg, F. *Work and the Nature of Man.* New York: World, 1966.

Hillebrand, W. "Der Stille Reformer." *Manager Magazine,* Nov. 1989, pp. 34–49.

Hirsch, F. *Social Limits to Growth.* Cambridge, Mass.: Harvard University Press, 1976.

Hirschman, A. *Exit, Voice, and Loyalty: Responses to Decline in Firms, Organizations, and States.* Cambridge, Mass.: Harvard University Press, 1970.

Hitotsubashi Shoten. *Kikai Gyokai Shushoku Shiken.* Tokyo: Hitotsubashi Shoten, 1984.

Hobsbawm, E. *Labouring Men.* London: Weidenfeld and Nicholson, 1964.

Hofstede, G. "Motivation, Leadership, and Organization: Do American Theories Apply Abroad?" *Organizational Dynamics,* 1980, 42–63.

Hofstede, G., Neuijen, B., Ohayv, D., and Sanders, G. "Measuring Organizational Cultures: A Qualitative and Quantitative Study Across Twenty Cases." *Administrative Science Quarterly,* 1990, *35*(9), 286–316.

Hollander, E. "Conformity, Status, and Idiosyncrasy Credit." *Psychological Review,* 1958, *65,* 117–127.

House, R., and Mitchell, T. "Path-Goal Theory of Leadership." *Journal of Contemporary Business,* 1974, *3*(4), 81–97.

Iacocca, L. *Iacocca: An Autobiography.* New York: Bantam Books, 1984.

Inohara, H. *Human Resource Development in Japanese Companies.* Tokyo: Asian Productivity Organization, 1990.

Itami, H. *Mobilizing Invisible Assets.* Cambridge, Mass.: Harvard University Press, 1987.

Jaggar, A., and Bordo, S. (eds.). *Gender/Bodyknowledge: Feminist Reconstructions of Being and Knowing*. New Brunswick, N.J.: Rutgers University Press, 1989.

James, W. *Pragmatism: A New Name for Some Old Ways of Thinking*. White Plains, N.Y.: Longman, 1907.

Japan Iron and Steel Federation. *The Steel Industry of Japan, 1990*. (Annual report.) Tokyo: Japan Iron and Steel Federation, 1990.

Japan Ministry of Finance. *Yuka Shoken Hohkoku Soran: Kawasaki Seitetsu Kabushiki Kaisha*. Tokyo: Japan Ministry of Finance, 1989.

Jelinek, E. *Women's Autobiography: Essays in Criticism*. Bloomington: Indiana University Press, 1980.

Johnson, A. "3M Organized to Innovate." *Management Review*, 1986, *75*, 38–39.

Joho Shisutemu Senta. *Shushoku Deta Tokuhon: Kagaku Yakuhin*. Tokyo: Joho Shisutemu Senta, 1988.

Jonas, H., Fry, R., and Srivastva, S. "The Person of the CEO: Understanding the Executive Experience." *Academy of Management Executive*, 1989, *3*, 205–215.

Jonas, H., Fry, R., and Srivastva, S. "The Office of the CEO: Understanding the Executive Experience." *Academy of Management Executive*, 1990, *4*, 36–48.

Kanter, R. *Work and Family in the United States*. New York: Russell Sage Foundation, 1977.

Kanter, R. *The Change Masters*. New York: Simon & Schuster, 1983.

Kanter, R. "When a Thousand Flowers Bloom: Structural, Collective, and Social Conditions for Innovation in Organizations." *Research in Organizational Behavior*, 1988, *10*, 169–211.

Kanter, R. *When Giants Learn to Dance*. London: Unwin, 1990.

Kanungo, R. *Work Alienation: An Integrative Approach*. New York: Praeger, 1982.

Kaplinsky, R. *Automation: The Technology and Society*. London: Longman, 1984.

Katz, D., and Kahn, R. L. *The Social Psychology of Organizations*. New York: Wiley, 1966.

Katz, D., and Kahn, R. *The Social Psychology of Organizations*. (2nd ed.) New York: Wiley, 1978.

Katz, R., and Van Maanen, J. "The Loci of Work Satisfaction." In P. Warr (ed.), *Organizational Careers: Some New Perspectives.* New York: Wiley, 1976.

Kiefer, C., and Senge, P. "Metanoic Organizations." In J. Adams (ed.), *Transforming Organizations.* Alexandria, Va.: Miles River Press, 1984.

Kilmann, R. H., Saxton, M. J., Serpa, R., and Associates. *Gaining Control of the Corporate Culture.* San Francisco: Jossey-Bass, 1985.

Kim, W., and Mauborgne, R. "Implementing Global Strategies: The Role of Procedural Justice." *Strategic Management Journal,* 1991, *12,* 125–144.

Klavens, R., Shanley, M., and Evan, W. "The Management of Internal Corporate Ventures: Entrepreneurship and Innovation." *Columbia Journal of World Business,* 1985, *20,* 21–27.

Klein, D. "Some Notes on the Dynamics of Resistance to Change: The Defender Role." *Concepts for Social Change.* Cooperative Project for Educational Development Services, no. 1. Washington, D.C.: National Training Laboratories, 1966.

Klein, J. "Parenthetic Learning: Toward the Unlearning of the Learning Model." *Journal of Management Studies,* 1989, *xx,* 291–308.

Klinger, E. *Meaning and Void: Inner Experience and the Incentive in People's Lives.* Minneapolis: University of Minnesota Press, 1977.

Knorr-Cetina, K. *The Manufacture of Knowledge.* Elmsford, N.Y.: Pergamon Press, 1981.

Knowlton, C. "Keeping the Fires Lit Under the Innovators." *Fortune,* Mar. 28, 1988, p. 45.

Koch, E. *Mayor.* New York: Warner Books, 1984.

Koenig, R. "DuPont Plan Linking Pay to Fibers Profit Unravels." *Wall Street Journal,* Oct. 25, 1990, p. 59.

Kolb, D., and Frohman, A. "An Organization Development Approach to Consulting." *Sloan Management Review,* 1970, *12,* 51–65.

Kono, T. *Strategy and Structure of Japanese Enterprises.* Armonk, N.Y.: Sharpe, 1984.

Kopelman, R. E., Brief, A. P., and Guzzo, R. A. "The Role of Climate and Culture in Productivity." In B. Schneider (ed.), *Organizational Climate and Culture.* San Francisco: Jossey-Bass, 1990.

Kotter, J., and Schlesinger, L. "Choosing Strategies for Change." *Harvard Business Review,* 1979, *57*(2), 106–114.

Kuhn, T. *The Structure of Scientific Revolutions.* (2nd ed.) Chicago: University of Chicago Press, 1970.

Lacey, H., and Schwartz, B. "Behaviorism, Intentionality, and Sociohistorical Structure." *Behaviorism,* 1986, *14,* 193–210.

Lacey, H., and Schwartz, B. "The Explanatory Power of Radical Behaviorism." In S. Modgil and C. Modgil (eds.), *B. F. Skinner: Consensus and Controversy.* New York: Falmer Press, 1987.

Landy, F., Barnes-Farell, J., Vance, R., and Steel, J. "Statistical Control of Halo Error in Performance Ratings." *Journal of Applied Psychology,* 1980, *65,* 506–601.

Lash, S. *Sociology of Postmodernism.* London: Routledge, 1990.

Latham, C., and Wexley, K. *Increasing Productivity Through Performance Appraisal.* Reading, Mass.: Addison-Wesley, 1981.

Latour, B. *Science in Action.* Cambridge, Mass.: Harvard University Press, 1987.

Laurent, A. "A Cultural View of Organizational Change." In P. Evans, Y. Doz, and A. Laurent (eds.), *Human Resource Management in International Firms: Change, Globalization, Innovation.* London: Macmillan, 1989.

Lawler, E. E., III. *Pay and Organizational Effectiveness: A Psychological View.* New York: McGraw-Hill, 1971.

Lawler, E. E., III. "What's Wrong with Point-Factor Job Evaluation?" *Management Review,* 1986, *75,* 44–48.

Lawler, E. E., III. *Strategic Pay: Aligning Organizational Strategies and Pay Systems.* San Francisco: Jossey-Bass, 1990.

Lawler, E. E., III, Ledford, G., and Mohrman, S. *Employee Involvement in America: A Study of Contemporary Practice.* Houston, Tex.: American Productivity and Quality Center, 1989.

Leibowitz, H. *Fabricating Lives: Explorations in American Autobiography.* New York: Knopf, 1989.

Lepper, M., and Greene, D. (eds.). *The Hidden Costs of Reward.* Hillsdale, N.J.: Erlbaum, 1978.

Lepper, M., Greene, D., and Nisbett, R. "Undermining Children's Intrinsic Interest with Extrinsic Rewards: A Test of the 'Overjustification' Hypothesis." *Journal of Personality and Social Psychology*, 1973, *28*, 129–137.

Levinson, D., and others. *The Seasons of a Man's Life*. New York: Knopf, 1978.

Levy, A. "Second Order Planned Change: Definition and Conceptualization." *Organizational Dynamics*, 1987, *15*, 4–20.

Levy, A., and Merry, U. *Organizational Transformation: Approaches, Strategies, Theories*. New York: Praeger, 1986.

Lewin, K. *Field Theory in Social Science*. New York: HarperCollins, 1951.

Lincoln, J., and Kalleberg, A. *Culture, Control, and Commitment: A Study of Work Attitudes in the United States and Japan*. Cambridge, England: Cambridge University Press, 1990.

Lippitt, R., Watson, J., and Westley, B. *The Dynamics of Planned Change*. Orlando, Fla.: Harcourt Brace Jovanovich, 1958.

Locke, E. A. "Personnel Attitudes and Motivation." *Annual Review of Psychology*, 1976, *26*, 457–480.

Lodge, C. G., and Vogel, E. F. *Ideology and National Competitiveness: An Analysis of Nine Countries*. Cambridge, Mass.: Harvard Business School, Publishing Division, 1987.

Lorsch, J. "Strategic Myopia: Culture as an Invisible Barrier to Change." In R. H. Kilmann, M. J. Saxton, R. Serpa, and Associates, *Gaining Control of the Corporate Culture*. San Francisco: Jossey-Bass, 1985.

Loveridge, R. "Business Strategy and Community Culture: Policy as a Structural Accommodation of Conflict." In D. Dunkerley and G. Salaman (eds.), *The International Yearbook of Organization Studies*. London: Routledge and Kegan Paul, 1981.

Loveridge, R. "Sources of Diversity in Internal Markets." *Sociology*, 1983, *17*, 44–62.

Loveridge, R. "Apocalyptic Change and Technological Innovation." Paper presented in the Workshop on Microsociology and Microeconomics, Institute of Science and Technology, University of Manchester, England, Sept. 1990a.

Loveridge, R. "Footfalls of the Future." In R. Loveridge and M. Pitt, *The Strategic Management of Technological Innovation*. New York: Wiley, 1990b.

Lu, D. *Inside Corporate Japan*. Tokyo: Tuttle, 1987.

Lublinski, D., Tellegen, A., and Butcher, J. "The Relationship Between Androgyny and Subjective Indicators of Emotional Well-Being." *Journal of Personality and Social Psychology,* 1981, *40,* 722–730.

Luthans, F., Welsh, D., and Taylor, L. "A Descriptive Model of Managerial Effectiveness." *Group and Organizational Studies,* 1988, *13,* 148–162.

Lynn, L. *How Japan Innovates: A Comparison with the U.S. in the Case of Oxygen Steelmaking.* Boulder, Colo.: Westview Press, 1982.

Lynn, L. "Multinational Joint Ventures in the Steel Industry." In D. Mowery (ed.), *International Collaborative Ventures in U.S. Manufacturing.* New York: Ballinger, 1988.

Lynn, L. "Technology and Organizations: A Cross-National Analysis." In P. S. Goodman, L. S. Sproull, and Associates, *Technology and Organizations.* San Francisco: Jossey-Bass, 1990.

Lynn, L., Piehler, H., and Zahray, W. *Engineering Graduates in the United States and Japan: A Comparison of Their Numbers and an Empirical Study of Their Careers and Methods of Information Transfer.* Final report to the National Science Foundation, grant no. SRS-84099836. Washington, D.C.: Government Printing Office, 1988.

Lyotard, J. *The Postmodern Condition: A Report on Knowledge.* Minneapolis: University of Minnesota Press, 1984.

McAdams, D. *Power, Intimacy, and the Life Story: Personalogical Inquiries into Identity.* New York: Guilford Press, 1985.

McGraw, K. "The Detrimental Effects of Reward on Performance: A Literature Review and a Prediction Model." In M. Lepper and D. Greene (eds.), *The Hidden Costs of Rewards.* Hillsdale, N.J.: Erlbaum, 1978.

McGregor, D. *The Human Side of Enterprise.* New York: McGraw-Hill, 1960.

Machiavelli, N. *The Prince.* (M. Musa, trans. and ed.) New York: St. Martin's Press, 1964. (Originally published 1532.)

MacIntyre, A. *After Virtue.* South Bend, Ind.: University of Notre Dame Press, 1981.

McMillan, C. *The Japanese Industrial System.* Berlin: de Gruyter, 1984.

McNutt, R. "Achievement Pays Off at DuPont." *Personnel,* June 1990, pp. 5-10.

Mahoney, T. "Multiple Pay Contingencies: Strategic Design of Compensation." *Human Resource Management,* 1989, *28,* 337-347.

Maidique, M. "Entrepreneurs, Champions, and Technological Innovation." *Sloan Management Review,* 1980, *21,* 59-76.

Mandler, J. *Stories, Scripts, and Scenes: Aspects of Schema Theory.* Hillsdale, N.J.: Erlbaum, 1984.

March, J. "Footnotes on Organizational Change." *Administrative Science Quarterly,* 1981, *26,* 563-597.

March, J. "Organizational Learning." Seminar presentation, Department of Psychology, University of Illinois, Mar. 1986.

March, J., and Simon, H. *Organizations.* New York: Wiley, 1958.

Marglin, S. "What Do Bosses Do?" In A. Gorz (ed.), *The Division of Labour.* London: Harvester Press, 1976.

Marsh, R., and Mannari, H. *Organizational Change in Japanese Factories.* Greenwich, Conn.: JAI Press, 1988.

Marx, K., and Engels, F. *Manifesto of the Communist Party.* London: Foreign Language Press, 1888.

Mason, M. "Autobiographies of Women Writers." In J. Olney (ed.), *Autobiography: Essays Theoretical and Critical.* Princeton, N.J.: Princeton University Press, 1980.

Maybury-Lewis, D., and Almagor, U. *The Attraction of Opposites: Thoughts and Society in Dualistic Mode.* Ann Arbor: University of Michigan Press, 1989.

Merei, F. "Group Leadership in Institutions." In E. E. Maccoby, T. M. Newcomb, and E. L. Hartley (eds.), *Readings in Social Psychology.* New York: Holt, Rinehart & Winston, 1958.

Merton, R. *Social Theory and Social Structure.* New York: Free Press, 1957.

Meyerson, D., and Martin, J. "Cultural Change: An Integration of Three Different Views." *Journal of Management Studies,* 1987, *24,* 623-647.

Miles, R. *Macro-Organizational Behavior.* Glenview, Ill.: Scott, Foresman, 1980.

Miles, R., and Snow, C. "Organizations: New Concepts for New Forms." *California Management Review,* 1986, *28*(3), 62–73.

Milkovich, G. "A Strategic Perspective on Compensation Management." *Research in Personnel and Human Resources Management,* 1988, *6,* 263–288.

Milkovich, G., and Newman, J. *Compensation.* Homewood, Ill.: BPI/Irwin, 1990.

Miller, C., and Schuster, M. "Gainsharing Plans: A Comparative Analysis." *Organizational Dynamics,* 1987, *16*(1), 44–67.

Miller, D., and Friesen, P. "Momentum and Revolution in Organizational Adaptation." *Academy of Management Journal,* 1980, *23,* 591–614.

Miller, D., and Friesen, P. "Structural Change and Performance: Quantum Versus Piecemeal-Incremental Approaches." *Academy of Management Journal,* 1982, *25,* 867–892.

Miner, J. *Theories of Organizational Behavior.* Hinsdale, Ill.: Dryden Press, 1980.

Mink, L. "History and Fiction as Modes of Comprehension." *New Literary History,* 1969, *1,* 556–569.

Mintzberg, H., and McHugh, A. "Strategy Formation in an Adhocracy." *Administrative Science Quarterly,* 1985, *30,* 160–197.

Mintzberg, H., and Waters, J. "Of Strategies, Deliberate and Emergent." *Strategic Management Journal,* 1985, *6,* 257–272.

Morgan, G. *Images of Organization.* Newbury Park, Calif.: Sage, 1986.

Mowry, D. *Alliance Politics and Economics.* New York: Ballinger, 1987.

Mulder, M. "Power Distance Reduction in Practice." In G. Hofstede and M. S. Kassem (eds.), *European Contributions to Organization Theory.* Assen/Amsterdam: Van Gorcum, 1976.

Munch, R. "Talcott Parsons and the Theory of Action, I: The Structure of the Kantian Core." *American Journal of Sociology,* 1981, *86*(4), 709–739.

Munch, R. "Talcott Parsons and the Theory of Action, II: The Continuity of Action." *American Journal of Sociology,* 1982, *86*(4), 771–826.

Myer, A. "Adapting to Environmental Jolts." *Administrative Science Quarterly,* 1982, *27,* 515–537.

Nadler, D. "The Effective Management of Organizational Change." In J. Lorsch (ed.), *Handbook of Organizational Behavior.* Englewood Cliffs, N.J.: Prentice-Hall, 1987, 358–370.

Nadler, D., and Tushman, M. "Beyond the Charismatic Leader: Leadership and Organizational Change." *California Management Review,* 1990, *32,* 77–97.

Navratilova, M. *Martina.* New York: Warner Books, 1985.

Nelson, R., and Winter, S. "An Evolutionary Theory of Economic Change." Cambridge, Mass.: Harvard University Press, 1982.

Nockolds, H. *Lucas: The First Hundred Years.* Mewton Abbot, England: David and Charles, 1976.

Nonaka, I. "Creating Organizational Order Out of Chaos: Self-Renewal in Japanese Firms." *California Management Review,* 1988, *30,* 57–73.

O'Dell, C. *People, Performance, and Pay.* Houston, Tex.: American Productivity Center, 1987.

Okochi, K., Karsh, B., and Levine, S. (eds.). *Workers and Employers in Japan: The Japanese Employment Relations System.* Princeton, N.J.: Princeton University Press, 1974.

Osigweh, C. "Concept Fallibility in Organizational Science." *Academy of Management Review,* 1989, *14*(4), 579–594.

Ouchi, W. *The M-Form Society.* Reading, Mass.: Addison-Wesley, 1984.

Ouchi, W. "The Economics of Organization." In P. Evans, Y. Doz, and A. Laurent (eds.), *Human Resource Management in International Firms: Change, Globalization, Innovation.* London: Macmillan, 1989.

Parsons, T. *The Structure of Social Action.* New York: Free Press, 1949.

Pascale, R. "The Paradox of 'Corporate Culture': Reconciling Ourselves to Socialization." *California Management Review,* 1985, *27,* 26–41.

Pascale, R. *Managing on the Edge: How Successful Companies Use Conflict to Stay Ahead.* New York: Viking Penguin, 1990.

Pasmore, W. *Designing Effective Organizations: The Sociotechnical Systems Approach.* New York: Wiley, 1988.

Pearce, J., and Robinson, R. *Strategic Management: Strategy Formulation and Implementation.* Homewood, Ill.: BPI/Irwin, 1988.

Pearson, A. "Tough-Minded Ways to Get Innovative." *Harvard Business Review,* 1988, *66,* 99–106.

Peters, T. *Thriving on Chaos.* New York: Knopf, 1987.

Peters, T. *Thriving on Chaos.* London: Pan Books, 1988.

Peters, T., and Waterman, R. *In Search of Excellence: Lessons from America's Best-Run Companies.* New York: HarperCollins, 1982.

Pettigrew, A. *Politics of Organizational Decision Making.* London: Tavistock, 1973.

Pettigrew, A. *The Awakening Giant: Continuity and Change in Imperial Chemical Industries.* Oxford, England: Blackwell, 1985.

Pfeffer, J. *Power in Organizations.* Hinsdale, Ill.: Dryden Press, 1981.

Piore, M., and Sabel, C. *The Second Industrial Divide.* New York: Basic Books, 1984.

Plachy, R. "The Case for Effective Point-Factor Job Evaluation, Viewpoint 1." *Personnel,* Apr. 1987, pp. 30–32.

Polanyi, K. *The Great Transformation.* New York: Holt, Rinehart & Winston, 1944.

Poole, M., and Van De Ven, A. "Using Paradox to Build Management and Organization Theories." *Academy of Management Review,* 1989, *14,* 562–578.

Popper, K. *Conjectures and Refutations: The Growth of Scientific Knowledge.* New York: HarperCollins, 1968.

Port, O. "Back to Basics." *Business Week,* June 16, 1989, pp. 14–18.

Porter, M. *The Competitive Advantage of Nations.* London, Macmillan, 1990.

Posner, B. "Right from the Start." *INC.,* Aug. 1988, pp. 95–96.

Prahalad, C., and Doz, Y. *The Multinational Mission: Balancing Local Demands and Global Vision.* New York: Free Press, 1987.

Prigogine, I., and Stengers, I. *Order Out of Chaos: Man's New Dialogue with Nature.* New York: Bantam Books, 1984.

Propp, V., *Morphology of the Folktale.* Austin: University of Texas Press, 1968.

Pucik, V. "White Collar Human Resource Management." *Columbia Journal of World Business,* 1984, *19,* 87–94.

Quinn, R. E. *Beyond Rational Management: Mastering the Paradoxes and Competing Demands of High Performance.* San Francisco: Jossey-Bass, 1988.

Quinn, R. E., and Cameron, K. "Paradox and Transformation: A Framework for Viewing Organization and Management." In R. E. Quinn and K. Cameron (eds.), *Paradox and Transformation: Toward a Theory of Change in Organization and Management.* New York: Ballinger, 1988.

Quinn, R. E., Denison, D., and Hooijberg, R. "Analyzing the Structure of Paradox: A Test of the Competing Values Framework of Leadership Roles." Unpublished paper, Business School, University of Michigan, 1990.

Quinn, R., Faerman, S., and Dixit, N. "Perceived Performance: Some Archetypes of Managerial Effectiveness and Ineffectiveness." Unpublished paper, Institute for Government and Policy Studies, Department of Public Administration, State University of New York, Albany, 1988.

Quinn, R., and Rohrbaugh, J. "A Spatial Model of Effectiveness Criteria: Toward a Competing Values Approach to Organizational Analysis." *Management Science,* 1983, *29*(3), 363–377.

Rabuzzi, K. *Motherself: A Mythic Analysis of Motherhood.* Bloomington: Indiana University Press, 1988.

Radnitzky, G., and Bernholz, P. (eds.). *Economic Imperialism: The Economic Method Applied Outside the Field of Economics.* New York: Paragon House, 1987.

Rapoport, R., and Rapoport, R. "Balancing Work, Family, and Leisure: A Triple Helix Model." In C. Derr (ed.), *Work, Family, and the Career: New Frontiers in Theory and Research.* New York: Praeger, 1980.

Rashad, A. *Rashad.* New York: Viking Penguin, 1988.

Rohlen, T. *For Harmony and Strength.* Berkeley: University of California Press, 1974.

Rosenwald, G. "A Theory of Multiple-Case Research." *Journal of Personality,* 1988, *56,* 239–264.

Rothenberg, A. *The Emerging Goddess: The Creative Process in Art,*

Science, and Other Fields. Chicago: University of Chicago Press, 1979.

Rue, L., and Holland, P. *Strategic Management: Concepts and Experiences.* New York: McGraw-Hill, 1989.

Runyon, M. *Life Histories and Psychobiography.* New York: Oxford University Press, 1983.

Russ, J. "What Can a Heroine Do? Or Why Women Can't Write." In S. Cornillion (ed.), *Images of Women in Fiction.* Bowling Green, Ohio: University Popular Press, 1972.

Russell, B., and Branch, T. *Second Wind: The Memoir of an Opinionated Man.* New York: Random House, 1979.

Ryohei, E. *Shin Jidai No Jinsai Ikusei Senryaku.* Tokyo: Sangy Noritsu Daigaku, 1988.

Saal, F., Downey, R., and Lahey, M. "Rating the Ratings: Assessing the Psychometric Quality of Rating Data." *Psychological Bulletin,* 1980, *88,* 413–428.

Sabel, C. *Work and Politics.* Cambridge, England: Cambridge University Press, 1982.

Sachs, J. Jewish parable told in the British Broadcasting Corporation Reith Lectures, November 1990.

Salner, M. "Adult Cognitive and Epistemological Development in Systems Education." *Systems Research,* 1986, *3*(4), 225–232.

Santalainen, T., and Hunt, J. "Change Differences from an Action-Research, Results-Oriented OD Program in High and Low Performing Finnish Banks." *Group and Organization Studies,* 1988, *13*(4), 413–440.

Sapienza, A. "Believing Is Seeing: How Culture Influences the Decisions Top Managers Make." In R. H. Kilmann, M. J. Saxton, R. Serpa, and Associates, *Gaining Control of the Corporate Culture.* San Francisco: Jossey-Bass, 1985.

Sarbin, T. (ed.). *Narrative Psychology: The Storied Nature of Human Conduct.* New York: Praeger, 1986.

Schaie, K. *The Course of Later Life: Research and Reflection.* New York: Springer-Verlag, 1989.

Schein, E. *Career Dynamics.* Reading, Mass.: Addison-Wesley, 1978.

Schein, E. "How Culture Forms, Develops, and Changes." In

R. H. Kilmann, M. J. Saxton, R. Serpa, and Associates, *Gaining Control of the Corporate Culture*. San Francisco: Jossey-Bass, 1985a.

Schein, E. *Organizational Culture and Leadership: A Dynamic View*. San Francisco: Jossey-Bass, 1985b.

Scherer, F. "Testimony Before the Committee on Ways and Means." U.S. House of Representatives, Washington, D.C., Mar. 14, 1989.

Scherer, F., and Ravenscraft, D. *Mergers, Sell-Offs, and Economic Efficiency*. Washington, D.C.: Brookings Institution, 1987.

Schneider, B. (ed.). *Organizational Climate and Culture*. San Francisco: Jossey-Bass, 1990.

Schneider, B., and Hall, D. "Toward Specifying the Concept of Work Climate: A Study of Roman Catholic Diocesan Priests." *Journal of Applied Psychology*, 1972, *56*, 447–455.

Schriesheim, C., House, R., and Kerr, S. "Leader Initiating Structure: A Reconciliation of Discrepant Research Results and Some Empirical Tests." *Organizational Behavior and Human Performance*, 1976, *15*(2), 297–321.

Schwartz, B. "Reinforcement Induced Behavioral Stereotypy: How Not to Teach People to Discover Rules." *Journal of Experimental Psychology: General*, 1982, *111*, 23–59.

Schwartz, B. *The Battle for Human Nature*. New York: W.W.Norton, 1986.

Schwartz, B. "The Experimental Synthesis of Behavior: Reinforcement, Behavioral Stereotypy, and Problem Solving." In G. H. Bower (ed.), *The Psychology of Learning and Motivation*. Vol. 22. New York: Academic Press, 1988.

Schwartz, B. *The Psychology of Learning and Behavior*. New York: W.W.Norton, 1989.

Schwartz, B. *Why the Best Things in Life Should Be Free*. New York: Atlantic Monthly Press, forthcoming.

Schwartz, B., and Lacey, H. *Behaviorism, Science, and Human Nature*. New York: W.W.Norton, 1982.

Schwartz, B., and Lacey, H. "What Applied Studies of Human Operant Conditioning Tell Us About Humans and About Operant Conditioning." In G. Davey and C. Cullen (eds.),

Human Operant Conditioning and Behavior Modification. New York: Wiley, 1988.

Schwartz, B., Schuldenfrei, R., and Lacey, H. "Operant Psychology as Factory Psychology." *Behaviorism,* 1978, *6,* 29–54.

Schweiger, D., and Ivancevich, J. "Human Resources: The Forgotten Factor in Mergers and Acquisitions." *Personnel Administrator,* 1985, *48,* 47–61.

Schwenk, T. *Sensitive Chaos.* New York: Schocken Books, 1976.

Scott, W. R. *Organizations: Rational, Natural, and Open Systems.* Englewood Cliffs, N.J.: Prentice Hall, 1981.

Seeman, M. "On the Meaning of Alienation." *American Sociological Review,* 1959, *24*(6), 783–791.

Segenberger, W., Loveman, G., and Piore, M. *The Re-Emergence of Small Enterprises.* Geneva: International Labour Office, 1990.

Shils, E. *Tradition.* Chicago: University of Chicago Press, 1981.

Shimada, H. "Japanese Industrial Relations – A New General Model?: A Survey of the English-Language Literature." In T. Shira (ed.), *Contemporary Industrial Relations in Japan.* Madison: University of Wisconsin Press, 1983.

Shutt, J., and Whittington, R. "Fragmentation Strategies and the Rise of Small Units." *Regional Studies,* 1987, *21,* 13–23.

Sills, B., and Linderman, L. *Beverly.* New York: Bantam Books, 1987.

Simon, H. *Administrative Behavior.* New York: Macmillan, 1957.

Singh, J., House, R., and Tucker, D. "Organizational Change and Organizational Mortality." *Administrative Science Quarterly,* 1986, *31,* 587–611.

Smith, A. *The Wealth of Nations.* New York: Random House, 1937. (Originally published 1776.)

Smith, D. *The Everyday World as Problematic: A Feminist Sociology.* Boston: Northeastern University Press, 1987.

Smith, K. K., and Berg, D. N. *Paradoxes of Group Life: Understanding Conflict, Paralysis, and Movement in Group Dynamics.* San Francisco: Jossey-Bass, 1987.

Sprinker, M. "Fictions of the Self: The End of Autobiography." In J. Olney (ed.), *Autobiography: Essays Theoretical and Critical.* Princeton, N.J.: Princeton University Press, 1980.

Srivastva, S., and Associates. *The Executive Mind: New Insights on Managerial Thought and Action.* San Francisco: Jossey-Bass, 1983.

Srivastva, S., and Associates. *Executive Power: How Executives Influence People and Organizations.* San Francisco: Jossey-Bass, 1986.

Srivastva, S., and Associates. *Executive Integrity: The Search for High Human Values in Organizational Life.* San Francisco: Jossey-Bass, 1988.

Srivastva, S., Cooperrider, D. L., and Associates. *Appreciative Management and Leadership: The Power of Positive Thought and Action in Organizations.* San Francisco: Jossey-Bass, 1990.

Starbuck, W., Greve, A., and Hedberg, B. "Responding to Crises." *Journal of Business Administration,* 1978, *9*(2).

Staw, B. "The Escalation of Commitment to a Course of Action." *Academy of Management Review,* 1981, *6,* 577–587.

Steiner, G., and Steiner, J. *Business, Government, and Society.* New York: Random House, 1988.

Stinchcombe, A. "Social Structure and Organizations." In J. March (ed.), *Handbook of Organizations.* Skokie, Ill.: Rand McNally, 1965.

Stone, A. *Autobiographical Occasions and Original Acts.* Philadelphia: University of Pennsylvania Press, 1982.

Taggart, W., and Robey, D. "Minds and Managers: On the Dual Nature of Human Information Processing and Management." *Academy of Management Review,* 1981, *6,* 187–195.

Taira, K. "Characteristics of Japanese Labor Markets." *Economic Development and Cultural Change,* 1962, *10,* 150–168.

Tanaka, T. "Development Managers in the Hitachi Institute of Management Development." *Journal of Management Development,* 1989, *8*(4), 12–21.

Taylor, F. *Principles of Scientific Management.* New York: W.W.Norton, 1967. (Originally published 1911.)

Teece, D. "Profiting from Technological Innovation." *Research Policy,* 1986, *15,* 285–305.

Thompson, J. *Organizations in Action.* New York: McGraw-Hill, 1967.

Thompson, V. *Modern Organization.* New York: Knopf, 1961.

Tosi, H., and Tosi, L. "What Managers Need to Know About

Knowledge-Based Pay." *Organizational Dynamics,* 1986, *14*(3), 52–64.

Trump, D. J. *Trump: The Art of the Deal.* New York: Warner Books, 1987.

Tuchman, B. *A Distant Mirror: The Calamitous 14th Century.* New York: Knopf, 1978.

Tuchman, B. "Biography as a Prism of History." In M. Pachter (ed.), *Telling Lives.* Washington, D.C.: Smithsonian Institution, 1979.

Turnbull, P. "The 'Japanisation' of Production and Industrial Relations at Lucas Electrical." *Industrial Relations Journal,* 1986, *17*(3), 193–206.

Turnbull, P. "Now We Are Motoring: The West Midlands Automotive Components Industry." Unpublished paper, Japanese Management Research Unit, Business School, University of Cardiff, Wales, 1989.

Turner, G. *The Leyland Papers.* London: Pan, 1973.

Turner, W. "Dimensions of Foreman Performance: A Factor Analysis of Criterion Measures." *Journal of Applied Psychology,* 1960, *44,* 216–223.

Tushman, M., and Anderson, P. "Technological Discontinuities and Organizational Environments." *Administrative Science Quarterly,* 1986, *31,* 439–465.

Tushman, M., and Nadler, D. "Organizing for Innovation." *California Management Review,* 1986, *28,* 74–92.

Tushman, M., Newman, W., and Romanelli, E. "Convergence and Upheaval: Managing the Unsteady Pace of Organizational Evolution." *California Management Review,* 1986, *29*(1), 29–44.

Vaill, P. B. *Managing as a Performing Art: New Ideas for a World of Chaotic Change.* San Francisco: Jossey-Bass, 1989.

Vaillant, G. *Adaptation to Life.* Boston: Little, Brown, 1977.

Von Bertalanffy, L. "The Theory of Open Systems in Physics and Biology." *Science,* 1950, *3,* 22–28.

Von Werssowetz, R., and Beer, M. "Human Resources at Hewlett Packard." In M. Beer (ed.), *Human Resource Management: A General Manager's Perspective.* New York: Free Press, 1985.

Vroom, V., and Yetton, P. *Leadership and Decision Making.* Pittsburgh, Pa.: University of Pittsburgh Press, 1973.

Wallace, M., and Fay, C. *Compensation Theory and Practice.* Boston: PWS-Kent, 1988.

Walton, M. "Beyond 'The Second Sex.'" *Philadelphia Inquirer,* Sept. 9, 1990, pp. 29–33.

Waterman, R. *The Renewal Factor.* New York: Bantam Books, 1987.

Waters, J. *Organizational Sanctions: A Process of Inquiry into Deviations.* Unpublished doctoral dissertation, Department of Organizational Behavior, Case Western Reserve University, 1976.

Watson, T. J. *A Business and Its Beliefs: The Ideas That Helped Build IBM.* New York: McGraw-Hill, 1963.

Watson, T. J., and Petre, P. *Father, Son & Co.: My Life at IBM and Beyond.* New York: Bantam Books, 1990.

Weber, M. *The Theory of Social and Economic Organization.* New York: Oxford University Press, 1947.

Weick, K. *The Social Psychology of Organizing.* Reading, Mass.: Addison-Wesley, 1969.

Weick, K. "Educational Organizations as Loosely Coupled Systems." *Administrative Science Quarterly,* 1976, *21,* 1–19.

Weick, K. "Obstacles to Strategic Renewal." Paper presented at the 50th annual meeting of the National Academy of Management, San Francisco, 1990.

Welbourne, T., and Gomez-Mejia, L. "Gainsharing Revisited." *Compensation and Benefits Review,* 1988, *20,* 19–28.

Westney, D. E., and Sakakibara, K. "Designing the Designers: Computer R & D in the United States and Japan." *Technology Review,* 1986, *89,* 24–31, 68–69.

White, H. *The Tropics of Discourse.* Baltimore, Md.: Johns Hopkins University Press, 1957.

Whittington, R. "The Fragmentation of R&D." In R. Loveridge and M. Pitt (eds.), *The Strategic Management of Technological Innovation.* New York: Wiley, 1990.

Wilkins, A., and Ouchi, W. "Efficient Cultures: Exploring the Relationship Between Culture and Organizational Performance." *Administrative Science Quarterly,* 1983, *28,* 468–481.

Williamson, O. *Markets and Hierarchies*. New York: Free Press, 1975.

Williamson, O. *The Economic Institutions of Capitalism*. New York: Free Press, 1985.

Womack, J., Jones, D., and Roos, D. *The Machine That Changed the World*. London: Macmillan, 1990.

World Commission on Environment and Development. *Our Common Future*. Oxford, England: Oxford University Press, 1987.

Yamaguchi, Y. *Kawatetsu: Shinayakana Chosen*. Tokyo: Asahi Sonorama, 1989.

Yeager, C., and James, L. *Yeager: An Autobiography*. New York: Bantam Books, 1985.

Yonekura, S. "The Japanese Iron and Steel Industry: Continuity and Discontinuity, 1850–1970." Unpublished doctoral dissertation, Harvard Business School, Harvard University, 1990.

Zaleznik, A. "Managers and Leaders: Are They Different?" *Harvard Business Review*, 1977, *55*, 67–80.

Zaltman, G., Duncan, R., and Holbek, J. *Innovations and Organizations*. New York: Wiley, 1973.

Name Index

Subject Index